FAITH IN THE MASSES

FAITH IN THE MASSES

Essays Celebrating 100 years of the CPUSA

Edited with an Introduction
by
Tony Pecinovsky

INTERNATIONAL PUBLISHERS, New York

Library of Congress Cataloging-in-Publication Data

Names: Pecinovsky, Tony, editor.
Title: Faith in the masses : essays celebrating 100 years of the CPUSA / edited and with an introduction by Tony Pecinovsky.
Description: New York : International Publishers, [2020] | Includes bibliographical references. | Summary: "Twelve essays covering aspects of the History of the Communist Party of the United States"—Provided by publisher.
Identifiers: LCCN 2020039190 (print) | LCCN 2020039191 (ebook) | ISBN 9780717808267 (paperback) | ISBN 9780717808274 (mobi) | ISBN 9780717808281 (epub)
Subjects: LCSH: Communist Party of the United States of America—History. | Communism—United States—History.
Classification: LCC JK2391.C5 .F35 2020 (print) | LCC JK2391.C5 (ebook) | DDC 324.273/750904—dc23
LC record available at https://lccn.loc.gov/2020039190
LC ebook record available at https://lccn.loc.gov/2020039191

ISBN 10: 0-7178-0829-7   ISBN-13 978-07178-0829-8
Typeset by Amnet Systems, Chennai, India

Table of Contents

Abbreviations

African Blood Brotherhood – ABB
American Indian Movement - AIM
American Federation of Labor – AFL
American Negro Labor Congress - ANLC
American Women for Peace – AWP
Black Panther Party - BPP
Civil Rights Congress - CRC
Communist Party of India – CPI
Communist Party of America – CPA
Communist Political Association - CPA
Communist Labor Party – CLP
Communist League of America - CLA
Communist Party, USA – CPUSA
Congress of American Women – CAW
Committee/Congress of Industrial Organizations – CIO
Committee for Environmental Information - CEI
Committee for Nuclear Information – CNI
Council on African Affairs – CAA
Croatian Fraternal Union - CFU
Free Speech Movement - FSM
House Un-American Activities Committee - HUAC
Industrial Workers of the World – IWW
International Labor Defense – ILD
International Workers Order – IWO
Jewish People's Fraternal Order - JPFO
Labor Sports Union - LSU
League of Struggle for Negro Rights – LSNR
National Alliance Against Racist and Political Repression – NAARPR
National Anti-Imperialist Movement in Solidarity with African
     Liberation - NAIMSAL
National Association for the Advancement of Colored People – NAACP
National Association of Base Ball Players - NABBP
National Negro Congress – NNC
National Student Association - NSA
Negro National League – NNL

Progressive Youth Organizing Committee - PYOC
Scientists Institute for Public Information – SIPI
Sharecroppers Union – SCU
Slovak Workers Society - SWS
Sojourners for Peace and Justice – SPJ
Southern Christian Leadership Conference - SCLC
Southern Negro Youth Congress - SNYC
Socialist Party, USA – SPUSA
Students for a Democratic Society – SDS
Student Non-Violent Coordinating Committee - SNCC
Trade Union Educational League – TUEL
Trade Union Unity League - TUUL
United Communist Party – UCP
Universal Negro Improvement Association – UNIA
W.E.B. DuBois Clubs - DBC
Women's International Democratic Federation – WIDF
Workers (Communist) Party of America - WPA
World Federation of Democratic Youth - WFDY
World Peace Council – WPC
Young Workers Liberation League - YWLL

FAITH IN THE MASSES

Introduction: Reclaiming History: A Century of the Communist Party

By Tony Pecinovsky

As I write this Introduction, a battle rages in the streets of America. Since the killing of George Floyd in late May 2020, millions of protesters have taken to the streets to confront police brutality, racism, and white supremacy. Though beaten with batons, tear gassed, pepper sprayed, shot with rubber bullets, and run-over (among any number of other civil liberties abuses), they persist. Despite the ongoing pandemic, COVID-19, and the justified fears associated with large gatherings, they persist. Their rally cry is "Black Lives Matter," a call that has brought in its wake a seismic quake strong enough to redefine the political terrain of struggle regarding the utility of police in modern society. Defunding police departments is now a majority sentiment. AFL-CIO central labor councils across the country are discussing the expulsion of police unions. Statues commemorating slave owners and racists are being torn down. Mississippi voted to remove the Confederate symbol from its flag. These are huge victories won against tremendous odds.

Recently, in St. Louis, Missouri – the city I choose to call home and raise my daughter in – a group of over 300 protesters marched through a gated community to the mayor's house. They were calling for her resignation. Just days earlier she had publicly shared the names and addresses of constituents calling for the defunding of the St. Louis City Police, thereby giving tacit approval to police harassment. The St. Louis Police Officers Association is led by the notoriously racist business manager Jeff Roorda, a close ally of the mayor. Though St. Louis is no stranger to racist police brutality and the concomitant outrage directed against it – recall the murder of Mike Brown in Ferguson (just a stone's throw from St. Louis) in 2014 – this protest was unique. Not because of the protesters, though. What made this protest unique were the white ambulance chasers, politely referred to as personal-injury lawyers, Mark and Patricia McCloskey. The couple had come out of their 18,000 square-foot mansion – originally built in 1909 as a wedding present for Anna Busch, the daughter of beer magnate Adolphus Busch – brandishing an AR-15 style rifle and a pistol. With fingers on the trigger, these up-standing paragons of St. Louis' ruling class and supporters of President Donald Trump, claimed to be the victims in this altercation. Like so many police, their lives were not in danger. Also like so many police, they felt emboldened, empowered, even entitled to threaten the use of deadly force on protesters who were predominantly Black – with no, or little consequence. The governor of Missouri is now suggesting that he will pardon the McCloskey's, who were charged with felonies. These actions, coupled with right-wing militias storming state capitols in Michigan, and elsewhere, as well as conspiracy theorists at Florida townhall meetings likening face mask regulations to so-called "communist dictatorships," signal a turn toward dangerous absurdity.

Not reported, in St. Louis or elsewhere, though, were the presence of actual Communists – early and consistent supporters of Black lives going back to at least the 1930s with the defense of the Scottsboro Nine. This point brings me to the book at hand *Faith In The Masses: Essays Celebrating 100 Years of the Communist Party, USA* and the continued relevance of the CPUSA.

To say that Communists have long fought for Black lives would be an understatement. The historical record is replete with example after example of Communists initiating and leading struggles on the "Negro question," African American equality, and Black liberation. As historian Gerald Horne notes, "despite its flaws, the [Communist] party was probably unparalleled in not just fighting racism in society but within the ranks as well."[1] Through organizations like the National Negro Congress,[2] the Southern Negro Youth Congress,[3] the Civil Rights Congress,[4] Sojourners for Truth and Justice,[5] the

1. Gerald Horne, *Black Liberation/Red Scare: Ben Davis and the Communist Party* (University of Delaware Press, 1994), 71

2. Erik S. Gellman, *Death Blow to Jim Crow: The National Negro Congress and the Rise of Militant Civil Rights* (University of North Carolina Press, 2014)

3. Sara Rzeszutek, *James and Esther Cooper Jackson: Love and Courage in the Black Freedom Movement* (University Press of Kentucky, 2015)

4. Gerald Horne, *Communist Front?: The Civil Rights Congress, 1946-1956* (Fairleigh Dickinson University Press, 1988)

5. Dayo F. Gore, *Radicalism at the Crossroads: African American Women Activists in the Cold War* (New York University Press, 2011)

Council on African Affairs,[6] the National Alliance Against Racist and Political Repression, and the National Anti-Imperialist Movement in Solidarity with African Liberation,[7] among many others, Communists consistently championed Black lives over the decades. Though the CPUSA's membership today hovers around 5,000 – a far cry from its peak – this aspect of its work has not changed, and partly explains why Samaria Rice – mother of the slain African American youth Tamir Rice – could be found at the CPUSA's 100th Anniversary Convention in spring 2019 thanking Communists for their ongoing support.[8]

Of course, the struggle for Black lives took many shapes and forms over the course of the CPUSA's 100 years. Many of those efforts are discussed in the following pages.

As a collection of essays celebrating the 100th anniversary of the birth of the CPUSA, *Faith In The Masses* continues and builds off the work of others. The collection of essays published by Monthly Review Press in 1993, titled *New Studies In The Politics And Culture Of U.S. Communism*, is one notable example. That project started as a daylong conference hosted by the Research Group on Socialism and Democracy in November 1989, for the CPUSA's 70th anniversary, and eventually made its way into book format. Of particular importance in that collection of essays is an analysis of the ongoing shift away from the "orthodox" or traditionalist school of historians characterized by Theodore Draper and Harvey Klehr who saw nothing more in the CPUSA than an "appendage of a Russian revolutionary power." Draper noted despairingly – and inaccurately – that "Nothing else so important ever happened to it [the CPUSA] again." Klehr continued in the same vein, making an academic career out of trying to tie nearly every aspect of CPUSA policy and history to Soviet espionage efforts. Contrasted with the "orthodox" or traditionalist school is what Michael E. Brown, an editor of the MR collection, called

6. Penny M. Von Eschen, *Race Against Empire: Black Americans and Anti-colonialism, 1937-1957* (Cornell University Press, 1997) and Nicholas Grant, *Winning Our Freedoms Together: African Americans and Apartheid, 1945-1960* (University of North Carolina Press, 2017)

7. Tony Pecinovsky, *Let Them Tremble: Biographical Interventions Marking 100 Years of the Communist Party, USA* (New York: International Publishers, 2019)

8. Michelle Zacarias, "CPUSA encourages building unity from the ground up in anti-oppression panel," People's World, June 26, 2019, https://www.peoplesworld.org/article/cpusa-encourages-building-unity-from-the-ground-up-in-anti-oppression-panel/

the "new historians" or the revisionist school. That latter group, which includes scholars such as Robin Kelley, Mark Naison, and Gerald Horne – and later Erik S. McDuffie, Dayo Gore, and Mary Helen Washington, among others – complicate the traditional anti-communist narrative. They add nuance to the lived experiences of Black and white Communists and their allies at the grassroots (and sometimes in higher party circles), while also modernizing the historiography of U.S. communism. As Brown points out, these "new historians" sought to "bring the history of Communism into line with *history* [*italic* in original]." As a result, they had "no choice but to write a history that includes the activists who formed the party, those of various backgrounds and persuasions who joined it in preference to other political options, those of varying degree of commitment who worked within and around party organizations, and the greater number of people – whether officially members or not – whose experiences of agency, moral urgency, and politics were influenced by it in the various settings in which they lived and felt the need to take action." Contrary to Draper and Klehr, these historians "represent a considerably expanded empirical field and a correspondingly different sense of what is involved in writing history."[9] The essays compiled in this collection continue to expand this "empirical field."

Also of note is the collection of essays edited by Robbie Lieberman and Clarence Lang, titled *Anticommunism And The African American Freedom Movement: "Another Side of the Story,"* published in 2009, at the time of the CPUSA's 90th anniversary. Lieberman and Lang, in their Introduction to that collection, make clear that their goal was "not simply to add to the litany of accounts of anticommunist attacks on movement activists and organizations," of which there are plenty. Their goal, much more ambitious, was "to illuminate the significant role of anticommunism in helping to determine the scope, shape, and personnel of the post-World War II black freedom struggle in the United States." As they argue, the "subordination and distancing" of the domestic struggle for African American equality away from the internationalist "organizations and activism that had been common" during the 1930s and 1940s "profoundly affected the shape of the struggle that is popularly known as the civil rights movement."[10] Of course, Lieberman and Lang build off the work of Gerald Horne,

---

9. Michael E. Brown (ed.), *New Studies in the Politics and Culture of U.S. Communism* (Monthly Review Press, 1993)

10. Robbie Lieberman and Clarence Lang (ed.), *Anticommunism and the African American Freedom Movement: "Another Side of the Story"* (Palgrave Macmillan, 2009)

Penny Von Eschen, and others who see the post-war anti-communist political repression as constraining the boundaries of domestic political discourse safely within the bounds of liberal, Western capitalism. As a result, Communist-led organizations championing Black civil rights and colonial independence in Africa, like the Civil Rights Congress and the Council on African Affairs, were deemed subversive; their leaders were harassed and imprisoned, while the organizations they led were eventually forced to dissolve. Regardless, by highlighting the various ways in which anti-communism served to constrain discourses on Black civil rights, Lieberman and Lang also a lay bare the confluence of interests constructed around the twin pillars of U.S. capitalism – white supremacy and red scare.

These same forces coalesce today and have found comfort in the largely incoherent utterances of the 45th president and his alt-right, racist supporters who now occupy strategic positions throughout the administration. Anti-communism is again a watchword, a motivating scare tactic used by the far-right to obscure, confuse, and tamp down even moderate efforts to alleviate the suffering associated with the current crisis engendered by capitalism's failures – the continued assault on Black lives and the still raging COVID-19 pandemic. This only partly explains the need for another volume of essays similar to the two mentioned above.

The obvious reason for another volume of essays is to celebrate the 100th anniversary of the birth of the Communist Party, USA. Very few organizations exist long enough to enjoy a centennial celebration. Fewer still enjoy this milestone moment when faced with decades and decades of concerted political repression. The criminalization of Communists in the public mind recalls a statement made by the Trinidad born, Black Communist Claudia Jones. In the early 1950s, as her friends and comrades faced long jail sentences, and as she was fighting deportation proceedings, Jones noted, "it is a crime to be a Marxist-Leninist" just as it is also a "crime" to be Black, as both are "daily convicted by a Government which denies us [our] elementary democratic rights."[11] This denial of "elementary democratic rights" was a means to an end. Dismantling the budding organizational infrastructure – through the CRC and the CAA, as well as Sojourners for Truth and Justice, for example – that bolstered collaboration between two key democratic forces, namely reds and Blacks, was the strategic goal of this civil liberties assault. At the heart of this collection – dissected from multiple perspectives – is a fuller understanding of the CPUSA's century long commitment to African

11. Pecinovsky, *Let Them Tremble…*, Ibid

American equality, an understanding needed now more than ever as the assault on Black lives continues.

*   *   *

Other topics, of course, are discussed throughout this volume. Chapter One provides a brief outline of the CPUSA throughout its 100 year existence, from 1919 to 2019. Notable moments and controversies are discussed here giving those less familiar with the broad depth and breadth of CPUSA history a general understanding of some momentous events. Communist-led organizations and prominent personalities are only briefly mentioned, as it is impossible to compress all of the CPUSA's history into one short essay. Of special note in this overview is the party's role in the 1930s during the Great Depression with the formation of the Unemployed Councils, and just a few years later the pioneering work of Communists in the formation of the steelworkers and auto workers unions. Unlike other histories of the CPUSA, Norman Markowitz and Tony Pecinovsky include a brief analysis of Communist activities throughout the 1960s, 1970s, 1980s, and into the 2000s, thereby challenging the myth of the party's demise post-1956.

Chapter Two is a political biography of the CPUSA's first executive secretary, C.E. Ruthenberg. Ruthenberg, an Ohio leader of the Socialist Party largely responsible for unifying the various parties and factions that emerged after the SP's split over participation in World War I, is largely forgotten today, partly a consequence of his passing at the age of 45 in 1927. As C.J. Atkins argues, Ruthenberg helped lay the organizational scaffolding for the building of "a party of action," what would become the CPUSA. That Ruthenberg left little in the way of philosophical or theoretical texts is highlighted by Atkins. Ruthenberg was a pragmatic organizer and Communist committed to the building of international socialism, not a polemicist, though his critiques could be sharp and biting. This chapter aims to rescue Ruthenberg and his legacy, which fell victim to party infighting, factionalism, and political erasure.

Chapter Three is an analysis of the CPUSA's 1932 presidential campaign, which saw William Z. Foster and James W. Ford running, respectively, for president and vice president. This essay compares the CPUSA to other political parties and questions the traditional definition of the role of political parties in liberal, Western democracy. As Josh Morris argues, the CPUSA "played by its own rules." Its goal was not simply just to amass votes, to win support for this or that policy or legislation, or to hold fundraising dinners and banquets. Rather, its goal was considerably more ambitious: to foment revolution. As part of the party's "Third Period" politics, the 1932 presidential campaign was viewed as a way to gauge U.S. workers' receptiveness to revolution, as well as the potential for CPUSA growth. During this time, Foster argued for the creation of a "Soviet America," while Ford argued for full equality for African Americans. Special attention is paid to Foster's visit to the Ford River Rouge Plant in Michigan and the ensuing Ford Hunger March led by the Unemployed Councils and CPUSA. During the march 60 people were injured and five were killed, including Joe York, an organizer with the Young Communist League. Indeed, the 1932 CPUSA presidential campaign provides an important example of the varying ways in which political parties can function during electoral campaigns, a function at odds with the current two party system and its constraining of political opportunities designed to limit participation by those that do not fit into this predetermined format.

Baseball is America's national pastime. In Chapter Four Al Neal provides a glimpse into the *Daily Worker*'s campaign to desegregate the diamond. First, Neal gives a brief overview of the history of the game, the emergence of separate white and Negro leagues, and the early reluctance of Communists to see sport as a valuable tool by which workers, young and old, could be organized to support African American equality and socialism. He also looks at the role of the rise of fascism in Europe, the perspectives of the Communist International (Comintern), and the transitions that took place within the pages of the *Daily Worker* as it became a foremost advocate for equality within sports during the Popular Front period. Black and white Communists, such as Angelo Herndon, Benjamin Davis, Jr., and Lester Rodney, factor heavily into Neal's analysis. As Nat Low wrote in October 1945, "Communists were the first to start the fight" to desegregate baseball. As such, America's national pastime, the players, and the fans, owe a debt of gratitude to the Communists who bravely challenged segregation on and off the field.

Chapter Five continues to highlight the CPUSA's long commitment to African American equality and Black liberation. Timothy V Johnson provides a historical analysis of the CPUSA's various approaches to the "Negro question." From the Black Belt Thesis and self-determination to the question of "centrality" and an "anti-racist majority," Johnson shows how Communists grappled with various aspects of the freedom struggle – theoretically, politically, and organizationally. In this chapter, Communist leadership of the Sharecroppers Union, the National Negro Congress, the Civil Rights Congress, Sojourners for Truth and Justice, the campaign to free Angela Davis, the National Alliance Against Racist and Political Repression, as well as the National Anti-Imperialist Movement in Solidarity with African Liberation, among other organizational formations, are discussed. Though Communist-led efforts through the NNC, CRC, and STJ, among others, faced unprecedented political repression, their impacts were felt for decades. Johnson also provides a contemporary analysis of recent CPUSA reports and resolutions dealing with the struggle for equality. He concludes that the party's "unquestioned commitment to equality" will help "chart the movement forward toward a society free of racism, discrimination, and exploitation."

One of the broadest Communist-led organizational formations throughout the 1930s, 1940s, and 1950s was the International Workers Order, a mutual benefit, fraternal society, and insurer with around 200,000 dues paying members. As Robert Zecker illustrates in Chapter Six, the IWO was unique in its commitment to anti-racism, and the fight against Jim Crow. Unlike other insurers, it actively challenged insurance policies that discriminated against Black, Latino/a, and Eastern European immigrants. Additionally, the IWO advocated for policies that if successful – like universal health care, generous unemployment and workers compensation packages, and robust social security benefits – would have made its existence redundant. The IWO did not see itself as just a mutual benefit, fraternal society, though. It saw itself as an advocate for socialism merged with a successful business model that caused envy among the more profit driven and racist insurers of the time. The IWO also provided an array of recreational programs, summer camps, and other cultural activities to its members. Unfortunately, the organization was hounded by the FBI, labeled subversive, harassed by the House Un-American Activities Committee, and eventually forced to liquidate – though its finances were impeccable and its insurance -policy business actuarially sound. The IWO provides proof of what is possible when a profitable company is run with socialist goals in mind. To its business competitors and political adversaries, the IWO was an organization that had to be destroyed lest its successful example infect the broader body politic.

Whereas Chapter Six provides a wide-lens analysis of the IWO, Chapter Seven focuses in on a very distinctive aspect of the Communist-led Civil Rights Congress: one of its leaders, Beulah Richardson, and two of her poems – "A Black Woman Speaks...

of White Womanhood, of White Supremacy, of Peace" and "Genocide." Probably best known for her film and stage roles, including
on *The Cosby Show*, Richardson's political art is largely ignored today.
However, like the playwright Lorraine Hansberry, Richardson saw
white supremacy, bourgeoisie femininity, and capitalism as mutually reinforcing. This partly explains her embrace of socialism and
friendships with prominent CPUSA personalities, such as William
L. Patterson and Louis Thompson Patterson. In this chapter Denise
Lynn dissects Richardson's poems and, notes their importance and
impact on the early 1950s struggle for Black civil rights – providing context for when and why they were written. Lynn also centers
Richardson at the heart of the Civil Rights Congress and Sojourners for Truth and Justice. Richardson's poems and politics were part
of the Black left's response to the Cold War and the constraining of
Black political discourse with the battering inflicted upon reds. This
chapter powerfully illustrates how Richardson's cultural and artistic influence was wielded on behalf of the struggle for equality and
exemplifies the way in which the CPUSA's embrace of culture and
art reached far beyond its dues paying members.

    Chapter Eight starts with a discussion of the 1935 Convention of
the Communist-led League of American Writers, the formation of
the American Writers' Congress, and the transition from a Marxist critique centered on "workers" to a critique of "the people." By
analyzing "revolutionary cultural practice" in the broadest terms
possible, Joel Wendland-Liu argues that Popular Front politics
resisted class determinism, as well as the submersion of other forms
of oppression into narrowly defined class relations. The role of art in
society is central to Wendland-Liu's analysis of cultural production.
Novelists, artists, musicians, photographers, playwrights, filmmakers, poets, journalists, educators, scholars, and critics affiliated
with or sympathetic to the CPUSA produced a body of work that
foregrounded the values of the exploited and oppressed and their
revolutionary actions, thereby challenging and recasting "symbols of
authority" that prefigure human liberation as the goal, not profit. In
this chapter, Wendland-Liu compares and contrasts the creative and
theoretical works of W.E.B. DuBois, Claudia Jones, Claude McKay,
H.T. Tsiang, Alexander Saxton and Lloyd Brown, among others.
Exploring the continuing influence of the cultural Popular Front, and
its various impacts, as Wendland-Liu contends, may help chart new
paths toward creating socialist consciousness in the 21st century.

    The authors of Chapter Nine Rachel Rubin and James Smethurst
also center their analysis on culture – on the cartoons of Ollie

Harrington, the Black left and the African American press during Jim Crow. As this chapter argues, Harrington, a well-known cartoonist, CPUSA member, and cultural critic, was an important artist of the Black radical tradition. Though red-baited, Harrington's cartoons were popular and widely circulated, especially in the Black press, an area of study often under considered. During the 1930s and 1940s, Black left publishers, editors, reporters, cartoonists, and columnists, many of whom happened to be Communists or close to the CP, shaped the trajectory of major African American newspapers and magazines, such as the *People's Voice*, the *Amsterdam News*, the *Chicago Defender*, the *Baltimore Afro-American*, *Michigan Chronicle*, and the *California Eagle*, and later *Freedomways*, among others. As a result, during the 1950s domestic red scare – with the corresponding constraining of acceptable political discourses – many of these same cultural producers were hounded, harassed, driven from their posts, and blacklisted. That Harrington, like Paul Robeson, and other well-known Black Communists, found more avenues for cultural expression within the world of 20th century communism complicates our understanding of U.S. history. According to the authors, Harrington's later days as a contributor to the *Daily World* and *People's World*, coupled with his life in the German Democratic Republic, was "more liberating than constraining." This is a significant acknowledgement; the shortcomings of U.S. Black civil rights, contrasted with the alternative offered by Eastern European state socialism adds nuance, especially as much of Harrington's later critiques were often ignored outside of the left and Communist press. In this chapter, a number of Harrington's cartoons, spanning his career, are contextualized, providing the reader with a better understanding of Harrington's political art.

Chapter Ten shifts gears away from the intersection of Black civil rights and cultural production. Instead, Elisabeth Armstrong focuses on women's international solidarity, with an examination of the Women's International Democratic Federation. The correspondences shared between Communists Betty Millard and Gita Bannerji, as well as the "primitive accumulation" involved in creating and fostering international relationships between disparate movements, organizations, and individuals from one continent to another are discussed here. From the late 1940s to the early 1950s, Millard and Bannerji both worked at the WIDF's central offices in Paris and then in Berlin, where it remained until 1991. Their political views, shared experiences, and commitments created a friendship that continued throughout their lives. According to Armstrong, Millard and

Bannerji's work for WIDF, as well as their ongoing correspondence, strengthened and affirmed a commonality of vision and purpose, which helped to sustain their activism during periods of political repression. Theirs is a love story centered on international solidarity, a story that exemplifies the bonds of comradery built countless times over by the 91 million members of WIDF. Unfortunately, theirs is also a story largely forgotten following the demise of Eastern European socialism and the alliances fostered by women's rights groups throughout the developing world. Armstrong also spends considerable text on the "Hands Off Korea" campaign and the 1951 WIDF report *We Accuse!*, which "galvanized women's organizations around the world to oppose the US military occupation of Korea."

Chapter Eleven makes yet another turn. It is often argued, within the "orthodox" school of historians of U.S. communism – as well as those sympathetic to socialism and the CPUSA – that whatever influence it may have had during the Great Depression and World War II heyday, the CPUSA became a marginal political force post-1956. In this chapter, Tony Pecinovsky challenges this narrative and argues that the CPUSA was far from marginal throughout the 1960s and 1970s. Highlighted is the successful wave of college and university Communist speaking engagements in the early 1960s. Communist-led youth groups, such as Advance, the Progressive Youth Organizing Committee, the W.E.B. DuBois Clubs, as well as the Young Workers Liberation League are discussed, as is the role of young Communists like Bettina Aptheker. Party leader Charlene Mitchell's campaign in 1968 as the first African American woman to run for president of the U.S., as well as the birth of the party-led National Alliance Against Racist and Political Repression (after the successful campaign to free Communist Angela Davis), and the National Anti-Imperialist Movement in Solidarity with African Liberation are also discussed. By examining an array of Communist activities throughout the 1960s and 1970s, Pecinovsky challenges the "myth of marginality" and argues for a reassessment of the historical record.

Chapter Twelve continues in this same vein, and touches on a topic largely neglected by historians of the CPUSA, i.e., the movement for environmental sustainability. Here we learn about the life and work of Virginia Brodine, an early proponent of environmental sustainability. Brodine, a life-long member of the CPUSA, started her organizing career in the party-led Congress of American Women, and became one of the most well-known environmental activists of the 1960s and 1970s. Throughout the 1960s and 1970s, Brodine edited and wrote for a wide array of environmental magazines and journals, including *Nuclear Information, Scientist and Citizen,* and later *Environment.* She also authored two books, *Air Pollution* and *Radioactive Contamination,* and numerous articles, and papers. She led grassroots environmental organizations, including the Committee for Nuclear Information, the Committee for Environmental Information, and Scientists Institute for Public Information. Her influence on Barry Commoner, the author of *The Closing Circle,* one of the most influential ecology books of the 1970s, is discussed, as is her work within the CPUSA where she advocated for a party environmental program, sometimes at odds with prominent party leaders. Brodine would live to see the Battle in Seattle against the World Trade Organization in 2000, a movement that brought trade unionists and environmental activists together to demand a just and sustainable society – something Brodine had committed her life to. Marc Brodine, Virginia's son who continued her work within the party, along with Tony Pecinovsky, co-author this chapter. They shed light on an important and neglected contribution Communists made to the modern movement for environmental sustainability.

*   *   *

As a collection of essays, *Faith In The Masses* is indebted to the various historians and activist-scholars who took time out of their academic and organizational responsibilities to celebrate the 100th anniversary of the CPUSA and contribute to this book. Like other collections, though, this book suffers from a number of weaknesses and shortcomings.

While this collection highlights the CPUSA's work on the "Negro question," African American equality, and Black liberation, it provides little insight into the party's work among the Latino/a community. Enrique M. Buelna's *Chicano Communists and the Struggle for Social Justice* is an excellent contribution to this history and should be read widely. Similarly, the party's work with the Japanese community deserves considerably more study. Josephine Fowler's *Japanese & Chinese Immigrant Activists: Organizing In American & International Communist Movements, 1919-1933* is an important book length study on early Communist involvement with Japanese Americans. Of course, the horrific treatment and internment of Japanese Americans during World War II, the party's unwillingness to challenge this treatment, coupled with the expulsion of Japanese CPUSA members, was inexcusable, as was the party's treatment of LGBTQ+ members for many decades. The treatment of Harry Hay and Bettina Aptheker are but two well-known examples of the latter. Internal sexism and a largely masculinist persona made up another set of weaknesses within the CPUSA that had to be challenged. Kate Weigand's *Red Feminism: American Communism and the Making of Women's Liberation,* Beth Slutsky's *Gendering Radicalism: Women and Communism in Twentieth Century California,* as well as Dayo Gore's *Radicalism at the Crossroads: African American Women Activists in the Cold War,* are important contributions to this neglected history. In line with what the party perceived as its responsibility as part of an internationalist movement, the CPUSA was also largely uncritical of the Soviet Union and the Eastern European states at too many critical historical junctures. While there is much to praise about these experiments in socialism, such as those efforts and accomplishments outlined in Kristen Ghodsee's *Second World, Second Sex: Socialist Women's Activism and Global Solidarity during the Cold War,* there is also much to criticize and condemn. This aspect of the CPUSA's record does not figure prominently in the current volume. Also absent from this collection is any extensive treatment of CPUSA splits, factional struggles, resignations, expulsions, and internal politics associated with all organizations big or small.

Of course, there are a number of other topics that could have easily been included in this collection, except for a want of authors and space. For example, the wide array of CPUSA affiliated youth/ summer camps is an important subject meriting discussion. While Robert Zecker mentions IWO run recreational camps in Chapter Six, to my knowledge Paul C. Mishler's *Raising Reds: The Young Pioneers, Radical Summer Camps, and Communist Political Culture in the United States* is the only book length study on this topic. Also missing from this collection is an analysis of the various Communist-led or affiliated ongoing adult, popular education institutions, such as the Jefferson School for Social Science. No book length study of these various initiatives and their impacts exists. The Red Scare in Hollywood is another topic deserving of more attention. Gerald Horne's *The Final Victim of the Blacklist: John Howard Lawson, Dean of the Hollywood Ten* and James J. Lorence's *The Suppression of Salt of the Earth: How Hollywood, Big Labor, and Politicians Blacklisted a Movie in Cold War America* are important contributions to this history. The party's role in the fight against fascism, during the Spanish Civil War and World War II, by contrast, have both been written about extensively. Maurice Isserman's *Which Side Were You On?: The American Communist Party during the Second World War,* as well as Robbie Lieberman's *The Strangest Dream: Communism, Anticommunism, and the U.S. Peace Movement, 1945-1963,* both cover a lot of important historical ground and raises a number of important questions regarding Communists in peace and war. Largely missing, however, is an analysis of the role of Communists in the 1960s and 1970s anti-Vietnam War peace movement. As I have written elsewhere, numerous Communists played important roles in the struggle for peace during this period. Not only did Arnold Johnson and Bettina Aptheker, for example, hold leadership positions in New Mobe and Student Mobe, respectively, other Communists, such as Herbert Aptheker – who led a delegation to Hanoi in 1965 – spoke out extensively against the war. The work of the party-led W.E.B. DuBois Clubs, as well as the Young Workers Liberation League, in the peace movement has yet to be given significant attention. Exposing the racist barbarity of apartheid South Africa, is another important topic that I wish could have been included in this collection. Penny M. Von Eschen's *Race Against Empire: Black Americans and Anticolonialism, 1937-1957*, as well as Nicholas Grant's *Winning Our Freedoms Together: African Americans and Apartheid, 1945-1960*, are excellent contributions to this history, especially as it relates to Paul Robeson, W.E.B. DuBois and Alphaeus Hunton's leadership of the Council on African Affairs. Unfortunately, the party-led National Anti-Imperialist Movement in Solidarity with African Liberation, founded in 1973, which continued the work of the CAA, has received little attention from historians. Similarly, Gerald Horne's *Communist Front?: The Civil Rights Congress, 1946-1956*, as well as his biography of William L. Patterson, *Black Revolutionary: William Patterson & the Globalization of the African American Freedom Struggle*, add a rich tapestry of detail to the history of the CRC. Like NAIMSAL, though, more work need to be done to update and connect this history to the 1970s party-led initiative, the National Alliance Against Racist and Political Repression. Similarly, the prominent role of Communists, such as Agnes 'Sis' Cunningham, in the folk revivalist movement deserve more attention. In general, the history of the CPUSA in the 1960s, 1970s, and 1980s, and on into the 2000s, needs to be chronicled and analyzed. While three chapters in this collection attempt to modestly shed some light on Communist activities during this period in U.S. history, much more remains to be done.

As the reader will undoubtedly note, there are no essays on the CPUSA and the labor movement in this collection. This is perhaps the most written about subject in U.S. Communist history. It was a deliberate choice of the editor to *not* include essays on this subject. The focus, instead, was to highlight aspects of CPUSA history given considerably less attention. For readers solely interested in CPUSA history as it relates to struggles within the AFL, and the building of the CIO, the steelworkers, the auto workers, longshore and maritime workers, teachers, etc., there are numerous excellent volumes that can be recommended, such as Clarence Taylor's *Reds at the Blackboard: Communism, Civil Rights, and the New York City Teachers Union*, Bruce Nelson's *Workers on the Waterfront: Seamen, Longshoremen, and Unionism in the 1930s*, Roger Keeran's *The Communist Party and the Auto Workers Union*, Rosemary Feurer's *Radical Unionism in the Midwest, 1900-1950*, as well as Judith Stepan-Norris and Maurice Zeitlin's *Left Out: Reds and America's Industrial Unions*. Like NAIM-SAL and NAARPR, the 1970s party-led initiative Trade Unionists for Action and Democracy and the publication *Labor Today* deserve more attention, as does the Wisconsin Steel Save Our Jobs Committee and the Congress of the Unemployed.

It is worth noting that this collection is *not* a "party history" written exclusively by CPUSA leaders. Rather, it is a collection of essays written by academic authors who specialize in various topics related to CPUSA history, as well as activist-scholars who happen to be Communists. This is an important distinction. This collection has been from its inception a collaborative endeavor, and the authors have been free to choose topics, personalities, and organizations of interest to them – so long as they relate to the history of the Communist Party, USA. That being said, as editor I do not necessarily agree with all of the authors or their sentiments. The only criteria – beyond the pursuit of academic excellence – is that the contributions in some way celebrate and add to the historiography of the CPUSA during its 100th anniversary.

Tony Pecinovsky, August 2020

Chapter 1

For Socialism, Peace, and Democracy: An outline history of the CPUSA

By Norman Markowitz & Tony Pecinovsky

1919 was a crucial year in history. A world war had ended a year before and a revolution for socialism was raging across a land that covered one sixth of the Earth's surface – a land then called Soviet Russia.

Throughout the world new parties emerged from existing socialist parties and anti-colonial movements; they united around the struggle for socialism and against imperialism. Ruling classes responded with red scares, the use of military and police force to suppress uprisings and peoples' movements with terror and murder. In the United States, the Communist Party, USA was born.

Who were the Communists?

America is a nation of immigrants and those who built the CPUSA came from the groups that made up the American people – old stock white protestant immigrants who could trace their family roots to colonial times; newer immigrants from what later became Germany and British colonial Ireland followed by immigrants from the new unified kingdom of Italy, the Czarist Russian and Austro Hungarian empires.

People of many nationalities – Irish, Germans, Italians, Finns, Poles, Czechs, Hungarians, and others; people of Roman Catholic, Orthodox Christian, and Jewish religious background. Many came to the United States fleeing poverty and persecution and they would continue those struggles. Some had been involved with socialist movements in the lands from which they came.

They would be joined by African American activists, who had faced the highest level of exploitation and oppression in the United States, fighting for three centuries against slavery and then Jim Crow; Indigenous peoples, Mexican Americans, and people from the

U.S. colonies of Puerto Rico and the Philippines; along with Japanese and Chinese Americans, all of whom were victims of violent, racist exploitation and oppression.

What made these activists different from members of the Socialist Party, the Industrial Workers of the World, two of the groups from which many CPUSA members came, and groups like the former Populist Party and progressive factions of the Republican and Democratic parties?

Those who joined the CPUSA learned from experience. The Socialist Party's inability to address the question of racism in the U.S. and imperialist war globally, and the IWW's policy of working for one big union and one big general strike that would smash the state/government and lead to a reorganizing of society through decentralized worker controlled collectives had failed. To them, a different kind of party, which the leader of the Soviet socialist revolution Vladimir Lenin called a vanguard party, was necessary to educate and organize the working class and create a new revolutionary worker's state if capitalism was to be defeated before it destroyed civilization through imperialist war.

The CPUSA during its first decade

In the first decade, 1919-1929, Communists, such as Charles Ruthenberg, helped to unify the numerous parties, factions, and groups into what would eventually become the CPUSA. Additionally, Communists fought to build radical industrial unions through the Trade Union Educational League and the American Federation of Labor. William Z. Foster, who had led the Great Steel Strike of 1919, the largest strike in U.S. history up to that time, emerged as a leader of the TUEL and later of the CPUSA. By 1929, the TUEL would transform into the Trade Union Unity League.[1]

Unlike the Socialist Party or other radical groups, U.S. Communists emphasized the oppression of what was then called the Negro people as a cornerstone of capitalist rule. They made the organization of Black rural and urban workers (sharecroppers and tenant farmers in the South and industrial laborers in the North) into unions a

---

1. Edward P. Johanningsmeier, *Forging American Communism: The Life of William Z. Foster* (Princeton University Press, 1994), James R. Barrett *William Z. Foster and the Tragedy of American Radicalism* (University of Illinois Press, 2001) and William Z. Foster, *Pages from a Worker's Life* (International Publishers, 1970)

central focus of their work; they also organized both Black and white working people to fight against all forms of racism.[2]

Communists saw themselves as a vanguard or advanced party of class conscious working people whose purpose was to educate, organize and help to coordinate the actions of workers in their struggle against capitalist exploitation and oppression. Theirs was an internationalists cause. With the aid of the Communist International, or Comintern, they saw themselves also as part of a world movement of vanguard parties seeking to fight international capitalism and imperialism in defense of all the world's working people.

Along with the building of existing trade unions within the AFL and the struggle to establish new, inclusive industrial unions – through the TUEL and later the Congress of Industrial Organizations – Communists also helped to establish organizations that would defend the civil rights and liberties of minorities, recent immigrants, and the foreign born. The International Labor Defense and the American Committee for the Protection of the Foreign Born were two such organizations. The ILD played a leading role in the first decade in the defense of Nicola Sacco and Bartolomeo Vanzetti, two Italian born anarchists falsely accused of committing a robbery in Massachusetts in which a paymaster was killed; both were sentenced to death. Among those fighting for Sacco and Vanzetti was a young African American lawyer, William L. Patterson, whose experience led him to join the CPUSA along with a woman who later became his wife, Louise Thompson Patterson, a leader in the International Workers' Order.[3]

---

2. Robin D.G. Kelley, *Hammer And Hoe: Alabama Communists During The Great Depression* (University of North Carolina Press, 2015), Mark Naison, *Communists in Harlem During the Depression* (University of Illinois Press, 2004), Erik S. Gellman, *Death Blow to Jim Crow: The National Negro Congress and the Rise of Militant Civil Rights* (University of North Carolina Press, 2014), Mark Solomon, *The Cry Was Unity: Communists and African Americans, 1917-1936* (University of Mississippi Press, 1998), Harry Haywood, *Black Bolshevik: Autobiography of an Afro-American Communist* (Liberator Press, 1978) and Nell Irvin Painter, *The Narrative of Hosea Hudson. His Life as a Negro Communist in the South* (Harvard University Press, 1993), among many other examples. For a documentary history, see: Philip S. Foner and James S. Allen (eds), *American Communism and Black Americans: A Documentary History, 1919-1929* (Temple University Press, 1987) and Foner and Herbert Shapiro (eds), *American Communism and Black Americans: A Documentary History, 1930-1934* (Temple University Press, 1991)

3. For more on Patterson, Louise Thompson, the ILD, and Sacco and Vanzetti, see: Gerald Horne, *Black Revolutionary: William Patterson & the*

The Pattersons played an important role in the struggles against racist and working class oppression for the rest of their lives, forming a community in Harlem with W.E.B DuBois, Paul Robeson, Langston Hughes and other African American artists, scholars, and intellectuals. After WWI and the rise of fascist regimes, murderous capitalist dictatorships that sought to destroy not only all people's movements but also representative government and the rule of law, these struggles became more crucial than ever.

The Great Depression and the First Great Upsurge

Many of the struggles in which Communists had played a leading role in the 1920s had ended in defeat. The 1926 Passaic, New Jersey silk strike[4] and the later Gastonia, North Carolina mill strike[5] had been violently crushed. Sacco and Vanzetti died in the electric chair in 1927. But Communists, strengthened by both the world Communist movement and a political structure of a revolutionary vanguard party that united them, learned from these setbacks.

Many working people on factories and farms, as well as professional people, journalists, teachers, writers, and artists, who had participated in these struggles, learned to respect Communists for both their words and their deeds, for their courage and commitment.

The capitalist media followed the lead of Secretary of Commerce and later President Herbert Hoover, who proclaimed "a new era" of permanent prosperity. He claimed corporations would deemphasize short term profits to produce better and cheaper products, workers would "democratize" capitalism by owning stocks and bonds, and the small number of poor would be generously cared for by private charity. This capitalist utopian dream collapsed in the great stock market crash of October 1929. Over the next four years, unemployment rose to more than a one-third of the work force, wages for the employed were slashed, and millions lost their savings.

Capitalists identify progress with individual initiative and the ability to take advantage of changing situations, avoiding both panic and inaction. Ironically, it was the CPUSA that took collective initiative

---

Globalization of the African American Freedom Struggle (University of Illinois Press, 2013) and Keith Gilyard *Louise Thompson Patterson: A Life of Struggle for Justice* (Duke University Press, 2017)

4. See: Jacob Zumoff, *The Communist International and US Communism, 1919-1929* (Brill Academic Publishers, 2014)

5. See: Gregory Taylor, *The History of the North Carolina Communist Party* (University of South Carolina Press, 2009)

to fight the depression while the capitalist class panicked. Capitalist predictions that the depression would be over in weeks turned into months and months into years. As a result, in March 1930 Communists in the U.S. and throughout the world organized "international unemployment day" to mobilize against the crisis. Demonstrations here drew hundreds of thousands of participants, surprising both their organizers and the capitalist power structure. Communists saw these demonstrations and strikes as actions to advance higher levels of organized struggle for social justice, not ends in themselves.

Shortly thereafter, Unemployed Councils led by Communist Herbert Benjamin organized in cities throughout the country to block the evictions of thousands of tenants who could not pay their rent. The Unemployed Councils, USA demanded work relief (public jobs for the unemployed) and home relief (aid for those who could not work, particularly women with dependent children and the disabled). In rural areas, Communists worked with others to block farm foreclosures.

The Unemployed Councils came forward with a new idea – unemployment insurance, which was so identified with the CPUSA that the conservative AFL leadership initially rejected the proposal and condemned it as Communist program. The Unemployed Councils were also integrated, often sending groups of Black and white activists to resist the evictions of both Black and white families from their homes. This was revolutionary, especially in the South.[6]

Beginning in 1935, the New Deal government of Franklin Roosevelt, elected three years earlier at the height of the depression, would enact unemployment insurance along with comprehensive public works, labor, and social welfare legislation (collective bargaining rights, social security, and later minimum wages, and the 40 hour work week), the most important victories for workers in U.S. history.

Roosevelt, whom Communists initially opposed (William Z. Foster and James W. Ford ran as the CPUSA's presidential candidates in 1932), would define these policies as an attempt to reform, humanize and save the capitalist system. The African American activist-scholar W.E.B. DuBois – who joined the CPUSA in 1961[7] – would later say

_____

6. For more on the Unemployed Councils, as well as other work among the unemployed, see: Fraser Ottanelli, *The Communist Party of the United States from the Depression to World War II* (Rutgers University Press, 1991) and James J. Lorence, *The Unemployed People's Movement: Leftists, Liberals, and Labor in Georgia, 1929-1941* (University of Georgia Press, 2011)

7. Gerald Horne, *Red & Black: W.E.B. DuBois and the Afro-American Response to the Cold War, 1944-1963* (State University of New York Press, 1986)

that they represented a surge in the direction of socialism. In a sense, both sentiments were correct.

While the benefits were significantly less than the CPUSA and others had advocated for, the leading role of Communists in the Unemployed Councils, and in the unions and community organizations, made the CPUSA the undisputed head of a domestic Marxist movement toward socialism. Many of the policies they advocated and fought for, policies which were considered farfetched or impossible in 1929, became realities by the end of the decade.

Communists and the early struggle against racism

In 1931, nine Black teenagers were arrested, accused of raping two white girls on a train near Scottsboro Alabama. They were almost lynched; during a show trial an all-white, all-male jury sentenced them to death.

The ILD took on the case when other groups would not; they employed distinguished appeals lawyers coupled with a massive, worldwide publicity campaign that saved the defendants lives. To Communists and their allies, the defense of the Nine symbolized a major blow against racist oppression, Jim Crow, and lynch law. To them, it was a struggle to make freedom and democracy real for all Americans – a call just a relevant today as the assault on Black lives continues unabated.

The ILD and the global Communist movement led demonstrations throughout the world to mobilize support for the Scottsboro Nine. Although there was no happy ending – the case dragged on through a number of trials and compromises – most of the Nine were eventually freed and no one was executed.[8]

For the first time since the 1850s, when the abolitionist movement brought the horrors of slavery in the U.S. to international audiences, an important example of racist oppression in the United States reached a global audience. The ILD's militancy brought millions of ordinary people – Black and white – into the struggle to free the Nine.

As the New Deal government advanced labor and social welfare reforms in response to the working class upsurge, Communists led in the formation of new civil rights groups, the National Negro

---

8. For more on Scottsboro, see: Horne, *Black Revolutionary...*, Ibid, James Goodman *Stories of Scottsboro* (Vintage Books, 1995), Mary Stanton, *Red, Black, White: The Alabama Communist Party, 1930-1950* (University of Georgia Press, 2019)

Congress, and the Southern Negro Youth Congress. Both groups sought to build alliances with and through the CIO, the Works Progress Administration, and other New Deal agencies. The NNC fought to advance the interests of African Americans in the fight for full political, economic, and social equality. This took the form of campaigns for a national anti-lynching law, an end to police brutality, segregation, and disenfranchisement in the South. They organized to eliminate racist policies and practices throughout society. Communists also played a leading role in the development of the Southern Negro Youth Congress, which fought similar grassroots battles to advance the struggles against segregation, disenfranchisement, and all expressions of racism.[9]

Although these and other militant civil rights organizations, which Communists helped to build, would be ruthlessly suppressed during the post-World War II period, many of their veteran activists would play important roles in the victories won during the great civil rights upsurge of the 1960s; many civil rights leaders cut their political teeth in Communist-led organizations like the NNC, SNYC and the Council on African Affairs.[10] Among others, leading African American Communists like James W. Ford, Benjamin Davis, Jr., Henry Winston, Louis and Dorothy Burnham, Ferdinand Smith, Claudia Jones, James and Esther Cooper Jackson and W. Alphaeus Hunton, emerged from these struggles.

Communists and the birth of the CIO

Communist Party activists struggled to build inclusive industrial unions since the birth of the CPUSA. By the early 1930s, a strike wave swept the nation. One of the most important of these strikes was the San Francisco General Strike, led by Harry Bridges, the Australian born leader of the International Longshore and Warehousemen's Union, who was thought to be a Communist. Though his CPUSA membership is contested, Bridges saw in socialism the

---

9. For more on the NNC and SNYC, see: Gellman, *Death Blow...*, Ibid, Sara Rzeszutek, *James and Esther Cooper Jackson: Love and Courage in the Black Freedom Movement* (University of Kentucky Press, 2015), and David Levering Lewis (ed), *Red Activists And Black Freedom: James And Esther Jackson And The Long Civil Rights Revolution* (Routledge, 2012)

10. For more on the CAA, see: Penny M. Von Eschen, *Race Against Empire: Black Americans and Anticolonialism, 1937-1957* (Cornell University Press, 1997) and Nicholas Grant, *Winning Our Freedoms Together: African Americans and Apartheid, 1945-1960* (University of North Carolina Press, 2017)

road to freedom and dignity for all working people, and he worked closely with CPUSA activists to win the strike.[11]

While many of the other 1934 strikes were viciously repressed, the increase in organization and struggle spilled over into the off year elections, which saw New Deal Democrats increase their numbers in Congress.

The Roosevelt administration responded to this working class upsurge by enacting the National Labor Relations Act (or the Wagner Act), which provided a democratic process for workers to organize trade unions and negotiate collective bargaining agreements. As a result of this legislation – coupled with grassroots organizing, the strike wave, and protests – union membership grew dramatically. Roosevelt also signed the Social Security Act, establishing old age pensions and unemployment insurance, which the Communist-led Unemployed Councils largely developed; he also created a Works Progress Administration, establishing the most ambitious and successful public works/public employment policy in U.S. history, the work relief program Communists had fought for; and legislation to provide aid to families with dependent children, the home relief that Communists and their allies had demanded.

These programs, while conservatives in Congress were able to limit their benefits, represented the greatest gains working people had won since the Civil War with the abolition of slavery. Communists were key to these victories.

How did Communists contribute to the consolidation of these gains?

Legislation is necessary, but not in itself sufficient to bring about social change. After the Civil War for example, the wartime Homestead Act, whose purpose was the distribution of public lands to landless laborers and workers, was used by speculators to exploit those whom it was supposed to benefit – poor white farmers, laborers, and newly freed African Americans. Abolitionists advanced and enacted the Fourteenth Amendment to the Constitution of the United States, which used the term "persons" to provide protection for the four million former slaves,

---

11. For more on Bridges and the San Francisco General Strike, see: Bruce Nelson, *Workers on the Waterfront: Seamen, Longshoremen, and Unionism in the 1930s* (University of Illinois Press, 1990), Mike Quin, *The Big Strike* (New York: International Press, 1991), and Vernon L. Pederson, *The Communist Party On The American Waterfront: Revolution, Reform and the Quest for Power* (Lexington Books, 2020)

freed by the Thirteenth Amendment. However, that Amendment was later twisted by the Supreme Court, which declared that corporations were "persons" in need of protection from state regulation.

Regardless, the early 1930s strike wave coupled with New Deal legislation and massive protests often led by Communists, emboldened a group of unions led by John L. Lewis, leader of the United Mine Workers, to call for a policy of organizing industrial unions at the AFL's 1935 convention. After the conservative AFL leadership voted this proposal down, Lewis and a number of unions walked out to form a Committee on Industrial Organization. But who would organize the unions? To his credit, Lewis realized that an alliance with the CPUSA, their experienced cadre, pre-established (and often secret) networks, and their commitment to organizing Black workers, the chances of forming industrial unions would increase dramatically. So, he met privately with CPUSA leaders Earl Browder and William Z. Foster and forged an alliance. It was decided that CPUSA organizers would represent the CIO as long as they did not use their positions to overtly recruit members to the party.

Lewis wanted to build industrial unions as an end in itself. Communists saw industrial unions as part of a process that would empower working people and help them advance toward a socialist society. Of the first 200 CIO organizers, roughly one-fourth were CPUSA activists, and they were among the most successful in building nascent organizing committees into functioning trade unions, winning union elections, and leading successful strikes. After attempts at reconciliation with the AFL failed, the CIO ceased to be a Committee and became a Congress of Industrial Organizations.[12]

President Roosevelt ran in 1936 on the major labor and social welfare reforms his administration had enacted; his enemies denounced him as a stooge of the Communists. He hit back, denouncing them as "economic royalists" for whom freedom and democracy meant only the protection of their wealth and power. While the CPUSA ran

---

12. On Communists and the early CIO, see: Judith Stepan-Norris and Maurice Zeitlin, *Left Out: Reds and America's Industrial Unions* (Cambridge University Press, 2002), Michael Dennis, *Blood on Steel: Chicago Steelworkers and the Strike of 1937* (John Hopkins University Press, 2014), Clarence Taylor, *Reds at the Blackboard: Communism, Civil rights, and the New York City Teachers Union* (Columbia University Press, 2013), Rosemary Feurer, *Radical Unionism in the Midwest, 1900-1950* (University of Illinois Press, 2006), Roger Keeran, *The Communist Party and the Auto Workers Unions* (Indiana University Press, 1980), William Z. Foster, *History of the Communist Party of the United States* (New York: International Publishers, 1952), among many other examples

its own presidential candidate, Earl Browder, it also distinguished between Roosevelt and the Republican candidate Alf Landon, who pledged to repeal New Deal reforms. The CPUSA saw Landon as leading the country toward fascism.

Roosevelt's and the Democrat's enormous landslide victory inspired working class activists to greater militancy and led to one of the most important strikes in American history, the General Motors Sit Down Strike in Flint, Michigan. Communist Party activists, such as Bob Travis, Wyndham Mortimer, and Henry Krause, were key leaders of this strike; their strategy and tactics led General Motors, then the largest industrial corporation in the world, to sign a collective bargaining agreement which established the United Automobile Workers Union.[13] After that U.S. Steel, the second largest industrial corporation in the world, also faced with a sit down strike, signed a collective bargaining agreement which established the United Steel Workers Union. Of course, Communists also helped to lead the Steel Workers' Organizing Committee and brought tens of thousands of workers into the new union.

The struggle to form inclusive industrial unions wasn't easy. The Ford motor company used its private army of police spies and thugs to terrorize union organizers, stalling UAW efforts. Republic Steel on Memorial Day, 1937 used private guards and the Chicago police to shoot and kill peaceful picketers, including one CPUSA member. This became known as the Memorial Day Massacre,[14] which the press sought to cover up. The CPUSA through its media, especially photographs and film shot by its affiliated Film and Photo League, fought to publicize.

These events reached the public through investigations of the Civil Liberties subcommittee of the Senate Labor Committee, headed by the Wisconsin Progressive Party Senator Robert La Follette, Jr. The La Follette Committee, which included Communist lawyer John Abt,[15] also focused on the actions of "private detective agencies" in infiltrating trade unions, creating provocations, and employing strike breakers.

------

13. Keeran, *The Communist Party…*, Ibid, and Wyndham Mortimer, *Organize! My Life as a Union Man* (Beacon Press, 1971)

14. Dennis, *Blood on Steel…*, Ibid, and Tony Pecinovsky, *Let Them Tremble: Biographical Interventions Marking 100 Years of the Communist Party, USA* (New York: International Publishers 2019)

15. John Abt and Michael Myerson, *Advocate and Activist: Memoirs Of An American Communist Lawyer* (University of Illinois Press, 1993)

The economic decline in 1937 saw unemployment rise sharply. Conservatives blamed the recession on New Deal labor and social welfare policies. Communists and New Deal supporters called the crisis a "strike by capital." In Congress, a conservative coalition made up of Republicans and Southern Democrats, was organized to roll back both the regulation of business and the new labor and social welfare policies. This conservative coalition developed two broad strategies which continue to this day. The first strategy embodied in the Senate Committee on non-essential expenditures led by Senator Harry Byrd of Virginia, was to attempt to systematically cut the budgets for New Deal agencies and programs which benefitted labor and the people, with the understanding that these cuts over time would see the programs lose both effectiveness and support on the principle of "to defund is to destroy." The second strategy was embodied in the House Un-American Activities Committee, led by Congressman Martin Dies of Texas; this committee held circus hearings to claim that the trade union organizing campaigns, the strikes, the public works programs, and other social legislation, were all the part of an un-American communist conspiracy to subvert and eventually take over the U.S. government. The Committee also began to compile large lists of names, which it sent to local business groups, veterans' organizations, local and state governments, and police. Their goal was to harass activists and target CPUSA members.

Was the CPUSA and its activists responsible for this backlash?

This assertion is a classic example of blaming the victim. The CPUSA did not bring about the recession of 1937. It did not play a leading role in the establishment of CIO unions to take them over. Instead, it advanced a broad People's Front or coalition program which helped to make victories possible. That Communists were compelled to keep their party membership private in many of these struggles was a response to the fact that informers, provocateurs, and police spies in the employ of both the corporations and local governments worked tirelessly to disrupt the various movements and organizations Communists helped to birth. Additionally, J. Edgar Hoover's FBI also worked behind the scenes with HUAC to subvert New Deal programs.

The Roosevelt Administration mocked HUAC and often refused to honor its contempt citations. Roosevelt realized by 1938 that the real enemies of his administration were powerful congressional Democrats, particularly Southerners, who thanks to the almost complete disenfranchisement of African Americans through literacy tests and the anti-democratic poll tax, were able to win election after election and through seniority become chairs of the major congressional committees, undermining progressive initiatives.

Roosevelt campaigned against these conservative Democrats in the 1938 primaries, hoping to replace them with administration supporters, but he was too late. The administration's refusal to fight against segregation and disenfranchisement in the South came home to haunt it. The conservative Democrats were re-nominated and the Republican Party made major gains in the 1938 congressional elections, enabling the conservative coalition to stalemate further progressive legislation and weaken a number of New Deal agencies. By fighting against these reactionary elements directly, or through allied organizations – such as the NNC, the IWO, various Communist-led CIO unions, etc. – the CPUSA's membership and influence grew considerably.

Communists for Peace and War

After the Hitler fascist regime in Germany launched a dictatorship based on extreme forms of racism and militarism, using terror and murder against its political enemies and the Jewish religious minority in particular, it also engaged in an enormous military buildup, threatening wars of conquest against its neighbors. The major European capitalist countries did nothing to stop Hitler.

The Soviet Union, on the other hand, called on the League of Nations for a policy of collective security, meaning international commitments to stop Hitler's and Mussolini's aggressions in Europe and the Japanese Empire's aggressions in Asia.

Communists in the U.S., like Communists everywhere, organized demonstrations and campaigns against Mussolini's colonial invasion of Ethiopia (1935), Japan's launching of a full scale war against China (1937) and Nazi Germany's savage and escalating persecution of Germany's Jewish minority. They called for consumer boycotts of goods imported from the fascist states. Communists also led campaigns against U.S. corporations (e.g., Standard Oil, GM, Ford, etc.) who made huge profits helping to build up the fascist war machines. These same multinational corporations also fought ferociously to prevent their workers from organizing unions. To Communists, these struggles were interconnected.

When Hitler and Mussolini backed General Francisco Franco's Fascist coup against the elected government of the Spanish Republic with tanks, bombers, and thousands of troops (1936), the

Soviet Union was the only major power to provide military aid to the Republic, which fought against great odds to survive. Communists throughout the world played the leading role in organizing anti-fascist volunteer brigades to fight alongside the defenders of the Spanish Republic. CPUSA members played the leading role in the mobilization of the Abraham Lincoln Brigade, organizing nearly 3,000 U.S. volunteers to fight against fascism in Spain – mostly fellow Communists.[16]

But the policy of collective security advanced by the Soviet Union and Communists throughout the world failed. British Prime Minister Neville Chamberlain advanced a policy of "appeasement." The major European non-fascist capitalist states gave the fascists what they wanted in order to avoid war and/or to ensure that war would be directed against the Soviet Union. They feared that collective security against fascism would advance socialist and communist parties, and coalition governments like the Peoples Front in Spain, and anti-colonial revolutions in India, Africa, and Asia. They also preferred to give up China to Japan in exchange for economic concessions rather than permit the Communist Party of China to lead the Chinese people to victory in a revolution for socialism and national liberation.

At the Munich Conference (1938) Chamberlain and Eduard Daladier, the British and French leaders, met with Hitler and Mussolini to dismember Czechoslovakia and give it over to Nazi Germany. The elected government of Czechoslovakia was not even allowed to attend the conference in which it was destroyed as a nation. Japan continued its undeclared war of conquest in China, killing millions, with no embargo or sanctions from any of the major capitalist countries.

From this the Soviet leadership concluded that the non-fascist capitalist states were seeking to unleash Nazi Germany against the USSR, a reasonable conclusion. As a result, the Soviet Union negotiated a non-aggression pact with Nazi Germany which the capitalist newspapers, most of whom had supported the Munich agreement, called "The Hitler-Stalin Pact."

---

16. For more on the Lincoln Brigade, see: Peter N. Carroll and James D. Fernandez, *Facing Fascism: New York & The Spanish Civil War* (New York University Press, 2007), Carroll, *The Odyssey of the Abraham Lincoln Brigade: American in the Spanish Civil War* (Stanford University Press, 1994) and Carroll, Michael Nash and Melvin Small, *The Good Fight Continues: World War II Letters From The Abraham Lincoln Brigade* (New York University Press, 2006)

Communist Parties throughout the world now defined the military confrontations as a war between rival imperialist blocs, while continuing to intensify their fight against militarism and racism. Nazi Germany invaded Western Europe in the spring of 1940. Those who supported the appeasement of Hitler at Munich now capitulated to him in Europe, establishing fascist collaborator governments and accepting occupation.

Communists at the same time used their organizational skills and experience, courage, and commitment, to play a leading role in developing anti-fascist resistance movements, which would grow into partisan fighting organizations in European and Asia/Pacific Island nations.

In the United States the CPUSA, targeted because of its anti-war stance, continued to mobilize workers in trade union struggles and intensified its anti-racist campaigns despite heightened political repression. Its continued solidarity with the Soviet Union and the world Communist movement after the non-aggression pact, cost it thousands of members, people who felt that the party had betrayed the anti-fascist cause.[17]

Other working class organizations initially opposed U.S. involvement in what was considered another European war. Prominent individuals, such as Norman Thomas, leader of the Socialist Party, and John L. Lewis, president of the CIO, also opposed involvement. Regardless, the CPUSA was not alone in its anti-war stance, though it has been vilified as such.

The principle opposition to U.S. support for the allied side came from the isolationist America First Committee, funded by large corporations that had been and wanted to continue to do business with Hitler and the Japanese Empire. The America First Movement drew its grassroots support from reactionary and openly pro-fascist, racist and anti-Semitic groups. Communists fought actively against these organizations and their anti-labor, racist activities, exposing their actions as an attempt to lay the groundwork for a fascist America.

The CPUSA through World War II

In June 1941, Nazi Germany, and its allies – with over three million soldiers – launched the military invasion of the Soviet Union, and thereby changed the character of the war. Communists understood this change and intensified their resistance activities in fascist and

17. Maurice Isserman, *Which Side Were You On? The American Communist Party during the Second World War* (University of Illinois Press, 1993)

occupied countries, as well as their work to build coalitions in allied and neutral countries. America First leaders like Charles Lindbergh, who virulently opposed U.S. aid to the Soviet Union under the lend lease program, also understood this changed character of the war. In the battle over lend lease aid to the Soviets, Senator Harry Truman said on the floor of the Senate, "if the Germans were winning we should support the Russians and if the Russians were winning we should support the Germans and that way let them kill as many as possible" (though, when this appeared in the press he repudiated the statement and said he did not want Hitler to win the war).

Even before the U.S. entered the war, following the attack on Pearl Harbor, Communist activists sought to mobilize the trade unions and all mass organizations to fight against the America First isolationists. Communists also took up President Roosevelt's call to make the U.S. the arsenal of democracy and win the battle of production, which given the U.S.'s industrial capacity, was essential to victory. Along with the sacrifice and heroism of an estimated 15,000 CPUSA members who served in the armed forces,[18] many in combat situations, these actions represented the highest form of patriotism and internationalism.

But the war at home between capital and labor, the war against racism and anti-Semitism, continued after Pearl Harbor. U.S. corporations dragged their feet on war production; they were worried that Hitler would win the war and that they would lose their European markets; their German and European subsidiaries continued war production for the Axis.

Communists fought to advance the Fair Employment Practices Commission, which the New Deal government had created in 1941 to integrate Black workers into the expanding war production industries. Struggle took many forms at the grassroots level. Communist trade unionists in defense plants worked to defend Black workers from racist foremen and to challenge racist attitudes among white workers; Communists like Thelma Dale, for example, challenged racist seniority policies in union contracts; they also fought to integrate union leadership.[19] Unfortunately, racism was often used against Communists in leadership struggles, as well as in wildcat strikes,

---

18. Isserman, *Which Side...*, Ibid. According to Isserman, nearly 1/5 of male communists were serving in the armed forces by January 1943. Ellen W. Schrecker and Phillip Deery, *The Age of McCarthyism: A Brief history with Documents* (Bedford / St. Martin's Press, 2016)

19. Dayo F. Gore, *Radicalism at the Crossroads: African American Women Activists in the Cold War* (New York University Press, 2012)

which were launched against African Americans in war production jobs. Communists, like Henry Winston and Claude Lightfoot, also fought to desegregate the armed forces.[20]

Conservative candidates made significant gains in the 1942 congressional elections and began to strike at progressive programs, eliminating the Works Progress Administration and the Farm Security Administration. Throughout this time, though, unions grew substantially, in part thanks to the War Labor Board's maintenance of membership policy, which compelled employers to accept union shops or lose their war contracts. In response, anti-labor groups and conservative politicians passed the War Labor Disputes Act over President Roosevelt's veto, which greatly reduced union rights to engage in political action while restricting union workplace activities. They also intensified their efforts to pass anti-union, open-shop laws at the state level using the term "right to work" as their rally cry.

To Communists, Franklin Roosevelt's victory was necessary to both save and advance the labor and social welfare gains of the New Deal, while also winning both the war and the peace. CPUSA activists supported the CIO's creation of a national political action committee, or PAC, which played a major role in mobilizing workers to defeat conservative candidates. In fact, CIO-PAC was able to organize Texas workers to force Martin Dies, founder and chairman of HUAC, out of Congress. It also brought President Roosevelt's campaign for an economic bill of rights to millions of working people. While the PAC failed to stop Southern segregationist Democrats from removing Vice President Henry Wallace from the ticket and replacing him with Senator Harry Truman, a centrist politician and product of the Kansas City Democratic / mob machine, it played an important role in re-electing Roosevelt and defeating Governor Thomas Dewey.

Mistakes and Leadership Problems in the CPUSA

During WWII, the CPUSA leadership supported the arrest and detention of Japanese Americans (including Japanese Communists) by the U.S.; Japanese American CPUSA members were also expelled. Nothing can be said to excuse this appeasement of racism by the CPUSA. All that can be said is that Communists later denounced this

20. See: Henry Winston, *Old Jim Crow Has Got To Go!* (New Age Publishers, 1941) and Claude Lightfoot and Timothy V Johnson (ed.), *Autobiography of Claude M. Lightfoot: Chicago Slums to World Politics* (New Outlook Publishers, 1985)

policy and made an apology to both the Japanese American people and Japanese American Communists.[21]

An internal problem also beset Communists. Earl Browder, general secretary of the CPUSA since the early 1930s, used his influence to transform the CPUSA into the Communist Political Association, abandoning Lenin's model of a revolutionary vanguard party for an association of trade union leaders, progressive intellectuals, and activists. Browder also called for a post-war policy of cooperation with the major centers of finance capital if they would accept and support progressive policies at home and abroad. Many party activists were confused by Browder's policies, which William Z. Foster strongly opposed. U.S. Communists began to present Browder's policies in discussions with comrades in liberated Europe during the war's final months, especially in France and Italy. There Communists had won mass support and were among the most powerful political forces. Jacques Duclos, a veteran leader of the Communist Party of France, wrote an article which sharply criticized Browder's policies and rejected them as a model for Communist Parties. To Duclos, it was one thing to participate with capitalist parties in post-war coalition governments to rebuild countries devastated by fascism and war. It was quite another to dissolve Communist Parties into political pressure groups. To him, this constituted a major victory for those whose appeasement and collaboration had led to the war and to all of the atrocities associated with it.

In 1945, immediately after the end of the war, U.S. Communists held an extraordinary convention to disband the CPA and reconstitute the CPUSA. Browder was expelled.[22]

Emerging Cold War and Red Scare

By the end of WWII, U.S. capitalism had emerged nearly hegemonic. Outside of the continental United States, it was now a devastated world; all major capitalist competitors – enemy and ally, alike – were either on the brink of bankruptcy or in ruins or both. Simultaneously,

---

21. For more on Japanese Americans and the CPUSA, see: Scott Kurashige, *The Shifting Ground of Race: Black And Japanese Americans In The Making Of Multiethnic Los Angeles* (Princeton University Press, 2010) and Josephine Fowler, *Japanese and Chinese Immigrant Activists: Organizing in America and International Communist Movements, 1919-1933* (Rutgers University Press, 2007)

22. James G. Ryan, *Earl Browder: The Failure of American Communism* (University of Alabama Press, 1997)

under the New Deal government, between 1933 and 1945 union membership had increased more than five-fold; as noted above, Communists played a leading role in organizing the emerging industrial unions. Further, during the war a system of progressive income and corporate taxation had been instituted; the administration also favored creating programs for national health insurance, full employment, federal education, and housing projects. CPUSA activists supported these programs and were crucial to winning grassroots support for them.

The tide was about to turn, though. The anti-communist trade union leader, James Carey, of the United Electrical Workers, predicted the future when in 1945 he said, "in this war [WWII] we fought with the communists against the fascists and in the next war we will fight with the fascists against the communists." That next war was the Cold War, which made permanent the war economy established just a few years prior. Soon the war-time alliance with the Soviet Union was broken. Over the next few years, newspaper headlines, radio newscasters, and movie newsreels screamed about Soviet spies stealing atomic secrets, the Communist takeover in Eastern Europe and China, war raging in Korea, and the emergence of Communist-backed national liberation movements throughout Asia, Africa, and Latin America. The U.S. ruling class, and their bought and paid for politicians, set their sights on domestic Communists, too, thereby initiating the Red Scare.

In the emerging Cold War world, domestic Communists were labeled "fifth columnists" determined to overthrow the U.S. government through "force and violence." Both the Republican and Democratic parties united behind these policies. The Communist Party fought against these developments by mobilizing support to repeal the Taft-Hartley Law, which rolled back key labor gains and barred Communists from serving as trade union officers.

As it became clear that the Truman Administration could not be dissuaded from destroying the New Deal coalition from above, Communists joined with disaffected New Deal liberals and progressives to form a third party, the Progressive Party, led by former Vice President Henry Wallace. Wallace ran on a program of advancing the New Deal's postwar program along with abolishing segregation and racism. The Progressive Party also advocated an end to the Cold War through a revival of wartime cooperation with the Soviet Union.[23]

---

23. For more on Wallace and the Progressive Party, see: Thomas W. Devine, *Henry Wallace's 1948 Presidential Campaign and the Future of Postwar Liberalism* (University of North Carolina Press, 2013)

The Truman administration won the election by moving to the left, supporting much of the Progressive Party's domestic platform, while soft pedaling its international Cold War policies. Truman's victory made everything worse; none of the promised expanded domestic programs were enacted. Communists and their allies, those who had helped to win the grassroots battles of the Great Depression, were purged from CIO unions; at that time Communists led about one-fourth of the CIO's then membership.[24] In 1948, the top leadership of the CPUSA were arrested, tried, and eventually imprisoned[25] – some went underground, others, such as Claudia Jones and Ferdinand Smith, were deported.[26]

Communists faced a long period of political repression, a period that continued long after Joseph McCarthy's downfall as an individual. Hundreds of Communists were arrested, thousands were harassed, spied on, and intimidated. That the CPUSA survived at all is a testimony to its resilience and strength. But Communists did more than just survive. They mobilized against great odds to fight against the Korean War and nuclear proliferation, and for democratic rights. Additionally, Communists continued their vanguard role in the fight for African American equality. The Civil Rights Congress, led by William L. Patterson, defended Rosa Lee Ingram, among other African Americans wrongfully convicted by Jim Crow courts. The CRC also published the historic document, *We Charge Genocide*, which was brought before the United Nations in 1951 – by Patterson and his good friend, and fellow Communist, Paul Robeson; the document was translated into many languages, and forcefully brought international attention to bear against the most egregious aspects of Jim Crow.[27]

Well into the mid-1950s, Communists continued to lead important grassroots organizations, such as the Jefferson School for Social Science (as well as other party-sponsored popular education

24. Stepan-Norris and Zeitlin, *Left Out...*, Ibid
25. For an analysis of the nature of the Smith Act trials, see: John Somerville, *The Communist Trials and the American Tradition: Expert Testimony on Force and Violence, and Democracy* (New York: International Publishers, 2000)
26. See: Carole Boyce Davies, *Left of Karl Marx: The Political Life of Black Communist Claudia Jones* (Duke University Press, 2008) and Gerald Horne, *Red Seas: Ferdinand Smith and Radical Black Sailors in the United States and Jamaica* (New York University Press, 2004)
27. Gerald Horne, *Communist Front?: The Civil Rights Congress, 1946-1956* (Associated University Presses, 1988)

institutions),[28] the International Workers Order,[29] Sojourners for Peace & Justice,[30] and the Council on African Affairs.[31] Communists – like Lee Lorch – would help desegregate public schools, too.[32] CPUSA members also campaigned for the international Stockholm Peace Petition – initiated by the Communist-led World Peace Council – and struggled against the expanding nuclear arms race, among other examples.[33]

By defending themselves against HUAC repression and the political show trials, by not accepting plea bargains or "confessing" their actions, Communists helped to bring about later Supreme Court decisions that defended the First and Fifth Amendment rights of all Americans. They sharply reduced the danger of an open fascist dictatorship in the United States. The CPUSA, even with many of its leaders imprisoned or underground or deported, and the mass organizations it had helped to create destroyed, not only survived but played an important role beating back the political straight jacket of McCarthyism. In short, their defense of the Bill of Rights benefited all Americans.

Though McCarthy was now dead, unfortunately J. Edgar Hoover remained director of the FBI. In response to Supreme Court rulings restricting public sector blacklisting and HUAC prison sentences, the FBI established a secret Counter-Intelligence Program (COINTELPRO) in 1956, which intensified its increased infiltration of Communist Party clubs; it also used burglaries, forged documents, and vigilante groups to sow divisions within the CPUSA, harass CPUSA members and their families, and encourage member resignations.[34]

---

28. Marvin E. Gettleman, "No Varsity Teams": New York's Jefferson School of Social Science, 1943-1956," *Science & Society*, Vol. 66, No. 3 (Fall 2002)

29. Robert M. Zecker, *"A Road to Peace and Freedom": The International Workers Order and the Struggle for Economic Justice and Civil Rights, 1930-1954* (Temple University Press, 2018)

30. Gore, *Radicalism at the…*, Ibid

31. Penny M. Von Eschen, *Race Against Empire: Black Americans and Anti-colonialism, 1937-1957* (Cornell University Press, 1997) and Nicholas Grant, *Winning Our Freedoms Together: African Americans and Apartheid, 1945-1960* (University of North Carolina Press, 2017)

32. Re Lorch, see: Pecinovsky, *Let Them Tremble…*, Ibid

33. Horne, *Red & Black…*, Ibid

34. Aaron J. Leonard and Conor A. Gallagher, *A Threat of the First Magnitude: Counterintellegence & Infiltration from the Communist Party to the Revolutionary Union – 1962-1974* (Repeater Press, 2018)

The dissemination of Soviet Premier Nakita Khrushchev's secret speech denouncing Joseph Stalin's crimes, coupled with internal factional struggles (primarily between William Z. Foster and John Gates, editor of the *Daily Worker*), along with crippling security measures, the elimination of membership lists, among other factors, undoubtedly weakened the CPUSA. However, by 1958-1959 Communists were beginning to regroup. They discussed their role in the emerging youth and student upsurge, and the Civil Rights Movement. The election of Gus Hall as general secretary in 1959, solidified this shift in direction.[35]

The CPUSA and the 1960s and 1970s: The Second Great Upsurge

Under the leadership of Gus Hall, Elizabeth Gurley Flynn, Benjamin Davis, Jr., William L. Patterson, Dorothy Healey, Arnold Johnson, Herbert Aptheker, and Henry Winston, among others, the CPUSA redoubled its efforts to rebuild. With the aid of Communist Parties and socialist countries – the Soviet Union, the Eastern European states, the Peoples Republic of China, and Cuba, especially – the CPUSA continued its decades long commitment to African American equality and civil rights. The early civil rights victories (the 1960 sit-ins, the 1961 freedom rides, the 1963 March on Washington, etc.) embodied the slogan "Freedom Now," while "We Shall Overcome," published by *People's Songs Bulletin* and sang by CPUSA ally and movement supporter Pete Seager,[36] became a slogan for both the upsurge and the domestic policies of the war on poverty and the great society. Communists also helped to found and fund *Freedomways*, the quarterly journal of Black liberation.

During this time Communists worked with the Student Non-Violent Coordinating Committee, Students for a Democratic Society, as well as the Southern Christian Leadership Conference, among other groups. Communists played an important role in Women Strike for Peace, which carried forward campaigns for nuclear disarmament, and against the U.S. blockade and war threats against the Cuban Revolution. While some historians have treated the role of former Communists in these and other organizations, few have

---

35. Pecinovsky, *Let Them Tremble...*, Ibid
36. Re Seeger and the CPUSA, see: David A. Graham, "Pete Seeger's All-American Communism," *The Atlantic*, January 29, 2014 and John Bachtell, "Pete Seeger and American communism," *People's World*, February 13, 2014

acknowledged the important involvement of CPUSA members. In reality, Communists and former Communists continued to work together in mass organizations throughout the 1960s.

Additionally, Communists spoke on hundreds of campuses to tens of thousands of students throughout the early and mid-1960s. "Ban the Ban (on Communist speakers)" became a rally cry on campuses across the country. Communist initiated and led youth groups, such as the W.E.B. DuBois Clubs, founded in 1964, mobilized young people to advance civil rights and fight for peace. As did CPUSA members in the National Mobilization Committee to End the War in Vietnam, or New Mobe, and Student Mobe – which organized one of the largest student strikes in U.S. history. Communists also helped to found and lead the National Chicano Moratorium Committee Against the Vietnam War.

CPUSA leaders, such as Herbert Aptheker and later Gus Hall and Jarvis Tyner, among others, risked their lives visiting Vietnam and wrote firsthand accounts of the brutality of the war being waged there. Additionally, in 1966 Communists were among the first GI's to refuse to be deployed to Vietnam; two of the Fort Hood Three were party members. Their actions spurred the genesis of the organized GI anti-war movement. Later the party-led Young Workers' Liberation League would organize a new generation of young people into the Communist Party.

In the larger civil rights and peace movements, Communists fought for broad united front coalitions with realistic goals. They opposed those in SNCC who voted to become an all-Black organization in 1965, as well as white anarchist and ultra-left oriented "new left" or "new communist" radicals who sought to import guerrilla tactics. CPUSA activists worked with the Black Panther Party, too; some BPP members would meet at CPUSA members houses. And noted Black lawyer, and CPUSA leader William L. Patterson, provided legal counsel to the BPP.

Communists also helped to lead the growing movement for environmental sustainability. Notable Communists, such as Virginia Brodine, not only helped to found environmental groups, they wrote for and edited prominent environmental magazines, such as *Scientist and Citizen* and *Environment*.

Communists continued to fight for a broad based people's coalition on both domestic and foreign policy. In 1968, Communist Charlene Mitchell became the first African American woman to run for President of the United States, a hallmark moment for civil rights and feminism. To many, another Black woman Communist, Angela

Davis, represented the bridge between the old and new generation of reds. After her arrest, and during the worldwide campaign that resulted in her acquittal – reminiscent of the campaign Communists led on behalf of the Scottsboro Nine – Davis became an international symbol of Black militancy, the fight for equality, and international socialism. Not only was she a CPUSA leader, but – along with Mitchell – she also helped to found in 1973 the National Alliance Against Racist and Political Repression, one of the most important civil rights organizations of the 1970s and 1980s. The NAARPR raised the issue of racist mass incarceration. Like the International Labor Defense in the 1930s and the Civil Rights Congress in the 1950s, the NAARPR defended victims of racist repression, such as JoAnne Little and Frank Chapman, among others. Other Communists, such as Judith LeBlanc, helped to lead the American Indian Movement and participated in the Stand Off at Wounded Knee.

Communists played a significant role in the creation of the Coalition of Black Trade Unionists and the Coalition of Labor Union Women, as well as Trade Unionists for Action and Democracy and the newspaper *Labor Today*. CPUSA leaders, like Henry Winston, made important contributions to the struggle for international solidarity with the birth of the National Anti-Imperialist Movement in Solidarity with African Liberation, which helped to spearhead the domestic South Africa divestment movement and worked in solidarity with the African National Congress and the South African Communist Party. The cross-Atlantic bond between ANC-SACP leaders and the CPUSA persisted through the demise of apartheid, and Communists, such as Angela Davis and Charlene Mitchell, would meet with Nelson Mandela after his release in 1990.[37]

In the 1980s

In the 1980s, while the AFL-CIO and much of the Democratic Party supported President Reagan's intensification of the global Cold War abroad and offered only token opposition to "Reaganomics" domestically, the CPUSA campaigned against the administration's arming of the Nicaraguan Contras and its support of the brutal dictatorship in El Salvador. Communists also joined with a growing peace movement to oppose the Reagan administrations nuclear arms buildup and its "Stars Wars" space shield, which given its Cold

---

37. The foregoing paragraphs regarding CPUSA activism during the 1960s and 1970s is taken from Pecinovsky's, *Let Them Tremble...*, Ibid

War escalation many feared would be used as a pretext to launch a nuclear first strike. Communist-led formations, such as the NAARPR and NAIMSAL, and the Congress of the Unemployed, continued to fight for racial equality, international solidarity (against apartheid South Africa), and relief for unemployed workers facing the brunt of factory closures, respectively.[38] Communists also helped organize Solidarity Day in March 1981, where an estimated 500,000 union members rallied and protested in Washington D.C. against Republican anti-union policies; for example, CPUSA leader Judith LeBlanc worked in the AFL-CIO's national office for months leading up to the march.[39]

Further, at a time when much of the left were denouncing the Soviet intervention in Afghanistan, the CPUSA stood largely alone in the U.S. in pointing to both the positive accomplishments of the Afghan revolution, and to the feudal conditions the so-called freedom fighters were seeking to restore as they advanced their holy war.[40] A key U.S. ally, strategic planner, fundraiser, and recruiter in this holy war was Osama bin Laden, who in 1988 created Al Qaeda. After the demise of the Soviet Union, bin Laden would bring his holy war to the United States resulting in the World Trade Center attacks and the loss of thousands of lives. Communists were in the frontlines of a post-9-11 protest movement calling for peace, while also trying to expose U.S. foreign policy decisions that lead to terror.

1991 and Beyond

After the dissolution of the Soviet Union (1991) propagandists for capitalism and imperialism proclaimed the final death of socialism and communism. It was "the end of history" they declared. These developments brought on a major crisis within the CPUSA, eventuating in a split with a number of prominent Communists – such as Angela Davis, Charlene Mitchell, and Herbert Aptheker – leaving the CPUSA and organizing the Committees of Correspondence.[41]

---

38. Pecinovsky, *Let Them Tremble...*, Ibid

39. Judith LeBlanc, author interview with Pecinovsky, 10/29/2019

40. For example, see: Phillip Bonosky, *Afghanistan – Washington's Secret War* (New York: International Publishers, 2001) and William Pomeroy, *Why Soviet Troops Are In Afghanistan* (National Council of American-Soviet Friendship, March 1980)

41. Daniel Rosenberg, "From Crisis to Split: The Communist Party, USA, 1989-1991," *American Communist History*, Vol. 18, 2019

Years later many would return to the CPUSA and/or continue to work closely with CPUSA members. After Gus Hall's death, CPUSA leaders, such as Sam Webb and Jarvis Tyner, made personal appeals to COC members in an attempt to heal old wounds.

The divisions within the CPUSA and the defeats within the world Communist movement were unprecedented. Despite this, Gus Hall called upon party activists to struggle for workers' rights and peace, and against racism, sexism, and war.

While the 1991 split further weakened the CPUSA, it weathered the storm and survived, and by the end of the decade initiated a new and exciting public access TV project called *Changing America.* Additionally, Communists participated in the Battle in Seattle.[42] They were among the thousands who protested in Florida after the George W. Bush "won" the election due to "hanging chads" and a Supreme Court decision ending the recount.[43] Communists also helped to lead one of the largest strikes of the 1990s, the UPS-Teamsters Strike in 1997,[44] which buoyed labor militancy, foreshadowing the change in AFL-CIO leadership to come by the early 2000s with the election of John Sweeney and Linda Chavez-Thompson.

In the early 2000s, Communists helped lead community-labor coalitions like Jobs with Justice, student groups like the Student Labor Action Project and the United States Student Association; and they held leadership positions in United For Peace & Justice, the National Youth & Student Peace Coalition, as well as Veterans for Peace. Communists took to the streets of Ferguson, Missouri after the murder of Michael Brown. They partnered with Black Lives Matter activists across the country to protest police brutality, and help African American activists get elected to local office.[45] More recently, as the nation reels from the COVID-19 pandemic, Communists are among the union organizers fighting to protect meat packers, their families, and all of us from the incompetence and callousness of the Trump administration.

42. Pecinovsky, *Let Them Tremble…*, Ibid

43. Pecinovsky was among the contingent of CPUSA members in Florida at that time.

44. Joe Henry, author interview with Pecinovsky, 2/10/2020. Henry worked full-time in the Teamsters national communications team during the strike; Henry was close to Ron Carey.

45. Pecinovsky, *Let Them Tremble…*, Ibid

Conclusion

A strong, vibrant CPUSA was essential to the establishment of inclusive industrial unions, social security, unemployment insurance, minimum wages, public works legislation, and skills training for millions. A vibrant CPUSA planted the seeds for the civil rights movement and served as a catalyst for the women's rights/women's liberation movement, the anti-war/peace movement, and the environmental movement. The CPUSA remains essential today and tomorrow to the advancement of all movements for economic and social justice, against racism, imperialism, and environmental destruction.

Those who sought to destroy the CPUSA after WWII and their kin today, have brought about the economic, environmental, and human rights crisis we currently face. The above is just a brief overview. There is much we can learn from the history of the Communist Party, USA as we celebrate a century of struggle for socialism, peace, and democracy.

Chapter 2

Building a Party of Action: C.E. Ruthenberg, First Leader of the CPUSA

By C.J. Atkins

At the time of his death in 1927, Charles Emil Ruthenberg was lauded as "one of the most indicted and imprisoned workers" in the history of the U.S. labor movement.[1] During his life, he was often spoken of – by both admirers and detractors – as "the most arrested man in America."[2] When he passed away suddenly at the age of 44, he cheated a Michigan prison of its next inmate and left a young Communist Party, USA – then called the Workers (Communist) Party – in mourning for its first general secretary. Yet today, few know his name.

Ruthenberg is buried in the row of graves behind the Lenin Mausoleum in Moscow's Red Square – symbolic, perhaps, of his exile from U.S. political history. A bronze urn bearing his remains is interred in the Kremlin wall beside those of other U.S. notables – early 20th century radicals like journalist John Reed and I.W.W. leader 'Big Bill' Haywood. Though Reed and Haywood remain staples in left and labor studies, Ruthenberg's life and work have received considerably less attention in the nearly 100 years since his death. This Ohio-born socialist played a pivotal role, however, in founding the Communist Party and helped ensure its survival in the dangerous years of the U.S. government's first Red Scare, which terrorized left-wingers and immigrants following the Russian Revolution and the strike waves that paralyzed U.S. capitalism in 1919.

No more than a handful of articles have been written about his life, and only one book length biography has ever appeared – *The*

---

1. William Z. Foster, "C.E. Ruthenberg." *Labor Defender*, April 1927, 53
2. Anna Damon, "How Ruthenberg, Founder of the ILD, Acted in Court," *Daily Worker*, March 9, 1935, 7

Day is Coming: Life and Work of Charles E. Ruthenberg, authored by a fellow founding CPUSA member, Oakley C. Johnson, in 1957.[3] Other Communist leaders and personalities have occasionally paid tribute to Ruthenberg in the pages of the party press over the decades, but outside of Communist circles, his contributions to the labor and anti-war movements of the United States have enjoyed scant recognition.[4]

One part of the explanation for why Ruthenberg has occupied a marginal role in the popular culture and history of the left (aside from the anti-communism that has regularly sidelined radical leaders), is the fact that he has been consistently downgraded in, or even erased from, the historical narrative offered by mainstream accounts of the Communist Party's foundation. The 1981 film *Reds* can be taken as an example. Anyone who has seen the movie has probably marveled at Warren Beatty's electric portrayal of the 1917 Bolshevik uprising and the clash between the dynamic personalities

---

3. Oakley Johnson, *The Day is Coming: Life and Work of Charles E. Ruthenberg* (New York: International Publishers, 1957). With his biography, Johnson intended to cement Ruthenberg's place in the pantheon of U.S. Communist leaders, perhaps sensing that Ruthenberg's work and contributions were fading from the memories of the party faithful. When he first appealed to the readers of the *Daily Worker* for help gathering materials in July 1940, he promised the book would be "an important contribution to the history of the Communist Party," and said it would stand alongside "such biographical and autobiographical writings" of luminaries as William Z. Foster, Big Bill Haywood, Earl Browder, and Mother Bloor. It took more than a decade and a half for him to complete the work. See: Johnson, Oakley. "Johnson Writing Book on Life of Chas. E. Ruthenberg," *Daily Worker*, July 5, 1940, 3

4. Other biographical sketches by CP-affiliated writers include: Max Bedacht, "C.E. Ruthenberg," *The Communist*, April 1927, 67-71; Jay Lovestone, *Ruthenberg: Communist Fighter and Leader* (New York: Workers Library Publishers, 1928), Robert Minor, "Our C.E.," *The Communist*, March 1935, 217-226, Elizabeth Gurley Flynn, *Debs, Haywood, Ruthenberg* (New York: Workers Library Publishers, 1939), Arthur Simson, "The 50-year memorial to Ruthenberg, a founder of CP," *Daily World*, March 5, 1977. Ruthenberg's son Daniel wrote a brief overview of his father's life in the mid-1930s, see: Dan Ruthenberg, "Charles E. Ruthenberg: Fighter for Socialism," *Ohio Marches Toward Peace and Progress: 1937 Yearbook* (Cleveland: CPUSA Ohio Historical Commission, 1937), 29-30. A non-CP account based on interviews with family members and Ruthenberg's papers at the Ohio Historical Society can be found in two works by Stephen Millett, "Charles E. Ruthenberg and American Bolshevism: 1917-1921" (Unpublished M.A. thesis, Ohio State University, 1970), and "Charles E. Ruthenberg: The Development of an American Communist, 1909-1927," *Ohio History* (Vol. 81, No. 3), 1972, 193-209

of John Reed and Louis C. Fraina; they are presented as the driving forces behind the CPUSA's founding as two separate parties in the summer of 1919.[5] The film was rightly lauded at the time of its release for breaking through the Cold War prejudices that were still standard in the 1980s, but the explanation for why the party had a "twin birth" was far more complex than the "immigrants vs. native born" divide that played out on screen. In that telling, inherited from Theodore Draper's book, *The Roots of American Communism*, the Communist Party of America under the Italian Fraina was an immigrant-dominated group out of touch with the American worker, while Reed's Communist Labor Party was led by English speakers and catered to the concerns of the U.S. born proletariat.[6]

Completely left out of the movie was the fact that the Ohio born C.E. Ruthenberg, as he preferred to be called, was one of the most prominent left figures in the country in 1919 and that he tirelessly worked for unity between the two parties before they were even established and long after. In the film, Fraina (played by Paul Sorvino) is seen showing up at the meeting of the now-expelled delegates of the Socialist Party's Left Wing to implore those present to

5. *Reds* was a telling of Reed's life and partially based on his account of the Russian Revolution: John Reed, *Ten Days That Shook the World* (New York: International Publishers, 2001 (1934))

6. Theodore Draper, *The Roots of American Communism* (New York: Transaction Publishers, 2003 (1957)). Draper's book has been credited with centering Italian immigrant Louis C. Fraina (later known as Lewis Corey) in the story of the CPUSA's founding, sidelining the major role played by Ruthenberg in those events. Warren Beatty's film, *Reds*, largely relied on Draper's version of events, and essentially erased Ruthenberg from its dramatic screen portrayal. Draper worked as assistant foreign editor of the *Daily Worker* and later of *The New Masses* in the 1930s after leaving academia. Though he never officially joined the CP, he remained in its orbit until the early days of World War II, the time of the Soviet-German Non-Aggression Pact. After serving in the U.S. Army during the war, Draper returned to his research, eventually producing *The Roots of American Communism* and *American Communism and Soviet Russia* with the financial support of Ford Foundation's Fund for the Republic. Draper relied heavily on original documents as well as close personal correspondence with James P. Cannon, a CP founder, factional opponent of Ruthenberg in alliance with William Z. Foster, and later a follower of Leon Trotsky. Upon retirement, Draper turned over his remaining research materials to historian Harvey Klehr, who produced a third volume Draper had planned focused on the CP in the 1930s and 1940s as well as other books on Soviet espionage. From 1962 to 1968, Draper was a fellow at the anti-communist Hoover Institution think tank at Stanford University.

not divide themselves, inviting them to join in the CPA's founding the following day. In real life, it was actually Ruthenberg, not Fraina, who showed up that night in an effort to avoid a split and establish a single party to win the American working class to socialism.[7]

Besides being slighted in Hollywood's box office telling of the CPUSA's establishment, another significant part of the explanation for Ruthenberg's relative obscurity in the annals of U.S. labor and Communist history is the fact that he died relatively young and left behind few doctrinal texts or autobiographical accounts of his life. Ruthenberg was known to hold his own in the raging factional clashes that characterized the socialist movement in the 1910s and 1920s, and he was as well-versed in the intricacies of Marxist theory as anyone. But he was more likely to be found speaking on the soapbox, convening a planning meeting, teaching a class, raising money, or editing a newspaper than arguing in the debate hall or writing ideological tomes.

Ruthenberg was an intensely practical organizer and agitator. That endeared him to his contemporaries but meant that the written record of his activities was typically focused on the issues of the day rather than larger theoretical questions treated in isolation. Ideology was baked into his strategizing and organizing. His articles and columns, which numbered in the hundreds, often displayed a mastery of the art and science of politics, but they were written so as to mobilize people in the moment. When party publishers wanted to rush his "collected works" out to the membership for study after his death, there were only a handful of pamphlets, convention reports, and trial testimony extracts which could be sent to press.[8] The rest of his works consisted of newspaper columns or party proclamations and programs on particular struggles. It took a year before International

<hr />

7. Max Eastman, "The Chicago Conventions," *The Liberator*, October 1919, 13. Eastman was present for all three conventions surrounding the CP's founding—those of the Socialist Party, the Communist Labor Party, and the Communist Party of America.

8. An advertisement that ran repeatedly in the *Daily Worker* in the days following Ruthenberg's passing, and for some years on the anniversary of his death, implored party members to "Read Ruthenberg's Books!" The titles on offer numbered but five. One was a transcript of his testimony before a court in 1919 when he faced criminal syndicalism charges, three were reports and summaries of remarks made at Communist Party conventions, and one was a recruitment pamphlet, *The Workers (Communist) Party: What It Stands For, Why Workers Should Join*. For an example of the advertisement, see: *Daily Worker*, March 7, 1927, 2

Publishers was able to collect enough of Ruthenberg's speeches and writings so that a thin volume could be issued as part of a series of books by revolutionary authors.[9] But even this collection vanished shortly after publication. Ruthenberg's legacy was, in part, a victim of the seesaw of late 1920s factional battles. When the key figure who had lionized Ruthenberg, expelled CP leader Jay Lovestone, fell out of official favor, his publications associated with Ruthenberg were expunged from the record along with him.

This relative lack of a textual legacy to pass on to future generations of Communists (or historians) was something even Ruthenberg's colleagues made note of at the time of his death. J. Louis Engdahl, editor of the *Daily Worker* newspaper, called Ruthenberg "an able organizer of labor for the social revolution," but lamented that, "If... routine duties had been lifted off Ruthenberg's shoulders...our party would certainly have had a greater literature from the pen of our fallen leader."[10] Alfred Wagenknecht, who had spent time behind bars with Ruthenberg in Ohio, spoke similarly of him: "No tasks were too routine, too ordinary, too small for him. He kept the books, receipted for dues and other income, edited the *Cleveland Socialist*, developed its circulation, participated in a dozen local committees,

---

9. Charles E. Ruthenberg, *Speeches and Writings of Charles E. Ruthenberg* (New York: International Publishers, 1928). Ruthenberg's book was Volume 10 of a series called "Voices of Revolt," that also included authors such as Robespierre, Ferdinand Lassalle, Karl Liebknecht, V.I. Lenin, Eugene Debs, and others. His installment featured a critical introduction written by Jay Lovestone, a close party ally of Ruthenberg and his successor as national secretary following his death. In the wake of Stalin's first round of purges in the Soviet Union in the late 1920s, Lovestone was expelled from the CPUSA, at least partially, over his close connection to Nikolai Bukharin, who had been removed as head of the Communist International. Lovestone was also charged with pursuing a policy of "American Exceptionalism," which was said to have held that U.S. capitalism was in some way immune to the natural crisis tendencies of the world capitalist system. After his expulsion, Lovestone went on to lead an opposition faction outside the Communist Party, then worked in various unions, and eventually became a right-wing official with the AFL-CIO and helped funnel money for the CIA to fund anti-communist activities abroad. Lovestone's expulsion and eventual turn to the right ensured that his volume of Ruthenberg writings never returned to print.

10. J. Louis Engdahl, "Ruthenberg Was an Able Organizer for the Social Revolution," *Daily Worker*, March 15, 1927, 6

himself kept a careful card file of every contact and of every worker's name and address he could get."[11]

Unsympathetic commenters later claimed such traits made Ruthenberg "humorless" and "power hungry."[12] Some of those who worked alongside him viewed things differently, however. Wagenknecht, a sometimes factional opponent of Ruthenberg, said he "understood clearly that although political leadership was paramount, to achieve organization and mass power, it was fundamentally necessary to weld and to rivet, to bind and tie the members into a solid unit by constant attention to every small and large practical and organizational detail."[13] From his days as a socialist agitator in Ohio straight through to his years heading the Communist Party, Ruthenberg was known as "a Party Man," someone whose constant attention was on moving people into the streets, the picket line, and the voting booth.[14]

In this essay, a brief sketch of Ruthenberg's life and historical contributions follows, consisting of three main parts. First, Ruthenberg's time as a labor activist and Socialist Party leader in Cleveland is reviewed. Attention is given to the life experiences that taught him the realities of class struggle, state repression, and political action. The second section examines Ruthenberg's central role in the founding of what eventually became the CPUSA and his extensive efforts to consolidate the various factions of the party into a single group. The final section takes a look at Ruthenberg's work to ensure the party survived the efforts of the U.S. government to destroy it during the first Red Scare. The essay concludes with a look at Ruthenberg's political legacy, which is defined first and foremost by his determination to build a united and open party of action in touch with the working class of the United States – in all its multicultural, multiracial, multinational, and multilingual reality.

Socialist agitator

Born the son of a Cleveland longshoreman on July 9, 1882, Charles Emil Ruthenberg missed entering the world as a German by only

_____

11. Alfred Wagenknecht, "Ruthenberg As a Practical Worker," *Daily Worker*, February 28, 1931, 2

12. James G. Ryan, *Earl Browder: The Failure of American Communism* (University of Alabama Press, 1997), 16, 19

13. Wagenknecht, 1931

14. Art Shields, "Life and Work of Ruthenberg," *The Worker*, April 20, 1958, 8-9

four months. His father, "Worker August Ruthenberg," as his name was recorded on his certificate of marriage to Wilhelmina Lau, had been a cigar maker and a lumber cutter in Brandenburg, Prussia. The couple arrived in the United States in March that year with eight children and moved to Cleveland, where August found work on the docks lining the shore of Lake Erie unloading iron ore arriving from Minnesota. Settling in a poorer area to the west of downtown, today known as the neighborhood of Cudell, August and his older sons spent the spring building a small wooden frame home for the family, the house where C.E. was born.[15]

Cleveland at the time of Ruthenberg's birth was at the forefront of the rapid changes American society experienced in the late 19th century. It was the place where progressive reformers and industrial tycoons alike were reshaping the world. Before the Civil War, Cleveland had been a hotbed of abolitionist activity, a refuge for runaway slaves, and a key stop on the Underground Railroad for escaped Blacks on their way to freedom in Canada. It played host to the National Women's Suffrage Convention in 1869 – the first national event to demand women's right to vote and hold office.[16] It was also, however, the place where monopoly capitalism was being established. In 1870, John D. Rockefeller founded Standard Oil Company in Cleveland, and by the time of Ruthenberg's birth, the company already controlled nearly 90% of oil in the United States and had its thumb on railroads across the country.[17] Rockefeller was shortly to become the world's first billionaire and Standard the world's first great industrial trust (and later the prime target of the "trust busters"). This dual legacy of long democratic traditions and emerging capitalist monopoly provided the context for Ruthenberg's politicization.

C.E.'s mother Wilhelmina was a devout Lutheran. She took the children to church every Sunday morning and ensured that C.E. was enrolled in Lutheran school at the age of six. August was more casual in his faith, apparently having said, "I know the life of Christ, and I try to follow it, but I don't need to go to church every Sunday to hear it all over again."[18] C.E. graduated from the Trinity Evangelical

---

15. Johnson, 1957, 7-11

16. David Van Tassel, "Introduction: Cleveland and Reform." *Cleveland: A Tradition of Reform*, edited by David Van Tassel and John Grabowski (Kent State University Press, 1986), 1-13

17. Steve Weinberg, *Taking on the Trust: How Ida Tarbell Brought Down John D. Rockefeller and Standard Oil* (New York: W.W. Norton & Company, 2008)

18. Johnson, 1957, 12

School in 1896, just before turning 14. His mother and the minister at Trinity urged him to enter the seminary and become a preacher of the gospel, but C.E. showed little interest in continuing his religious education. He had done well in school and hoped to go on to college, but the family had no money. So, as is typical for many youth in working class families, C.E. went straight to work. His first job was a low-paying position in a bookstore on Superior Avenue. He earned enough to enroll in night classes at a local business school, taking bookkeeping, accounting, and typing. Biographer Oakley Johnson said that C.E.'s friends of that time recalled him being determined to find an office job and even dreaming of becoming a businessman. "He shared in the illusions of capitalist-minded America at the turn of the century," Johnson wrote.[19] His night school credentials and lack of formal training did not get him far in the business world, however. When his father August died in 1898, C.E. had no choice but to take whatever work he could get – office job or not. A brother-in-law got him on as a carpenter's helper in a picture frame factory working 10 hours a day trimming and polishing frame molds.

After more than a year, Ruthenberg caught the attention of a manager at the plant who moved him into an office position. Shortly thereafter, Ruthenberg scored a position at another firm with better pay, a job that actually used some of the skills he had picked up in night school – bookkeeper and salesman for a publishing house. He was soon made delivery and sales manager, overseeing salesmen in Ohio, Michigan, and Indiana. He stayed with the company, Selmar Hess Publishing, for eight years, developing his administrative and executive abilities there during the day and continuing his self-education at night. Though his formal schooling ended when he was 16, Ruthenberg had continued studying on his own, becoming part of the pool of 'working class intellectuals.' By this time, he was spending more of his Sundays at the library than at church with his mother. He read about how people made it (or, more often, didn't) in the world of big business, while also mixing more historical books into his studies. Though struggling to make a living in the world of commerce, Ruthenberg at the time still "believed in the ideals of *laissez-faire* capitalism and Social Darwinism." Among his favorite authors were Thomas Jefferson, Thomas Paine, Ralph Waldo Emerson, and Henry David Thoreau, "but their ideas of freedom, justice, and dignity were hard to reconcile with the materialistic values of the profit motive in business."[20]

---

19. Ibid, 14
20. Millett, 1972, 194

By this time, Ruthenberg was husband to Rosaline "Rose" Nickel, a friend of one of his sisters, and father of a son named Daniel. "Dandy," as C.E. nicknamed his son, told Oakley Johnson years later that during this time, he remembers his father living by the creed of the agnostic and humanist orator Robert G. Ingersoll: "Happiness is the only good. The place to be happy is here. The time to be happy is now. The way to be happy is to help make others so."[21] A plaque bearing Ingersoll's words hung on the wall of C.E.'s home library. Daniel said that "instead of merely reading" Jefferson, Paine, and the rest, "my father believed with them and acted on their principles."[22] The younger Ruthenberg wrote of his father in 1937: "The Americanism of C.E. Ruthenberg was not the Americanism of the dollar-chasing exploiters, of blood-smeared generals, or lying, treacherous statesmen, of swindling office-holders, or of tax-dodging capitalists. His Americanism was that of the Declaration of Independence, that of Thomas Paine, of [Ralph Waldo] Emerson, of [Mark] Twain…and [Walt] Whitman."[23]

It was around this same time that Ruthenberg struck up a friendship with a fellow salesman at Selmar Hess named MacBain Walker who would push his world outlook in a different direction. A university educated man who wore his atheism with pride, Walker cynically prodded C.E. about his "idealist" leanings. When the two sparred, Ruthenberg championed Cleveland's reform mayor of the day, Tom Johnson, saying that while there was need for social improvement – like the breaking up of the trusts and the end of "special privilege" – the system of free enterprise still worked and meritocracy ensured success to those who deserved it. He often pointed to their employer, Selmar Hess, an immigrant who built up his publishing house from nothing, as proof. Walker wasn't buying it, though, and suggested Ruthenberg check out Karl Marx. His notion of socialism wasn't all that developed, but Walker continually pushed the idea to Ruthenberg that they and the rest of the workers in Cleveland's industries were being "robbed," exploited and cheated of the "full product of their toil." The disagreements between the two friends escalated into a full-on debate over the virtues of capitalism and socialism, held before an audience of salesmen on the floor of the publishing plant. By a vote of the workers, Walker was handed the victory. Stung from being bested, Ruthenberg promptly went to the library to read up on Marx. The debate cost him his job

21. Johnson, 1957, 18-19
22. Ibid, 19
23. Dan Ruthenberg, 30

once the general manager of Selmar Hess found out about it. C.E. next found work for a roofing company, again working in the sales department.[24]

The year was 1908. Beginning to see how the class struggle played out on the job and continually losing in his intellectual jousts with Walker, Ruthenberg became more and more disillusioned with the social and economic system of capitalism. Having initially prepared for a life as a minister, Ruthenberg now traded the Bible for Marx's *Capital*, borrowed from his local library. When asked by a prosecutor years later how he had been converted to socialism, he answered: "Through the Cleveland Public Library." It was during this time that he began to tell others he was a socialist, though he remained an advocate of Mayor Johnson's reformist "municipal socialism," whereby city owned power plants and garbage incinerators were the stuff of social change. Over the next several months, Ruthenberg worked out his own ideological understanding of the world, sometimes quite publicly.

When Mayor Johnson's administration bought out the private streetcar company in Cleveland but refused to honor a 2-cent-per-hour raise that the old owners promised, the workers went on strike. The local chapter of the Socialist Party of America, which had been founded in 1901 and rapidly spread its influence across the Midwest and other parts of the country, backed the workers. Ruthenberg was sympathetic but thought the workers were shortsighted. He wrote in the *Cleveland Citizen*, a trade union newspaper, that "Johnson has changed the street railway system in Cleveland from one conducted for the profit of the stockholders only to one conducted in the interests of the whole people." The editors of the paper wrote back to Ruthenberg, chastising him and saying he should not write about things he knew "nothing about." They said he "should not attempt to criticize socialism without a fair knowledge of the philosophy." Ruthenberg responded, saying he saw Johnson's measures as a means to "clear the way for socialism," closing his response with: "For the social *evolution*, may it reach socialism in our time." Robert Bandlow, one of the *Citizen* editors, sent Ruthenberg one last letter in their public exchange, writing: "Social evolution is a slow process that may and will be hastened by revolution. You should enroll yourself as a member of the Socialist Party and stand with us for the social revolution in our time."[25]

---

24. Johnson, 1957, 21
25. All quotes cited by Johnson, 1957, 24-25

In January 1909, when he was 27, Ruthenberg took Bandlow up on his challenge. Communist journalist Art Shields, who worked with Ruthenberg, recalled, "That was a turning point in Ruthenberg's life. And he kept his eyes fixed on the goal of socialism from the day he joined the Socialist Party. His hatred of capitalism and his vision of the Cooperative Commonwealth that is to be ran through almost every speech he made after that."[26] Ruthenberg now put the organizational and managerial experience he'd gained in the business world to work for socialism. After a full day at the roofing company, Ruthenberg started his second shift at the local Socialist Party headquarters – talking up the party's campaigns before crowds on street corners, writing articles for the party press, and participating in every committee meeting he found out about. He also dug deeper into the works of Marx, Friedrich Engels, and other socialists. MacBain Walker, the co-worker who'd debated Ruthenberg, said: "I communicated these 'poisonous' doctrines to Charles, but the pupil was soon ahead of the teacher...I would say that in two years, C.E.R. knew much more than I ever knew about such things. He...introduced me to scientific socialism...and continued to get more and more enthusiastic until he gave up business to devote his whole energies to the cause."[27]

Because of his devotion to the organization, articulate public speaking abilities, efficient management skills, and fluency in English (a valued trait in an organization dominated by newer immigrants), Ruthenberg rose quickly through the Socialist ranks. A year after joining, he was elected to the City Central Committee and was nominated as the party's candidate for Ohio state treasurer, running on a platform that called for unemployment insurance several decades before that reform was eventually won. "The capitalist class knows no other law than the law of profits," he said in a column in August 1910. "The workers have the power to place on the statute books a compulsory insurance law, but they cannot secure such a law by voting for the candidates nominated by parties owned and controlled by their employers." Just as workers needed unions, so they needed the Socialist Party: "They must have their own political

---

26. Shields, 8
27. Cited by: Michael O'Malley, "Charles E. Ruthenberg, the Clevelander Who Founded the American Communist Party is Remembered Both as an Incredible Visionary and a Bitter Antagonist," *Cleveland Plain Dealer*, January 21, 1996

organizations to fight their political battles just as they have their own industrial organizations to fight their industrial battles."[28]

Sixty thousand people cast their ballots for him, and Ohio tallied more votes for the Socialist Party in that election than any other state, making it the country's first "Red State."[29] Following the 1910 campaign, Ruthenberg became a perennial candidate for the Socialist Party, running for governor of Ohio in 1912, U.S. senator in 1914, Congress in 1916 and 1918, and mayor again in 1911, 1915, 1917, and 1919. During his first run to lead Cleveland, the *Plain Dealer* asked Ruthenberg how he came to "take up the doctrine of socialism." Ruthenberg responded: "It wasn't a speech or a pamphlet that made me a Socialist. It was study. I wanted to be a minister, and I became a student of the Bible. I studied the Bible, all that I could find written about the Bible. Then I studied evolution and literature on sociology. Then I lost my desire to be a minister, and I can say that it was hard study that made me a Socialist...I am hoping, like all Socialists, for the co-operative commonwealth, and I recognize in Socialism the next step in the evolution of mankind."[30]

During these years, Ruthenberg's politics became increasingly more radical, moving him from the Socialist Party's moderate wing to its left. He began to argue that it was the economic functioning of capitalism – overproduction of goods matched with the inability of the working class to consume them – that was creating the conditions that would lead to a social and political revolution. He became an outspoken advocate of trade unionism and the duty of the party to help labor struggles. When the International Ladies' Garment Workers Union struck the textile factories of Cleveland for five months in the summer of 1911, Ruthenberg and the Socialist Party held constant street meetings to support the strikers and rouse public opinion against employers' decisions to bring in armed mercenaries to fight the workers. "With political power in their hands, the workers would quickly win this strike, or any other strike!," he proclaimed.[31]

His understanding of the political economy of capitalism was increasingly matched with a certainty that workers must have their own party to bring about change. He began to see the Socialist Party

---

28. C.E. Ruthenberg, "Accident Insurance and Political Action," *Chicago Daily Socialist*, August 15, 1910. In *Speeches and Writings*, 21-22

29. Johnson, 1957, 37

30. Ruthenberg, quoted in "Becomes Socialist Instead of Pastor," *Cleveland Plain Dealer*, September 25, 1911

31. Ruthenberg, quoted in Johnson, 1957, 45

as workers' political organ, responsible for educating them about
the nature of the system and articulating their demands.[32] He organized a Socialist Sunday School that offered a few hours of political
education in the principles of Marxism and revolutionary songs
for parents and children alike.[33] "The capitalist system," he wrote
in October 1912, "stands for industrial slavery." The old parties –
Democratic, Republican, and Progressive – could not bring about the
end of exploitation and bondage of private ownership of the means
of production: "The emancipation of the working class can only be
won by the working class itself."[34] The Ohio party moved decisively
to the left, influenced by Ruthenberg's growing embrace of revolutionary politics. Probably not coincidentally, he was arrested by
Cleveland police for the first time during this period, dragged down
from a soapbox in 1913. He was taken to the station but let go hours
later. Upon his release, Ruthenberg promptly returned to the same
street corner to carry on his agitation.[35]

When World War I broke out in Europe in the summer of 1914,
all the political work of Ruthenberg, the Socialist Party, and the
entire left movement around the world was changed forever. Within
a week of the war's start, he was already addressing a rally 3,000
strong in Cleveland denouncing it as a capitalist struggle for markets
and a fight for the redivision of colonies by the imperialist powers.
The war immediately disrupted international trade and combined,
at least temporarily, with one of capitalism's periodic downturns.
Rising prices for food, growing unemployment, and the spread
of homelessness became the immediate issues around which the
local party branch in Cleveland organized. Ruthenberg launched a
new newspaper, the *Socialist News*, which gave extensive coverage
to unemployment (which had tripled in only one year), winning
new support for the SP from the Cleveland Federation of Labor,
which started marching in the Socialists' May Day demonstrations
in 1915 and 1916.[36] In the spring and summer of 1916, Ruthenberg
spearheaded a campaign to collect signatures to help put a CFL referendum on the ballot creating a minimum wage for city employees.
By August, the CFL announced that more than half of the signatures

---

32. Millett, 1972, 196
33. Ibid, 197
34. C.E. Ruthenberg, "Economic Emancipation," *Ohio Socialist Bulletin*,
October 1912. In *Speeches and Writings*, 34-36
35. O'Malley, 1996
36. Johnson, 1957, 94-95

needed had been turned in by "Secretary C.E. Ruthenberg of the Socialist Party."[37] The referendum made it to the ballot and passed.

At the national level, though, the Socialist Party was already showing some internal cracks over the question of war by the beginning of 1916. A number of leaders in the party were becoming less vocal as to where they stood, talking in vague terms about maintaining military preparedness in order to safeguard peace. Running for the party's National Committee, Ruthenberg staked out an unequivocal position: "It is our work to show that capitalist war is a fruit of an industrial system based upon production for profit, with all that that implies in the shape of competition with the capitalists of other nations, and to oppose it with all our power."[38] By March, the war danger exploded on the U.S.'s southern border, as American troops invaded Mexico, ostensibly to capture Pancho Villa. Ruthenberg, of course, denounced the move, telling a cheering crowd in Public Square, "There is no reason why any man should go down into the hell of war to fight for the dollars of the ruling class."[39]

The "Pancho Villa Expedition" lasted 11 months, ending just in time for the United States to finally, and fully, enter the European conflict on April 4, 1917. The Socialist Party called an emergency convention to meet in St. Louis three days later. Left and right were split over the war, with a substantial pro-war grouping quitting the party. Ruthenberg and some other anti-war delegates pressed party leaders to state definitely whether they were opposed to all militarism and war, but SP leaders Morris Hillquit, Adolph Germer, and Victor Berger managed to short-circuit the effort.[40] Any suggestion that opposition to the war should be mobilized for a revolutionary overthrow of capitalism was going too far for them. Neither left nor right had sufficient power to force their views at the convention. Eventually, an anti-war unity resolution was passed, but its language was so compromised that no one was really satisfied. The resolution went just far enough, though, to provide the U.S. government the evidence it needed to claim the Socialist Party was obstructing the war effort. The Espionage Act was used to suppress the party and other groups like the Industrial Workers of the World, but the now-consolidated SP Left Wing fought back and devoted itself to the anti-war cause completely.

---

37. Ibid, 96-97

38. Ruthenberg, quoted in Johnson, 1957, 103

39. Ruthenberg, quoted in O'Malley, 1996

40. Earl Browder, "Ruthenberg's Struggle Against War," *Daily Worker*, February 28, 1931, 5

Ruthenberg emerged from the emergency convention as one of the Socialist Party Left Wing's most outspoken figures and a nationally known opponent of the U.S. government's involvement in World War I.[41] Back in Cleveland in May, he issued an incontrovertible anti-imperialist – and anti-capitalist – manifesto before a crowd of thousands in Public Square:

> This is not a war for freedom. It is not a war for the liberties of mankind. It is a war to secure the investments and profits of the ruling class of this country…The only reason we are in this war now is because it is to the interests of the ruling class, the capitalist class of this country, to have us in this war…We of the Socialist Party are…working towards this end, that out of the chaos of this war there may come a new society, a new world, a new organization of the people, which will end the cause of war by ending the private ownership of the industry which brings war into existence.[42]

Along with his party comrade Alfred Wagenknecht, he was promptly arrested as mounted police charged through the masses of assembled people. Up to this point, Ruthenberg had still been working the double shift – spending days at his regular job and evenings and weekends volunteering for the party. His anti-war crusade put an end to that. His employer, which by this time was a garment manufacturer, the Printz-Biederman Company, made him an offer. A manager dangled a block of shares in the company worth $10,000, an immediate pay raise of $5,000, and a promise to eventually make Ruthenberg a vice president of the company if he would drop the war issue and quit the Socialist Party. In 2020 inflation-adjusted dollars, that amounted to over $200,000 of stock and a salary boost of more than $100,000 per year. Ruthenberg's response to his boss's bribe was as should have been expected. Shortly thereafter, he became a full-time salaried organizer for the Socialist Party.[43]

The government stepped up its repression of the Socialists, banning their newspapers from the mail and indicting Ruthenberg, Wagenknecht, and Ohio state organizer Charles Baker for their speeches.

------

41. Alexander Trachtenberg (ed.), *The American Socialists and the War* (New York: Rand School of Social Science, 1917)

42. C.E. Ruthenberg, "Fight the War!" May 27, 1917. In *Speeches and Writings*, 40-41

43. This story was told to Oakley Johnson by Ruthenberg's brother-in-law, Ernst Brandt. See: Johnson, 1957, 117-118

C.E. Ruthenberg speaks against the United States' entry into World War I at a meeting in Market Square, Cleveland, Ohio, October 28, 1917. | Courtesy of Ohio History Connection, Charles E. Ruthenberg Collection

Rose and Daniel Ruthenberg, wife and son, were hounded by federal agents to turn over C.E. He dodged the police long enough to address yet another anti-war rally before turning himself in. The Ohio Three were charged with obstructing the draft by encouraging young men not to register for military service. At the trial, they remained defiant. Ruthenberg repeated the speech that had landed him in court, while Wagenknecht predicted the eventual demise of the system they were protesting: "We know that capitalism is fashioning the hempen rope, will act as its own hangman, its own embalmer, its own gravedigger."[44] A swift conviction in July handed them all a sentence of one year in the Canton Workhouse. They were among the hundreds of Socialists and other radicals prosecuted for opposing the war during that period.[45] The Ohio case was appealed all the way to the

---

44. Wagenknecht, quoted in: Phil Bart, "The S.P.'s St. Louis Convention of 1917," *World Magazine* (*Daily World*), April 23, 1977, M-4

45. Several people who would go on to be prominent figures in the history of the Communist Party were among the activists swept up in the government's dragnet. Earl Browder, future CPUSA leader, and his brothers were locked up in Kansas City. Rose Pastor Stokes, an early woman leader of the Communist Party, was jailed for penning a letter to the newspaper saying the government was "for the profiteers." Louis C. Fraina, later to play a prominent role in the CP's founding, was arrested in New York City for speaking to a group of conscientious objectors. These and others are discussed by Draper, 1957, 95

U.S. Supreme Court. From that time until his death a decade later, Ruthenberg was constantly either behind bars or facing imminent imprisonment. While he awaited the decision of the Supreme Court, Ruthenberg launched yet another campaign for Cleveland mayor, running on a platform of "Socialism, Peace, and Democracy." Unofficial polls showed he might pull off a win, and one newspaper even prepared a proof page in case of a Ruthenberg victory. He ended up with nearly 28,000 votes out of 100,000 cast in a three-way race, an impressive accomplishment in the midst of the patriotic hysteria being whipped up by government war propaganda.[46]

During 1917, Ruthenberg also encountered Lenin for the first time. In March, tsarism had been overthrown in Russia, but the world press was talking about the return of an exiled agitator named V.I. Lenin to Russia and the possibility of a second revolution – a socialist revolution. All summer long, the pages of the New York Socialist Party paper, *The Call*, were filled with Lenin's appeals to the workers, soldiers, and peasants of Russia to rise up and end the imperialist war and take power into their own hands through new representative bodies, the Soviets. On November 7, 1917, the Soviets, led by Lenin and his Bolshevik Party, made their move, seizing power and overthrowing the provisional government that had succeeded the tsar's regime. The first act of the new revolutionary state was to issue its Decree on Peace, calling for the immediate end to the war. Electrified by the Russian Revolution, Ruthenberg authored a resolution passed by the SP Cleveland local on November 25 declaring the Bolsheviks' peace effort offered the "only hope of saving our civilization from destruction" and swearing the Socialists' uncompromising support: "We hail the policy of their [Russia's] present government as the true expression of proletarian action, and pledge ourselves to do all in our power to assist in wiping out capitalist imperialism and establishing the civilization of the future, the commonwealth of the workers united irrespective of nationality."[47] If opposition to the war had been the litmus test of conviction for the SP's Left Wing before November 1917, afterward it was support for the revolution in Russia.

Rather than just cheering on Russia from the armchair, though, Ruthenberg took action. His goal was to convince workers in Ohio

---

46. Johnson, 1957, 125

47. C.E. Ruthenberg, "Cleveland Socialists Greet Bolshevik Revolution," *Socialist News*, November 25, 1917. Reproduced in: Philip S. Foner (ed.), *The Bolshevik Revolution: Its Impact on American Radicals, Liberals, and Labor* (New York: International Publishers, 2017 (1967)), 55

of how the struggle of workers in faraway Petrograd was linked to the battles faced at home. Ruthenberg hurried around the state in the weeks that followed, speaking to gatherings about the significance of what was happening in the world and urging other party locals to adopt resolutions modeled on that of Cleveland. He maneuvered to help SP activists on the ground to head off Right Wing leaders' efforts to tamp down support for the Bolsheviks.[48] In early January 1918, he wrote: "Things are moving fast in the world. Governments and thrones are rocking...The Socialist movement the world over is wielding more power than ever before in its history. The future belongs to the workers...Our task is to build the working class movement in Cleveland."[49] He felt the chance was at hand to build up workers' confidence and end the war at the same time. He was sure of advance, even though the top body of workers in the U.S. – the American Federation of Labor – was still solidly pro-war and did whatever it could to dilute any militancy that might pop up in union ranks.[50]

Ruthenberg's organizing was abruptly halted on January 14, though, when the Supreme Court's ruling in his case came down. It upheld his conviction and those of Wagenknecht and Baker and ordered them to report to the Canton Workhouse. Over 3,000 workers packed Cleveland's Market Square under heavy snowfall to mark the three men's surrender to U.S. marshals. They were kept behind bars until the following winter, though between bouts of torture and solitary confinement, Ruthenberg was still able to stay involved in party work through his wife Rose's visits and her smuggling of articles he wrote for the press. She became more active in the party and was elected a state delegate.[51] In June, the Ohio Socialist Party state convention met in a park outside the gates of the prison and was addressed by Eugene V. Debs, the SP's most famous national leader. The speech Debs made in Canton that day was the one that would send him to jail and make

48. Johnson, 1957, 129

49. Ruthenberg, cited by Johnson, 1957, 130

50. Robert Phillipoff, "The First Decade," *Highlights of a Fighting History: 60 Years of the Communist Party USA* (New York: International Publishers, 1979), 3-9

51. An article in the *Socialist News* in January 1919 celebrating Ruthenberg's release from prison obliquely referred to Rose's stepped-up activism: "With our State Secretary back on the job, reinforced by the work of his heroic wife and comrade, the work should progress as never before." See: Marguerite Prevey, "The Great Work Ahead," *The Ohio Socialist*, January 1, 1919, 2

his fight for free speech an international *cause célèbre*. Thousands listened as he praised "our most loyal comrades" in the Workhouse who were "paying the penalty for their devotion to the cause of the working class." He mocked the U.S. government's war propaganda, saying that Ruthenberg, Wagenknecht, and Baker had shown "that it is extremely dangerous to exercise the constitutional right of free speech in a country fighting to make democracy for the world." He told the crowd, "They may put those boys in jail and some of the rest of us in jail, but they cannot put the Socialist movement in jail."[52]

Ruthenberg emerged from the Canton Workhouse in December 1918, with Rose Ruthenberg, Gene Debs, and a few other close friends retrieving him and the other two leaders. Incarceration had only made C.E. more determined to push ahead with turning the Socialist Party at the national level into an action oriented organization, something more than an electoral vehicle for reform minded office seekers. He embarked on a speaking tour around the state, appearing in Youngstown, Columbus, Toledo, Sandusky, and Lorain. A "Reconstruction Organization Campaign" was launched to win 10,000 readers for the party newspaper. Mass rallies were held to demand freedom for political prisoners still behind bars. Educational seminars were convened to spread the news of what was going on in Soviet Russia.

It was amid this whirlwind of activity during the winter of 1918-19 that Ruthenberg first read Lenin's *Letter to American Workers*.[53] The Russian leader reminded workers in the U.S. of their "great, really liberating, really revolutionary" fight for independence from British colonialism in 1776, which "gave the world an example of a revolutionary war against feudal subjection." Lenin urged American workers to give the world a new example by throwing off the "billionaires, these contemporary slave owners," by ending capitalism.[54] Learning from Lenin as he had earlier learned from Marx, Ruthenberg

---

52. Eugene V. Debs, "Speech by Eugene V. Debs, June 16, 1918," Criminal Case Files, United States of America v. Eugene V. Debs, U.S. National Archives Identifier 2641497. In September 1918, Debs was convicted under the Espionage Act and sentenced to ten years in prison. After losing a Supreme Court appeal, he was sent to the Atlanta penitentiary in April 1919, from which he ran for president in 1920 as "Convict No. 9653," and scored nearly a million votes, still a historic high for a socialist candidate.

53. Johnson, 1957, 138-139

54. V.I. Lenin, *Letter to American Workers* (New York: International Publishers, 1934), 9-10

became convinced of the need for a 'party of a new type' to carry out a political, economic, and social transformation of society.

He penned an 11-part serialized feature in the pages of *Socialist News* under the headline, "After the War – What?" in which he sought to link up the possibilities that came from recent changes in the functioning of capitalism, centralized and planned due to the urgencies of war, with workers' self-organization and their fight for political power. It was the duty of the Socialist Party, he argued, to be their instrument:

> The halo of capitalism has been smashed by the war. Men have found that the industrial order under which they live is not the permanent and unchangeable thing they thought it to be... The struggle of the working class will henceforth be a political struggle for control of the state because it must gain control of the government before it can hope to establish democracy in industry...The work the workers have to do in this country, the way to freedom, is through building a class conscious political movement which will carry on the work of educating the workers to an understanding of the system of exploitation which now exists and the class character of the government and to organize the workers for the struggle to wrest control of the government out of the hands of the capitalist class.[55]

Militant strikes were sweeping the country during this period, often under left leadership: the packinghouse strike (1918) and the Great Steel Strike (1919), both headed by William Z. Foster; the Seattle General Strike of 1919; and others. Unprecedented change seemed to be in the offing. In January, Ruthenberg declared the Bolsheviks to be the "gravediggers of capitalism" and builders of "the new world." Connecting the principles of Marxism he had long sought to master with the actions of the vanguard party in Russia, Ruthenberg said that if the doctrines of Marx and Engels were put down on paper and compared to the movement Lenin was leading, it would be obvious that "Bolshevism is Marxian Socialism in action."[56]

The revolutionary impulses of Ruthenberg the agitator and others inspired by the Bolshevik example were pushing in a direction that

---

55. C.E. Ruthenberg, "After the War—What?" *Socialist News* (Vol. 4, Nos. 210-215, 217-221), December 7, 1918 to February 22, 1919, https://www.marxists.org/history/usa/parties/spusa/1918/1207-ruth-afterthewar.pdf

56. C.E. Ruthenberg, "The Bolshevists: Grave-Diggers of Capitalism," *The Ohio Socialist*, January 29, 1919, 4

went against the cautious instincts of the moderates who headed the Socialist Party at the national level. The growing division between the SP's activist base and the establishment in New York portended a struggle that would see the movement split down the middle in only a few short months and give birth to not one, but two new radical parties.

Communist founder

Support for the Left Wing was rapidly consolidating among the Socialist Party membership well beyond the bounds of Ohio in early 1919, driven by dissatisfaction with what was seen as the luke-warm way the leadership had met the issue of imperialist war, its half-hearted embrace of the workers' revolution in Russia, and its failure to support industrial trade unionism. The factional schism first emerged into the open in the New York district, where the party apparatus was controlled by the old guard leadership, but many grassroots locals and foreign language branches were firmly com-mitted to the Left. The catalyst for a Left Wing break was an earlier vote by some Socialist aldermen in New York to approve war fund-ing (the fourth Liberty Loan) and their support for a Victory Arch monument in Manhattan. The giant socialist parties of Europe that had made up the Second International were torn apart by the war in 1914; in the U.S., the same process played out similarly but on a much smaller scale in 1919.

A "Left Wing Manifesto and Program" was adopted in February that denounced the opportunism of the "moderate" party leadership and scolded the latter for missing out on the great "awakening of labor" that was underway. It said that under the drastically different conditions of the post-war world, the Socialist Party had to reorga-nize itself, "urge the workers to turn their craft unions into industrial unions," and "teach, propagate, and agitate exclusively for the over-throw of capitalism and the establishment of socialism through a proletarian dictatorship."[57] Recognition of the Soviet Republic, opposition to any U.S. military intervention against it, and affilia-tion to the new Communist International were further principled positions laid out in the program. Ruthenberg saw the document as

---

57. "Manifesto of the Left Wing Section of the Socialist Party of America," *The Ohio Socialist*, February 26, 1919, 2. The document still displayed strong elements of the syndicalist path that was predominant in the IWW, the old Socialist Labor Party, and other radical trends. It almost equated industrial unions to the Soviets in Russia.

the basis for organizing the membership to revolutionize the Socialist Party and make it into a real working class political organ. He ensured the Manifesto was immediately printed in the pages of the *Ohio Socialist* and the Cleveland *Socialist News*.[58] One SP local after another, one state district after another, signed on to the Manifesto. The national leadership of the party prevaricated, unwilling to commit to an agenda that now had obvious majority support but also fearful of provoking an organizational split.

Ruthenberg carried on with his local organizing work while at the same time maneuvering the minefield of national party politics. With May Day approaching, he sought to consolidate the gains made in building alliances with local trade unions in recent years. Nineteen different street protests were organized in April to demand freedom for Eugene Debs, who was about to be locked up over his speech outside the Canton Workhouse. The events were all oriented toward ensuring a massive turnout for a gigantic May Day rally to showcase the Socialist program for working class progress locally and build Ruthenberg's latest mayoralty campaign. On the bright, sunny morning of May 1, as many as 100,000 (depending on whose numbers you trust) men, women, and children marched in Cleveland's Public Square. Banners proclaiming "Workers of the World, Unite!" and "Help for the Unemployed!" were hoisted aloft by the crowd. Among the lines of marchers were even uniformed soldiers just home from the war carrying the red flag. At the head of the first column, leading the march, was Ruthenberg.

Before he could even mount the rostrum to address the rally, authorities made their move. Police on horseback stormed into the square swinging clubs. U.S. army tanks rolled into the crowd as cars full of more club-wielding men arrived on scene. Marchers were sent running, quite literally, for their lives. A reporter for the mainstream *Cleveland Plain Dealer* later described the attack: "I saw men and women brutally beaten, though they made no resistance. I saw the blood flow in sickening streams at the city's busiest corner."[59] Two workers were killed by the armed squads and over 200 more were injured.[60] One hundred and thirty four people were arrested, including Ruthenberg. Of those apprehended, 131 were foreign born; most of them would eventually be deported. While the crowd was being

---

58. Johnson, 1957, 140

59. Ted Robinson, quoted in O'Malley, 1996

60. Elizabeth Gurley Flynn wrote that the number of dead was three, including the two workers and a child. Verification could not be found. Flynn, 1939

dealt with at Public Square, a gang of men in plainclothes – rumored to be paid by the Chamber of Commerce – ransacked Socialist Party headquarters. Ruthenberg wrote shortly afterward, "The workers of Cleveland who are striving to throw off the yoke of oppression and exploitation have received their baptism in blood."[61] He was indicted on a trumped-up charge of "assault with intent to kill." No evidence was presented that he actually had struck anyone, only a claim that he had urged workers a month earlier to "organize in the industries and form a workmen's council."[62] The proceedings went nowhere, and the charge was eventually dropped.

Ruthenberg was thus fresh out of jail, again, as the Left Wing stepped up its drive against the old guard in the SP. The bloody police repression of May Day in Cleveland became a catalyst for mobilization and catapulted Ruthenberg and the Ohio Socialists to the position of leading figures in the national Left Wing. A party-wide referendum on affiliation to the Communist International won by a margin of 10-1, while vote-by-mail elections for the SP's National Executive Council saw the Left Wing sweep 12 of the 15 seats and four out of five international delegates. Louis C. Fraina of Boston was the top vote getter, with Ruthenberg coming in second. With momentum on their side, Ruthenberg of Cleveland, Fraina of Boston, and Maximilian Cohen and John Reed of New York forged ahead in their campaign to remake the Socialist Party from below with a "National Conference of the Left Wing," to be convened in Manhattan on June 21.[63] The old leadership of the SP was not going down without a fight, however. After being totally rejected by the party membership, they declared the elections fraudulent and nullified the results. Hoping to pull the rug from under Ruthenberg and the Left before they could act, Morris Hillquit, dean of the old guard moderates, gave the signal to his deputy Adolph Germer, the SP's National Secretary, to initiate a purge, saying, "Let

---

61. C.E. Ruthenberg, "The Cleveland May Day Demonstration," *The Revolutionary Age*, May 10, 1919, 4

62. "Clifford and Ruthenberg Held For Grand Jury Indictment," *The Ohio Socialist*, May 28, 1919, 1, 4

63. "Call for a National Conference of the Left Wing," *The Revolutionary Age*, April 26, 1919, 1. The organizers—Locals Boston, Cleveland, and the Left Wing Section of Local New York—were clear and deliberate in setting their goal: "The purpose of the Conference is to formulate a national declaration of Left Wing principles, form a national, unified expression of the Left Wing (a sort of General Council—not a separate organization) and concentrate our forces to conquer the Party for revolutionary Socialism."

us clear the decks."[64] Reed's *New York Communist* newspaper – the first party body to embrace the communist label – responded to Hillquit: "When the time comes for clearing the decks, we will handle the mop."[65]

The party leadership launched an offensive that summer before the new Executive Committee members could be seated. Over the course of several weeks, the old guard expelled the entire Socialist Party organizations of the states of Michigan, Massachusetts, and Ohio, the powerful Chicago city local, several New York branches, numerous smaller city locals, and at least seven foreign language federations. By the middle of 1919, the split of the Socialist Party was a reality – a split carried out by the Right Wing leadership. Total SP membership had stood at 109,589 in January; in July, by Germer's own admission, it was only 39,750.[66] An Emergency Convention was set for Chicago on August 30.

Ruthenberg and the other representatives of the Left Wing arrived in New York for the National Left Wing Conference in June. A new "Left Wing Manifesto" was prepared that drew largely on the previous document but sought to debunk claims that they were just cheerleaders for Russia, emphasizing that the Left Wing was "the product of the experience of the American movement…invigorated by the experience of the proletarian revolutions in Europe." It again declared the SP was infected by "parliamentarism." Displaying the political immaturity of the Left Wing, the document was still constrained by some of the same sectarian syndicalism carried over from the IWW that had defined the first.[67] Another glaring failure in hindsight, this Manifesto (like the first) made no mention of the

64. Hillquit, quoted in Johnson, 1957, 158

65. *New York Communist*, May 24, 1919, 7

66. Adolph Germer, "Report to the National Executive Committee," August 27, 1919. Cited by Draper, 1957, 158

67. Syndicalism is an offshoot of union activism that sees the overthrow of capitalism happening largely via industrial action by workers through trade unions. The union is held to be the primary vehicle for revolutionary change. In the United States, the Industrial Workers of the World was the most prominent organizational representation of syndicalist theory and practice. There were many IWW veterans in the Socialist Party Left Wing and in the new communist parties. Early Communist Party programs still contained some holdovers from this thinking but paired it with the notion of the vanguard political party that would lead the revolution. These syndicalist leanings took on their most tangible form in the insistence by some Communists to form separate "revolutionary" trade unions to oppose and compete with the American Federation of Labor. The disconnect between

oppression of Black Americans, mass lynchings across the old Confederacy, or the segregation of Socialist Party branches in the South.[68]

When it came to strategy, the leadership of the Left Wing struggled to maintain flexibility. No sooner had they been expelled from the SP than their own internal tactical differences came to the fore. The Russian Socialist Federation, an SP language-based affiliate, made a motion at the New York conference to immediately constitute the Left Wing as a new party – a communist party. The proposal was rejected after a tense vote. Reed, together with Benjamin Gitlow of New York, were determined to go to Chicago and take back control of the whole Socialist Party and were not yet willing to give up and start a new party from scratch. Ruthenberg, along with Wagenknecht, voted with Reed and Gitlow, but endeavoured to hold the two factions together for the fight that was still to come. Ruthenberg hoped the Left Wing could keep the SP from being stolen by the Right, but he was practical about the matter and knew that most of the levers of power were still in the hands of the old National Executive. He believed the Left Wing should try to take the seats that belonged to them, but they should also make preparations to form a party to succeed the SP if such a course of action became unavoidable.[69] He thus also signed a statement calling for "all revolutionary elements" to convene in Chicago on September 1 to either join the Socialist Party under its new revolutionary leadership or to rally for the foundation of a new Communist Party of America.[70]

Though officially the new National Council that was elected at the conference left the meeting united around both a plan and a backup plan, the reality was that the different factions almost immediately went off in their own directions. The Russian Socialist Federation and the Michigan SP promptly formed a committee to prepare a founding convention for September 1, set up a headquarters at the Russian Federation building on Blue Island in Chicago, and established a new newspaper, *The Communist*. The first issue, already branding itself as the "Official Paper of the Communist Party of America,"

---

syndicalism and Marxism was eventually resolved in favour of the latter in the CPUSA.

68. For background on segregation and the SP, see: Sally Miller, "For White Men Only: The Socialist Party of America and Issues of Gender, Ethnicity, and Race," *The Journal of the Gilded Age and Progressive Era*, Vol. 2, No. 3, 283-302

69. "The Communist Party and Communist Labor Party," *The Communist*, September 27, 1919, 10-12

70. *The Revolutionary Age*, July 19, 1919. Cited by Draper, 1957, 169

said the majority at the Left Wing Conference had "weakly neglected to sever their connections with the reactionary" leadership of the SP and said their policy of trying to "capture the old party machinery and the stagnant elements" was a struggle for "false unity." It declared that "no other course is possible" but to meet in Chicago and organize a new party.[71] The National Council, on which Ruthenberg sat, meanwhile, made a last-ditch effort to negotiate with the SP Executive under Germer to persuade them to hand over control of the party to its rightfully elected new leaders. They were met with a flat out refusal. On July 28, the National Council faced up to the writing on the wall and voted 5 to 2 – with Ruthenberg in the affirmative – to go to Chicago and establish a new party. Fraina did not vote but sided with the majority. Benjamin Gitlow, with the backing of Reed and Wagenknecht, held out and still planned to show up at the Socialist convention on August 30. Should they fail to seize control, they would then also form a communist party, but not the one being planned on Blue Island Avenue. It was now a predetermined outcome that three parties would emerge out of the conventions in Chicago at the end of summer.

Germer opened the Socialist Party convention on August 30 at Machinists Hall, prepared to repel any effort by the Left Wing to seize control of the proceedings. Security was tight, with special white cards from the leadership needed to enter, on top of any state-issued delegate credentials. The police were kept on call in case they were needed.[72] Despite the walls put up by Germer, the Left Wing minority group led by Reed, Wagenknecht, and Gitlow insisted on staging a raid and taking the seats they had been elected to. When they met the night before to plan their attack, Ruthenberg was there. Though he had already voted to set about founding a separate party, in the interests of unity and to preserve the bonds between the two factions of the Left, he agreed to serve on the steering committee. No one doubted they would all be denied their seats on the Executive Committee of the SP, and so the minority group had also rented a room downstairs from the official meeting, anticipating they would need a place to set up their own party.

Journalist Max Eastman described the mood of the SP convention as "a little apologetic throughout, a little wan and anxious, and yet at the same time indignant of criticism – about what you might

---

71. "Call for a National Convention—For the Purpose of Organizing the Communist Party of America," *The Communist*, July 19, 1919, 1

72. "Police Under Direction of Adolph Germer Open National Convention of the Socialist Party," *The Ohio Socialist*, September 10, 1919, 1

expect of the mother of twins."[73] After a wave of forced police ejections and walkouts, by August 31, most of the Left Wingers who had shown up for the convention were now literally out of the party. The irony of socialists calling the police against fellow socialists was apparently lost on the party establishment.[74] At 6 p.m., 82 delegates convened in the billiard room of Machinists Hall and established a new communist party. Having just stormed the gates upstairs, the atmosphere among delegates was ecstatic; the meeting "had a little of the quality of a revival meeting" with those present "singing and shouting and feeling that the true faith was about to be restored in their hearts and homes."[75] Contentious debate over the program and how to attain membership in the Communist International, or Comintern, however, hardened the tenor of the sessions. Two days later, the new group got its name: Communist Labor Party of America.

Historian Theodore Draper, in his *Roots of American Communism*, wrote, "In a sense, the Communist Labor Party lost its reason for existence by coming into existence."[76] Though the CPUSA disagreed with Draper's account of its history on many points, about this one he was most certainly right.[77] The reason the Left Wing had split was over the question of whether control of the Socialist Party could still be won. The events of the last two days had proven decisively that it could not. So, why go about setting up a separate communist party when a convention was already arranged to found one the next morning? Personalities, weeks of animosity, and the contentious

---

73. Eastman, 5

74. It was not lost on the Machinists union that had rented the space out to the Socialist Party for its convention. During the proceedings, the executive board of Die and Tool Makers Lodge No. 13 sent a stern letter, saying: "We protest against the harboring and use of police in this hall. This hall is the property, as well as the sanctuary, of a progressive and militant labor organization, based upon the class struggle...We cannot let the police remain as your protectors..." Quoted by Eastman, 10

75. Ibid

76. Draper, 1957, 179

77. When it was published, Draper's 1957 book was critically reviewed in the *Daily Worker*, with its chief shortcomings seen as the "cold and somewhat shallow" way it treated the men and women involved in founding the party and their motivations to build a better world, its overly sympathetic account of Louis C. Fraina and the inflated role given him in the party's founding, and the conclusion that the U.S. Communist movement was forever "surrendered to Russian leadership." Ruthenberg biographer Oakley C. Johnson also had a back-and-forth debate with Draper in the pages of the CPUSA's theoretical journal, *Political Affairs*, in March and May 1959.

issue of the foreign language federations all played a role by this point. Ruthenberg, probably the only Left Wing leader present for both founding conventions, put a motion on the floor at the first session that the immediate order of business should be to unite with the other communist convention. With the practical sense of an organizer, Ruthenberg sought to stop the two parties from starting down the path of inward-looking factional disputes from the very day of their birth – especially when the political and economic situation in the country was crying out for a radical party of action that could play a leadership role in the labor uprisings roiling industry. Ruthenberg had gone to his fellow communists – still small-c at this point – to appeal for the formation of a single party of socialism. After a long debate that night, the group, led by Reed, spurned Ruthenberg's overture by a vote of 37-21 and proceeded to outline an agenda for their new party. Wagenknecht, Ruthenberg's Ohio comrade and Canton prison mate, was elected Executive Secretary. Though that first attempt was in vain, Ruthenberg never stopped pushing for a united, open party in touch with the masses.

At noon the next day, the founding convention of the Communist Party of America opened at the Russian Socialist Federation headquarters, affectionately called the Smolny Institute after the Bolshevik's Petrograd headquarters during the 1917 revolution. The meeting hall was decked out in red banners bearing revolutionary slogans. Portraits of Marx, Lenin, and Leon Trotsky hung above the stage. Eastman said it was characterized "by a spirit of youthful but sophisticated efficiency...a consciously expert convention [that] showed the rest of them what a convention was supposed to be."[78] Just as the meeting was about to open, the Chicago Police Red Squad burst into the hall. It was later said that the police supplied the most convincing argument about which of the three conventions that weekend was seen as the greatest threat to the existing social order: "The Right Wing was protected by the police, the Left Wing was ignored, but the hall of the Communist convention was raided, photographs taken, decorations and revolutionary placards destroyed, and two men arrested."[79] The delegates stared at the police for a few moments, and then a brass band struck up the "Internationale" and everyone started to sing and cheer. After the excitement died down a bit, Louis Fraina made the opening keynote with the following words: "We now end, once and for all, all factional disputes. We are

---

78. Eastman, 5
79. Ibid, 14

at an end with bickering. We are at an end with controversy."[80] Of course, with two separate communist parties founded just 18 hours apart, it was clear that the division and factionalism were far from over.[81]

Ruthenberg, recognized as the most prominent national figure of the group and its ablest organizer, was elected the first executive secretary of the new Communist Party of America.[82] Fraina, the propagandist, was made editor of the party press. While some CPA members continued to trade barbs with their CLP siblings,[83] Ruthen-

---

80. Ibid

81. Even within the CPA convention, there were divisions. Though detractors and opponents have long dismissed the CPA as a Russian immigrant-controlled body in comparison to the more "American" CLP, the reality was that the foreign language federations and the mostly English-speaking National Left Wing Council headed by Ruthenberg and Fraina were roughly equal in size at the CPA convention. A third, smaller group was the Michigan party organization, which was defined by often contradictory ideological leanings that demanded immediate revolution but more often in practice advocated the short-term reformist politics carried over from the SP. Though smaller, the Michigan group held the balance of power at the convention on several votes. They threw their support behind a move by the federations to block any appeal for unity with the CLP. Outvoted, Ruthenberg, Fraina, and Jay Lovestone resigned from a convention committee in protest. The federations and Michigan realized the stakes involved and reversed their position. Another appeal was made to the CLP, but negotiations came to nothing. As for the final results of the Executive Council elections to control the party, the language federations had two representatives while non-federationists occupied five seats—disputing the notion of total federation control. See: Draper 1957, 182-184; also Ferguson, I.E. "The Communist Party Convention," *The Communist*, September 27, 1919, 4

82. Ruthenberg was already likely to be elected Executive Secretary of the Socialist Party of America had the Left Wing been able to take the seats they had been elected to in that party, so his position of leadership in the CPA was largely assured from the start. Describing the elections at the CPA convention, I.E. Ferguson wrote: "C.E. Ruthenberg of Cleveland was chosen for the important post of National Secretary. Comrade Ruthenberg has a record of service in the Socialist Party which has made him a national figure in the Socialist movement for many years. Already elected by a very large vote as International Delegate and Executive Committeeman, Ruthenberg now takes these offices in the Communist Party." Ferguson, 5

83. As an example, see "The Plea for Communist Unity," *The Communist*, October 4, 1919, 6: "The Communist Labor Party continues its meaningless pleading for Communist unity by the two Communist parties 'on a basis of equality' (whatever that may mean). It has already been made clear that the very creation of the Communist Labor Party was a calculated act against

berg wanted to get down to work, which meant concentrating on the actual problems facing workers and linking them up with a party armed with organization and ideology. He told members that their program declared the Communist Party to be a party of action and said they needed to "prove by our deeds that this is no idle boast." The goal had to be "action, and more action."[84] The Communist Party would only grow stronger, he argued, if it proved itself worthy of workers' support.

Building a party of action in the face of repression

While Ruthenberg and other Left Wingers were consumed with the fight for control of the SP and preparing for the establishment of a new party, the instruments of state repression were also hard at work. The Ohio legislature passed a "criminal syndicalism" law, a forerunner of the later Smith and McCarran Acts used to persecute Communists during the Cold War, that made it a crime to "advocate violence" to achieve social change. When Ruthenberg returned from

Communist unity. … a miserably designed coup d'etat to out-Communist the Communists. … dastardly and traitorous." The polemic was published unsigned, so it is not known whether it was a statement of the CPA or the work of the editor, Fraina. Another example, also unsigned, was an attack on John Reed in November in which "Jack the Liar" was denounced for claiming the CPA sought to "create a foreign working class movement in the United States" and that it was "an artificial grouping of foreign-born workers." See: "Jack the Liar," *The Communist*, November 22, 1919, 3. Ruthenberg himself largely limited his comments on the division to a letter circulated to CPA branches and locals, rather than in the public party press. He laid out why he believed the Left Wing SP members who had organized the CLP were responsible for the split in Communist ranks, but he refused to close the door on bringing everyone back together again: "The Communist Party [CPA] yields to no other organization in its desire to bring together in one organization every man or woman in the country who agrees that it is through an organization founded upon Communistic principles that the freedom of the workers alone can be won. … Communist Unity is still possible. The delegates of the Communist Labor Convention are responsible for the organization of a third party. If they are Communists in principle, let them step aside." See: "Circular Letter to All Branches and Locals of the CPA from C.E. Ruthenberg, Executive Secretary, October 7, 1919, https://www.marxists.org/history/usa/parties/cpusa/1919/10/1007-ruth-toall-branches.pdf

84. Ruthenberg, C.E. "Circular Letter to the Members of the Communist Party of America," October 15, 1919, https://www.marxists.org/history/usa/parties/cpusa/1919/10/1015-ruth-tocpamembers.pdf

the Left Wing Conference in July, he had been arrested and charged with distributing copies of an African American Socialist publication, *The Messenger*, which was accused of advocating a "Soviet form of government." At the same time, New York prosecutors unveiled their own case against Ruthenberg, labeling him a "criminal anarchist," with the June Left Wing Manifesto offered as proof. The state's Criminal Anarchy Law had been passed in 1902 in the wake of President William McKinley's assassination. Ruthenberg posted bail and went back to his organizing work while awaiting his next trial. During the summer and fall of 1919 then, as he was founding the Communist Party and focused on moving its members into the labor struggles raging during those months, Ruthenberg had the threat of prison again hanging over his head.

    U.S. Attorney General A. Mitchell Palmer and his deputy J. Edgar Hoover mobilized the full force of the government to crush the Communists before they could make any progress. Between October 1919 and January 1920, massive raids were carried out against Communists, anarchists, socialists, syndicalists, and leftists of every stripe. More than 10,000 people were swept up in the government's dragnet, and hundreds of foreign born workers deported in America's first Red Scare. Both CPA and CLP headquarters were trashed by federal agents, and Ruthenberg and several other top party leaders were arrested.[85] But the sight of thousands being dragged from their homes and thrown into crowded jails sparked an indignant response from many quarters. The American Civil Liberties Union was founded in response to the Palmer Raids. As soon as he was out on bail, Ruthenberg rallied party members and class conscious workers to "Help Defend Your Comrades!" In an appeal, he declared: "The ruling class of this country is making a desperate effort to disrupt the Communist Party. It believes that if it can put the officials of the organization in prison the party will disintegrate."[86] With the courts breathing down his neck, Ruthenberg orchestrated a fundraising drive for a national legal defense fund, asking workers to send every

---

85. Instead of its usual numbers and administrative data, Ruthenberg's weekly column in the party newspaper carried a notice in the December 6th issue announcing: "Again Comrade Ruthenberg is held away from his office by the courts...No individual in the labor movement in the United States has been more shamelessly hounded than Comrade Ruthenberg." See: "The Party Organization," *The Communist*, December 6, 1919, 7

86. C.E. Ruthenberg, "Help Defend Your Comrades!" *The Communist*, December 13, 1919, 7

penny they could. Added to his list of responsibilities was now secretary of the Communist Defense Committee.

The raids had a devastating effect, driving most Communist leaders underground or locking them behind bars and sending many
rank and file members fleeing. Of the 60,000 who had left the SP
under the banner of the Left Wing in 1919, only about 10,000, combined, remained in the CPA and CLP by 1920.[87] The situation was
made worse by ongoing internal sectarianism and factionalism. The
threat of joint destruction, however, forced many in the CPA and
CLP leaderships to realize that they would be stronger together in
a single organization. Ruthenberg, as always, was at the center of
efforts to bridge the divide between the two parties. His negotiations with the CLP resulted in an agreement to forge an immediate
working unity between the two groups and a plan to hold a joint
convention later in the year. But the whole effort was scuttled by
the tendency of some of his party comrades – especially among the
Russian Federation in Chicago – to turn inward during the period of
repression. The government onslaught had "deepened the tendency
for the Party to become merely a propaganda society."[88] Ruthenberg
was determined that the party keep its eyes set on the class struggle
while also fighting for its own survival; he continued to believe that
workers would only come to support and defend the Communist
Party if they saw it as a vehicle for their own struggles. He combat-
ted the proclivities of some to turn the party into a fan club for Soviet
Russia or a debating society committed to 'pure principles' that simply waited for economic crisis to deliver workers into its hands.[89] He

_____

87. William Z. Foster, *History of the Communist Party of the United States*
(New York: International Publishers, 1952), 176

88. C.E. Ruthenberg, "Seven Years of the Communist Party of America,"
The Workers Monthly, September 1926, 483-485

89. Typical of the crude understanding of Marxism that defined this viewpoint was a May Day article from the "anti-Ruthenberg majority" headlined
"The Party Crisis," which stated: "We must try to reach the workers with
our propaganda—we don't expect to make much of an impression on them
at present. Well and good. We shall continue our agitation, confident that
the social forces, the economic disintegration of world capitalism since the
war—and which can no longer succeed in rehabilitating itself—will compel
the masses to listen to our message. ... The masses will come to us in good
time. ...What we will not do...is to go to the masses now, 'seek contact with
them' and lead them into the Communist movement at the expense of sacrificing our principles, policies, and aims. If the 'secessionists' [Ruthenberg
and allies] do succeed in splitting the party—if they do succeed in winning most of the rank and file with them—why that will only mean that

said the Communist Party "should be not a party of closet philoso-
phers but a party which participates in the everyday struggles of the
workers, and by such participation injects its principles into these
struggles and gives them a wider meaning."[90] In May 1920, Ruthenberg offered blunt criticism of those who held the opposite outlook:

> It may be said, in all candor, that up until this time our zeal
> has been more in the direction of faithful imitation of phrases
> than in Communist expression of the class struggle as it devel-
> ops from day to day in the United States...The vaguest sort of
> phrases will serve the purposes of celebrating the Russian rev-
> olution, which has been too much the exclusive concern of our
> public meetings. But only the most precise phrases of imme-
> diate application will challenge the attention of millions of
> workers...Let no one dismiss the present struggle in the party...
> It is a life and death struggle to save the party from the grasp
> of Russian nationalists who have made a demagogic merger of
> nationalistic and ultra-revolutionary phrases, but to whom the
> building of a real party to take part in the class conflict in the
> United States is meaningless...Our crying need is a more pre-
> cise and understandable expression of Communism as part of
> the everyday working class fight in the United States.[91]

Ruthenberg held no sympathy for those who wanted to play at revolution or preferred the underground life of persecuted martyrs.
The party was losing contact with the mass of American workers
at a moment when its experienced organizers were needed most
– exactly what the Red Scare repression was intended to achieve.
Finding allies in the CLP with a similar mindset, especially his old
Ohio comrade Wagenknecht, Ruthenberg proposed a Unity Conference. There were still intense debates to be had over strategy and
tactics and the approach to trade unionism, but a new body bringing
together a big part of the CPA and the CLP was founded in the spring

---

the majority of the rank and file were themselves not fully ready to accept
Communist theory and practice. It will only mean that the real Communists
remaining will close ranks and march unflinchingly onward to the goal."
See: "The Party Crisis," *The Communist* (Majority Faction edition), May 1,
1920, 2, 8

90. C.E. Ruthenberg (writing as David Damon), "Make the Party a 'Party
of Action'," *The Communist* (Minority Faction edition), April 25, 1920, 4

91. C.E. Ruthenberg (writing as David Damon), "Communist Party Criticism," *The Communist* (Minority Faction edition), May 15, 1920, 2

of 1920 – the United Communist Party – with Ruthenberg once more selected by his peers to serve as leader.[92] It would still be some time before the remainder of the CPA – the sectarians and the language federations that insisted on their autonomy – would rejoin the fold and a truly united Communist Party emerge in the United States.

The process of overcoming the sectarianism and isolationist politics was helped along by Lenin with the publication of his *"Left-wing" Communism: An Infantile Disorder* in 1920, though it did not appear in English until the following year. A declaration of war on ultra-left hang-ups the world over, the book struck at precisely the kind of 'purist' politics that Ruthenberg had been battling. Lenin condemned some Communists' refusal to dirty themselves with participation in bourgeois democracy or work in reactionary trade unions. Electoral and trade union struggles, he said, were essential for winning workers and changing the balance of forces required to move toward socialism. Communists had to maneuver and compromise as necessary to advance the cause of the working class and never mistake their own "desire, their ideological-political attitude, for actual fact." The take-home message: "Work wherever the masses are to be found."[93]

The internal debates of the UCP were hardly settled, but the State of New York demanded that the Communist leaders turn their attention back to the repression at hand. In October 1920, Ruthenberg was finally tried on the charge of criminal anarchism that had been leveled at him nearly a year before. A guilty verdict was essentially a

---

92. Two figures who had played such prominent roles in the period of the CP's founding, John Reed and Louis C. Fraina, no longer figured largely in internal affairs after 1920. John Reed died in October in Moscow. He had been serving as representative to the Comintern and contracted typhus while in Baku. Fraina, meanwhile, disappeared mysteriously under a cloud of espionage accusations and, eventually, charges concerning the embezzlement of Comintern funds. He resurfaced years later back in the United States, working as an editor named Joseph Charles Skala and then as an economist called Lewis Corey who wrote books on the decline of capitalism during the Great Depression. He remained on the fringes of the CPUSA in the early 1930s and then toyed with James P. Cannon's Trotskyists and Jay Lovestone's expelled Communist opposition group. By 1940, he had turned on Marxism completely and found work with the Meat Cutters union in the early 1950s. The government tried to deport him during the McCarthyite "Second Red Scare," but he died before it got the chance. See: Draper 1957, 297-302

93. V.I. Lenin, *"Left-wing" Communism: An Infantile Disorder"* (New York: International Publishers, 1940 (2005)), 37-41

foregone conclusion. Never letting an opportunity for agitation and propaganda to pass him by, though, Ruthenberg declared to the court:

I have merely this to say for myself, that I have in the past held certain ideals for a reorganization of society on a new basis. I have upheld those ideals and gone to prison for them when they were connected with the late war. I have stood by those principles in which I firmly believe, and I still stand for those principles irrespective of the result of this particular trial...I realized from the beginning of this trial, as I have in any other trial that I have taken part in as a defendant, that this court, and all the instruments of this court, are merely a part of that organization of force which we call the capitalist state...I accept this as a case of class justice, a case of the use of the organized force of the state in order to suppress the desires of those who today are suffering under the oppression of the present system. I will accept the sentence in that same spirit of defiance, realizing that I go to prison because of support of a great principle that will triumph in spite of all the courts, in spite of all the organizations of the capitalist class.[94]

Along with New York party leader I.E. Ferguson, Ruthenberg was convicted by "a carefully picked jury of business men" who sentenced him to an indeterminate sentence of 5 to 10 years.[95] Ruthenberg became Prisoner 71624 at Sing Sing State Penitentiary. While he was locked up, the UCP and the remaining CPA faction in Chicago finally united, pushed along by the Comintern. The name Communist Party of America was maintained for the new organization. The major split that had kept Communists apart since their divorce from the SP was finally overcome, but similar divisions reappeared later under the guise of a debate over whether or not to maintain dual legal and illegal (i.e. underground) party structures. There were some who argued that the CP should only emerge from underground when it could openly advocate armed insurrection. From behind bars, Ruthenberg made clear his preference and drafted a new program for an open, aboveground party. If existing out in the open where workers could find them required Communists to stop talking of

---

94. C.E. Ruthenberg, "A Case of Class Justice," October 1920 (mis-dated as March 1920). In *Speeches and Writings*, 48-49

95. "Two More Political Prisoners," *The Toiler*, November 6, 1920, 9

violence and forcible overthrow, then Ruthenberg had no qualms about doing so.[96] He ended up serving 18 months before an appeals court judge said he should never have been found guilty in the first place and ordered him released pending retrial. When he left Sing Sing in the summer of 1922, Ruthenberg showed up at party head-quarters and immediately resumed his duties as head of the Workers Party (the name for the CP's aboveground organization).

Forty days later, he was apprehended yet again, this time at a con-vention of the underground CPA in Bridgman, Michigan, at which he was arguing for Communists to fully come out into the open and eliminate the underground party completely. The Justice Depart-ment had planted a spy at the meeting and managed to discover its location. When the feds struck, Ruthenberg and the others were paraded through the streets in handcuffs. A few weeks later, William Z. Foster, the labor leader famous for leading the Great Steel Strike of 1919, was seized in Chicago, and taken back to Michigan with the others (he had also been at the convention but left early). Foster had joined the party in 1921 while Ruthenberg was at Sing Sing. With two of the most well-known working class leaders in the country jailed, one of the biggest labor defense campaigns in history was launched, the so-called "Michigan Defense." The ACLU offered its services to represent the indicted Communists, and prominent fig-ures such as Elizabeth Gurley Flynn of the Workers Defense Union, Eugene Debs of the Socialist Party, Robert Buck of the Chicago Fed-eration of Labor, John G. Brown, secretary of the Farmer-Labor Party, and many more signed on to the cause.

The backdrop for the raid was an ongoing wave of militant labor struggles across the country. At the time, well over one million work-ers were out on strike in various industries: 500,000 coal miners, 400,000 railroad shop men, and 200,000 textile workers. The gov-ernment seemed determined to decapitate labor by removing those leaders seen as most capable of 'exploiting' unrest.[97] Foster was tried first, with Ruthenberg called by the defense as a witness. He tes-tified for four days, using his allotted time to educate the jury on the nature of capitalism, the functioning of governments and courts under capitalism, about how capitalism itself called forth revolution because of its own contradictions, and about the virtues of American

---

96. C.E. Ruthenberg and Max Bedacht (writing as David Damon and James Marshall), "Problem of Communist Organization," *The Communist*, July 1922, 24

97. This account of the Bridgman Convention and the Michigan Defense were provided in Johnson, 1957, 154-155

C.E. Ruthenberg at the 1924 convention of the Workers Party in St. Paul, Minnesota. At the time, Ruthenberg was the party's executive secretary. | Communist Party USA Archives, Tamiment Library, New York University

democratic constitutional principles. The end result: a hung jury and a mistrial. The mistake of letting working people onto the jury was not repeated for Ruthenberg's trial – only property owners were allowed. This time, Ruthenberg was almost prevented from speaking altogether, and the government got the guilty verdict it wanted. Appeal was made to the Michigan Supreme Court, but the verdict was upheld. Ruthenberg entered Jackson State Prison in January 1925 to serve a three- to ten-year sentence. But in a stunning reversal, 20 days later, U.S. Supreme Court Justice Louis Brandeis ordered that Ruthenberg be granted bail. After the payment of $7,500, Ruthenberg was out again and back to lead the now totally aboveground Workers (Communist) Party.

The threat of reimprisonment, however, never went away. Lenin was said to have written to the *Daily Worker* that, "The Communists of America prove by their long prison terms, to which the bourgeoisie sentence them for communist agitation and propaganda, what capitalist democracy really means. They are tearing the masks from it and are exposing it as a reign of trust kings and speculators amid the subjection of the masses."[98] As the "most arrested man in

98. The quote was attributed to Lenin by Jay Lovestone in 1928, though I can find no source for it in either the *Collected Works of V.I. Lenin* or the

America," Ruthenberg seemed to be the living example of Lenin's dictum. Regardless of the ever present shadow of prison gates, he never hesitated to carry on organizing.

Throughout the 1920s, he continued in his push to turn American Communists outward, to keep their attention focused on the mass movements of workers and the oppressed. He spearheaded a $100,000 fundraising campaign to launch the *Daily Worker* newspaper, which published its first issue on January 21, 1924. He became a herald for united front politics, advocating Communists' involvements in efforts to establish a broad Farmer-Labor Party. His was also a voice for equality for African Americans at a time when still far too few left leaders – including Communists – were taking up the fight for Black freedom or challenging the lynch rule of Jim Crow. Ruthenberg had no respect for the arguments of some socialists that racism was a problem that could only be solved after the revolution, and he understood the multiple layers of oppression that weighed on Black workers. He argued: "The Negroes are not only a part of the most bitterly exploited section of the working class, but they are in addition, oppressed as a race. The Workers (Communist) Party supports the organization of the Negroes for their fight against exploitation as a part of the working class and against the special discrimination to which they are subjected. It demands complete social equality for the Negro."[99]

Death and legacy

In early 1927, Ruthenberg's tireless work came to an abrupt and untimely end. At a meeting of the party's political committee on February 27, he was jotting down notes when William Z. Foster told him that he looked pale. His only response was that he was "kind of under the weather."[100] A couple of hours afterward, he collapsed and was taken to the hospital for emergency appendectomy surgery. He died three days later, March 2, of acute peritonitis. He was only 44 years old. A black banner headline stretched across the front page of the *Daily Worker* the next morning: "RUTHENBERG IS DEAD."[101] Only two weeks prior, Irish writer T.J. O'Flaherty had noted that "he

archives of the *Daily Worker*. See: Jay Lovestone, "Ruthenberg, Revolutionary Chief," *Daily Worker*, March 2, 1928, 1

99. C.E. Ruthenberg, *The Workers (Communist) Party: What It Stands For, Why Workers Should Join* (Chicago: Workers (Communist) Party, 1923), 13

100. Recounted by Johnson, 1957, 177-178

101. *Daily Worker*, March 3, 1927, 1

looked the picture of health" and "seemed destined to play a leading role in the party" for many years to come.[102] The editorial staff of the *Daily Worker* lamented, "We expected to write soon that he had gone to prison again because of his loyalty to the cause of workers…But death does not release its prisoners."[103]

For days, the party press was filled with reports from memorial meetings across the country, remembrances by close comrades, tributes from unions and progressive organizations, and condolences from several foreign parties.[104] Upton Sinclair, famed novelist and author of *The Jungle*, said "our capitalist government has lost one of its predestined victims."[105] The director of the ACLU, Forrest Bailey, wrote, "The death of C.E. Ruthenberg is a distinctive loss to the aggressive front of labor…He is the sort of man that cannot be replaced."[106] The American Negro Labor Congress expressed sorrow at the loss of a man it counted as "one of the upstanding and fearless leaders of the Communist Party who always has taken a very clear position in defense of the Negro people of this country."[107] And an outfit known as the United Council of Working Class Housewives said Ruthenberg inspired "working class women to take their place in the struggle, side by side with the working man."[108] Messages came in, too, from Eugene Debs, Norman Thomas, and others. Locals of the Steelworkers, Bakers, Millinery Workers, and other unions declared they were in mourning for a great labor leader. A Ruthenberg Recruiting Drive to enroll new members into the Workers (Communist) Party was launched.

Two massive funerals took place, with thousands of workers packing Chicago's Ashland Auditorium and New York's Carnegie Hall. The remains were cremated and sent to Moscow, with further memorial gatherings along the way in Europe in Bremerhaven, Bremen,

102. T.J. O'Flaherty, "Current Events," *Daily Worker*, March 3, 1927, 1

103. Daily Worker Editorial Staff. "In Memoriam," *Daily Worker*, March 3, 1927, 1

104. Notices and reports in the *Daily Worker* during March 1927 suggest no less than 20 memorial meetings were held coast-to-coast, from Seattle to St. Louis to New York, and points in between.

105. "Upton Sinclair Respects Loyalty," *Daily Worker*, March 3, 1927, 2

106. "Forrest Bailey [sic] Recognizes His Value," *Daily Worker*, March 5, 1927, 2

107. "American Negro Labor Congress Feels It Has Lost Great Friend," *Daily Worker*, March 7, 1927, 2

108. "Inspired Working Class Women," *Daily Worker*, March 3, 1927, 1

Hamburg, and Berlin.[109] A final grand farewell was held in the Soviet capital, with tens of thousands paying respects, a Red Army honor guard, a brass band playing "The Internationale," and Comintern head Nikolai Bukharin delivering the eulogy.[110] The bronze urn containing Ruthenberg's ashes was interred in the row of honor inside the Kremlin wall behind Lenin's mausoleum.[111]

In the United States, meanwhile, factional infighting carried on, with Ruthenberg's memory and legacy one of the casualties. Immediately after his death, a battle for leadership ensued between one of his close associates, Jay Lovestone, and labor veteran Foster. Lovestone prevailed, initially, assuming the role of general secretary. He hoped to leverage Ruthenberg's prestige to cement his own position and so portrayed himself as the dead leader's disciple and rightful successor. He attached his name to every imaginable Ruthenberg tribute article, pamphlet, book, or event. Within a few years, he was expelled from the party over his supposed theories of "American Exceptionalism," but the affairs of the American Communists had also become entangled by that time in the Stalin-Trotsky-Bukharin fight in the Soviet Union. As much as his domestic politics, it was Lovestone's close connection to Bukharin that helped do him in once Stalin made a move against the Comintern leader.[112] Foster, too, came in for a scolding by Stalin for his factionalism and was passed over for the leadership after Lovestone's ouster. That left Earl Browder from Kansas as the new general secretary. He would head the party until his own downfall 15 years later.

After Lovestone was purged in 1929, his works immediately disappeared from the party, including those which had promoted the study of Ruthenberg's contributions and writings. During Browder's tenure, the party press talked above all about Browder. But even once Foster eventually became the top CPUSA leader after World War II, there was no major effort to revive Ruthenberg. The two men had spent a considerable part of Ruthenberg's final years on opposing sides of many key questions, trade union and united front political

---

109. J. Louis Engdahl, "High Honor Paid Ruthenberg By Moscow Museum of Revolution," *Daily Worker*, June 2, 1927, 1

110. "Address of Comrade N. Bukharin At the Funeral of Comrade C.E. Ruthenberg," *Daily Worker*, May 18, 1927, 3

111. J. Louis Engdahl, "World Leaders Guard Ashes of C.E. Ruthenberg," *Daily Worker*, May 18, 1927, 1, 3

112. Edward P. Johanningsmeier, *Forging American Communism: The Life of William Z. Foster* (Princeton University Press, 1994), 245-247

Ruthenberg's death was announced in a banner headline edition of the Daily Worker, March 3, 1927. | Daily Worker Archives, Courtesy of People's World

work key among them.[113] When Foster published his official *History of the Communist Party of the United States*, the name of Ruthenberg –

---

113. For some background discussion on the differences, see Ruthenberg's account: C.E. Ruthenberg, "From the Third Through the Fourth Convention

perhaps the most pivotal figure in the party's founding and the person who helped hold it together during the first Red Scare – was mentioned a mere eight times in 600 pages.[114] Oakley C. Johnson's 1957 biography of Ruthenberg was the last major effort to remind party members of his contributions, but even it was plagued by the proscription on mentioning forbidden names, such as Louis C. Fraina and Jay Lovestone; they had both become staunch anti-communists, so their misdeeds cast a shadow over any effort to comprehensively assess the decade of the 1920s. Not since Lovestone's downfall has the CPUSA or its associated bodies republished any significant part of Ruthenberg's work.[115]

The U.S. Communist movement owed (and owes) a lot to C.E. Ruthenberg, even though his contributions may have faded from memory. More than any other leader in the party's formative years, he worked to keep it united and its attention turned constantly outward. He was an organizer by nature, determined to build a party of action that planted itself firmly in the struggles that moved the working class in the here and now while always striving toward revolutionary social transformation. He was also a bridge between the positive traditions of American democratic thought, the pioneering work of the old Socialist Party, and the revolutionary politics of the Leninist 'party of a new type.'

Ruthenberg once said that the Communist Party had been founded too early in the United States, that it was not yet prepared for the role history had assigned to it. Being established in 1919, it preceded most of the Communist parties of Europe, for instance, by a year or two or more. The movement in the U.S., he wrote, developed in a "hip-hip-hurrah fashion," driven by people energized by the need to break from the Socialist Party officialdom but not yet united among themselves. The draconian response to dissent taken by the old SP bureaucrats pushed everything to the fore on a sped up schedule, thus "the issues which were fought out within the Socialist parties of Europe were consequently fought out in the United States between the two Communist Parties."[116] The ideological immaturity

of the Workers (Communist) Party of America," *The Workers Monthly*, October 1925, 531-538

114. Foster, 1952, Index, 592

115. One of few exceptions was the inclusion of a 1924 article from *The Liberator* entitled, "The Revolutionary Party," which appeared in *Highlights of a Fighting History*, 1979, 21-24

116. C.E. Ruthenberg (writing as David Damon), "The Communist Party and its Tasks," *The Communist*, July 1921, 25-27

of many of the founders and their divergent ideas about what the role of the new party should be led to bitter division in a period of intense government repression. Ruthenberg, along with others, managed to navigate those fights as well as the terror of the Justice Department and stitch together a single Communist Party by the end of the 1920s. They achieved it just before the Great Depression struck, a time when the CPUSA achieved its greatest impact and influence. Without the work of leaders like Ruthenberg, it is doubtful the party would have been ready for the great battles to stop fascism and Jim Crow or win unemployment insurance, Social Security, and industrial unionization.

Through all the years of factionalism, sectarianism, and repression, Ruthenberg maintained his stance in favor of a united, legal, and practical party. Though some, like Fraina and Lovestone, would fade into obscurity or ignominy, Ruthenberg remained dedicated to building a fighting organization committed to the goal of winning socialism in the United States. He was of course a combatant in the divisive internal battles of the CP's first decade. His hands weren't always clean, and he was not some pure figure to be canonized. But he consistently fought to achieve unity – from his days in Cleveland all the way up to his death. He was a devoted Marxist but had little sympathy for those who, on the basis of protecting their supposedly revolutionary principles, would have made the party into little more than a debating society. "The knowledge gained in study classes," he wrote in his last *Daily Worker* column, "must be carried into the actual class struggle." [117] That combination of theory and practice is the legacy of C.E. Ruthenberg.

---

117. C.E. Ruthenberg, "Our Proletarian Friends," *Daily Worker*, February 28, 1927, 4

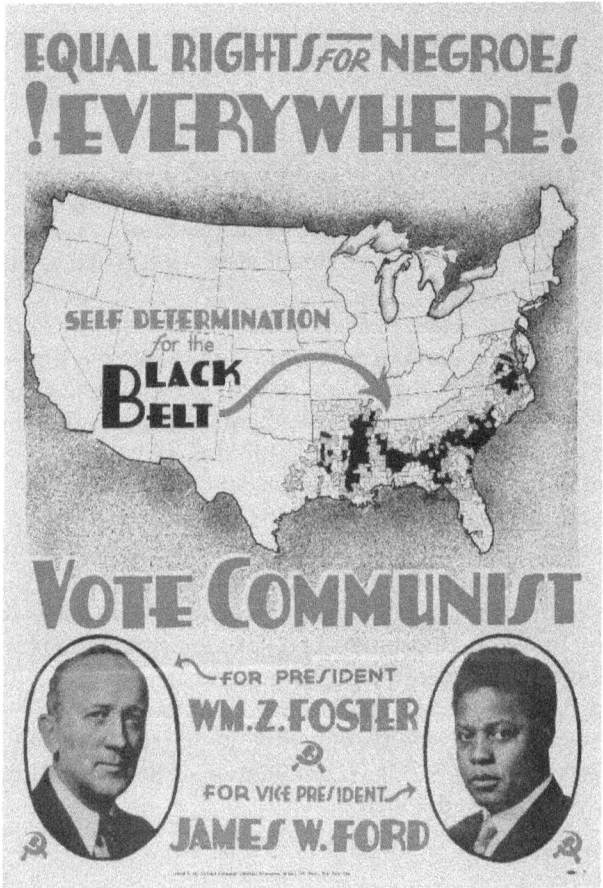

1932 CPUSA Foster / Ford Campaign poster

Chapter *3*

Playing by Our Own Rules: The Communist Party's Presidential Campaign in 1932

By Joshua Morris

The historiography of the Communist Party of the United States of America is a complex and often contradictory narrative. Edward Pintzuk accurately described the early studies as narratives of "continuous setbacks."[1] One of the earliest theses, put forth by Theodor Draper in the 1950s, remains one of the most dominant: the CPUSA was the product of the Communist Party of the Soviet Union and for better or worse served as a front for the ideals of Soviet foreign policy. This narrative has since been dubbed the "traditionalist" view on American Communism. Later scholars, such as Robin Kelly, Fraser Ottanelli, James Barrett, and Randi Storch, examined the internal party functions and the personal lives of Communists at the grassroots to discern civil versus political activism. These "revisionist" scholars benefitted from the fact that since the mid-1990s, research on American Communism has renewed vigor as more people began to tell their stories, the Russian Center for the Preservation and Study of Documents of Recent History (RTsKhIDMII/RGAJPI) digitized its archives on the CPUSA (now widely available around the world through Marxisthistory.com), and new methods of interpreting history, such as an emphasis on personal experiences, became more widely used. From the historiography, we get a glimpse of the party's international connections, a separation between its upper and lower leadership, the general effectiveness of the party's organizing drives for labor and against racism, and its ineffectiveness in capturing the minds and hearts of Americans as a political party. Despite this rich scholarship, one of the least discussed aspects of

---

1. Edward Pintzuk, *Reds, Racial Justice, and Civil Liberties* (MEP Publications, 1997), 9

American Communist history is the electoral programs and the campaign platforms promoted in national elections by the CPUSA and the effect their campaigns had on American politics. To this end, we have only limited scholarship and it is the purpose of this essay to expand on that scholarship.

The CPUSA engaged in American politics in a manner profoundly different from other political parties, including labor parties such as the Socialist Party of America and the Socialist Workers' Party, to the extent that one might legitimately ask "did the CPUSA even run elections in the manner that we understand electoral activity?" This study began with the question of "how did the Communist Party conduct an electoral campaign in 1932?" This question quickly turned into a philosophical one: Just what exactly *is* an electoral campaign to a political party that openly advocated revolution and substantive societal change? If we define campaigns by the nature in which they are practiced by the two dominant American parties, Democrat and Republican, then the definition becomes straightforward: an organized effort to get an individual or policy voted into office or law, respectively. But if we accept this definition and examine the CPUSA's engagement into American electoral politics in 1932, it becomes clear that the CPUSA *did not run an electoral campaign with the goal of being voted into office.* For Communists electoral campaigns, as a means to an end, performed the function of drawing in the attention of American voters by offering radical alternatives to the solutions presented by Democrats, Republicans, and progressive socialists. The campaigns attempted to attract American citizens and workers into the orbit of the party's auxiliaries where they could be exposed to Communist ideology, literature, theory, and organizational methods. In short, the process was about ideology and its goal was education and recruitment, a means to an end.

It is not just because the CPUSA was a "radical" party that it engaged in politics this way, nor can the party's actions be solely the result of a relationship held in the international Communist movement centered around the Communist International. Though both elements have been argued extensively in the party's historiography, particularly by traditionalist historians such as Draper and David Shannon, focusing on them exclusively ignores another fundamental component to party history: the structure of the party itself. When one observes the campaign of presidential candidate William Z. Foster and vice presidential candidate James Ford, the party's approach can only be described as the *antithesis* of campaigning in the conventional sense that most Americans were and still are accustomed to.

This essay argues that the CPUSA ran their own electoral program by their own rules for three interconnected reasons.

First, the party's history in the movement to advance socialism in the United States between 1919-1928 separated the party's political tiers, based in New York City, from its more civil-activist lower tiers, based in the Midwest and the South. The CPUSA's emphasis on Leninist democratic centrism characterized the nomination process through secret ballot; where decisions were made in private then submitted to the majority for approval. This division allowed the party to function as a flexible and broad civil activist organization in large rallies, while maintaining a rigid organization dedicated to acute political goals. Second, the orientation of the party in the throes of the Comintern had a direct effect on how the party viewed its role and its prospects for revolution in America. Finally, the dire situation of the Great Depression by 1932 gave the party the most convenient excuse for abandoning previous approaches to electoral campaigning, and instead allowed it to engage in a more radical, revolutionary, and aggressive campaign best evidenced by William Z. Foster's rallies at the Ford River Rouge factory during its historic 1932 hunger march. For the CPUSA, the 1932 campaign was not a campaign for the office of President, but rather a campaign for revolution in America.

Democratic Centralism in Ideology and Practice

A political party, according to V.O. Key in his text, *Politics, Parties and Pressure Groups*, and according to Grier Stephenson Jr. in *Introductions to American Government*, exists because of three basic "functions" or activities. These functions "help to socialize voters into politics and form public opinion" on a range of ongoing issues; these are "socialization," "electoral," and "governmental" functions.[2] Socialization is the means by which a party makes itself present in the minds of public opinion and passes on its ideological practices. Electoral functions integrate party officials into the eyes of voters by placing them behind specific issues. Finally, governmental functions allow a political party's structure and methodology to influence the policies and coherence of the government as a whole – should they win office.[3] These general categories create the very idea of what a polit-

2. Grier Stephenson Jr., "Interest Groups and Party Politics" in *Introductions to American Government* (CA: Northwest, 2002), 214-215

3. V.O. Key, *Politics, Parties, and Pressure Groups* (NY: Crowell, 1964), 656

ical party *does* or *should do*. With these three functions in mind, the CPUSA retained the clear identity of an American political party, but that is where the similarities between it and the dominant American parties cease.

Stephenson also defines political parties by their structure, which invariably limits him to discussing the Republican and Democratic Parties as standards and all deviations from which are determined to be "third parties."[4] In Stephenson's portrayal, a political party "is not a single organization, but [rather] a broad family of related formal organizations and informal groups." Third parties on the other hand, "have been little more than temporary vehicles for a particular candidate or issue." While Stephenson does credit third parties with having "an important role in influencing the actions of major parties," they nevertheless retain the identity of a sideline role; influential to the same extent that a fan might be to his sports team on the sidelines, rooting for victory despite impossible odds.[5] It is here where the CPUSA stands out from the crowd of sidelined political groups, as the party as an organization was certainly *not* a broad family of interrelated organizations throughout its lifetime (unless we consider all sects of Communist and labor groups to be the 'broad' category), nor was it (nor did it see itself as) a temporary vehicle for one candidate or another. The methodology and organization of the Party separated it from the general category of what Stephenson calls a "third party," and created visible differences between existing portrayals of both American party types.

The CPUSA's organizational methodology paralleled European Communist Parties so close that its differences to traditional American political groups likely stood out larger to American political scientists than any policy it advocated. The party defined its organizational method as *democratic centralism*, a phrase that referred to a form of party centralism mirrored from the Soviet Union's actual governing bodies. It was thus this structure that created the image of the party in the eyes of the public, both in practice and in potential policy. Historian of grassroots American Communism Randi Storch described the party's democratic centralism as "an elaborate, hierarchical structure...which fit [recruits] at its bottom while connecting them to a leadership in the Soviet Union, at the top. There stood the Communist International."[6] Despite their clear size limita-

---

4. Stephenson, 215
5. Ibid, 216
6. Randi Storch, *Red Chicago: American Communism at its Grassroots, 1928-1935* (University of Chicago Press, 2007), 18-19

tions and placement in a completely separate realm from European working class struggles, the CPUSA for the most part mimicked the organizational structure of European parties, particularly because of their support from and interdependency to the Comintern – which in their eyes provided them legitimacy in the global movement for socialism.

The hierarchy of the party itself detailed the inner workings of democratic centralism as a political methodology.[7] At the top of the party sat the Central Executive Committee, also known as the CEC or simply CC. The CC was made up of three branches, with the general secretary in the executive position over each branch, of which Earl Browder held the title during the 1932 election. The CC's main tasks involved a process of secret ballot voting and publishing directives for the overall party ideology and annual activities. While in form the party's political system appeared rigidly hierarchical, in practice it was much more divided – split between a theoretical and internationalist sect based out of New York City and a more labor oriented syndicalist segment based heavily out of Chicago. While the CC effectively controlled party functioning nationally and internationally, they did not necessarily have control over regional Communist leaders and especially their lead organizers in the labor movement.[8]

For our purposes here, it is important to consider that William Z. Foster's nomination to the Presidential ticket in 1932 was made by a CC secret ballot taken most likely in February 1932, one month before his campaigning began. The same secret ballot nominated Foster in 1928, and likely as well in 1924.[9] It is no surprise, then, that Foster began his 1932 electoral campaign in March, in Detroit, two months prior to accepting his formal nomination by the party. While each district of the party held their own voting procedures by region, the democratic centralist hierarchy of upper party decision making remained unchallenged at the national level.

From the top, each branch of the party split into regional, followed by local "political committees" or Polcoms, which "oversaw Party policy between CC meetings, and an even smaller Secretariat [that]

---

7. Image in Storch, 21

8. For more details on the division of the American Communist movement into various worlds of experience, see: Joshua Morris, "The Many Worlds of American Communism" (Dissertation, Detroit, Wayne State University, 2019), Proquest.com.

9. William Z. Foster, "Acceptance to the Nomination of President," in *Acceptance Speeches, 1928* (Workers' Publishers Library, 1928)

ran the Party's daily activities" in each respective region.[10] Beneath Polcoms were upper district branches and committees, of which 18 existed between 1928-1936. They also all grew out of urban cities; New York City was the largest of the 18 districts, followed closely by Chicago and then Detroit.[11] District conferences were held annually and voted via write-in ballots "for anywhere from fifteen to nineteen Party members to lead them." Once picked, this district commit-tee went on to elect its own executive committee "of three to seven leaders, whom they called the Secretariat or Buro." The Secretariat divided its members according to specific party responsibilities. This was precisely where the division between the upper and lower tiers of the CPUSA created two different worlds of experience. Under the upper district branches were the city based branches who elected their own leadership. These groups, in contrast to the upper branches, "were organized by neighborhood and shop groups, known as nuclei or units." The individuals voted into the position of the city Secretariats were typically those from the rank and file who showed the most promise as opposed to who were the most ideolog-ically sound or "ideal" charismatic figure. Organizational practice, experience, and most importantly a strong dedication to working class activism in the surrounding community thus formed a criti-cal component to party leadership potential at the lower branches. Because of the requirement of experience, most lower branch leaders came into the party already having established a foothold in their local community struggles. In addition to having experience, lower branch Secretariat leaders also "participated in the activities carried on by their nuclei as well as the work organized by leaders at the [upper] district level" and in this sense facilitated some semblance of cooperation between the upper and lower tiers.[12] Between 1928-1935, the number of lower district sections increased from five to 13, which reflected the party's overall growth from under 600 members in the mid-1920s to a few thousand by 1934, a product of the party's heightened activism and popularity.[13]

Finally, beneath the city district branches were the Nuclei, where everyone usually started either on the street or shop scene. There were both shop, or workplace, and street/community nuclei, both of which did not necessarily collect dues nor issue membership cards. Nuclei were "units of ten to fifteen people," whose main goal was

---

10. Storch, 19
11. Ibid, 19
12. Storch, 20
13. "District Secretariat Minutes", February 14, 1933, in Storch, 20

to "bring Communist ideals to factories, schools, and residential areas throughout the city." In Presidential campaigns, their task was the distribution of political literature and the promotion of policies endorsed by the party that particular year.[14] As with city branches, nuclei typically voted, via secret ballot, between three to five leaders to command the overall direction and tasks of the regional local.[15] The nuclei branches brought the party's existence into a direct heading with grassroots organizing and carried with it a strong push for increased involvement in labor organizing. An important distinguishing feature between street nuclei and their more party oriented city districts was how the lower branches of the party mirrored a civil rights organization much more so than a political one. At a time when the Trade Union Unity League was the party's sole organ for organizing workers into a national union, the nuclei served as shop based recruitment centers that aimed at specific strikes, worker grievances, and education in industrial unionism.

In many ways the organizational structure of the party, split into upper and lower branches with different functional forms, likely handicapped efforts at electoral politics more than it aided it. The starkest feature of the party's electoral politics was that candidates nominated for office were typically picked by higher bodies of the party, not the local they came from. And they usually ran successive campaigns, despite changes in popular opinion or development at the grassroots. Foster, for example, having experience mainly with just steel workers and packing shed workers, ran in 1924, 1928, and 1932 to represent the so-called 'vanguard of the proletariat.' Earl Browder, who sat as the party's general secretary for nearly a decade with much less organizing experience than Foster, ran in both 1936 and 1940. John Schmies, the party's candidate for Mayor of Detroit, unlike Foster, did not enjoy a large presence in the campaigning process, and little is left behind as to when or by what branch his nomination was voted in via secret ballot. These campaigns, however, were predicated on the context in which they were initiated as opposed to a specific policy or idea, which tended to not change much throughout the Third Period and the Popular Front. Although the means to achieving the goal shifted from campaign to campaign, the goal of erecting socialism on the ashes of American capitalism always remained the same.

---

14. Vaughn Davis Bornet, "The Communist Party in the Election of 1928," *Western Political Quarterly*, Vol. 11, No. 3, September 1958, 519

15. Storch, 20

Even into the 1970s, the party's structure produced the same result, with Gus Hall running four times from 1972-1984. In all of these cases, it is only high ranking party members who had established a reputation among existing members of the party from their political activism and labor organizing who managed to make it to high office nomination. The low ranking nominations, evidenced by John Schmies, paled in comparison to the high ranking ones, typically only netting temporary national attention. As well, in most cases, the nomination process occurred at party levels above the locality of the person nominated.[16] As Storch shows, there was little chance of a member joining in 1928 and eventually finding their way onto a Presidential ticket. Foster and Browder had been lucky to join the party during its formative years, in addition to taking on leadership roles not because of their ideological genius but because of their track records of organizing experience with American workers. Unless one brought to the American Communist movement an extensive resume of working class experience, the upward mobility of the CPUSA's democratic centralism was virtually non-existent.

Structure was not the only handicap. Resistance to party policy or candidate nominations were enough to have someone expelled. James P. Cannon, founding member of the CPUSA and upper branch division leader, found himself expelled in 1928 for his disapproval of Foster as a candidate and Stalin as an international leader. Cannon went on to found the American Trotskyist movement subsequent to his expulsion, but for the most part his career as a Communist among labor groups fell apart; an unfortunate, but common, outcome among the radical left. Cannon's expulsion at the upper level also masked the multitude of expulsions done at lower levels. While this contributed to a solidified and unified party by 1929 and arguably set the pace for the party's subsequent years of organizing success, at the same time the movement was held together by perceptions of loyalty to both the party and the internationalism of the Communist movement.[17]

In a very real way, the party's division was visibly broken into political and civil activist camps. This development occurred between 1919 and 1921 as the CPUSA grew up through an intense period of factionalism and government repression – dividing regional sentiments

---

16. Earl Browder's self-nomination in 1936 and 1940 is the exception to this. Likely, Browder was taking Stalin's approach to leadership of the Party, which meant asserting authority as a "revolution from above" perspective

17. James Cannon, *A History of American Trotskyism* (Pathfinder Press, 2002), ix

about practical paths for socialism but encouraging Communists to maintain "unity" above all else. During the 1930s, by the time policy debates found themselves at lower district levels, upper districts had usually already concluded a decision and local divisions were obliged to either accept it or reject it; no formal process existed for proposing counter candidates or counter debates.[18] Although city branches also voted via secret ballot and created their own Secretariat just like the upper divisions, the alienation of the lower branches to the upper branches of the party should not be overlooked. In her oral history interviews, lower branch party organizer Dorothy Ray Healey expressed how the organization of the party prevented anyone from "hear[ing] the minority position…all you ever heard was the one position which [the CC] had agreed upon."[19] Russel Brodine, a party organizer and member of his local Communist Musicians Club, also experienced a fundamental disconnect to the upper party's directives:

We decided to organize a Communist Club among students. We found a couple of others willing to join us. The Party's leadership considered it important that we not be active publicly as communists. However, we were publicly active anti-fascists, and were, of course, suspected by some of being Communists. One of our members was warned not to associate with the crowd. [But], she ignored this instruction.[20]

At these grassroots levels, following the party's line was more a matter of showing allegiance to "the movement" than showing support for a particular policy or candidate. This occasionally reached limits, as with Brodine, where the policies and identity of the party were disconnected from the activism that it promoted (whereas grassroots members saw promoting anti-fascism and identifying as Communist as one and the same, leaders drew a line between such actions). Most party members at lower levels seemed to share the same sentiments with regard to passively accepting party policy but practicing it subjectively at the local level. In numerous cases, disobeying the party's instruction was useful and necessary when it seemed practical, and

18. Storch, 22

19. Dorothy Ray Healey, *Dorothy Healey Remembers Oral History Interviews*, Tape 3, Side 2, October 24, 1972 (UCLA Oral History Special Collections, 2012)

20. Russel Brodine, *Fiddle and Fight* (New York: International Publishers, 2001), 32

the lack of repression against ideas that turned out fruitful gave a certain level of leeway between actions at these lower branches. Such a perspective may have been tolerated to a degree at lower divisions, but such activity would have been grounds for expulsion, as was the case with Cannon, at the upper party branches.

Still, for others, the alienation between upper and lower branches was a reality but not powerful enough to break one's commitment to the ideals of the movement. Beatrice Lumpkin, long time party member and autobiographer, expressed her "joy in the struggle" despite any loose ties the party had between its branches. For Lumpkin, these kinds of issues did not become "problems" until people "began looking back onto the Party" and trying to examine where the party made mistakes. The story of the party's unity, she contends, "has been kept out of most history books," and it is this more unified narrative she is accustomed to "because [she] lived through it."[21] Lumpkin's view comes from that of an internal and passionately devoted party member, but it does help expand the ways party members viewed and experienced their complex organization. Though she downplays its role in defining party history, Lumpkin nevertheless accepts that certain internal limitations did exist, such as a tendency of leaders to make decisions without fully understanding the local context of a strike or demonstration. Peggy Dennis as well held her own reservations about internal party issues, particularly debates about ideology and national policy. For Dennis, the "factionalism" and "unprincipled struggle for power" by party leaders such as Foster and Lovestone, presented a larger practical challenge than any organizational division between upper and lower districts, which she believed was predominantly a theoretical matter.[22]

Part of the lesson we can take from this, which benefits from the post-1980s scholarship on the CPUSA, such as Storch, Edward Pinzuk, as well as the autobiographies of party members, is how a complex hierarchy fostered divisions which then characterized the party's ability to function and relate to its members at the local, grassroots level. While the upper branches of the party concerned themselves with the Comintern and the ideology of international Communism, the lower branches were inevitably more concerned with regional and local struggles. For those who were involved in

---

21. Beatrice Lumpkin, *Joy in the Struggle* (New York: International Publishers, 2013), 69

22. Peggy Dennis, *The Autobiography of an American Communist* (Berkley: Creative Arts Book Co., 1977), 163-164

the party because of what it stood for, such as Peggy Dennis, Emma Tenayuca,[23] and Dorothy Healey, these divisions undermined the overall goals. For them, the division was eventually enough to cause their leaving of the party by the 1970s (Tenayuca left in the 1940s). For others like Lumpkin as well as regional party organizers such as Armando Ramirez and Marc Brodine, the CPUSA's overall purpose as an agitator to the currents of American politics was enough to overcome its complexity and shortcomings.[24] For the 1932 election, this division helped to cultivate support for revolution at lower party branches as a civil activist movement – a movement that fought against racism and unemployment but was often isolated from the more ideological aspects of achieving communism, which was advocated by the two nominated candidates: William Z. Foster and James W. Ford.

The Candidates: Foster and Ford

William Z. Foster grew up destined to be an organizer and a leader. Born to a family prone to moving frequently, he left school at the age of 10 to become the apprentice to a die sinker for professional shop grade bits. At age 13 he took a job in a lead factory. Between 14 and 24 he worked a series of jobs that gave him experiences as a member of the American working class, from a plant fertilizer for agricultural farmers in Pennsylvania to a streetcar motorman in Manhattan. At age 20, Foster joined the burgeoning Socialist Party of America in 1901. At the time, the Socialists were the largest labor political force in the country, with the grandfather of the Pullman Rail strike, Eugene V. Debs, at its head. Foster remained with the Socialists until joining the International Workers of the World in 1909, and then left

---

23. A close associate of Dorothy Healey, Tenyuaca is most famous for her role in the organization of UCAPAWA locals for Texas pecan-shelling workers in the mid-1930s. For her work, see· Joshua Morrio, "The Choitest Shaw, The CPUSA and Agricultural Unionism, 1934-1949" (Master's Thesis, California State University, Pomona, 2010)

24. The prime example of building socialism for most CPUSA members was Russia, which was rife with internal divisions throughout its early years of existence; between 1917-1923, then again between 1926-1928. It is plausible that those who found themselves passionately devoted to the cause could justify internal CPUSA divisions by suggesting that it was a natural product for all growing Communist Parties.

professional organizations entirely for a career in union organizing in 1911.[25]

The height of Foster's early organizational career was the 1919 steelworkers strike. For organizational strategy, Foster used his experience organizing packinghouse workers to think on a big scale. The key to success, exclaimed Foster, was a national strike campaign led by a council that represented the bulk of the nation's steel unions. Though the American Federation of Labor was skeptical about the strategy and did not give Foster all the funds he requested, he did get approval to organize and began the campaign in Gary, Indiana, and Chicago. With Foster's guidance, the national council signed up over 100,000 steel workers by mid-year. When demands presented to U.S. Steel were rejected, over 250,000 steel workers went on strike in September. The authorities responded by repressing the strike and the effort ultimately failed. The strategy, however, and response to it by workers could not be ignored. Afterwards, Foster organized relief councils to collect aid for steel workers' families – an act that made him a working class hero in many circles and attracted the attention of Earl Browder, who at the time was learning more about a splinter faction of the Socialist Party that became the forerunner to the CPUSA between 1920 and 1921.

Browder invited Foster to join him in 1921 on a trip to the Soviet Union, where the Communist International was hosting its first major assembly of Communist Parties in Moscow. Upon returning to the U.S., Foster joined the CPUSA and was quickly appointed as executive officer of the party's Trade Union Educational League. The TUEL in the early to mid-1920s functioned as an educational branch of the party; providing leaflets, books, and the *Daily Worker* to shops and street organizations. Foster was instrumental in establishing the general strike strategy of the TUEL, and its various local organizations.[26] Foster however transformed it by 1928 into the Trade Union Unity League, with the explicit goal of creating a council to represent the various unions of the nation collectively. Because of his activism and notoriety among both party members and working class groups, Foster was placed as the Presidential candidate for

---

25. A good history of Foster's early work can be found in the CPUSA's official published history, *Highlights of a Fighting History: 60 Years of the CPUSA* (New York: International Publishers, 1979)

26. William Z. Foster, "Strike Strategy: A Pamphlet by the Trade Union Educational League, 1926,"http://www.marxists.org/archive/foster/1926/strikestrategy/index.htm

the party in 1924 and 1928 prior to the 1932 election.[27] As previously stated, Foster's nomination was done via secret ballot by the highest branches of the party plenum, and most certainly via the approval of the Comintern.[28]

Unlike Foster, James W. Ford was nominated to the position of Vice President as part of a broader campaign strategy, as pointed out by historian Mark Solomon:

> In 1932 the Communist Party ran dozens of black candidates in every region for everything from alderman and mayor to lieutenant governor and governor to members of Congress. All the Party candidates stressed the issues of unemployment insurance and racial equality. Getting elected was not a serious goal. In Ford's words, [campaigns] were a means to "mobilize workers in the struggle for their immediate needs." When asked about chances for the Party's black candidates, Ford replied, "The Communist Party is not stupid; we know that better than 4 million Negroes in this country cannot vote…and besides this, there is a great anti-Negro sentiment which the Party goes up against when it puts forth Negroes as their candidates."[29]

Ford thus benefitted from an overarching strategy by the CPUSA to endorse Black candidates in order to attempt to place the issue of racial equality directly on the ballot box. This does not mean we can simply overlook the historic importance of his nomination. Ford's nomination was the first for an African American to the executive ticket of a major party in the 20th century and the second in the history of the United States behind Frederick Douglass.

Similar to Foster, Ford had a rich history with the party and helped contribute to its shift in policy between electoral seasons (1928 and 1932). While Foster was campaigning in 1928, Ford attended the Comintern's 4th and 6th Assemblies of the sixth congress in Moscow as a delegate, where he was placed as the head of the Comintern's Negro Commission. There, along with delegates from other Communist Parties, Ford helped create the Third Party policy of "self-determination and sovereignty of the black belt," a

---

27. William Z. Foster, "An Open Letter to John Fitzpatrick," *The Labor Herald*, Vol. 2, No. 11: January 1924, 6-8

28. The methods of Party nomination is discussed in the later section: *Democratic Centralism, In Ideology and in Practice*

29. Mark Solomon, *The Cry Was Unity: Communists and African-Americans, 1917-1936* (University of Mississippi Press, 1998), 218

canon policy whereby African Americans living in the Southern United States constituted a disenfranchised nation. Ford considered the question of African American sovereignty to be merely "an academic matter," and he did not believe that an end to Jim Crow would solve the racial problem. Ford saw utility in the fiery rhetoric of self-determination and the recruitment of young African Americans such as Hosea Hudson by the early 1930s seemed to confirm this assessment. This reality became amplified by the Scottsboro case in 1931.[30] For the party, the Scottsboro case became a platform for demanding civil rights for African Americans and was replicated in many of their presidential campaign posters.[31]

By the early months of 1932, the CPUSA's electoral machine was already beginning to show signs of life with Foster calling for rallies and hunger marches in Detroit and New York City. Now that we know the candidates more personally in addition to the party structure which permitted the rise of such candidates, we can move into discussing how the party's electoral campaign was built *on their own rules*.

The CPUSA and International Communism, 1928-1932

In 1928, the CPUSA ran a relatively moderate political campaign out of its then headquarters in Chicago. The only extensive scholarly work done on this campaign was written by Vaughn Davis Bornet, in 1958. According to Bornet, the lack of scholarship on the CPUSA's electoral program obscured "the real nature of the Communist Party in American political life...in spite of the millions of words written about it."[32] Foster stated his personal belief about the purpose of the party in elections in his acceptance speech during a resolution meeting in May 1928:

> We are not going into the national election campaign solely for the purpose of getting votes...we also have other bigger objectives...Our aim must be to arouse the class consciousness of the masses in a political sense and to mobilize them for the struggle

---

30. Ibid, 68

31. See, Foster / Ford presidential flier: The image used depicts the Party's utility of the Third Party Policy in conjunction with its presidential campaign.

32. Vaughn Davis Bornet, "The Communist Party in the Election of 1928." *Western Political Quarterly*, Vol. 11, No. 3, September 1958, 514

on all fronts. Vote-getting is only one aspect of this general mobilization of the workers.[33]

Foster's statement depicts the general attitude the party had toward the 1928 election, an election that was conducted during the late roaring 1920s, and almost immediately prior to the Great Depression. An election for the Republicans or Democrats, according to Foster, would mean that "for the next four years there will head the government an unscrupulous figure adept at utilizing misery and devastation for imperialist purposes."[34] In short, an election for anyone but the Communist Party would result in a continuation of capitalism *as it was*. This portrayal led Bornet to conclude that "the political campaign of 1928 had neither a beginning nor an ending point for the Communist Party," since the beginning and end policy for the campaign remained unchanged: general resistance to capitalism.[35]

For 1928, the goal in the election was to "register the extent of [the] Party's support in the working class by mobilizing the maximum number to vote for [party] candidates."[36] It was essentially a litmus test on the palatability of the Communist Party as an organization among the American working class. Part of this was shaped by the existence of the Socialist Party, which for over 25 years had participated in national elections. The Socialist Party taught that "the workers could vote their way to emancipation" by electing progressive and labor oriented candidates. This platform was seen in the Socialists' electoral programs for 1908, 1912, and again in 1916 when Eugene V. Debs ran for president while in jail for protesting against World War I. The Socialists thus created the perception among the American left that radical politics was *American* politics radicalized. The rise of the Bolsheviks to power in 1917, and the success of the Red Army in the Russian civil war transformed these perceptions. The Communist Party emerged as a result of secession by the Left Wing of the Socialist Party. As such, the CPUSA remained constantly critical of its former ally after 1921. Whereas the Socialists campaigned for an American government with a socialist face, the CPUSA campaigned for "a new state, a new government of workers and farmers; in short, a Soviet Government of the United States."[37]

---

33. William Z. Foster, *Acceptance Speeches of the Workers (Communist) Party* (National Election Campaign Committee, 1928), 11, in Bornet, 514
34. Bornet, 515
35. Ibid, 514
36. Bornet, 518
37. Ibid, 518

In October 1931, the 13th Plenum of the CPUSA Central Committee outlined a narrative of world history that depicted a "decaying
capitalism and rising socialism."[38] The CC did not make any new
resolutions until after the 1932 election, so their 1931 statement
represents their most direct resolution for party activity during the
election period. It should be noted, as Theodore Draper pointed out,
that the 13th Plenum's resolution was merely a reflection of a resolution passed by the Central Committee of the Communist Party of
the Soviet Union just months prior.[39] Together, both the CPSU and
CPUSA resolutions concluded that Communist Parties around the
world had one principle failure: a general failure to consolidate organization among an influenced and partially radicalized proletariat.
For the Soviet Union, the influence was their existence as the world's
first revolutionary government. For the CPUSA however, the focus
was on the 11 million unemployed and the inclination American
workers have toward change under such conditions.[40] Both resolutions also highlight how the CPUSA's policy direction was part of a
broader movement than just the American geopolitical landscape. Its
domestic platforms were invariably linked to its international goals.

The resolution of 1931 dictated specific objectives for Party activity
that aimed to build membership as well as create an identity and
affinity among unemployed Americans. Coinciding with this was
the subtle push for international recognition and support of the
Soviet Union – which up to that point had still been deemed a rogue
state by Western governments. As the resolution concluded, "political and revolutionary crises are identical," and as such party leaders
needed to "construct [a] 'political crisis' as a necessary intermediary
stage between the revolutionary upsurge and revolutionary crisis."[41]
This objective created the basis for re-engaging in American electoral
politics in a way profoundly different from 1928. Whereas the 1928
election platform emphasized the perceived weaknesses and failures
of Democratic and Republican politicians, the 1932 election program
focused on the weakness and failures of the CPUSA and the inability of major parties to combat the worst effects of the Depression.[42]
By publicly identifying the "weak situation of [the] Party in relation

---

38. "Resolution of the 13th Plenum of the Central Committee", *The Communist*, October 1931, 818
39. Theodore Draper, *Roots of American Communism* (Viking Press, 1958),
109
40. "Resolution of the 13th Plenum of the Central Committee," 819
41. "Resolution of the 13th Plenum of the Central Committee," 820
42. Bornet, 515

to the masses," the CC attempted to reiterate the interconnectivity between political action and revolutionary activism and used this view to contrast the CPUSA against the "other political parties" and their methods. Whereas in 1928 it was a matter of fighting *against* capitalist politics, 1932 was a matter of fighting *for* revolutionary politics. This meant the promotion of strikes, rallies, and marches.[43]

An early article to come out during the developmental period of the CPUSA's 1932 campaign strategy was Max Bedacht's "Leninism and our Party." Submitted to *The Communist* in January, 1930, Bedacht asserted that the CPUSA lived in a part of the world where "capitalism developed under extremely favorable conditions," emphasizing the vast natural resources, the "comparatively higher wage and living standard," and the isolationism of the U.S. from European endeavors.[44] A by-product of this uniqueness, according to Bedacht, was an unradical proletarian movement. Instead of seeing the rise of powerful Communist Parties like Europe, the political and economic privileges of the American proletariat "led the American worker to the conclusion that his proletarian existence [was] not the result of social conditions but of individual qualities."[45] Bedacht's article highlighted, unlike the CC's later resolution, the reality that right from the beginning the party's efforts to reach American workers was first a battle of the mind and heart; the battle of politics came in as a close second. Bedacht of course does not portray hopelessness in the party's efforts, rather he emphasized this "illusion" of social divisions based on quality and how it masked the various actual struggles.

Bedacht's article also highlights the different manner by which Marxism as a political ideology came into the United States versus Europe. For Americans, Marxism came as a "philosophical school" that seemed to parallel the various other political and economic philosophies pervasive throughout American socioeconomic theory. Europe, on the other hand, experienced it as a "science of a proletarian revolutionary movement." Bedacht points to differences to make this assertion, such as how the CPUSA and the Socialist Party were socially identified as "just another political party" in contrast to the government-building and highly popular socialist political groups of

---

43. "Resolution of the 13th Plenum of the Central Committee," *The Communist*, October 1931, 820

44. Max Bedacht, "Leninism and Our Party," *The Communist*, January 1930, 11 (accessed at the Walter P. Reuther Library, Wayne State University, Detroit)

45. Ibid

Europe. This suggests that according to Bedacht and his party contemporaries in 1930, Leninism in the United States implied a different
form of political organization where the practices and policies were not
simply the promotion of revolution, but in practice were the *antitheses
to* or the *negation of* the dominant political groups in America.[46] Going
into the 1930s and the deepening crisis of the Great Depression, Communist writers like Bedacht gave direction, meaning, and purpose to
a political effort that in the past was grounds for treason.

By February of 1932, the path chosen by the CPUSA took on
international implications with the publication of the *Communist
International*'s "Thesis on Parliamentarianism." The large issue for
European Communist Parties was the question over involvement in
parliamentary procedure, as it had been so ever since the end of the
Soviet Union's civil war in the early 1920s. The decision stipulated
how "parliament can in no way serve as the arena of struggle for
reform," but that because of parliament's general support among the
masses, "the bourgeoisie is forced to have some of its policies in one
way or another passed through parliament." This results in a constant "haggle for power" among ruling groups.[47] To a small extent
this mirrored the sentiments of leaders when the CPUSA ran for
president in 1924 and 1928; but both times Foster echoed the notion
that the purpose of campaigning was one step in a larger process of
building a revolutionary movement. He wrote:

> It is important, should the possibility present itself in any of the
> state or local elections, to elect Communist candidates, so that
> they can utilize the legislative bodies as a forum wherefrom to
> acquaint the workers with the inequities of capitalism and the
> necessity of the Communist program.[48]

The release of the Comintern's decision on parliamentary activity in
1932 forced the CPUSA to realign its role in politics into an approach
that exploited the efforts of other parties to "haggle for power" and
instead press the immediate needs and demands of the American
people.

---

46. Bedacht, 13
47. "Thesis on Parliamentarianism, Resolution of the Communist International," *The Communist*, February 1932, (accessed at the Walter P. Reuther
Library, Wayne State University, Detroit)
48. William Z. Foster, "Acceptance Speeches" in Bornet, "The Communist Party in the Election of 1928," *Western Political Quarterly*, Vol. 11, No. 3,
September 1958, 517

Also, in February the *Communist International* released its "Results of 1931 and Prospects for 1932 in the USSR," a report on the ongoing development of the 5 Year Plan started in 1928. Less important for the CPUSA was the internal developments of the USSR than the depiction of capitalism in 1931 and 1932 as "a system [that] discredited itself."[49] In April of the same year, the periodical released another issue with a headline title of "War and the Immediate Task of Communist Parties." Both the "Results" and the "Immediate Task" articles highlight a myth that was pervasive across all Communist groups; that the Soviet Union was under the threat of war by Western nations.[50] This myth continued up through the 1930s and reached its height with the CPUSA's endorsement of the Soviet invasion of Poland in 1939 as a means for preventing war with Germany. As the years got closer to the electoral year of 1932, this perception of imperialist war heavily influenced the basis of the CPUSA's foreign policy stances, particularly a non-interventionist approach that focused on recognizing the political legitimacy of the USSR.

The international influences and connections to the CPUSA are important to consider as we move into the examination of the campaign itself from March to July of 1932. Communist Parties are by their nature never national parties, though they do spring up as from time to time as national groups. The ideology of Communist Party practice was fundamentally internationalist while its success and experiences at the local level were rooted in the conditions and needs of American citizens. Thus while the internationalist nature of the CPUSA's organization caused their participation in a national election to reflect the goals the party hoped to achieve internationally, the direction of the campaign as well as subsequent recruitment successes of the party was driven far more by the grassroots response of workers and community members to the visible acts of repression and violence by the state.

The Campaign for Revolution

By 1932, the ongoing conditions of the Great Depression provided the CPUSA the perfect stage in which to advance its Third Period national policies of campaigning against mainstream and "centrist"

---

49. "Results of 1931 and Prospects for 1932 in the Union of Soviet Socialists Republics," *The Communist International*, Vol. IX, No. 2: Feb 1st, 1932, 35

50. "War and the Immediate Task of Communist Parties," *The Communist International*, Vol. IV, No. 6: April 1st, 1932, 179 (accessed at the Walter P. Reuther Library, Wayne State University, Detroit)

progressives such as the Socialist Party. The conditions of the Depression also permitted the CPUSA to run a campaign with more flexibility in its militancy than it could in previous years. Whereas in 1928 Foster could only warn about the possible dangers of allowing capitalist politicians to win, by 1932 many of those perceived dangers were no longer theoretical – at least in the minds of some 10 million unemployed American citizens sprawled out across the nation. Unemployment, homelessness, and the Dustbowl created conditions where the average American family was stretched to its limits, and initial responses by the Hoover Administration did little the quell the worst effects of these conditions. Unemployment alone peaked at 23.6 percent in 1932, nearly 80,000 registered as unemployed in Detroit alone.[51] Urban centers in the Midwest, such as Detroit and Chicago, were hit particularly hard because of cutbacks in production, layoffs, and speedups by the major industrial giants that lay hold over the region.

To respond to the unemployment crisis early in the electoral season, the CPUSA jump started the process of building Unemployed Councils by distributing a pamphlet titled *Fighting Methods and Organizational Forms of the Unemployed Councils: A Manual for Hunger Fighters*. The Councils built their demands on unemployment insurance, equal wages regardless of sex and race, citizenship to all, free gas, lighting, and water, as well as a national rent freeze with eviction protection. More specific demands included a six hour day without pay reduction for all mine, railroad, and youth workers and a full commitment to combatting racial, sexual, and ethnic discrimination. These stipulations represented how CPUSA leaders idealized the vision for mobilizing the American people on a national scale. Much of the immediate demands, however, reflected highly specific and regional circumstances of the Great Depression. For example, the pamphlet emphasized that "broad general demands must be kept in the forefront of each struggle for even the smallest demand." Among the immediate demands were the establishment of regional cash relief offices for families and the pooling of resources to investigate specific cases of eviction and denial of government relief, resistance to layoffs for shop floor and mining workers, resistance to expulsion for non-payment of dues to unions and veterans organizations, free use of public dormitories for homeless youth and the YM-YWCA, as well as public demonstrations against war and for issues that benefit working and unemployed citizens. Politically, the Unemployed

---

51. "How the Depression Changed Detroit," *The Detroit News*, March 3, 1999

Councils called for all political candidates to endorse the Workers' Insurance Bill, which sought to provide unemployment protection for those still employed and form the basis of a broader Unemployment Bill.

Foster and Ford's campaign focused on these key areas of party presence where the Unemployed Councils were building promise: New York City, Detroit, and Chicago. Of all the events on Foster's short-lived campaign trail, none other best represented the methodology of the party than the Ford Hunger March in Detroit. Throughout the first few years of the 1930s, the party's national efforts, dictated by the party's acceptance of Comintern directives on Parliamentarianism and the need for the party to become one *of* the workers, culminated into a series of hunger marches organized by its local district committees and their Unemployed Councils. While New York had some of the party's largest marches, reaching as high as 110,000 demonstrators demanding food and relief,[52] Detroit's demonstration in March resulted in a political and social conflict that focused national attention on the Unemployed Councils and was part of a series of events leading up to the full unionization of the American auto industry later in the decade.

On March 6, a Sunday, Foster met with the Detroit local branch's CC to outline the plans for the next day. Foster's campaign platform was later published as a text by International Publishers, titled *Toward Soviet America*. "The capitalists will never voluntarily give up control of society and abdicate their system of exploiting the masses,"[53] Foster told party members, auto workers and others. One of the greatest threats to the American worker, Foster insisted, was the "social fascism" of the American Socialist Party and its devious program that would not alleviate the burden of unemployment but rather would deepen the economic crisis with its failed ideological program. Indeed, the perception of the Socialist Party's "gradualness" toward revolution created the opposite of the CPUSA's approach to electoral politics. While the Socialists held public conventions on Woodward Avenue, Foster declared that the CPUSA would instigate a "revolutionary force" by uniting with the Unemployed Council of Detroit and the Auto, Aircraft, and Vehicle Workers of America Union – what would become the UAW. Of course, the Council was staffed and organized primarily by the CPUSA's Michigan District and shared friendly relations with the

---

52. Lumpkin, 57
53. William Z. Foster, *Toward Soviet America* (New York: International Publishers, 1932)

local labor movement. The three together called for a demonstration set for March 7, with their eyes set on Ford Motor Company's
River Rouge Complex; a massive industrial marvel built in 1917
and by 1932 still the single largest industrial factory in the world.[54]
Foster, mayoral candidate John Schmies, and the YCL arrived early
Sunday morning, March 6, to distribute leaflets and give a speech
in preparation for the next day. Upon arrival, Foster set up a stage,
delivered his opening speech and began taking demands from the
marchers which included rehiring of the unemployed, an end to the
factory's racial hiring practices, coal for use in the factory during
winter, and the abolition of company spies and security forces. Foster
"intended to send a small committee to present to Henry Ford" at the
march and told the marchers to prepare themselves.[55] March 7 was
cold, but around 4,500 workers gathered outside of the City of Dearborn, roughly one mile away from the Rouge Complex. They carried
signs that screamed "give us work" and "tax the rich." Not long into
the demonstration, the Dearborn police arrived with revolvers and
clubs in hand. Once the crowd of workers began throwing rocks at
the Dearborn police, however (one of which hit police chief Harry
Bennett in the head), the police retaliated. The *Detroit Times* reflected
on the way police brutality fostered radicalism among the demonstrations, reporting that "with hundreds of hungry men in line, little
was required to kindle violence. The opposition by the Dearborn
police evidently changed an orderly demonstration into a riot."[56]

Media sources at the time conveyed the march as a "riot" that
broke out because of "communist instigators." Maurice Sugar, attorney for the families involved and a local CP lawyer, recalled his
personal experience of the ordeal in his book *The Ford Hunger March*.
While the *Detroit Times* claimed that "Communists inflamed by Foster hurl[ed] stones and clubs in prearranged outbreaks," and that
"six shots were fired by a communist hiding behind a parked car,"[57]
Sugar remembered it differently. He wrote:

> Knowing that not a single policeman was shot at – much less
> shot – while four workers had been shot and killed, and scores
> more shot and wounded, I began to wonder where the *Times'*

54. Maurice Sugar, *The Ford Hunger March* (Berkley: Meiklejohn Civil Liberties Institute, 1980), 30

55. Sugar, 32

56. "Ford Riot," *Detroit Times*, March 9, 1932

57. "Riot at Ford Plant", *Detroit Times*, March 7, 1932

reporter had gotten his information. Not a single shot was fired by any "agitator" or "Communist."[58]

Paul D'Amato offers some insight from an internal-party view on how the police repression was both expected, and typical for such a demonstration:

> The idea that strikes and social movements are caused by "outside agitators" or a minority of "trouble makers"…conveys the idea that ordinary people are too happy with their lot to want to fight against their own oppression, but are gullible and therefore easily duped by "Machiavellian" leftists.[59]

In short, while the media focused on Foster's presence at the march as a precursor to what became a riot, they simultaneously ignored the workers, their demands, and Foster's role as an electoral candidate trying to appeal to his base.

The *Daily Worker*, the party's national newspaper, had its own portrayal of the event. "Ford cops use tear gas against 800 unemployed" ran the headline for March 8. Ignoring the rock throwing and supposed gunfire, the *Worker* claimed that fighting broke out simply while trying "to release a worker arrested for distributing leaflets." A day after the event, the *Worker* issued a call for local community members to "organize for defense against the boss' terror drive" at the Detroit CP headquarters. There, a banner laid out across the speaker's floor that read "smash Ford-Murphy police" and "Ford gave bullets for bread." The riot that broke out, Communists explained at their rally, was the result of a general policy by police and employers to "shoot and jail those who organize and resist."[60]

Following the event, both local and national CPUSA leaders were sought for charges of inciting the riot. Foster managed to make it out of Michigan and avoid arrest, but Schmies was not so lucky. Arrested and jailed, then released, then arrested again, then given a trial, then a retrial, Schmies' ability to continue campaigning for the rest of the year was shattered. On March 13, a week after the riot, nearly 100,000 people marched at funeral processions that led out of the CPUSA's headquarters in downtown Detroit. For Foster and the party, despite the loss of life which included four CPUSA

---

58. Sugar, 41

59. Paul D'Amato, *The Meaning of Marxism* (Haymarket Books, 2006), 20

60. "Ford Cops Use Tear Gas on 800 Unemployed," *The Daily Worker*, March 8, 1932

members, the event proved to be a victory. To them and much of the national party leadership, the funeral procession demonstrated the effectiveness of the March 7 demonstration in raising the attention of the Detroit masses beyond the 800 unemployed workers involved in the riot. In just a few days, it seemed, the masses of Detroit had been roused into political consciousness against police brutality and the efforts of Henry Ford to squash out local union drives. The *Detroit Times* also reflected on the funeral parades as a victory for the Communists, placing a national spotlight on the party in a manner not seen before:

> The people chanted "we wanted bread; Ford gave us bullets." Thousands of right arms, with fists clenched, were raised in the Communist salute as the caskets were carried from the Ferry Avenue hall.[61]

On June 20, Detroit CPUSA activist John Frey caught attention for setting up a rally in Ann Arbor in coordination with the Michigan Federation of Labor and the Economics Department at the University of Michigan. Frey discussed "the causes of unemployment," but his conference remained mostly academic and removed from the masses of unemployed workers standing in line waiting for food and jobs.[62] Lacking a big figure like Foster as well as agitated, hungry workers, Frey's conference resulted in low attendance. The rally did, however, show the ongoing relevance of the party's stances toward particular community groups throughout Detroit, particularly the Unemployed Councils and other organizations which sought legal protections for both the employed and unemployed. By July, the Detroit Grand Jury released its official report on the March 7 incident and charged that "no indictments" would be issued for either side. They did, however, conclude that the entire riot was "initiated, organized and conducted by the so-called unemployment councils... [which] professed belief in the doctrines of the Communist Party." [63] In no small twist of irony, the CPUSA received credit in the form of criticism by the media and city courts, and praise from sympathetic workers and academics in and around Detroit.

---

61. "10,000 Parade Peaceably for Ford Rioters," *Detroit Times*, March 13, 1932

62. "John Frey Plans Labor Forum in Ann Arbor," *Detroit Free Press*, June 20, 1932, 4

63. Sugar, 129

On May 28, Foster made his first public appearance since the Ford Hunger March with James Ford at his official acceptance speech to the nomination of presidential candidacy, in the birthplace of the CPUSA: Chicago. As was typical with party procedure, the nomination was merely the official seal on an already established decision. Emphasizing six platforms, Foster declared that the party represented an answer to the nation's conditions of "starvation and misery," particularly for the "Negro masses."[64] The platforms were reprinted in *The Communist* later that month:

1) Unemployment and Social Insurance at the expense of the state and employers; 2) Against Hoover's wage-cutting policy; 3) Emergency relief, without restrictions by the government and banks, for poor farmers and exemption of poor farmers from taxes; 4) Equal rights for the negroes and self-determination for the Black Belt; 5) Against capitalist terror and all forms of suppression of political rights of workers; 6) Against imperialist war, for the defense of the Chinese people and the Soviet Union."[65]

Following the announcement of the party's formal demands, Foster tied in his 1928 proclamation about maintaining hope in the Democrats or Republicans to the conditions of the Depression and claimed that "The Communist Party [was] the only Party that foretold the present crisis."[66]

After depicting the Depression in strong, emotional language, such as "a scene of wholesale mass starvation," Foster pointed to the Soviet Union as the "only country free from crisis." Reflecting the party's overall enthusiastic support for the Soviets, the Soviet society was depicted as a paradise where "the workers had abolished all exploitation" and the "industries flourish[ed] to an unparalleled degree under the world-famous Five-Year Plan."[67] Aspects of James Ford's policy on the self-determination of African Americans also permeated both speeches, with claims that the "Negro people [were]

---

64. William Z. Foster, "Acceptance Speech, 1932" in *May Acceptance Speeches of Communist Candidates for President and Vice President*, December 1932 (accessed from Deering Library Special Collections, Political Pamphlets P105719), 2

65. "Draft of Party Platform," *The Communist*, May 1932, 422-424

66. William Z. Foster, "Acceptance Speech, 1932," 13

67. Ibid, 16

the hardest hit by present crises."[68] To this end, Ford focused on "increases in lynching and Jim-Crowism" throughout the country and the need "for the unity of white and negro toilers." To contrast himself against other progressive choices, Ford condemned the Socialist Party as the "Bosses' Party of Jim-Crowism."[69]

Foster finished his speech by re-emphasizing the internationalist nature of the party and the overall Communist movement:

> The Communist Party of the United States is a section of the world Party of Lenin, the Communist International. (*Applause.*) It is a brother Party of the great Russian Communist Party which blazed the way for the world revolution. It is also a brother Party to the heroic Japanese Communist Party, now so courageously combatting the imperialist war, to the Chinese Communist Party now controlling great stretches of China, [and] to the German Communist Party fast preparing the millions of German workers for the Revolution. Today the American Communist Party is still relatively small, but in its hands rests the future of the producing millions in this country. (*Loud Applause – prolonged ovation – singing of the Internationale*).[70]

Foster continued his campaign after Chicago by visiting New York City for the annual summer hunger march, which had been a staple of the CPUSA's New York branch as early as 1930. Beatrice Lumpkin recalled that despite the party's low numbers leading into 1932, "the Communists were like the yeast used to make bread," and their push for demonstrations resulted in numbers totaling over 110,000.[71] Lumpkin's memories of the cause for peoples' desperation was the pervasive hunger and the "hidden homelessness" of American families suffering the worst elements of the Depression. Unlike the 1920s, when couples got married during the Depression "they often remained in their parents' apartment." The result was that "families doubled up, [sometimes] even unrelated families, each paying half the rent."[72] Foster responded to such conditions in a speech to the New York district; directing the local Young Communist League to assist the city's various Unemployed Councils with "putting

68. James Ford, "Acceptance Speech, 1932" in *May Acceptance Speeches of Communist Candidates for President and Vice President*, December 1932, 5

69. Ibid, 8-9

70. Foster, "Acceptance Speech, 1932," 32

71. Lumpkin, 57

72. Ibid, 58-59

furniture back, [and] restoring evicted families to their apartments." The Councils then proceeded to stage strikes and protests in front of landlord's residences and worked to control access to power and water lines to ensure street level control over local utilities. Lumpkin, at the time a YCL member, remembered the demonstrations "were always multiracial,"[73] as a result of the party's public campaign for racial equality. The remainder of the summer saw similar marches staged in Chicago and Boston, with Foster and Ford making regular appearances.

Throughout the campaign, rival Marxist groups such as the Communist League of America remained ideologically distant from the CPUSA's public work but maintained support for it by participating in rallies and recruitment drives. For example, on January 9, 1932, the CLA criticized Foster and Ford for advocating open trade with the Soviet Union as a means for combating domestic unemployment.[74] Later that month, the CLA sent their delegate representative Frank Buckley to attend the CPUSA's and ILD's United Front Conference to Fight Against Criminal Syndicalist Laws at the Peoples' Auditorium in Chicago.[75] The two organizations even exchanged accusations against one another in mid-1932 over the death of a worker, Michael Semen, after a New York CLA meeting on August 7, even though attacks by conservative protestors were frequent in that area.[76] After the election, the CLA indicated its displeasure over the "distressingly low vote" for both the CPUSA and SPA, which collectively failed to break the 1912 vote number for Eugene V. Debs; long considered a watershed moment in American socialist history.[77] Ultimately, though the CLA may have held its reservations about the CPUSA during the election such as the unlikely development of making it on the ballot of numerous key states and fielding less support than the SPA. Expelled party member, James P. Cannon concluded on November 5, 1932 that "the workers must be told to vote

---

73. Ibid, 60

74. "Capitalist Politicians Favor Credits; Stalinists Mark Time," *The Militant*, 5 No. 2 (January 9, 1932), 1

75. "Chicago Stalinists Disrupt Conference," *The Militant*, 5 No. 2 (January 30, 1932), 2

76. National Committee, CLA, "Slander the Opposition as Murderers of Two Workers at N.Y. Street Meeting," *The Militant*, 5 No. 35 (August 27, 1932), 1

77. Martin Abern, "The Elections and Labor's Struggle: What the Presidential Vote Means for the Workers," *The Militant*, 6 No. 5 (February 4, 1933), 2

communist," and he continued to use CPUSA popularity as a barom-
eter of public sentiment regarding socialism.[78]

Part of what made the CPUSA's campaign so attractive was the
placement of the party's "Negro Question" at the front and center
of the campaign. This set it so far outside of mainstream politics that
they naturally gained attention – both welcomed and unwelcomed.
The party's nomination of James Ford as Vice President remains a
prime example of how serious the CPUSA took its effort to politicize
the plight of African Americans and the injustices of Jim Crow. The
subsequent rise in membership among Black voters attests to the
strategy's overall success. Additionally, Communist lawyers continued to fight localized racial discrimination through the International
Labor Defense and brought together numerous Black workers who
were hesitant to join an organization that claimed to be a political
party. The 1932 campaign decisively thrust the CPUSA into the spotlight and took attention away from alternative socialist organizations
like the SPA, CLA, and IWW.[79] Subsequently, the fight against racism
diffused into communities as Communist lawyers such as Benjamin
Davis, Jr., worked to create legal precedents against Jim Crow and
racial discrimination. Throughout the Third Period and Popular
Front ending Jim Crow remained a canonical CPUSA political tenet.

The campaign reached a stalemate by the end of summer, with
much of the momentum behind the hunger marches influencing
the direction and reform of not just the Roosevelt Administration's
approach to the New Deal but also the labor movement in specific
areas like Detroit. Part of the complexity of American communist
history, particularly that involving the CPUSA, is how actions and
events usually carried multiple meanings to the various people
involved. Foster's campaign in Detroit was aimed at radicalizing
Detroit workers and directing their attention toward Communist
answers to the Depression. Foster's campaign was *more successful*
however in directing the attention of people toward ongoing injustices, such as racism, police brutality, and the hegemonic influence
of corporate power. The militancy forged at the Ford Hunger March
was repeated in Flint, in 1936, and again back at the Rouge Complex
in 1941 when Ford Motor Company became the last of the Big Three
auto manufactures to cave to union demands.

---

78. "Class Against Class in the Presidential Elections: Communist Vote
Will Test the Policy of the Stalinists"

79. Nell Irvin Painter, *The Narrative of Hosea Hudson: The Life and Times of a
Black Radical* (W.W. Norton & Co., 1993), 95–100.

Results and Meaning

By the end of 1932, Foster and Ford's campaign netted the highest election numbers in the party's history; a record still held to this day. The CPUSA netted 102,785 popular votes, 0.26 percent of the total and nearly all of which were based heavily in urban areas like Chicago and Detroit.[80] Defeated by the Socialist Party, which got over 880,000 votes, the CPUSA nevertheless outdid its previous performance of 48,551 in 1928.[81] The increase reflects how the party managed to become more integrated among certain groups of working class American voters, particularly urban working class voters and African American voters in Chicago and Detroit. Additional votes also went hand in hand with increased membership. Between January and Foster's acceptance speech in May, Chicago alone saw an increase of 2,009 – a margin of 79 percent.[82] Both of these developments translated into victories for the party, despite marginal numbers by comparison. Following the logic of the party's Third Period philosophy of engaging with American voters, increased votes combined with increased recruitment meant an overall increase in the perception of legitimacy by American workers. In tandem was the obvious fact that increased membership meant increased *ability* for activism. The resulting party work in the building of the California agricultural union movement and maintaining annual Hunger Marches up through 1936 serves as good evidence to the party's notion that growth was an indicator of success.[83]

For African American Communists like Hosea Hudson, the campaign's increasing popularity meant increased action to gain membership regardless of the setting. On November 7, 1932, Hudson and the Birmingham party district organized an Unemployed Council meeting on the courthouse lawn. Within a matter of hours, the speakers were arrested, and the meeting broken up by city police. Birmingham Communists turned to the Masonic Temple on

80. David Leip, "U.S. National Election Statistics, 1932" in *Dave Leip's Atlas of U.S. Presidential Elections*, http://uselectionatlas.org/RESULTS/national.php?year=1932&f=0&off=0&elect=0 (accessed 4/13/14, 12:21pm);
    also verified by "Electoral College Box Scores 1789-1996", available from U.S. National Archives' Website
81. David Leip, "U.S. National Election Statistics, 1928" in *Dave Leip's Atlas of U.S. Presidential Elections*
82. Storch, 162
83. For more on the CPUSA's work in unionism, see: Joshua Morris, "The Shortest Straw, The CPUSA and Agricultural Unionism, 1934-1949" (Master's Thesis, California State University, Pomona, 2010)

the corner of 17th and 4th, which offered the CPUSA space in their auditorium under contract for the remainder of the year. Numerous setbacks such as these, particularly with police and local officials, riddled Communist organizing efforts in the South. When Hudson approached his church's pastor, Reverend Patterson, about holding a lecture in support of the Scottsboro Nine, he faced outright rejection. Patterson worried that the white community of Birmingham would respond harshly with full retaliatory force and insisted that the church would not involve itself in further dividing the community. To get around the pastor, Hudson invited his speaker, David James, to have a quick announcement at a private event for the church right after Hudson's quartet finished a song. James was a member of the ILD and a CPUSA spokesman for the Scottsboro case. When he reached the podium to speak, he told the mostly young Black audience that they should organize, educate, and arm themselves with the methods of revolution as a means for preventing job loss. When a young church attendee, Reuben Patterson, criticized James' stance as divisive against whites, the church's deacons intervened and ended the speech. Despite the disruption, threats by racist groups, and failed attempts to get Reverend Patterson on their side, Hudson noted a steady increase in Birmingham membership in the subsequent months.[84]

The party, however, cannot credit its increased numbers solely to political campaigning. Rather, it was due to both circumstance and practice: the CPUSA capitalized on the conditions of the Great Depression by advocating a revolutionary approach to politics; a radical left turn off-road when the existing options appeared to lead nowhere. Running for president was a means to measuring the palatability of revolution among American workers, and it ultimately showed them that at least some American workers could be swayed to their cause. This sort of a test could only have been done by conducting their electoral campaign as it was done, for *revolution* as opposed to simply for *president*. Campaigning by their own rules in such a manner meant organizing marches and strikes, not speeches and dinners. It meant envisioning a new government, instead of merely a new leader. Foster's *Toward Soviet America* depicts his campaign goal in its very title. The structure of the party, the development of international Communist ideology up to 1932, and the conditions of the Depression worked in tandem to produce the party's strategy and methods, best evidenced by Detroit's Hunger March.

---

84. Painter, *The Narrative of Hosea Hudson...*, Ibid, 129–30.

Something historians of the CPUSA need to consider is how the political efforts of the party in electoral periods, including when they do not nominate a candidate, helps to define the party within American politics. When we look back on Stephenson's depiction of the three functions of a political party, the CPUSA certainly retains all of them. They create an image of themselves in the eyes of the electorate, they rally candidates behind specific goals and policies, and they allow their physical structure to influence the ways they perform their politics; all for better or for worse. Additionally, they fall out of Stephenson's depiction of a "Third Party" in that they were certainly more than just a temporary platform for a single issue. Of course, "revolution" can be considered a single issue, but the means and prospects for achieving said revolution changed from election to election, as we witnessed by just looking between 1928 and 1932. Finally, the CPUSA separates itself from the Democratic and Republican Parties in that it is not a loosely organized structure, but rather has a history of being a rigidly hierarchical organization with sympathies beyond that of the American state. The CPUSA's history carves a unique experience of the political party organization in American politics and provides a counterweight to perceived norms and traits of dominant and third party groups.

Chapter 4

"First to start the fight": Communism, the Daily Worker, and Baseball

By Al Neal

Introduction: The beginnings of baseball

The sound of polished walnut striking stitched cowhide – hurled at up to 100 miles per hour. The awed silence broken abruptly by the sound of a thousand gasping breaths held in momentary anticipation. The smell of sweat and salted peanuts walloping all six senses. The booing of some, and the cheering of others can only signify a singular activity: an afternoon spent at the great American ballpark.

Baseball, America's national pastime, has captured the imagination of children, fostered unlikely friendships – beyond economic class distinctions – and has, at times, provided much needed comfort during moments of crisis for over 150 years.

The earliest mention of the game came in the form of a diary entry by a Princeton University student in 1786. "A fine day, play baste [sic] ball in the campus but am beaten for I miss both catching and striking the ball."[1] A scribbled note, in a way, marked the beginning.

And whilst we may applaud the ability of professional baseball to bring people, from all backgrounds, together, we would be remiss if we did not note that for much of the game's early existence there were two histories: the Negro leagues and the white leagues.

The game grew in popularity during the mid-1800s, the New York Knickerbockers being one of the first organized baseball teams.[2] By 1857, 16 New York clubs formed the National Association of Base

---

1. "Base Ball" Played at Princeton, https://protoball.org/1786.1
2. "Gotham Club Rules (1837), https://protoball.org/Gotham_Club _Rules_(1837)

Ball Players,[3] the first organization to govern the sport and establish a championship competition.

As early as the 1840s, African American's had been playing ball by Madison Square, and by 1859 had formed three Brooklyn Clubs: the Unknown Base Ball of Weeksville, The Henson Club of Jamaica, Queens, NY, and the Monitor Base Ball Club of Brooklyn.[4]

Growing alongside this budding sports phenomenon were political hostilities. Civil War was on the horizon and would soon tear the nation asunder. Following the 1860 election of President Abraham Lincoln, seven slave owning states seceded and formed the Confederate States of America – eventually, they were joined by Arkansas, North Carolina, Tennessee, and Virginia.

While the war's initial blow to organized baseball was minimal during the first year, by 1862 teams struggled to organize games and field players. Young able bodied men were needed in the war effort. Of course, while the organizational operations of baseball were hindered, the game itself grew in popularity within Union and Confederate encampments.

It should come as no surprise that soldiers organized ball games when off duty, or to shake off their pre-battle jitters. In his 1863 diary, Henry Squire, 72nd New York Infantry, wrote: "I have been playing base ball [sic]. The weather is pleasant, but it looks like snow or rain." Union sharpshooter Jacob Wallace Smith, with the 7th Company, 1st Battalion, New York, wrote in his 1863 diary while stationed in Virginia: "Had inspection at 2 oclock [sic]. Went up to Rapphanoc [sic] Station with Leut [sic] Pickard, and play at (base) ball."[5]

In the decades following the end of the American Civil War – with the emancipation of African Americans and the eradication of slavery as a legal institution – baseball rooted itself firmly in postbellum America. The game gripped the attention of all.

However, the racist tendencies which emerged from Southern states determined to constrain Reconstruction – the newly gained, at

---

3. Marshall D. Wright, *The National Association of Base Ball Players, 1857-1870* (McFarland, 2000) and https://www.baseball-reference.com/bullpen/National_Association_of_Base_Ball_Players

4. Ryan Whirty, "Brooklyn's African-American baseball tradition didn't start with Jackie Robinson," *Brooklyn Daily Eagle*, April 15, 2014, https://brooklyneagle.com/articles/2014/04/15/brooklyns-african-american-baseball-tradition-didnt-start-with-jackie-robinson/

5. Henry Squire Diary, 1863 (Ms2011-103), Virginia Tech Special Collections and University Archives Online, http://digitalsc.lib.vt.edu/CivilWar/Ms2011-103

a bloody cost, constitutional rights, and freedoms of African Americans – infected organized baseball as well.

Only two years had passed since the end of the Civil War. And within that period, the previously unwritten rule of banning African American players from the game was cemented in the official records of the NABBP's 1867 convention. In its report, the Association's nomination committee wrote:

It is not presumed by your committee that any club who have applied are composed of persons of color, or any portion of them; and the recommendations of your committee in this report are based up this view, and they unanimously report against the admission of any club which may be composed of one or more colored people.

The reasoning behind the discrimination:

If colored clubs were admitted there would be in all probability some division of feeling, whereas, by excluding them no injury could result to anybody, and the possibility of any rupture being created on political grounds would be avoided.[6]

We are safe in assuming that "some division of feeling" can only mean frustrations and perhaps, even jealousy at the skill of African American ballplayers by their white counterparts. Ego, especially during competition, can become fragile. Perhaps, this is an early example of what is now called white fragility? Additionally, that the excluding of African Americans from the Association was not seen as injurious – that only white players could be injured by the addition of Black players – serves to further dehumanize and affirm long-standing racial prejudices towards people of color into the realm of sport.

Preempting such an official stance was the application for membership in the NABBP by the all-Negro

Pythian Base Ball Club from Philadelphia, PA, one of the earliest Negro league baseball clubs founded in 1865.

Octavius V. Catto, the Pythian's promoter took the initiative in an effort to loosen the restrictions which made it difficult for Negro teams to get permits to hold public games. Catto, a Civil War veteran,

---

6. Seymour, Harold, *Baseball: The Early Years* (Oxford University Press, 1960)

founded the Pennsylvania Equal Rights League in 1864, and viewed baseball as a unifying element; a way to bridge the gap between white and Black America. He also used civil disobedience tactics, including sit-ins,[7] whilst working to desegregate Philadelphia's trolly system. He said:

> We shall never rest at ease, but will agitate and work, by our means and by our influence, in court and out of court, asking aid of the press, calling upon Christians to vindicate their Christianity, and the members of the law to assert the principles of the profession by granting us justice and right, until these invidious and unjust usages shall have ceased.

It is only natural that he would take this spirit of moral authority with him into organized baseball, and it was a backlash against this passion for equality that would see Catto murdered at the age of 32,[8] a tragic precursor foreshadowing the violence inflicted upon the Civil Rights Movement of the 20th century.

From its inception, the idea of baseball was seen by many as a herald of racial peace and cooperation, only to be thwarted by contempt for equality, which created two tracks of baseball history.

By 1885, the Cuban Giants established the first Black professional baseball team. It was followed by the first Negro league, the National Colored Base Ball League, in 1887. Although the Cuban Giants were the first professional Black team,[9] the first professional Black player, Bud Fowler, never played for them, though he was recruited several times throughout his career. Fowler signed with the Binghamton, NY team, a mixed minor league team early in 1887, and took the field in spring of that year. Early coverage was driven entirely by racism.[10] A quote in the April 1887 edition of *Sporting Life* read: "Joe

7. Jerrold Casway, "September 3, 1869: Inter-racial baseball in Philadelphia, SABR Virtual, https://sabr.org/gamesproj/game/september-3-1869-inter-racial-baseball-philadelphia

8. Stephan Salisbury, "A monument at last for Octavius Catto, who changed Philadelphia, *The Philadelphia Inquirer*, September 25, 2017, https://www.inquirer.com/philly/entertainment/arts/a-monument-at-last-for-octavius-catto-the-activist-who-changed-philadelphia-20170925.html

9. Paul Browne, "July 21, 1886: 'A Glorious Victory': Cuban Giants beat the Red Stockings," SABR Virtual, https://sabr.org/gamesproj/game/july-21-1886-glorious-victory-cuban-giants-beat-red-stockings

10. Brian McKenna, "Bud Fowler," SABR Virtual, https://sabr.org/bioproj/person/200e2bbd

Ardner, in one game he played, shows himself to be…far superior to the 'coon' Fowler on second base."[11] By July, Fowler was cut from the team. In its coverage of Fowler's ouster, the *Boston Herald* wrote: "The 'colored gentleman' in question is the present phenomenal second baseman of the Montpeliers, and the above is a most decided compliment for him. Considering his superiority as a base-ballist [sic], it is reasonable to suppose that jealousy and not prejudice against color influenced the weak fellows of the Binghamton club."[12]

This scene would be repeated for the next serval decades, into the so-called "roaring twenties." On February 13, 1920, Andrew 'Rube' Foster, a hall of fame pitcher turned team owner, along with several other African American ball club owners joined together to form the Negro National League.[13] Foster's baseball career showed he was a powerhouse on and off the pitching mound. Coverage of Foster in the 1907 *Indianapolis Freeman* read:

> Rube Foster is the pitcher of the Leland Giants, and he has all the speed of a [Amos] Rusie, the tricks of a [Hoss] Radbourne [sic], and the heady coolness and deliberation of a Cy Young, What does that make of him? Why, the greatest baseball pitcher in the country; that is what the best ball players of white persuasion that have gone up against him say.[14]

With 24 professional teams, the NNL held four colored World Series from 1924 through 1927 against the Eastern Colored League:

1924 – Kansas City Monarchs beat Hilldale Club, 5 games to 4 games (1 tie)
1925 – Hilldale Club beat Kansas City Monarchs, 5 games to 1 game
1926 – Chicago American Giants beat Atlantic City Bacharach Giants, 5 games to 4 games (2 ties)
1927 – Chicago American Giant beat Chicago American Giants NNL 5-3 Bacharach Giants ECL

---

11. Ibid
12. Ibid
13. Matt Kelly, "The Negro National League Is Founded," National Baseball Hall of Fame and Museum, https://baseballhall.org/discover-more/stories/inside-pitch/negro-national-league-is-founded
14. Ibid

Throughout those years, Black teams drew huge crowds, but the white baseball agents, holding all authority over when and where games could be played, tightly controlled the attendance revenues, rarely sharing the profit with Black teams and owners. Of this problem Foster commented:

> The wild, reckless scramble under the guise of baseball is keeping us down, and we will always be the underdog until we can successfully employ the methods that have brought success to the great powers that be in baseball of the present era: organization.[15]

Taking out his frustrations by banging the keys of his typewriter, Foster wrote several articles for the *Chicago Defender*, founded in 1905 and considered one of the most important Negro newspapers. Within its pages, Foster highlighted the ills faced by Negro ball clubs, and called for more to be done, especially in creating space for Black ball games to be held, which would in turn benefit local communities. He wrote:

> It is very necessary that we have parks to play in. Without them there would be no incentive for one to attend…These ballparks must be furnished in way which will pass along pay…to be giving employment to a profession when it must…yet one cannot get the men to come together and try and cement some place for the betterment of the game. We cannot get along without organization.[16]

Unfortunately, as the 1920s headed into the 1930s, the NNL was hit with several controversies – lack of African American umpires, scheduling issues, and favoritism, among them. In the not-to-distant future the Great Depression loomed, which ultimately spelled disaster for the league. The NNL folded in 1931, primarily due to the economic pressure placed on it by dwindling ticket sales. By 1932, the Negro Southern League was the only African American league to survive that year's baseball season.

Amid the financial and personal ruinations caused by the 1929 stock market crash, the smoldering embers of class consciousness

---

15. Ibid

16. "Andrew Rube Foster Scrapbook, 1910-1981," National Baseball Hall of Fame and Museum, https://collection.baseballhall.org/PASTIME/andrew-rube-foster-scrapbook-1910-1981#page/4/mode/1up

began to forge organic Black and white unity across industrial cities nationwide. Well aware of the negative economic toll the Depression would have on the working class, the Communist Party, USA, who from its founding in 1919 aimed to create Black and white working class unity, formed national Unemployed Councils and led a burgeoning mass movement against the ravages of capitalist exploitation, the primary cause of the tumult.

As the CPUSA leader, William Z. Foster, put it: "The manifold activities of the Unemployed Councils, besides making a burning national issue of unemployment insurance, also resulted in securing many immediate relief concessions to the unemployed all over the country…They [the capitalist class] were dealing with an awakening working class."[17]

An "awakening working class" was ripe for change. The ideals of Karl Marx, Friedrich Engels, and V.I. Lenin were being embraced by tens of thousands. The CPUSA recognized this change in class consciousness, and in turn, focused its efforts on grassroots organizing. They hoped to create a Soviet America.

Yet, their egalitarian cause was apt to overlook, or undervalue, certain aspects which define the average interests of working people – baseball was a case in point. And it is from this perspective where we will trace the CPUSA's trajectory from dismissing the importance of sports, to becoming one of the leading forces behind the integration of America's national pasttime.

Communists, the *Daily Worker*, and early sports coverage

Gunshots broke the evening silence of October 24, 1917. With shots heard round the world the working people of Czarist Russia took to the streets in revolutionary fervor whilst soldiers, exhausted by the physical and emotional toll of the Great War, stormed the Winter Palace, taking control of the provisional government established by the February Revolution eight months earlier.

The October Revolution of 1917 single handedly changed the course of modern history and called into question the notion that Western, liberal capitalism as the only viable economic model. The revolution was certainly nuanced, and the movement of Soviets championed by Lenin in the April 7, 1917 issue of *Pravda* embedded an idea in the minds of working people globally. Lenin wrote:

---

17. William Z. Foster, *History of the Communist Party of the United States* (New York: International Publishers, 1952)

The masses must be made to see that the Soviets of Workers' Deputies are the only possible form of revolutionary government, and that therefore our task is, as long as this government yields to the influence of the bourgeoisie, to present a patient, systematic, and persistent explanation of the errors of their tactics, an explanation especially adapted to the practical needs of the masses.

As long as we are in the minority, we carry on the work of criticizing and exposing errors and at the same time we preach the necessity of transferring the entire state power to the Soviets of Workers' Deputies.[18]

John Reed, an American reporter on assignment for *The Masses* and founding member of the CPUSA, was present on the streets of Petrograd as the revolution unfolded; he was enthralled by Lenin and the Bolsheviks. To him, this crucial historical moment meant: "No matter what one thinks of Bolshevism, it is undeniable that the Russian revolution is one of the great events of human history, and the rise of the Bolsheviki a phenomenon of world-wide importance."[19]

Two years after this Bolshevik phenomenon captured the world's attention – and the sympathy of U.S. workers[20] – the revolutionary organizations that would eventually become the Communist Party, USA were formed on September 1, 1919, in the industrial mecca of Chicago, Illinois.

Looking back at the early years of the Communist Party, William Weinstone, a founding member wrote:

The war (World War I) and the proletarian revolution in Russia, followed by the revolutions on the continent, had a great impact on the workers in the U.S. Their fighting spirit rose, and though it did not reach the tumultuous heights of Europe, it was expressed in the vast strike movement…[21]

---

18. In Lenin's *Collected Works* (Progress Publishers, 1964), Volume 24, 19-26

19. John Reed, *Ten Days that Shook the World* (New York: International Publishers / Boni & Liveright, 1919)

20. Philip S. Foner (ed), *The Bolshevik Revolution: Its Impact on American Radicals, Liberals, and Labor* (International Publishers, 2017)

21. William Weinstone, "Formative period of CPUSA," *Political Affairs*, September-October 1969

This impact upon the U.S. working class also led to an examination of the previous attempts and mistakes made by the Socialist Party and the International Workers of the World, when confronting the systemic nature of racism. At the 1922 Convention of the Workers (Communist) Party of America (the aboveground, legal arm of the CP), the official program addressing the "Negro question" began with "an analysis of the history of Negro oppression in the South" and declared that Communists "would support Negroes in their struggle for liberation and will help them fight for economic, political, and social equality."[22] A similar analysis would soon provide the ideological thrust needed in the fight to desegregate baseball.

The early years of domestic communism centered on building organizational unity among the various parties and factions, creating a political platform for the working class, and instilling a sense of revolutionary purpose in American society. Party members, however, were also part of labor unions, fraternal societies, and workingmen's associations, and – like other Americans – found time to enjoy sports. Many party members were of Eastern European and European descent and brought with them a love for football (soccer), tennis, and field and track, too.

Within the editorial pages of the June 25, 1921 edition *The Toiler*, an Ohio socialist newspaper predating the *Daily Worker*, there is the tiniest mention of sports: "In Moscow, the factory workers have formed a sport club which counts 3,500 members."[23] That was it. Just a mention of what American workers' counterparts were up to in what was soon to be called the Union of Soviet Socialist Republics.

Unfortunately, within the pages of the party's early newspapers, a hard political line was taken. The minuscule reportage of sport activities, and the concomitant, though limited, advertisements for community games and schedules, were often framed as distractions from the class struggle. In short, workers were the victims of bourgeois sports, a new "opiate of the masses," thereby equating Karl Marx's well-known reference to organized religion with organized sport.

Across the Atlantic, though, Communists were taking a different approach. *Rote Fahne*, official publication of the German Communist Party, devoted one page each week to workers' athletics. "More than a million German Workers are now organized in athletic clubs that are strictly of a working class nature," it was noted. Conversely, the October 7, 1922 issue of the *Worker*, disparagingly noted, American

22. Ibid
23. *The Toiler*, June 25, 1921

workers "still prefer to hand over their money to baseball kings, prizefight promoters and other professional sport profiteers."[24] In short, workers who enjoyed sports were mocked and ridiculed for their seeming lack of class consciousness.

It was not until the formation of the Young Communist League in 1920, and the Young Workers League of America in 1922, that the topic of sports would be given more than just a cursory – and largely negative – mention within the pages of the party's newspapers.[25]

In 1924, the *Daily Worker* became the party's main print organ and sports became a topic of discussion as part of the "With the Young Workers Column," a section devoted to the news and activities of young Communists. Youth were intrigued by the Russian youth (Komsomol) movement, and its use of organized sports as a recruiting and organizing tool. In the January 22, 1924 issue of the *Daily Worker* it was noted:

There is tremendous interest in sport in Russia, particularly track sport, rowing, and football. But the sports organizations are broader than any party and the husky young communists are leaders in this world as well as in the political.

There is no valid reason why friendship for Marx should mean enmity for [Albert] Spalding [American baseball pitcher, manager, and founder of Spalding sporting goods]. Sport is a wide avenue of approach thru [sic] which thousands of youth can be influenced to take their first steps towards communism in America.[26]

Though slowly and only piecemeal, a new political framework was emerging. Sports were increasingly being viewed as a tactic to build revolutionary, working class consciousness, a counterbalance to the capitalist criminality embedded within the early years of professional and organized sports. This new framework encouraged domestic Communists, young and old, to organize their own sports movements.

Not surprisingly, this movement began in New York. The February 27, 1924 *Daily Worker* headline read: "Muscular Party of Athletes, is Conference Aim, N.Y. Communists Start Sport Movement." "The

---

24. "Give the Turks Constantinople," *The Worker*, October 7, 1922
25. "Agenda For the First National Convention of the Young Workers League of America," *The Young Worker*, Vol. 1. No. 3. (May 1922), 18
26. "The Youth in Russia," *The Daily Worker*, January 22, 1924

revolutionary youth of America must have sound bodies," declared
the Athletic League of the Finnish Federation of the Workers' Party.
It was added, "the capitalist class spends millions of dollars for the
bourgeois sport movement in order to bring the young men and
women where it can preach patriotism and hatred of the revolutionary movement to them." This was an attempt to build collective
identity with bourgeois sporting institutions among youth; Communists figured they should do likewise. "In America it is our duty
to start organization of a Workers Athletic League that is controlled
by our party and the Young Workers League. Some comrades might
think that when we organize an athletic club into our midst our
activities in the class struggle cease. But experience shows us different," it was argued. The 1918 Civil War in Finland was singled out
as an example. There sporting clubs were often the first to fight for
the rights of the working class, and Communist activity increased,[27]
as unity and collective identity through sport strengthened the
organization.

This debate was an early inclination that party members were not
as divided on the question of organized sports within capitalism as
some had previously thought. By 1926, Communists began to take
note of the "sports question" and formed the Labor Sports Union.
This formal acknowledgement by Communists regarding the importance of sports clubs helped awaken the spirit of working class unity
in the fight against Jim Crow racism. With this acknowledgement
came the first mentions of creating equality within professional
sports, and the breaking of the color line.

At the bottom of page three of the July 29, 1926 issue of the *Daily
Worker* a few paragraphs were devoted to challenging racism in
tennis. In the article, titled "Labor Sports Union Moves to Break
Bar of Color in Games," it was noted, "To erase the color line from
tennis courts the Labor Sports Union is calling a conference of all
tennis players in Chicago interested in breaking the tradition of
racial separation in the world of tennis. The union has taken this
step to challenge the precedent set by the American Lawn Tennis
Association in excluding Negro Players." It was added that this initiative would be "followed by similar steps in other sports."[28] By

27. "Muscular Party of Athletes is Conference Aim," *The Daily Worker*,
February 27, 1924
28. "Labor Sports Union Moves to Break Bar of Color in Games," *The
Daily Worker*, July 29, 1926

this time, Communists had also started their own Workers' Soccer Association.[29]

Despite these positive steps, coverage of big league baseball was a few years away. And *Daily Worker* staff reporters continued to negatively typify sports coverage. To them, workers needed a class conscious analysis of sports as an institution, not a love of the game. YCL coverage of the 1928 World Series between the St. Louis Cardinals and New York Yankees, boiled down to:

> Though the means of this professional capitalist 'sport,' the capitalists were able to hoodwink the greater part of the American workers to eat, sleep, and talk nothing…but baseball for a week…Baseball is still a method used to distract workers from their miserable conditions.[30]

Unfortunately, the "miserable conditions" were about the get worse. Black Tuesday loomed. As the Great Depression strangled America's economy and workers, sports coverage in the pages of the *Daily Worker* turned towards addressing the overwhelming impact of mass unemployment, union strikes, and President Woodrow Wilson's weak response to the crisis. Of course, the battle for racial equality was not forgotten. In summer 1929, the headline "Labor Athletes Fight Race Discrimination; Want Negroes Meet" was seen on page two of the July 16 edition of the *Daily Worker*. Unlike the major sports leagues, the Communist-sponsored LSU actively sought to include African Americans. As the article notes, "Far from restricting Negro athletes in its athletic meets or its general program, the Labor Sports Union, a workers' sport organization, is making special efforts to secure entries from Negro sport clubs for its Third National Track and Field Meet…" It was added, "The Labor Sports Union is opposed to race discrimination and will fight it on the sports and social field."[31]

As the new decade unfolded, towing economic and social misery in its wake, writers for the *Daily Worker* were becoming less dogmatic in their analysis of sports, especially in the breaking down of Jim Crow barriers in baseball. Taking a trip to Ebbet's Field in Brooklyn

---

29. Gabe Logan, "C'mon, You Reds: The U.S. Communist Party's Workers' Soccer Association, 1927-35," *Journal of Sport History*, Vol. 44, No. 3 (Fall 2017)

30. "World Series: New York takes on St. Louis," *The Daily Worker*, October 10, 1928

31. "Labor Athletes Fight Race Discrimination: Want Negroes at Meet," *The Daily Worker*, July 16, 1929

to watch and report on a game between the Brooklyn Dodgers and New York Giants, *Daily Worker* reporter Ben Field wrote in 1933, "Are these 'bad elements?' Many are workers who have so identified themselves with their team that they cannot sleep or eat when the team losses. The leanness of American life under capitalism drives them to this fever." Many Communists were still struggling to understand why.

Unlike his predecessors, Field took his analysis of baseball one step further and alluded to an issue which would soon become the paper's sports page social justice crusade. "You spot a few Negro fans. Negro workers made good athletes. But where are the Negroes on the field?," he asked. "The Big Leagues will not admit Negro players. There is something else to chalk up against capitalist controlled sports," he concluded.[32] This passing remark was, indeed, a significant step for the paper.

Unbeknownst to Field, however, there were other global factors that would soon push Communists towards a deeper appreciation of sports. On January 30, 1933, Adolf Hitler became Chancellor of Germany. Thus, began the barbaric and murderous campaign to create the Third Reich under Nazi rule. To ensure that fascism would firmly root itself in German culture, Hitler, through his youth organization, seized organized sports as a means to disseminate fascist propaganda.[33] To him, it was Aryan superiority over all other races in physical might and fight.

The Emergence of the Popular Front in *Daily Worker*'s Sports Coverage

A storm was brewing across Europe. The violent and barbaric ideology of fascism was slowly gripping power and upending the momentary and uneasy peace enforced by the Treaty of Versailles. The thought of a second global war was unthinkable – to both world leaders and workers – and many were determined to preserve peace through negotiated compromise and appeasement. By 1935, the Nazis had suppressed all opposition parties in Germany; the arrest

---

32. Ben Field, "The Brooklyn Dodgers win a game," *The Daily Worker*, August 29, 1933

33. Anspach, Almog and Taylor (edited and updated by Balser and Santalbano), "Football and Politics in Europe, 1930s-1950s," Soccer Politics, https://sites.duke.edu/wcwp/research-projects/football-and-politics-in-europe-1930s-1950s/

and execution of opposition leaders followed, mainly German Communists following the Reichstag fire on February 27, 1933.

On the morning of July 25, 1935, over 500 Communists from around the globe gathered in the Teverskoy District of Moscow and entered the historic House of Unions to attend the 7th congress of the Communist International. Wilhelm Peick, a member of the Communist Party of Germany living in exile in Moscow, delivered the congress's opening remarks. He noted:

> The defeat of the German proletariat and the establishment of the fascist dictatorship in Germany was the greatest event that marked these first years of crisis in the capitalist countries…the more fascism arms, the more frantically the bourgeoisie arms for new wars, the more rapidly grows the will of the labouring mases to fight against fascism and for socialism.[34]

The overarching theme of the congress was the united fight against fascism in the form of a Popular Front offensive. Georgi Dimitriov, a Bulgarian communist, was one of the main theorists of this strategy.[35] In short, to Communists the Popular Front was a broad coalition of different political forces – leftist to centrist – united to defeat the spread of fascism globally.

Particular attention was given to youth. As noted above, at the heart of Nazi ideology was the belief in Aryan superiority. By the time Hitler took power, Germany's football federation, the Deutscher Fusball-Bund, had already declared its support for fascism; all Jewish players, team owners, and sponsors were banned. Additionally, the Federation implemented rules requiring all opposing teams to perform the Nazi salute as a show of fidelity to the Nazi cause. According to one analysis, "The consensus was that German soccer helped stabilize the Hitler regime…"[36]

By exploiting the reach of sport, Nazi propaganda was able to increase its influence far and wide, a reality belatedly acknowledged by some within the world Communist movement in general and the CPUSA in particular.

At the Comintern Congress Georgi Dimitriov highlighted this weakness and noted that Communists needed to act swiftly to

---

34. "VII Congress of the Communist International," (Moscow: Foreign Languages Publishing House, 1939)

35. Georgi Dimitriov, *Selected Works* (Sofia Press, 1972)

36. Anspach, Almog and Taylor, Ibid

prevent further corruption of youth. He told the assembled delegates and guests:

> We have underestimated the enormous importance of the youth in the fight against fascism. We have not always considered the special economic, political, and cultural interests of the youth.
>
> All this has been utilized very cleverly by fascism, which in some countries, particularly in Germany, has inveigled large sections of the youth onto the anti-proletarian road.[37]

How would Communists answer such a pressing and frightful question regarding youth? As became clear, sports was part of the answer.

After a week of discussion focused on preventing the spread of fascism, on August 20, 1935 the congress laid out its resolution on "The United Front Against Fascism and War." The resolution provided Communists, especially young Communists, with a new direction. They were instructed:

> To take effective measures to overcome the sectarian secludedness [sic] of a number of Young Communist League organizations, to make it the duty of the Young Communist League members to join all mass organizations of the working youth (trade union, cultural, sports organizations) formed by bourgeoise-democratic, reformist and fascist parties, as well as by religious associations, and to wage a systematic struggle in these organizations to gain influence of the broad masses of the youth [thereby] mobilizing it for the struggle against militarization and forced labour camps and for the improvement of its material conditions, for the rights of the young generation of workingmen, while striving to establish for these purposes a broad united front of all non-fascist youth mass organizations.[38]

Following the resolution outlined by the congress, the CPUSA was tasked with reevaluating its approach to issues affecting the domestic working class and youth, and to distance itself from the reputation of being "foreign." To build a Popular Front against fascism, Communists needed to be seen as an American institution. Their leadership

---

37. Dimitriov, Ibid
38. Ibid

in the American Youth Congress[39] was part of this process, as was the *Daily Worker*'s sports coverage. For some sports fans, the CPUSA's "Americanization" began in earnest with its sports coverage in the *Daily Worker*.

Shortly after the congress' conclusion, *Daily Worker* columnist Mike Gold critiqued the party's sports coverage to-date. He did not pull any punches.

> Many [party members] seemed to think…it was a waste of time and valuable space to discuss baseball. Snobbism! In the circles in which these comrades move…[they] never meet anybody who is interested in baseball. It happens, however, that baseball is the American national game. I would say that nine out of every ten American workers follow it intensely, as well as other sports.

> You can condemn them for it, if you are built that way, and you can call baseball a form of bourgeois opium for the masses. But that doesn't get around the fact that…the vast ocean of Americans of whom we are as yet a minority, adore baseball. What are we going to do, insist that they give up this taste? Are we going to maintain our isolation and make Americans stop their baseball before we will condescend to explain Communism to them? When you run the news of a strike alongside the news of a baseball game, you are making American workers feel at home. It gives them the feeling that Communism is nothing strange and foreign…let's loosen up. Let's begin to prove that one can be a human being as well as a Communist.[40]

Shortly thereafter, the *Daily Worker* began printing a weekend edition, aimed at reaching a broader audience – shedding some, though not all, of its editorial "Snobbism." And on Sunday, January 12, 1936, readers woke up to a new beginning for the paper, an edition filled with editorial cartoons, comic strips, puzzles, and above all else, a Sports Page.

---

39. Robert Cohen, *When the Old Left Was Young: Student Radicals and America's First Mass Student Movement, 1929-1941* (Oxford University Press, 1993), and Gil Green's interview in *New Studies In The Politics And Culture Of U.S. Communism* (Monthly Review Press, 1993)

40. Mike Gold, "What's Wrong with Baseball," *The Daily Worker*, August 31, 1935

But it would take the love of baseball, and a nascent understanding of communism by a young New York University student by the name of Lester Rodney, to fully articulate the transformative power of a *Daily Worker* sports page.

"First to Start the Fight," the *Daily Worker* and Lester Rodney

The Brooklyn Bridge catches the eye. It holds your attention, and creates a sense of pride, and longing. More importantly, the bridge transports you to the home of the famed Brooklyn Dodgers. And it is here where we meet a young Lester Rodney, who eventually became the most unlikely, and most influential sports editor in *Daily Worker*'s history.

As a student at NYU during the Great Depression, it was hard for Rodney to avoid talk of political "isms," though, as he put it, "I was in my twenties before I even knew what a communist was."[41]Regardless, during this period, radical political thought occupied the minds of many working people and youth. Rodney became part of an intellectual milieu discussing the cause and searching for a solution to the economic crisis faced by millions of workers, a crisis that seemed systemic. In turn, with Communists then gaining prominence in cultural, artistic, and intellectual circles, students like Rodney began to think about creating a system that would prevent future crisis, perhaps socialism.

Like millions of other Americans, the Great Depression ruined his family's economic stability, thereby awakening his class consciousness. Additionally, Rodney was working odd jobs and going to school at the same time, which further opened his mind to radical ideas like socialism. Then everything changed. He met his first Communist organizer on the corner of 42nd street and Grand Central Station. As Rodney later wrote, "He wasn't at all like the popular image I had of Communists…he was saying something along the lines of 'don't you think it's ridiculous for a country as rich as ours to have so many people out of work? We Communists believe there are reasonable alternatives to the callous capitalism that benefits the few and keeps creating wars and economic crises. Do you know what socialism is, what it proposes?'"[42]

---

41. Irwin Silber, *Press Box Red, The story of Lester Rodney, the Communist who helped break the color line in American Sports* (Temple University Press. 2003)

42. Ibid

With the curiosity of a young reporter, Rodney approached and asked the man a few questions. He was impressed by the organizers' patience and his answers. After an hour of talk over cake and coffee, Rodney began to seriously consider the party's platform, learning about its political ideas. He also read the *Daily Worker* for the first time.

The sports writing did not leave a good impression. As Rodney explained, the sports page was written at that time in a very concrete, facts and figures only style. It was less conversational due to the *Daily Worker*'s once a week coverage of sports. The frequent return to political editorializing, demonizing sports as a capitalist institution, turned Rodney off.

Part of this editorial stiffness stemmed from a slow shift toward Popular Front activity, something some party hardliners had not yet warmed up to. As a diehard Dodgers baseball fan, Rodney took it upon himself to write a scathing review of the sports coverage to the *Daily Workers* editor, Clarence Hathaway. As Rodney would mention decades later, his mistake in all of it was putting his home address on the envelope for a reply.

Hathaway responded with an invitation to meet in person. After some brief discussions, Rodney was offered an opportunity to write for the sports page, and so began his career with the *Daily Worker*. Almost immediately, the paper's coverage of sports broadened, softened up its tone, while still providing a working class analysis.

In short time, Rodney would become a prominent voice calling out racism in the big leagues, and the Jim Crow color line hampering the game's potential – and talent. According to Rodney, here was no regular coverage of African American ballplayers to be found in the major newspapers nationwide:

Never a mention that these (Negro) players were barred from advancing to the major or even minor league. No incredulous editorials blasting this un-American discrimination, no investigative articles listing the qualified and overqualified black players, no queries addressed to the commissioner (of baseball), the league presidents, team owners, managers, and the white players. The conscience of American Journalism on baseball's apartheid ban, sorry to say, was not in the hands of America's major daily newspapers.[43]

---

43. Ibid

The moral ambiguity shown by some of history's great sports writers was soon to be challenged. On August 12, 1936, the *Daily Worker* made an announcement that would soon send shivers down the back of big league baseball:

OUTLAWED BY BASEBALL!
The Crime of the Big Leagues!
The newspapers have carefully hushed it up!
One of the most sordid stories in American Sports!
Though they win laurels for America in the Olympics – though they have proven themselves outstanding baseball stars – Negroes have been placed beyond the pale of the American and National Leagues.
Read the truth about this carefully laid conspiracy.
Beginning next Sunday, the *Sunday Worker* will rip the veil from the "Crimes of the Big Leagues" – mentioning names, giving facts, sparing none of the most sacred figures in baseball officialdom.[44]

So started the *Daily Worker*'s campaign. In the week following the announcement a taste of the type of investigative sports writing the expose would employ was done by *Daily Worker* sportswriter Ted Benson, as he cornered National League president Ford Frick and asked: "is there anything in baseball to prevent an owner who has 100 percent control of his club from employing Negro ball players?" Taken aback, Frick acknowledged that there were no such written rules. "Beyond the fundamental requirement that a major-league player must have unique ability and good character and habits," Frick said, "I do not recall one instance where baseball has allowed race, creed, or color to enter into its selection of players."[45] The first domino fell.

This type of coverage would continue, and the response from readers, as well as baseball fans, intensified. Some readers called for a full-scale organizing campaign to end Jim Crow baseball. Fans wanted words coupled with action.

This evolving escalation of tactics would come to fruition with hundreds of Communists, union members, and baseball fans, picketing outside ballparks. Soon hundreds of thousands – perhaps,

44. "Nazi Insults to Negro Stars Condemned by Herndon," *The Daily Worker*, August 12, 1936
45. Communist Party Oral Histories, Lester Rodney, New York University Tamiment Library, https://wp.nyu.edu/tamimentcpusa/lester-rodney/

millions – of petition signatures would be gathered calling on the Commissioner of Baseball, Judge Kenesaw Landis, to desegregate America's national pastime.[46]

Rodney broke down the process: First, to elevate awareness of the Jim Crow color line in baseball, which was being discussed in African American newspapers and magazines. Second, to give comprehensive coverage of the Negro Leagues, focusing on the playing abilities of star Negro athletes. And finally, to challenge the notion that white players and managers would not take the field with Black teammates.

Adding fuel to the fire was the success of the Black athlete Jesse Owens, who took home four gold medals at the 1936 Olympics in Berlin. Hitler bristled at Blacks besting Nazi athletes. The *Daily Worker*'s reportage gave readers a glimpse of the evils of fascism, too. It drove home the very real possibility of a similar scene at home – if racism and fascism were not confronted and defeated simultaneously. As Angelo Herndon put it:

NAZI INSULTS TO NEGRO STARS CONDEMED BY HERNDON – Urges [Alf] Landon's Defeat to Halt Reaction in American

Discrimination against Negroes in the Berlin Olympics was cited yesterday as an example of what fascism would mean in the United States by Angelo Herndon, chairman of the Youth Committee of the Communist Election Campaign Committee, in a statement calling for the defeat of the [William Randolph] Hearst-Landon forces in the 1936 elections.

Herndon, a former Georgia political prisoner, new firsthand the barbarity of Jim Crow. He added, "The Nazi Olympics have given American Negro youth a picture of what they may expect in the United States if the reactionary forces represented by the Liberty-League-Hearst-Landon combination triumph." To Communists racism was just a veiled form of fascism, which gave the campaign to desegregate the diamond an international character – a hallmark of the Communist-led defense of the Scottsboro Nine a few years earlier. The article continued, "The triumph of fascism in the United States would mean that the persecution and discrimination suffered

---

46. William Weinbaum, "Rodney pushed for MLB integration," *ESPN*, February 24, 2010

by the Negroes in certain Southern states would be intensified many times…"[47]

Along with breaking down the color line in Baseball, Rodney had another goal. He wanted to establish the *Daily Worker* as a sports paper of record, to broaden its non-CPUSA readership.

And so, it would go for the next two years. The campaign slowly picking up steam and influence, though most owners in Major League Baseball were vehemently opposed to desegregation. By 1938, more newspapers were confronting the league's segregation. Simultaneously, YCL members began swarming the streets around ball parks in New York and elsewhere with leaflets highlighting the *Daily Worker's* campaign; these leaflets included printed comments by ballplayers, managers, and owners.[48]

A year later, the *Pittsburgh Courier* jumped into the fray with Wendell Smith taking over their sports section. He paid close attention to the fight to desegregate baseball, whilst ignoring Rodney and the *Daily Worker*. In contrast to the *Courier's* cold shoulder, the *Daily Worker* often reprinted Smith's coverage, and gave readers updates on the movement to end Jim Crow Baseball through the *Courier's* "With the Campaign!" announcements:

> Another sensational interview with a manager on the Jim Crow question here tomorrow – Doc
> Prothro, manager of the Phillies, tells Wendell Smith of the *Pittsburgh Courier* a few things that will help the gathering momentum of the forces of sportsmanship that will blast the last remnants of discrimination out of baseball. Doc, incidentally, is from Memphis, Bill Terry's hometown – but there's a difference.[49]

The color line shattering quote pulled out of Prothro by Smith made it clear that only those at the top echelon of professional baseball wanted to keep the game status quo. Smith quoted the Phillies managers: "The Majority of managers would hire negro stars if given permission."[50]

In spring 1939, the campaign to break baseball's color line entered the halls of government with the introduction of a resolution by New York State Senator Charles Perry of Harlem (the resolution was

47. "Nazi insults…," Ibid
48. Communist Party Oral Histories…, Ibid
49. "With the Campaign!," *The Daily Worker*, July 29, 1939
50. "With the Campaign," *The Daily Worker,* July 31, 1939

actually drafted by the *Daily Worker*'s Albany, NY, correspondent Mike Singer). The resolution read in part:

> The legislature of the State of New York has from time to time enacted legislation designed to prevent racial discrimination in the various branches of the government as well as in private industry and labor unions and…there are in the United States many baseball players whose skill is equal to or surpasses that of many now playing in the many leagues of organized baseball but who are prevented from seeking or finding employment therein…this discrimination is against the expressed intention of the State of New York.[51]

And whilst this campaign was the vision of Rodney, CP, YCL, International Workers Order, National Negro Congress, and adjacent union members primarily in CIO locals – i.e., the Popular Front coalition then coalescing around the party – were the vital foundation to its eventual success. It was the YCL and party activists who organized the petition drives, and demonstrations, with the *Daily Worker*'s sports page encouraging it, promoting it, covering it, and pushing it forward.[52]

The immediate involvement of CPUSA members in the CIO, particularly through Communist-led unions like the National Maritime Union and the Fur and Leather Workers' Union, was instrumental in exposing the fight to desegregate baseball to a wider audience.[53] Of course, Black Communists, such as Paul Robeson and Benjamin Davis, Jr., were key to the campaign's success, too.[54]

In 1940, the work continued at a furious pace, and was strengthened by the New York Trade Union Athletic Association, which threw its hat into the ring when it initiated the Committee to End Jim Crow in Baseball and pledged to help collect one million signatures.[55] This widening of the campaign demonstrated the broad tactical flexibility of Communists, as well as the fluidity with which dues paying CPUSA members and non-party activists within the party's milieu

51. *The Daily Worker*, May 21, 1939
52. Communist Party Oral Histories…, Ibid
53. Communist Party Oral Histories…, Ibid
54. Benjamin Davis, Jr., *Communist Councilman From Harlem* (International Publishers, 1991), 132-134
55. Communist Party Oral Histories…, Ibid

gravitated together and intersected around issue-based campaigns. Though war was on the horizon, Rodney could feel a breakthrough coming.

Daily Worker readers often wrote letters to the editor regarding the color line in baseball, too. They created a juxtaposition between the backdrop of Black soldiers – now overseas fighting against fascism, though still in segregated units – whilst at home they were blocked from playing professional baseball. Though Commissioner Judge Landis was known as a shrewd, powerful man, and an avowed racist, he was still susceptible to public pressure, especially during a time of war. A May 6, 1942 *Daily Worker* letter had the following headline: "Time for Stalling is Over, Judge Landis." The author noted:

Negro soldiers and sailors are among those beloved heroes of the American people who have already died for the preservation of this country and everything this country stands for – yes, including the great game of baseball.

So, this letter isn't going to mince words.

You may file this away without comment as you already have done to the petitions of more than a million American baseball fans. You may ignore it as you have ignored the clear statements of the men who play our national pastime and the men who manage the teams. You may refuse to acknowledge and answer it as you have refused to acknowledge and answer scores of sports columns and editorials in newspapers through the country.

Yes, you may ignore this. But at least this is going to name the central fact for all to know.

You, the self-proclaimed "Czar" of baseball, are the man responsible for keeping Jim Crow in our national pastime. You are the one who, by your silence, is maintaining a relic of the slave market long repudiated in other American sports. You are the one refusing to say the word which would do more to justify baseball's existence in this year of war than any other single thing. You are the one who is blocking the step which would put baseball in line with the rest of the country, with the United States government itself.

There can no longer be any excuse for your silence, Judge Landis…[56]

The letter, coupled with the campaign initiated by Rodney and the *Daily Worker*, may have ruffled Landis' feathers. For, just a few months later he spoke with Brooklyn Dodgers manager Leo Durocher, who previously mentioned in a *Daily Worker* interview that he was ready to hire a Black ballplayer when given the green light. Following this chat, Landis decried that there was no formal rule barring Black players from the big league, which was a lie. Unfortunately, Rodney was not there to call Landis' bluff. He had been drafted into the Army. Along with an estimated 15,000 other Communists,[57] Rodney served with honor. Regardless, the tide had turned – whether Landis wanted to admit it or not. Being quietly discussed in locker rooms and owners' offices was the prospect of signing the first Black ball player. Brooklyn Dodgers owner Branch Rickey, who included the *Daily Worker* among his regular newspapers[58] saw the writing on the wall. The future of the game would be both Black and white, thanks to the help of reds.

Whilst Landis swept aside the petitions, pickets, letters, and protests, others involved in the running of the game watched, and waited. Judge Landis died of a heart attack in 1944. In 1945, the New York State legislature passed the Quinn Anti-Discrimination Act, making discrimination based on race, creed, or color unlawful. Baseball was mentioned directly, as a form of employment, meaning Black ball players could no longer be barred from the big leagues legally.

On a remote South Pacific island in 1945, Sgt. Lester Rodney with the 52nd Field Hospital, received an unexpected cable from the United States mainland: "Congratulations. Dodgers yesterday signed Jackie Robinson…You did it!"[59]

Simultaneously, well-known Black Communists Robeson and Davis, were part of a celebratory reception with Robinson with "about 25 trade union, Negro, progressive and Communist leaders." According to Davis, Robinson "commended Robeson for his

---

56. "Time for Stalling is Over, Judge Landis," *The Daily Worker*, May 6, 1942

57. Ellen W. Schrecker, *The Age of McCarthyism: A Brief History With Documents* (Bedford / St. Martin's, 2001), 176

58. Lee Lowenfish, *Branch Rickey: Baseball's Ferocious Gentleman* (Bison Books, 2009)

59. Silber, *Press Box Red…*, Ibid

contributions...and said a few kind words about me..." As a councilman, Davis had been instrumental in a city council resolution calling for desegregating baseball. Robeson and Davis had also been key to organizing a protest at the New York Vanderbilt Hotel, where "baseball magnates" had gathered for their annual meeting.[60]

Jack Roosevelt Robinson, who would wear the #42 for the Brooklyn Dodgers become the first African American ballplayer to play in Major League Baseball. The color line was broken November 1, 1945 as Branch signed Robinson to Montreal Royals, and on April 15, 1947 he would make his first at-bat for the Dodgers in Ebbet's Field.

Two months later back in New York, the new Commissioner of Baseball took the breaking of the color line a step further by explicitly stating, "I believe Negroes should have chances like everyone else. The arrangements are yet to be worked out, but I believe this is a free country and everybody should have a chance to play its favorite pastime."[61]

The *Daily Worker*'s front page reveled in the success. Nat Low wrote:

It may have more of an effect than even the singing of Marian Anderson or Paul Robeson. And if this great medieval fortress of Jim Crowism has been breached, let all good Americans know that the Communists were the first to start the fight...I hope this lesson will teach Americans that the Communists are useful citizens who form the core of a healthy democracy.[62]

Two years after receiving the cable announcing the end of Jim Crow in baseball, Sgt. Rodney, now *Daily Worker* Sports Editor, took his seat at Ebbet's Field to cover Jackie Robinsons first Major League game in his "On the Scoreboard" column. He wrote, "it's hard this opening day to write straight baseball and not stop to mention the wonderful fact of Jackie Robinson."

You tell yourself it shouldn't BE especially wonderful in America, no more wonderful for instance than Negro soldiers being with us on the way oversees through submarine infested waters in 1943. And that never seemed "wonderful," just sensible, necessary, and right.

---

60. Davis, *Communist Councilman...*, Ibid
61. Nat Low, "Words Fine, Mr. Chandler; ACTION Needed," *The Daily Worker*, May 5, 1945
62. Nat Low, "The Low Down," *The Daily Worker*, October 26, 1945

It's quite possible to be stupid about something like this. After chatting with Jackie on the field the first day he was in a Dodger uniform and becoming overwhelmed with the feeling of pressure and tension thrown fully upon his broad shoulders by the spotlight of publicity, the scrambling photographers oblivious of all else, even the kids pushing for autographs at his every move, it took no remarkable perception to know that beneath Jackie's smile was at least a little wish to be let alone and treated just like any other rookie, on his merit. And I decided then and there to start writing less about him in my Brooklyn stories.

But that didn't seem quite right. It didn't square with the inescapable feeling that the readers WANTED to know about him. A conflict.

Then up in the press box Saturday, his second day in uniform, when the special warm applause continued to roll down from the Ebbet's Field stands every time he went to bat though he had been doing nothing spectacular, another writer sitting near me, a right enough guy, said, "I wish they would stop that already and just treat him as another ball player." I suddenly knew he was wrong. The conflict evaporated.

For like it or not, Jackie Robinson was not "just another ball player" down there. Not yet! The continuing cheers from the 25,000 strong cross-section crowd was actually expressing America's great inherent sense of sportsmanship, equality, and Bill of Rights democracy, if you will, was insisting on expressing it fully when given the dramatic concentrated chance to do so.

The repetition and re-emphasis that worried my well-meaning friend carried with it the awareness that Negro Americans hadn't been allowed to play down there before, that everything WASN'T smooth and equal for either the Negro people or Jackie Robinson. Consciously or not, it carried an answer to [racist Senators Theodore] Bilbo and [John] Rankin and their northern counterparts; it carried decent human feeling down to Robinson on the field and a message to every magnate in the big leagues.

In the surprising – yes surprising to me too – depths of the cheers for Robinson was the real democracy of the vast majority of our people, a democracy sometimes blurred, stultified, confused, rationalized, and diverted, but still in there waiting for a chance to come through.

And here it was!

You can't ask people to measure, to control their democracy. Cheer on for a while, you people of Brooklyn! Cheer on, democracy!

And when the Dodgers go to Boston and Philadelphia and Cincinnati and Chicago and Pittsburgh and St. Louis, there'll be special cheers when Jackie Robinson steps out of the visiting dugout.

And maybe we were wrong about Jackie's own feelings. The cheers and commotion add to the pressure he's under, sure, but he knew what he was doing when he started fighting for a big league job, when he became the first, the forerunner, knowing he had to be better than just good enough.

The cheers may make it a little tougher on Robinson, the athlete, in a way. But the cheers are saying something, something that will make it easier for Negro players to come, for the day when there'll be no special pressure upon an American ballplayer whose skin happens to be dark.

I guess Jackie must know that.[63]

And there it was, the ten year campaign to break the color line in baseball was victorious. Just as importantly, it was also a victory for the Popular Front initiated and led by Communists, despite their early misgivings. A similar strategy was used across the pond, too. Baseball was desegregated, and fascism was defeated – in no small part due to the valiant sacrifices of Communists.

Conclusion

To say members of the CPUSA are un-American, un-patriotic, and not deserving of the rights afforded to all other political parties belies the

---

63. Lester Rodney, "About Jackie and the Cheers," *The Daily Worker*, April 15, 1947

historical record – at least when it comes to desegregating America's favorite pastime. Though Communists initially struggled with sport as a collective molder of identity, shared values, and teamwork, they quickly saw the error in this line of thought. Spurred on by Popular Front strategies – as well as the embrace of sport by Communists throughout the world – CPUSA membership grew dramatically, as did its acceptance beyond actual dues paying cadres. During this time, Communists became "the left," a position they would hold well into the early 1950s. Whilst much has and can be said about the overall success of the Popular Front, and its near demise post-World War II with the onset of Cold War and Red Scare, at least for baseball loving party members, it worked.

American Communists played a pivotal role fighting Jim Crow on and off of the field. Whilst we should not ignore the initial missteps and mistakes made by party leaders and the editorial board of the *Daily Worker,* by dismissing social and cultural activities – like baseball – we also should not minimize the contribution of Communists to desegregating the diamond.

Communist initiated direct action brought public pressure to bear on a seemingly insurmountable social justice campaign. Unfortunately, while the color line in baseball was broken in 1945, the foul stench of racism in sports persists. It wasn't that long ago that Colin Kaepernick, former San Francisco 49'ers quarterback, took a knee during the National Anthem to protest the continued assault on Black lives. He said:

> I am not going to stand up to show pride in a flag for a country that oppresses black people and people of color. To me, this is bigger than football and it would be selfish on my part to look the other way. There are bodies in the street and people getting paid leave and getting away with murder.[64]

As of this writing, Kaepernick remains unsigned. It's anybody's guess if he will ever take the football field again. Obviously, racial, and sexual discrimination in sports is not a thing of the past. Female players of the U.S. Women's National Soccer Team are fighting for equal pay and an end to gender discrimination. Minor league

---

64. ESPN.com News Service, "Colin Kaepernick protests anthem over treatment of minorities," *The Undefeated,* August 27, 2016, https://theundefeated.com/features/colin-kaepernick-protests-anthem-over-treatment-of-minorities/

baseball players are fighting for a living wage, alongside fast food workers in the Fight for $15. These are just a few examples.

For Lester Rodney, though, it was the love of the game and the rapport he established with the ballplayers that drove his reportage, not his CPUSA membership. The *Daily Worker* provided the vehicle for him to live out his convictions in action. As Rodney put it:

> I never thought of myself as a "Communist sportswriter…" I was a sportswriter. Sure, your political leanings will inform some of the things you write, even in sports writing…I was a sportswriter who happened to be writing for a communist newspaper…if I had constantly ground an ideological axe (which isn't my style anyway) the first thing to cross a ballplayer's mind when he saw me would have been "Communist," and I never would have been able to establish the rapport I had with so many different athletes over time.[65]

Above all, at the heart of 1930s and 1940s Popular Front Communism was coalition building, especially in the fight to defeat Jim Crow. Communists influenced and impacted American society in numerous ways. They fought for social safety nets, civil liberties, workers' rights, peace, and equality. And they initiated the modern campaign to desegregate the diamond, while training a whole generation of activists who would help lead the Civil Rights Movement of the 1960s.

Every year on April 15, as the nation celebrates Jackie Robinson Day and as every baseball player wears the #42 out onto the field, remember, it was a 25 year old kid from Brooklyn who took his love of baseball, merged it with his political and moral convictions, and began a little known crusade in the pages of the *Daily Worker* to break the color line.

---

65. Silber, *Press Box Red…*, Ibid

Chapter **5**

The Communist Party and the African American Question

By Timothy V Johnson

Introduction

The Communist Party, USA, throughout its 100 year history, has made inestimable contributions to the advancement and development of democracy in the United States. Its efforts to build the movements to organize labor, advance the cause of peace, and support various anti-intervention causes, are each worthy of recognition. However, one can argue that its most significant impact has been felt in the struggle against racism. Placing the struggle against racism (and for an all-sided equality) at the fore of their program set the Communist Party apart from nearly all other organizations that existed at the time of its birth in 1919. That many of its positions, radical when first posited, are now accepted as legitimate in the mainstream of American thought, is a testament to the party's vision, struggle, and sacrifice.

This essay endeavors to evaluate and provide an overview of the CP's theoretical positions on the African American struggle for equality; how that theoretical understanding translated into political programs; and the struggle within the party and in the mass movement to effect change in the wider society. As such, the focus of this essay is primarily on theory. That is, how the CP theorized African American oppression and, secondarily, how that theory was translated into practice.[1]

---

1. For those seeking detailed examinations of the party's activities in the African American community from 1919 through the 1930's, see: Mark Solomon, *The Cry was Unity: Communists and African Americans, 1917-1936* (University of Mississippi Press, 1998), Mark Naison, *Communists in Harlem*

Social Democratic Beginnings

The Communist Party, USA was the national expression of an international movement that began with the Russian Revolution of 1917. During World War I, social democratic organizations throughout the world began splitting over the issue of whether to support their own governments. After the war (and the Russian Revolution), most of the social democratic parties that had opposed the war sided with the Russian Bolsheviks and formed the Third International, or Comintern.

As in other countries, left-wing social democrats in the United States formed the nucleus of the Communist Party. With regard to the issues of racism and African American oppression, they essentially continued the social democratic approach, which was, in essence, encapsulated by an oft-quoted statement by Eugene V. Debs, "We have nothing special to offer the negro, and we cannot make separate appeals to all races."[2] Though his comment was often interpreted as dismissive, Debs was a stalwart opponent of racial discrimination. In the same article, he added, "…so thoroughly is the south permeated with the malign spirit of race hatred that even socialists are to be found, and by no means rarely, who either share directly in the race hostility against the negro, or avoid the issue…"[3] Debs' overall position was that racism would eventually be resolved in the context of the class struggle and the implementation of socialism. In other words, racism would be resolved *en passant*, and it would be a diversion from the class struggle to raise it prematurely.

Many social democratic local organizations, especially in the South, were segregated, and many nationally known social democratic leaders openly expressed racist sentiments. Although the issue of racism was rarely debated at social democratic conventions, when it was brought to the floor these racist attitudes were prevalent.[4] Yet there were socialist leaders who actively spoke out against racism, including W.E.B. DuBois, Hubert Harrison, and A. Philip Randolph. In a

---

during the Great Depression (University of Illinois Press, 1982) and Robin Kelley *Hammer and Hoe: Alabama Communists during the Great Depression* (University of North Carolina Press, 1990). Unfortunately, there is no overall study of the CPUSA and African Americans covering the Post-War era.

2. Eugene V. Debs, "The Negro and the Class Struggle," *The Internationalist Socialist Review*, (#5, 1903), 260

3. Ibid, 257

4. For a more detailed discussion of this issue, see: Timothy V Johnson "'Death for Negro Lynching!' The Communist Party, USA's Position on the African American Question." *American Communist History*, December 2008

series of articles for the *New York Call*, Harrison called upon socialists to "champion the cause of the African American and that the Socialists should undertake special efforts to reach African Americans as they had done with foreigners and women." He concluded, "Politically, the Negro is the touchstone of the modern democratic idea."[5]

Another left-wing organization, not a constituent contributor to the CP, was the Industrial Workers of the World. They had a more enlightened position on African Americans but disdained political activity in favor of labor organizing. Nevertheless, they were quite ahead of the Socialist Party on the issue of racism. A pamphlet issued by the IWW in 1919 noted "the IWW is not a white man's union, not a black man's union...but a working man's union."[6] It was also written into the IWW bylaws that a member could not be excluded based upon race or nationality.

Initial Communist Party Positions

In 1919, two communist parties were founded in the United States: the Communist Party of America and the Communist Labor Party. The CPA was majority foreign born (encompassing many of the foreign language federations of the SP), while the CLP was primarily composed of native born Americans. Reflecting their social democratic ideological lineage, both parties viewed the African American question as merely an extension of the class question. At the founding of the CLP, there was no mention of African Americans or racial oppression.[7]

Ironically, the CPA was the first to pay specific attention to African Americans. Although they offered no clear-cut program to appeal to African Americans and continued to see racial oppression as merely an expression of class oppression, they apparently thought it was deserving of special attention. In their founding program in 1919, they noted:

In close connection with the unskilled workers is the problem of the Negro worker. The Negro problem is a political and

_____

5. Hubert Harrison, "The Negro and Socialism: The Negro Problem Stated," *New York Call*, November 28, 1911, 6

6. Paul Heideman (ed), *Class Struggle and the Color Line* (Chicago: Haymarket Books, 2018), 154-155

7. "Minutes of the Founding Convention of the Communist Labor Party of America, Aug. 31 — Sept. 5, 1919, *The Ohio Socialist* [Cleveland], no. 85 (Sept. 15, 1919), 2-3

economic problem. The racial oppression of the Negro is simply the expression of his economic bondage and oppression, each intensifying the other. This complicates the Negro problem, but does not alter its proletarian character. The Communist Party will carry on agitation among the Negro workers to unite them with all class-conscious workers.[8]

By 1921, the CLP (now renamed the United Communist Party after merging with a faction of the CPA) had initiated an analysis of the African American question. In their 1921 program and constitution, under a section entitled "Negro Problem," they refer to African Americans as "the most exploited people in America" and "an out-law race." They add that, "The task of the United Communist Party is to break down the barrier of race prejudice that separates and keeps apart the white and the Negro workers, and to bind them into a union of revolutionary forces for the overthrow of their common enemy."[9]

A two part article appearing in the 1921 UCP publication *Communist* was the first attempt at an overall analysis of the African American question. Written by John Bruce and J.P. Collins (pseudonyms), it began with the following statement:

The solution of the Negro Problem lies, as in the case of most social suffering, in the abolition of Capitalism. But to be satisfied with this conclusion, and present the same as a cure-all to the masses will not do. The masses do not understand our theories, and the bourgeois grip upon them cannot be loosened merely by the statement of such truths.[10]

The article continues with an historical analysis of slavery and Jim Crow that attempts to explain the attraction of racialism/nationalism (as opposed to class identity) to African Americans, stating that, "As a result of the bestial treatment accorded them, the mass of Negroes has developed a profound hatred, not so much of the class that caused their sufferings, as of the race to which his oppressors

8. Communist Party of America. Manifesto and Program (Chicago: CPA, 1919)

9. United Communist Party of America. Program and Constitution. (Chicago: UCP, 1921), 18

10. Bruce, John and J.P. Collins, *Communist*, November 1921, 18

belong."[11] This is followed by a brief discussion of three major African American organizations (the UNIA, NAACP, and the African Blood Brotherhood), and the role of the church, before concluding that, "Bearing in mind all these factors it is easy to account for the racialism of the Negro and the almost complete lack of class consciousness…"[12]

The second part of the article addresses the process of how to bring African Americans into "our camp." The authors highlight the significance of the struggle to free Africa, the struggle for social equality, and the struggle for equality within the trade union movement. Most important, in their view, is the political struggle: "To achieve equality he must organize his power everywhere…in the South to gain political freedom…in the North to get better material conditions…Thus we see that the Negro struggle takes on the aspect of a racial as well as a class struggle. Fundamentally it is, of course, a struggle against Capitalism and Imperialism."[13]

In their conclusion, Bruce and Collins note:

> The conquest of political equality in the South and colonies, will bring the right to organize, right to vote, and freedom of speech which will not be conceded by the planter-barons, accustomed to holding the Negroes in peonage, without the bitterest struggle – a struggle which will rock to the very foundation that hideous regime.[14]

There are a number of significant takeaways from this article. First, it was the beginning of a serious theoretical analysis of the African American question – one grounded in history, politics, and Marxist theory. Second, it moved toward an understanding of the national importance of the struggle to democratize the South. Third, it demonstrated the beginnings of an understanding that the struggle against African American oppression was distinct, while at the same time, intertwined with the broader class struggle. Fourth, it was an early attempt (although not fully theorized) to link the issue of African Americans with the masses of colonized people. The path forward would have to come to terms with how Communists articulated those relationships in Marxist theory and in political practice.

---

11. Ibid, 18
12. Ibid, 20
13. Bruce, John and J.P. Collins, *Communist*, December 1921, 16
14. Ibid

At the second convention of the Workers (Communist) Party of America in 1924 (the party resulting from a merger of the UCP and the CPA), the political program was expanded to include the African American question. The WPA acknowledged that "The Negro workers of this country are exploited and oppressed more ruthlessly than any other group...The Worker's Party will support the Negroes in their struggle for liberation and will help them in their fight for economic, political, and educational equality."[15]

Their statement is particularly noteworthy for its use of the word "liberation," a term which had hitherto not been utilized. The WPA also passed a resolution which went beyond economic factors. The resolution declared:

> The twelve million Negroes in the United States constitute an oppressed race, and as such they require and demand special attention...The Workers Party pledges itself to strive, both in the process of its regular work and also by the creation of special organs of press and organization, for the following ends...[16]

There follows an enumerated, programmatic list of demands, including equal membership in trade unions, equal wages, voting rights, opposition to lynching, and an end to all racial discrimination.

Thus, shortly after their founding meetings, both organizations were searching for a way to approach the oppressive conditions of African Americans. It is logical that, in 1919, the CPA was the first to recognize the complexity and importance of this issue. Since the majority of the CPA membership was drawn from foreign language associations (mostly foreign born and many Eastern Europeans), they had also been the targets of ethnic prejudice in the United States. In addition, they were familiar with the experience of minority peoples based on their own history in Eastern Europe, which V.I. Lenin (referring to Russia) termed a "prison of nations."

It is significant to note that the CLP had no African-descended people at its founding convention, whereas Otto Huiswood, an Afro-Caribbean, was a founding member of the CPA. Most importantly, Huiswood was an associate of the African Blood Brotherhood, also founded in 1919 by Cyril Briggs. Huiswood forged connections with the ABB and served as a liaison between the ABB and the Communist Party. Huiswood also built relationships with

---

15. Workers Party of America, Theses. Program. Resolutions (Chicago: CPA, 1924), 83-84
16. Ibid, 125-126

Asian Communists (including M.N. Roy, an Indian Communist, and Sen Katayama, a Japanese Communist, both of whom would later become important contributors to the Communist approach to the African American question). The ABB and Asian Communists greatly influenced African American Communists as well as the CPA's thinking on the role that racial/national minorities play in the Communist movement.[17]

Enter the Comintern

In 1919, the Communist International was formed in Moscow in the wake of the Bolshevik Revolution. The call for the first congress affirmed, "The world situation now requires the closest contact between the different parts of the revolutionary proletariat and the complete unity of the countries in which the revolution has triumphed."[18] The congress enumerated a series of points to which a party had to adhere to be affiliated with the Comintern. The goal was to create an international organization of Communist parties that would function under the discipline of the Comintern.

Contrary to right-wing interpretations, the Comintern was not simply an extension of the Soviet Party. In reality, the Soviet Party held sway over the Comintern because it was the most prestigious party and the only one holding state power. But each constituent member had the freedom to voice their opinions on the issues at hand. And most parties, especially the relatively recently founded and inexperienced parties (like the CPUSA), sought out the Comintern for advice on organization, strategy, tactics, structure, and political program. Additionally, the structure and leadership of the Comintern committees were comprised of Communists from across the world.

At the Comintern's second congress (1920), Lenin introduced a draft thesis on the National and Colonial Question, outlining broad principles that the Soviet government was implementing in formerly oppressed areas of Czarist Russia. He proposed that Communists should support movements of national liberation and invited further discussion on a number of oppressed nationalities, including the "Negroes in America." John Reed, representing the CLP, responded to Lenin's assertion:

17. Minkah Makalani, *In the Cause of Freedom* (University of North Carolina Press, 2011)

18. Bertil Hessel (ed.), *Theses, Resolutions & Manifestos of the First Four Congresses on the Third International* (Humanities Press, 1980), 2

If we consider the negroes as an enslaved and oppressed people, then they pose us with two tasks: On the one hand a strong
racial movement and on the other a strong proletarian, workers'
movement whose class consciousness is quickly growing. The
Negroes do not pose the demand of national independence. A
movement that aims for a separate national existence, like for
instance the 'Back to Africa' movement that could be observed
a few years ago, is never successful among the Negroes. They
hold themselves above all to be Americans. They feel at home
in the United States. That simplifies the tasks of communists
considerably.[19]

Reed was countering Lenin's brief intervention, which seemed
to categorize the African American question within the context of
a national (or ethnic) question. Reed's counter-reasoning was that
categorizing it as a national question would lead to a "racial movement," instead of a class movement. This was consistent with the
CLP approach.

At the fourth congress of the Comintern in 1922, the question was
once again brought to the table. That congress was attended by two
African-descended people, Otto Huiswood, leading member of the
CPA, and Claude McKay, a member of the ABB. Huiswood clearly
placed the African American question in the realm of a national/
colonial question: "In the Negro question we have before us another
phase of the race and colonial question to which no attention has
been paid heretofore."[20] He continued by arguing that the "Negro
question" was fundamentally an economic (class) issue, but was
complicated by the racial (national) aspect. He also stressed its international implications by highlighting the influence of the African
American struggle on the anti-colonial struggles in Africa and the
Caribbean. Speaking on behalf of the Negro Commission (of the
Comintern), Huiswood proposed the recognition and support of
all forms of the Negro movement that weaken capitalism, the organization of Black workers in trade unions, that Communists' work

---

19. *Second Congress of the Communist International: minutes of the proceedings, Vol. 1* (New Park, London, 1977), 123-124

20. Otto Huiswood, "Speech to The Fourth Congress of the Third Communist International, Moscow, November 25, https://www.marxists.org/
history/etol/newspape/internationalist/pamphlets/Com-Int-&-Black-
Lib-OptV5.pdf

among Blacks be carried out mainly by Blacks, and that an international conference of Blacks be organized.[21]

McKay, who was not a communist, spoke in generalities but, reflecting on the significance of the Comintern's actions, acknowledged, "In 1918 when the Third International published its Manifesto and included the part referring to the exploited colonies, there were several groups of Negro radicals in America that sent this propaganda out among their people."[22]

The fourth Comintern congress passed a resolution on "The Black Question," which posited,

> The Communist International represents the revolutionary workers and peasants of the entire world in their struggle against the power of imperialism – it is not just an organization of the enslaved white workers of Europe and America, but is as much an organization of the oppressed non-white peoples of the world, and so feels duty-bound to encourage and support the international organizations of the black people in their struggle against the common enemy.[23]

The resolution declared (1) that Communists were committed to supporting all African American struggles that weakened capitalism, (2) the Comintern pledged itself to fight for racial equality, and (3) it urged the convening of an of international conference/congress to be held in Moscow.

The appearance of Huiswood and McKay at the Comintern Congress was a response to growing criticisms of the American party over its lack of attention to the African American community. Complaints by African American party members found receptive ears in the Comintern among Russian Communists and, especially, among Asian Communists. Shortly after the fourth congress, Lovett Fort-Whiteman, an African American Communist who had come to the Soviet Union for training, was approached by members of the Comintern and urged to organize for the Negro congress that had been suggested by Huiswood and seconded by the Comintern. The plan was to launch a new organization aimed at political work in the African American community, to be called the American Negro Labor Congress. The ANLC would provide an organizational vehicle to enable Communists to organize in the African American community,

---

21. Ibid
22. Ibid
23. Hessel, *Theses, Resolutions & Manifestos…*, Ibid, 328-331

as well as the political base for the organizing of the proposed international conference/congress.

The national convention of the WPA was convened in Chicago in August 1925. No doubt prodded by the Comintern, the WPA unfolded its most ambitious analysis and program concerning the African American community. "Negro Work" was listed as one of the "areas of work." The convention report noted that African American members had been sent to the fifth Comintern congress and an African American farmer was sent to a convention of the Peasants International. Special party schools which targeted African American activists were founded, specially targeted literature had been produced to improve the recruitment of African Americans, and an organizer had been sent into the South to work with African Americans. Most importantly, a subcommittee of the Central Executive Committee was created to oversee Negro work. Their report confirmed that, "In accord with the instructions of the Communist International, most of our work has been carried on in connection to the American Negro Labor Congress."[24]

In a lengthy analysis of the African American question, the party highlighted the significant role that African Americans' labor played in the development of the United States, their role in the Civil War, and their increasing role in the organized labor movement. The party noted:

> The Negro has played an important role in American history. First, his labor transformed the Southern wilderness into an empire. More than a score of heroic slave revolts enrich the forgotten pages of American history. The smoldering fire of slave rebellion was one of the immediate forces impelling the first centralization of the government of the capitalist republic – the adoption and the formation of the national army.[25]

For possibly the first time, the party highlighted the active role that African Americans played in the building of the U.S. Although the program recited the usual afflictions put upon them, it also stressed the active role of resistance that had run as a thread throughout the African American experience. It called for more active measures in recruiting African Americans into the party and stated:

---

24. *Report of the Central Executive Committee to the 4th National Convention.* The Fourth National Convention of the Workers (Communist) Party of America (Chicago, Daily Worker Publishing, 1925), 17-18

25. Ibid, 115

All slogans of equality which are current among the Negro masses, or which can be awakened among them, which express the aspirations for equal rights and equal treatment of Negroes in political and economic life and in public customs, are placed among the demands of the Workers (Communist) Party.[26]

Next came a lengthy list of democratic demands including, in what may be a first for a predominately white political organization, "the abolition of all anti-intermarriage laws."

It concluded by reporting that the party would center its activities around building the American Negro Labor Congress, which would work to establish connections between the struggles of African Americans and workers, and between African Americans and Blacks across the diaspora and in Africa. The statement powerfully asserted:

The aim of our Party in our work among the Negro masses is to create a powerful proletarian movement which will fight and lead the struggle of the Negro race against exploitation and oppression in every form and which will be a militant part of the revolutionary movement of the whole American working class…to broaden the struggles of the American Negro workers and farmers, connect them with the struggles of the national minorities and colonial peoples of all the world and thereby further the cause of the world revolution and the dictatorship of the proletariat.[27]

The American Negro Labor Congress, whose creation was first suggested by the Comintern (with nudging from Black Communists), began organizing for its founding conference in early 1925. Beginning in May, regular articles ran in the *Daily Worker* announcing informational meetings being held across the country to build for the conference. Lovett Fort-Whiteman, chief organizer of the ANLC, announced that its primary purpose was "to establish in the minds of both the white and black workers a spirit of amicability and class solidarity."[28]

Its founding was attended by approximately 33 credentialed delegates. The organization was heavily burdened by attacks from the

26. Ibid, 119
27. Ibid, 123
28. "Negro Labor Congress Head Reports Glowing Prospects for Coming Chicago Meet," *Daily Worker*, October 7, 1925, 3

AFL, social democrats (in the African American community), and religious leaders. Although it suffered from organizational issues and personality conflicts among its leaders, the ANLC was able to build several active locals (most notably in Chicago and New York City). The *Daily Worker* heavily covered its activities, printing over 400 articles on the ANLC during the five year existence of the organization. In spite of a few successes, it was disbanded in 1930. Historian Mark Solomon commented: "Life was hard for the ANLC from the start, and despite some accomplishments. It never got better."[29]

The Comintern Re-enters

The Communist Party's theory, strategy, and approach toward the African American question went through a radical transformation based on resolutions passed by the Comintern in 1928 and 1930. Those resolutions made it clear that African Americans were an oppressed nationality who were entitled to the right of self-determination. The 1930 resolution clearly stated,

> the Negro question in the United States must be viewed from the standpoint of its peculiarity, namely, as the question of an *oppressed nation* [with racial distinctions and social antagonisms]…This introduces into the American Negro question an important, *peculiar* trait which is absent from the national question of other oppressed peoples. Furthermore, it is necessary to face clearly the inevitable distinction between the position of the Negro in the *South* and in the *North*…The struggle of the Communists for *the equal rights* of the Negroes applies to all Negroes, in the North as well as the South. The struggle for this slogan embraces all or almost all of the important special interests of the Negroes in the North, but not in the South, where the main Communist slogan must be: *The Right of Self-Determination of the Negroes in the Black Belt* [*italic* in original].[30]

The demand for self-determination was consistent with the Comintern's position that oppressed nations and nationalities were entitled to this right. In the case of African Americans, it was determined that they were an oppressed nationality and that the geographical

29. Mark Solomon, *The Cry was Unity: Communists and African Americans, 1917-1936* (University Press of Mississippi,1998), 56

30. *The Communist Position on the Negro Question: Self-Determination for the Black Belt* (CPUSA, New York, 1935), 41-64

area where they represented the majority (an area partially covering several states of the South and colloquially referred to as the "Black Belt") was an oppressed nation. The resolution clearly stated that Communists did not necessarily advocate separation or the formation of a distinct political nation – only that the people who inhabited that area had that right if they so choose.

The majority of the inhabitants of the Black Belt (African Americans) lacked the right to vote, had no protection of their safety, and were denied most basic democratic rights. The resolution clearly implied that if they secured these rights, they would be in a position to make this determination for themselves. Thus, the demand for the "right" to self-determination was not a demand to separate.

These new resolutions provided clarity and direction for party activity in African American communities and also provided a theoretical basis for a program. In addition, the 1928 resolution made it clear that,

> [t]he time is ripe to begin within the Party a courageous campaign of self-criticism concerning the work among the Negroes…An aggressive fight against all forms of white chauvinism must be accompanied by a widespread and thorough educational campaign…to stamp out all forms of antagonism, or even indifference among our white comrades toward Negro work.[31]

While other left organizations like the IWW had opposed racism, the Communist Party became the first to actively wage an internal struggle to fight racism within its own ranks.

On the international scene, these new resolutions must be viewed in the context of the Comintern's overall international strategy. They were entering into what has been called the Third Period, when it was believed that capitalism was on its last leg and only needed to be shaken to be brought down. Alliances with liberal and social democratic political forces were frowned upon and communist parties throughout the world began launching more militant (some would later say 'sectarian') actions.

Thus, the party was now equipped with a clear ideological prism through which to view the African American question. Additionally, the party would seek to place itself in the vanguard of organizations

---

31. Ibid, 6

that stood uncompromisingly for complete equality for the African American people.

At an anti-lynching conference called by the ANLC in St. Louis on November 17, 1930, the ANLC was transformed into the League of Struggle for Negro Rights. The League's program, mirroring the party's new direction, called for equal rights for African Americans throughout the entire country as well as for self-determination for African Americans in the Black Belt.[32] It was in the ensuing period that the party earned its sobriquet as the "Party of the Negro people."

Perhaps the most well-known campaign undertaken by the party, with its allied organization the International Labor Defense, was the defense of the Scottsboro defendants. These were nine young African Americans who had been unjustly accused of the rape of two white women in Scottsboro, Alabama in 1931. In the ensuing years, the *Daily Worker* ran more than 4,000 articles on the legal case and the movement to free the defendants. The party succeeded in turning the Scottsboro case into an international story, with *Daily Worker* articles being reprinted in thousands of Soviet Union newspapers and other Communist Party newspapers around the world. In this and other campaigns, the CPUSA was able, for the first time, to put an international microscope on the lynching mentality and blatant racism prevalent in American society.

In addition to the Scottsboro campaign, the party also organized struggles against numerous instances of police brutality against African Americans throughout the country. Nearly every issue of the *Daily Worker* carried some local story of police or governmental racist abuse. The party organized protests against evictions, with Communists playing the leading role in organizing communities to return furniture to the apartments of those evicted and engaging in physical altercations with the police. As a result of these interventions, the party began to develop the reputation for being the most stalwart defender of the rights of African Americans. This identification was so strong – and the connection of Communists and racial equality so enduring – that 30 years later, when the Civil Rights Movement gained steam in the South, there was an immediate connection in the public mind between Communists and integration. Hence the infamous posters produced by segregationists proclaiming "Communism = Race Mixing."

According to historian Mark Naison, "Communists organized eviction resistance, relief bureau sit-ins, protests against job

---

32. *Equality, Land and Freedom: A program for Negro liberation* (League of Struggle for Negro Rights, 1934)

discrimination, rent strikes, consumer boycotts, and demonstrations against segregated hotels, restaurants, and recreation facilities."[33] These activities, mostly concentrated in the North, were attempts to bring to life the party's uncompromising position on equal rights for African Americans.

In the South, while also upholding the "equal rights" program, the party was also tasked with implementing the self-determination program. They chose to focus on organizing sharecroppers into a union. Party organizers concentrated in Alabama, forming the Alabama Sharecroppers Union.[34] The logic was that to wage a struggle against the landowners (with a democratic demand for the confiscation of large landholdings), the sharecroppers would first have to be organized. In the early 1930's, the SCU conducted several strikes and by 1931 there were 14 locals and 149 members in Tallapoosa County, 12 locals and 137 members in Dadeville, as well as locals in East Tallahassee, Lee, Macon, and Chambers Counties. By 1935, there were 12,000 dues paying members of the SCU.[35]

The organizing of African American sharecroppers was one of the most dangerous initiatives that the party undertook. Organizing in the South was extraordinarily perilous. Most local law enforcement agencies (sheriffs) were directly or indirectly connected to the Ku Klux Klan and other racist organizations. Many sharecroppers in the SCU were murdered, assaulted, or jailed. Organizers were subject to the same treatment. There were several armed battles (resulting in casualties on both sides) between the SCU and law enforcement – most notably at Reeltown and Camp Hill, Alabama.

B.D. Amis, an African American party leader based in Philadelphia, reported on party work in the South for the journal *Communist International*. He wrote:

The Party has established organizations in the South. The creation of a sharecroppers' union of several thousand is an advance in the building of organizations of struggle in the Black Belt. Although our southern organizations are weak, they are,

---

33. Mark Naison, "Harlem Communists and the Politics of Black Power," *Marxist Perspectives*, Fall 1978, 20

34. For a detailed examination of the Sharecroppers Union, see: Timothy V Johnson, "We Are Illegal Here: The Communist Party, Self-Determination, and the Alabama Sharecroppers Union," *Science and Society*, 77(4), 454-479

35. Ibid, 467, 473

nonetheless, becoming a more known force to the Southern Negro toilers and white workers.[36]

The Popular Front

In 1935 a major change in policy at the Comintern affected all communist parties. With the goal of fashioning tactics that could defeat a rising fascism, the Comintern advocated for the creation of Popular Fronts, formations in which Communists, socialists, and liberals could unite to defeat fascism. This spelled the end of the Third Period, when ultra-leftism and sectarianism had dominated.

Within the context of the party's role in the African American struggle, this translated into downplaying the demand for self-determination and building broad coalitions that included liberal and religious elements in the African American community. The LSNR was disbanded and the party focused its energy on founding the National Negro Congress. The NNC included labor leaders such as A. Philip Randolph, academics, social work activists, and religious leaders, as well as trade union leaders and activists. It functioned as a form of the Popular Front in the African American community.

The Popular Front spelled doom for the SCU. While the Popular Front proved to be a successful strategy in the North, both in the African American and the labor movements, the South had few "liberal" forces with which to ally. The SCU initially merged with the Farmers Union of Alabama, then was dissolved into the United Cannery Agricultural Packers Allied Workers of America. In the context of these mergers, the SCU lost its militancy and its ability to attract sharecroppers.

During World War II, under the leadership of Earl Browder, the party began to moderate many of its positions, envisioning a situation where capitalism could slowly evolve into socialism without class struggle. In January 1944, Browder wrote an article in *Political Affairs,* the party's theoretical journal, dismissing the slogan of self-determination, implying that African Americans had made the choice to integrate into American society. This sparked a debate on self-determination within the party that was carried out through the magazine's pages. Self-determination was one of the issues that was part of an overhaul of the party's ideology and politics. Browder also asserted that a Communist Party was no longer a necessity and led

---

36. B.D. Amis, "How we carried out the decision of the 1930 C.I. Resolution on the Negro Question in the U.S." *The Communist International*, May 5, 1935, 500

the transformation of the organization into the Communist Political Association, which would function as a pressure group within national politics.

In 1944, at the convention of the newly formed Communist Political Association, there was a session on "The South." The presentation made no mention of self-determination, but instead focused on the growing unity of whites and African Americans under the developing Democratic Front. During the discussion following the presentation, William L. Patterson, an African American party leader, forecasted, "There is going to arise a clear and distinctive differentiation between those Negroes who are seeking to divide national unity by asking the Negroes to follow a line of their own, and those forces that are linking the Negro together with all other elements of national unity."[37]

The final resolution on the South from the CPA stated, "Growing industrialization and the advance of the progressive labor movement below the Mason and Dixon line, and the increased unity of Negro and white, of worker, farmer and businessman, are reinvigorating the political life of the South."[38]

In 1945, the French Communist Party published an article that was critical of Browder's theories; shortly after, Browder was expelled, and the CPUSA was re-established. Many identified the dropping of the self-determination position directly with Browder's revisionism and, after his expulsion, it was re-adopted in 1946. At a 1946 National Committee meeting, numerous CP leaders, including William Z. Foster, James E. Jackson, Edward Strong, and William Patterson spoke on the importance of the right of self-determination in relation to the Black Belt. The resolution that passed stated:

As always, the Communist Party stands firmly in the forefront of the struggle for full economic, social and political equality for the Negro people. In fighting for their equal rights, the Negro people are becoming more unified as a people...Their fight for liberation from oppression in the Black Belt – the area of Negro majority population – is a struggle for full nationhood, for their rightful position of full equality as a nation.[39]

---

37. *The Path to Peace, Progress and Prosperity: proceedings of the Constitutional Convention of the Communist Political Association* (Communist Political Association, 1944)

38. Ibid, 118

39. *The Communist Position on the Negro Question* (New Century Publishers, 1947), 11

In the ensuing decade there was, again, a series of discussions within
the party on self-determination, this time prompted by the Supreme
Court ruling (1954) of *Brown vs. Board of Education*, which called for
the integration of schools (and by implication the desegregation of
U.S. society) and, most significantly, by the burgeoning Civil Rights
Movement, centered in the South, which was demanding desegregation and voting rights. The Montgomery Bus Boycott (1955-56)
helped launch a national grassroots movement and propelled leaders such as Dr. Martin Luther King, Jr. to the forefront of movements
fighting for democratic rights.

In 1957, ahead of the party's 16th convention, a series of *Discussion
Bulletins* were published which allowed party members to express
their opinions on the program. The African American question was
widely addressed in these bulletins. Doxey Wilkerson, a CP leader
and scholar, wrote in relation to self-determination for the Black
Belt, "It is an untenable position, demonstrably undermined by the
whole course of development of the Negro people during the past
quarter-century."[40]

Wilkerson analyzed population shifts, social advances of the
African American people, and trends in African American political
movements. He concluded:

Thus, for the past quarter-century our Party has been hob-
bled by a theoretical position on the Negro question which is
contradicted by its actual and prospective course of development, which operates to further our isolation from the Negro
people, and which we are now coming to understand was an
incorrect, doctrinaire application of Marxist principles on the
national question in the first place. We do, indeed, need to
"re-appraise" – in fact, to abandon – this unreal and disorient-
ing theoretical outlook.[41]

By 1957, African American party leader Benjamin Davis, Jr., proposed at a CP National Committee meeting, "It would seem that the
slogan of self-determination should be abandoned and our position
otherwise modified and brought up to date."[42]

In preparation for the for the party's 17th convention (1959), the
National Committee published a pamphlet entitled, "Theoretical

40. Doxey Wilkerson, "Time to Reappraise CP Position on Negro Question," 16th National Convention Discussion Bulletin, Nov. 1956 (CPUSA), 5
    41. Ibid, 7
    42. Harry Haywood, *Black Bolshevik* (Liberator Press, 1978), 607

Aspects of the Negro Question in the United States." It included a detailed essay by James Jackson (former lead CP organizer in the South and a founder of the Southern Negro Youth Congress), a draft resolution, and excerpts from the ensuing National Committee discussion.

Jackson wrote, "The Negroes in the United States are not constituted as a nation. Rather, they have the characteristics of a racially distinctive people or nationality who are a historically determined component of the American nation in the United States." He continued,

> To conclude that the Negro people in the U.S. are not a nation is not to say that the Negro question is not a national question. It is indeed a national question. The question is, however, a national question of what type, with what distinguishing characteristics, calling for what strategic concept for its solution.[43]

Jackson sought to address the concern that this new analysis lessened the importance of the African American struggle. He noted:

> A special feature of the American road to socialism is revealed in the fact that the requisite preparation of the forces for effecting fundamental social change in the system necessitates the completion of the bourgeois-democratic norms of political, economic and social development for the South in general and the Negro people in particular. Furthermore, a condition for accomplishing the prerequisite unity of the American working class with its class allies for advanced social struggle is to level the main rails of the color bar. The struggle of the Negro people for the democratic goals of political, economic and social equality feeds into the general stream of the historic working-class cause of our time – a powerful current which raises the torrential power of the whole cause of social advance.[44]

Overall, the National Committee approved of Jackson's restatement of the party's position. Charlene Mitchell, a delegate from California who would go on to become a major national leader of the party, questioned certain aspects of Jackson's analysis. She posited that,

---

43. James Jackson, "New Features of the Negro Question in the U.S." in *Theoretical Aspects of the Negro Question in the United States* (CPUSA, 1959), 3
44. Ibid, 11

"...the Party has to answer the question of whether or not the slo-gan of self-determination, if it is not correct now, was ever correct." Referring to the party's previous position she added, "I have not been sufficiently satisfied that this is no longer true." Mitchell then proposed a series of meetings across the country to further discuss the resolution.[45] Recalling that discussion more than 50 years later, Mitchell wrote:

Under the rubric of the demand for self-determination, the Par-ty's activities focused on the African American community... the prestige of the Party, as being one of the few interracial organizations that fought for African American rights, was established...I was just concerned that dropping the demand would change the way the Party viewed the African American question in a fundamental way.[46]

It took the party 12 years of debate to revise its position on the African American question by dropping its demand for the right to self-determination in the Black Belt. There were several practical prob-lems which elongated the timeframe for that change. The party had been under increasingly strenuous repression by the federal gov-ernment from the end of World II until the late 1950s. Many top party leaders (national and local) were jailed and/or imprisoned for much of that period. Some went underground in an effort to main-tain a continuity of leadership. In addition, following the Browder era, there was more than a decade of intense factionalism within the party as members adjusted themselves to the new international dynamics – particularly the onset of the Cold War, the Khrushchev's revelations about Stalin-era crimes, and party members' expulsion from most AFL-CIO union leadership positions.

In reality, the self-determination position had a reduced practi-cality with the ending of the Third Period. The Popular Front era forced the Communist Party to broaden its outreach to a larger population – within and outside of the African American com-munity. The National Negro Congress was a body that was more reflective of the Northern African American community (although there were chapters throughout the urban South) and was more concerned with the agenda that would later be emphasized by the Civil Rights Movement. The youth version of the NNC, the Southern Negro Youth Congress, among whose leaders was James

45. Ibid, 25
46. Charlene Mitchell, *An Organizer's Life* (unpublished manuscript), 67

Jackson, focused more on issues of labor organizing, voting rights and anti-lynching than on the land-based issues which had once motivated the SCU.

In 1946, the NNC merged with the ILD and another rights organization to form the Civil Rights Congress. The CRC was a forerunner of many of the legal defense organizations that proliferate today. Following the pattern of the ILD's defense of the Scottsboro defendants, the CRC mobilized public opinion, organized mass rallies, and provided legal defense to victims of racism, police brutality, and anti-communist repression. As with the Scottsboro case, they waged campaigns of justice for Rosa Lee Ingram, the Martinsville Seven, and Willie McGee – turning them into household names among the Left, progressive and African American communities.

In 1949, the CRC led a mass march of 3,000 people demanding civil rights legislation be enacted by the U.S. Congress. In 1951, the CRC and its head, Communist William Patterson, along with artist/activist Paul Robeson, presented a petition to the United Nations entitled *We Charge Genocide: The Crime of Government Against the Negro People*, which documented the many crimes of racist violence committed and/or sanctioned by the U.S. government. The CRC had chapters in many large cities throughout the U.S. and its activities were widely covered in the African American press and the *Daily Worker*. In the course of its existence (1946-1956), the *Daily Worker* ran over 3,000 articles chronicling the CRC's activities.

In many ways, the NNC/SNYC and CRC provided both transition and continuity to the modern Civil Rights Movement. An examination of the archives of the SNYC demonstrates that many activists who later became locally and nationally well known (including Rosa Parks), gained their initial activist experiences through the SNYC. Thus, although these organizations were short-lived, they left a legacy still evident today. In the McCarthy era it was difficult for Communists to act openly so these organizations provided an organizational outlet for Communist activists in the African American and broader Left communities.

Many Communists participated in the developing Civil Rights Movement in the 1960's – although usually as individuals and not as open Communists. The central area of concern was that they wanted to avoid the right wing's redbaiting of the movement. Even so, many party leaders (locally and nationally), through contacts developed in the 1940s and 1950s, frequently consulted with movement activists and leaders.

In the 1968 presidential election, the party decided to run its own candidates, Charlene Mitchell and Michael Zagarell (as the respective presidential and vice presidential candidates). Mitchell, an African American activist then based in New York and Zagarell, a white youth activist from New York, continued the party's legacy, begun in the 1930s, of running an integrated presidential ticket that symbolized Black/White unity.

Perhaps the most significant party activity in the African American community during the 1960s and 1970s was the defense campaign waged against the persecution of Angela Davis. Davis, a party member and professor at the University of California, was arrested in connection with a 1970 failed attempt to free several political prisoners from the California corrections system. Several people were killed in the incident. Although Davis had no connection to the incident, she was arrested and put on trial, with the death penalty as a possibility. The party immediately organized a campaign to release Davis on bail and to pressure the state of California to drop the charges. All across the country rallies, demonstrations, petition drives, and pickets were organized demanding the freedom of Davis under the slogan, "Free Angela."

After a trial, Davis was acquitted and released. The Free Angela Davis Committees were reorganized into the National Alliance Against Racism and Political Repression in 1973, which began campaigns to free other political prisoners throughout the United States and the world. The campaigns of the Free Angela committees and the NAARPR brought a large number of African American youth into the party. Both organizations were led by Charlene Mitchell. Mitchell, who had earlier worked as an organizer in Los Angeles, had in the late 1960s organized a party club called the Che-Lumumba Club. This was an all-Black club active in South Central Los Angeles. Although the existence of an all-Black club was controversial within the party, which had always insisted on racial integration, it was allowed due to special circumstances. The Black Power Movement had created a political environment in the African American community, especially among radically inclined young, urban, northern African Americans, that was suspicious of predominately white organizations. The All-Black club was viewed as a transition for these youths into the party.

During this period, the party also rallied support for the Black Panther Party, then under violent attack by police departments across the country and the FBI. The party spearheaded a broad coalition of organizations into a vehicle called, "The Committee to Defend the Right of the Black Panther Party to Exist." The committee assisted in organizing public events and fundraising for legal defense expenses.

Party members also took an active participation in the anti-Vietnam War movement by participating in mass anti-war organizations. The party was responsible for creating a defense committee for the Fort Hood Three, three youths (one white, one Latino, and one African American) who refused orders to go to Vietnam. This case was especially used to organize anti-war sentiment in the African American community.

Another intervention into the African America community centered around the freedom of South Africa and the developing anti-apartheid movement. In 1973, the National Anti-Imperialist Movement in Solidarity with African Liberation was founded. This was another initiative by the party to create a mass movement capable of mobilizing the American people to act against apartheid and colonialism in Southern Africa. NAIMSAL was active in cities across the country and sponsored or participated in numerous nationwide actions.

The party's activity in the African American community and its stalwart opposition to racism did not lessen as it dropped the self-determination position. In attempting to grapple with the theoretical ramifications of the change, the party sought to clarify what was new in its developing position. The eventual result was the development of the theoretical category of "centrality." This was hinted at in James Jackson's previously cited presentation to the CP National Committee in 1959. Jackson wrote:

> [A] condition for accomplishing the prerequisite unity of the American working class with its class allies for advanced social struggle is to level the main rails of the color bar. The struggle of the Negro people for the democratic goals of political, economic and social equality feeds into the general stream of the historic working-class cause of our time a powerful current which raises the torrential power of the whole cause of social advance.[47]

Jackson's point was to offer a theoretical connection between the class struggle (to overthrow capitalism) and the struggle against racism and for equality. His point was that the overthrow of capitalism was contingent upon the unity of the working class and that unity had to be constructed on the basis of opposition to racism and to the advocation of equality. This theory was encapsulated by the term

---

47. Jackson, op. cit., 11

"centrality," which was interpreted as meaning that the struggle against racism and for equality was central to the successful prosecution of the class struggle.

The issue of centrality and a new concept of an "anti-racist majority" would spawn major political debates within the party in the 1980s and early 1990s. Unfortunately, just as in the debates over self-determination in the 1940s and 1950s, these discussions occurred in an atmosphere of intense factionalism as these later debates took place within the framework of the dissolution of socialism in the Soviet Union and Eastern Europe. Communist parties across the world were re-assessing Marxism-Leninism, the viability of socialism, the necessity of a Leninist party, and other existential issues.[48]

The Anti-Racist Majority

The phrase "anti-racist majority" was initially used by Jarvis Tyner (although colloquially, not theoretically), then CP candidate for governor of New York, in 1978. In response to a series of racist attacks in New York City, Tyner issued a statement proclaiming, "Our program is aimed at mobilizing the peace-loving and anti-racist majority and not sanctioning the violent acts of a minority of racists elements in our society."[49]

The main statement of the CP's 24th convention (1987) said, "Most white people reject racism, as they understand it. They reject the basic premise of white supremacy."[50] While the resolution was confirming what social scientists had been stating for some time – that an increasing number of white Americans rejected the idea of superior/inferior races – some thought that definition of "racism" was shallow and ignored new forms of racism, i.e., opposition to affirmative action, denial of present day racial discrimination, etc. Critics also questioned the use of the term "majority" – was that inclusive of racial minorities? If so, then the majority of whites could still harbor racism. Thus, what did it really mean? Following the resolution, the *People's Daily World* was replete with stories demonstrating the

---

48. For a fulsome interrogation of the factional fight, see: Danny Rosenberg's "From Crisis to Split: The Communist Party, USA 1989-1991," *American Communist History*, (18:1-2), Mr-Je 2019

49. Victoria Missick, "Politicians, big biz blamed for racist attacks in NYC," *Daily World*, September 6, 1978, 6

50. Central Committee, CPUSA, "Political Resolution," *Political Affairs*, April 1987, 15

actions of the "anti-racist majority" in response to some particular local racist outrage.

The anti-racist majority concept was discussed at length at a 1990 CP conference on "Equality and Empowerment" organized by the African American Equality Commission.

A month earlier, in the party publication *Dialog*, created to discuss contentious issues within the party, Anthony Monteiro, an African American leader of the CPUSA, slightly reconfigured the notion by limiting it in reference to those progressive movements developing in the U.S. He referred to the confluence of those movements as demonstrative of a "new anti-racist consensus."[51] Thus, he seemed to be characterizing the mass movement, not the U.S. population in general.

In his summary remarks at the conference, Gus Hall, CPUSA national chair, concluded:

> On the anti-racist majority. I have not used this concept for some time because it is so difficult to pinpoint what each of us thinks it is. If we consider all those who are not racist in the broadest sense, then I believe it is a valid concept...I don't believe anyone thinks about this concept as a white anti-racist majority. I think most start calculating the numbers by including the 60 million who are victims of racial and national oppression...Therefore, I don't think "anti-racist majority" is a scientific phrase.[52]

In his closing remarks at the conference, Robert Lindsay, chair of the African American Equality Commission, concluded:

> Take the question of an anti-racist majority. We debated that for three years. I don't think we need to continue the debate. Gus has said that there is no scientific basis for it. That's true. There is no scientific basis for it. Everything shows the contrary. It's ludicrous to come up with such a formulation. But, here we go again, we're going to raise the "anti-racist consensus." Now, what does that mean, when we put out a formulation like that?[53]

---

51. Anthony Monteiro, "A New Consensus against Racism," *Dialog*, September 1990, 14

52. Gus Hall, "Special Remarks," *Equality & Empowerment, Part II* (CPUSA, 1990), 3

53. Robert Lindsay, "Summary," *Equality & Empowerment, Part II* (CPUSA, 1990), 20

Unfortunately, since the discussion was largely viewed through the lens of factionalism, the opposing side never closely examined the nuance in Monteiro's arguments. What was meaningful in his argument was that the increasingly advanced unity of progressive movements, including a broad array of the nationally oppressed and whites, was beginning to incorporate the struggle against racism into their analyses. Organizations formed around the environment, gender, and other issues were all beginning to include anti-racism at the center of their programs. In essence, this was a testament to the groundbreaking work done by the party over the decades. Instead, Monteiro's contribution was viewed as merely an attempt to clean up Hall's errors.

Centrality

The notion of centrality – that the struggle against racism is central to the class struggle – became the formulation that replaced self-determination. This concept was always interpreted by the party as an explanation for the developing dialectics between these two struggles. At a Central Committee meeting in 1983, Henry Winston, explained:

> The question of the centrality of Black liberation is a very import-ant question and this explains why it is being discussed with such vigor. What is the problem? It should be understood that what is not being questioned is that the multi-national working class is the leading force in society and the pivot around which the struggle against monopoly capitalism, as well as the social-ist transformation of society depends. What is being proposed is the unity of Black and white in struggle against the corpora-tions. The decisive question involved here is the unity within the class as a precondition for the struggle against racism in every form manifested. In short, the unity of Black and white is the pivot around which class unity becomes possible.[54]

Another explanation of centrality was delivered in 1975 by James Steele, then the head of the Young Workers Liberation League (the party's youth group). Steele, explained:

---

54. Henry Winston, *National Committee Report* (CPUSA, 1983)

At every decisive juncture, victory or defeat has been determined by the degree to which Black-white working class and
democratic unity was built on the basis of the fight for the equal
rights of Black people and the special responsibility of whites
on fighting racism.[55]

As expressed by the party, in speeches and in print, the centrality
of the struggle against racism and for equality was always contextualized within the class struggle. Yet some in the party began to
question the validity of that position. At the Equality and Empowerment conference, Gus Hall admitted,

I don't think we have found the solution to an acceptable formulation. The question is: if the struggle against racism is
central to everything, where does that leave the class struggle
and the working class? We have to find a formulation that does
not replace or substitute the basic concept of the class struggle
or the historic role of the working class, while in no way mini-
mizing the struggles against racism and for equality.[56]

Ironically, Hall and others were arguing against a position that no
one in the party had expressed. This deepened the suspicion of some
that behind this proposition of an anti-racist majority and the attack
on centrality was a reevaluation of the significance of the struggle
against racism. By the next party convention, the use of the term centrality had been dropped. In 1999, the CPUSA program stated under
"Racism and the struggle for equality":

Racism and racist violence, chauvinism, bigotry and discrimination and of every kind have always been an integral part of
U.S. capitalist reality. It is perhaps clearer today than ever that
working-class unity in the struggle to eradicate these evils is
critical for progress in the fight against monopoly capitalism
and for socialism."[57]

---

55. James Steele, "Report on Centrality of Black Liberation and the Fight
Against Racism," *Youth Unite for the Right to Earn, Learn, and Live!* (YWLL,
1975), 46

56. Gus Hall, "Special Remarks," *op. cit.*

57. Gus Hall, "Report to the Convention of the Communist Party, USA,"
https://web.archive.org/web/19980201234530/http://www.hartford
-hwp.com/cp-usa/docs/report-1.html#Z11

In the Party's 2006 program (still in effect) it reappeared. The program stated, "the struggle for equality and against racism in relation to African Americans has played a central role in the entire struggle for democracy and progress.[58] Although in 2008, *Political Affairs* editor Joe Sims listed centrality as one of the worst ideas in Marxism. According to Sims:

> Centrality of the African American people. Theorized in the 1970s and 1980s by Communist theoreticians of the national question, African American centrality had different interpretations, but tended to place the national question over and above the class question. At its best it stressed the central role of fighting racism as part of the struggle for class and national unity, the importance of which can be seen in the Obama candidacy. At its worst it placed undue emphasis on working in the African American community (by whites) and to give up fighting racism among whites.[59]

By the 29th convention (2010) centrality, although not in the party program, was still being used. In the report on the fight for equality. Jarvis Tyner declared:

> You know comrades, the fight against racism has always played a central role in the overall struggle for unity; defeating racism has always been decisive to advancing the class struggle. Our nation is going through a major transition politically and as we have been saying, through struggle a new era of progressive reform is possible but the fight against racism and for unity is decisive.[60]

The resolution from the 29th convention fell short of recognizing Tyner's intervention. It resolved that "the Communist Party USA reaffirms that the struggle against racism and national oppression is *essential* to the struggle of the working-class for democracy

58. The Road to Socialism USA, https://www.cpusa.org/party_info/party-program/

59. Joe Sims, "Worst and Best of Marxism #4," *Political Affairs*, August 2008, https://paeditorsblog.blogspot.com/2008/08/worst-and-best-of-marxism-4.html

60. Jarvis Tyner, "The Fight Against Racism: new challenges, new features, new possibilities," May 27, 2010, https://www.cpusa.org/party_voices/the-fight-against-racism-new-challenges-new-features-new-possibilities/

and socialism [*italics* added, T.J.]." *Essential* presumably meaning "extremely important," according to one dictionary.[61]

There were no resolutions from the 30th convention (2014). The resolutions of the 31st convention (2019) took a major step forward in re-establishing the party's historic position. In a resolution on "Special Oppression and the Struggle for Equality and Democracy," it noted, "As Communists we consider the fight against special oppression and for full equality as fundamental to all working class and people's struggles." It is assumed that fundamental, according to the dictionary, meant central or necessary. The resolution on "For Unity Against Racism," went further, proclaiming "the CPUSA vows to make the fight for unity against racism the core of, and central to, all of its work going forward..."[62]

The Communist Party has a long history as being in the vanguard in the struggle against racism and for African American equality. As would be the case for any organization travelling a new path, there have been detours, side-steps, and mis-directions. However, its unquestioned commitment to equality has always allowed it to make corrections and to chart the movement forward toward a society free of racism, discrimination, and exploitation.

61. Communist Party Resolves: Build united action against racism and for unity, https://www.google.com/search?client=safari&rls=en&q=cpusa+resolutions+29+convention&ie=UTF-8&oe=UTF-8

62. Resolutions adopted by the 31st Convention of the Communist Party USA, https://www.google.com/search?client=safari&rls=en&q=cpusa+resolutions+30+convention&ie=UTF-8&oe=U

Chapter **6**

"Faith in the Masses": The International Workers Order

By Robert Zecker

Once upon a time there was a workers' run mutual insurance society that lobbied for universal, publicly funded health care. Its interracial membership enjoyed affordable accident, sickness, and funeral policies, as well as access to low cost medical, dental and optometrist clinics, but they also appreciated their society's militant lobbying for full equality for African American and Hispanic members. The society, known as the International Workers Order, orchestrated anti-lynching and fair employment campaigns uniting white, Black, and Latino members in advocating an inclusive, progressive Americanism. The IWO offered, too, a panoply of recreational activities to its members. These activities ranged from sports leagues to art classes to musical and drama troupe, what the Office of Special Services' Foreign Nationalities Branch called "a diversified program of social-cultural activities." The World War II spy agency cited a *Daily Worker* article celebrating the International Worker Order's vast array of recreational programs.[1]

While agents of the federal government kept a wary eye on the IWO, which it accurately noted had been founded in 1930 by members of the Communist Party, USA, throughout industrial America, many other working-class people with few other options for affordable accident, sick and funeral policies saw the Order as a godsend. By 1948 the Order claimed 180,000 members offering minimal dues

---

1. Wayne State University, Walter P. Reuther Library, Don Binkowski Papers, Box 4 Folder 4-29, OSS/FNB report, July 11, 1944, FNB to Director of Strategic Services, "Communist-Line IWO Reorganizes to Emphasize Nationality."

for some security.[2] The IWO's defense of social insurance, public housing, and workers' collective bargaining rights also won it many grateful enrollees, its Communist leadership notwithstanding. Party members in leadership positions such as Max Bedacht, Rubin Saltzman and Louise Thompson Patterson saw their 180,000 members as much more than figures on an actuarial table.

The fragility of life in mine and mill helps account for the attraction of the Order, as when a disabled miner from Lansford, Pennsylvania, wrote to the IWO's welfare fund for assistance. Other members were helped finding doctors or even affordable electric blankets. Dozens of IWO members wrote to the organization's national headquarters looking for help even in the "prosperous" early 1950s. By this date, the IWO was under government harassment for alleged "subversive" activities, but rather than part of an international Communist conspiracy, tens of thousands of members saw the Order as a means of assistance in desperate times. Just as Steve Nelson, jailed under the Smith Act as a Communist, said when he was organizing Pennsylvania coal miners in the Depression, few workers cared if he was "red" so long as he was a dependable union ally. So, too, the IWO won the allegiance of members by providing for their needs.[3]

The International Workers Order was born in 1930 out of the CPUSA's Language Department work seeking to sway existing ethnic fraternal societies to adopt the most progressive stance on unemployment, old age pensions, and other deficiencies of capitalism. Prior to the adoption of New Deal legislation such as the Social Security Act, the minimal insurance policy of ethnic fraternal societies such as the Croatian Fraternal Union or Jewish Workmen's Circle were often all that stood between working families and complete destitution. Already in the late 1920s, the Language Department tried to move fraternals to more militant positions advocating government unemployment insurance. Progress, however, was slow, with the South

2. Cornell University, Kheel Center, IWO Collection, Box 46, *Jewish Fraternalist*, November 1948, 3-4, "Department of Justice Evades Justice" by Peter Shipka; Box 31, Folder 11, letter, Gedalia Sandler to Henry Wald of Atlanta, January 31, 1949.

3. Steve Nelson, James Barrett and Rob Ruck, *Steve Nelson, American Radical* (University of Pittsburgh Press, 1981), 65-66, 76-79, 163-165; Cornell, IWO, Box 20, Folder 19, letters, May 8, 1953, Fanny Goldenzweig, IWO Sick Benefit Department, to A. Harvan, secretary, Lodge 2004, Lansford, Pennsylvania, and June 1, 1953, Harvan to Karol Korenič on behalf of Frank Schubak; Box 4, Folder 6, letters, January 11, 1953, Isaac Galperin to IWO and January 26, 1953, Dave Greene to Galperin; Box 4, Folder 5, letter, February 16, 1951, Greene to Stella Fidyk.

Slavic Bureau in 1928 noting out of 70,000 CFU members, only 400 could be reckoned party members. The situation in the Slovenian National Benefit Association was even more discouraging, with 100 party members out of 68,000 members.[4]

In the late 1920s and even into the early Depression, attempts to "bore from within" Italian, Puerto Rican, Hungarian and other societies seem to have yielded little results. A few Polish Workers' Clubs were said to be under party control, Bolesław Gebert, later head of the IWO's Polonia Society, reported. More typical was the Bulgarian comrades' assessment to the Language Department: "We need a good live wire for our secretary," they pleaded.[5]

But in 1930, with the Depression adding thousands more unemployed to the soup lines every month, the party began to turn the fraternal societies into more effective vehicles for providing tangible relief. When thousands of CFU members found themselves out of work, the party's Frank Borich stepped in with a plan to "immediately work out the program for those unemployed members... unable to pay their dues." He noted lodges had done nothing to help unemployed members and called on leftists in the CFU and other fraternals to make motions to "reduc[e] the pay of Bureaucrats and to use this...for the dues of unemployed members."[6]

Gebert, who had been a charter member of the Communist Party in 1919,[7] backed Borich's plan, adding these steps should be taken "to develop the sharp struggle among workers in C.F.U. for the Social Insurance and against the fascists and social-fascists in the

4. Library of Congress, Communist Party USA collection, Reel 109, Delo 1454, Yugoslav Language Bureau Questionnaire (1928); Reel 65, Delo 905, Report of "Mass Work Among the Jugo-Slavs" (no date, 1926); "To the Investigation Committee of the CEC, On the Workers' Progressive Bloc" in the CFU, February 4, 1926.

5. Ibid., Reel 154, Delo 2014, minutes, Language Department meeting, May 9, 1930; Reel 130, Delo 1684, "Questionnaire sent to language fractions – Polish Fraction" and "Questionnaire – Czechoslovak Fraction" (1929.); Reel 109, Delo 1449, "Questionnaire – Hungarian Fraction" (1928.) Reel 129, Delo 1683, letter, November 26, 1929, B. Mitcheff to Language Department, Reel 102, Delo 1342, letter, March 13, 1928, Alfred Wagenknecht to Jay Lovestone.

6. Ibid., Reel 151, Delo 1961, letter, March 15, 1930, F. Borich, South Slavic Fraction, to Central Committee, CP. See, too, Reel 109, Delo 1454, "The Benefit Organizations" section of minutes, plenum, South Slavic Faction, Workers (Communist) Party of America, March 10-11, 1928, 3-9; Reel 162/1, Delo 2161, minutes, South Slavic Bureau meeting, October 1, 1930.

7. WS, Binkowski Box 4, Folder 4-14, Bill Gebert biography, April 15, 1932. Sent by Gebert to Executive Committee, Communist International.

organization." Social insurance was a frequent demand of the IWO and its predecessor ethnic organizations. The program for unemployed members' dues relief was adopted, and the Language Department added all fraternal members should twin this call with a demand for enactment of social insurance and unemployment relief, plus the end of sheriff's evictions. In the second winter of the Depression such campaigns were welcomed by jobless Croatians, Poles, and others.[8]

As established fraternal societies dragged their feet on aiding destitute members, the need for a more militant organization became apparent. In his 1930 report on "The Work of the Communist Fractions in Fraternal Organizations," Marcus Jenks argued although fraternal organizations "are organized for the purpose of mutual aid, sick and death benefit etc.," they often actually

are an aid to the capitalists and government, because in reality they help to divert the struggle of the workers from fighting for social insurance and social laws in general. Who does not know that in this, the land of the billionaires, in America, there is no social insurance for workers, and also less protection of the lives of the workers than in any other capitalistic country in the world. And to a large extent it is due to the fact that there is no struggle going on for the establishment of laws for social insurance for workers, unemployment aid etc.[9]

A different kind of self-insurance society, one that would fight for members in the streets and legislative halls, was born in these party deliberations – the International Workers Order.

Factional fights in the Jewish Workmen's Circle were the proximate cause of the birth of the Order. In 1950, Lucy Davidowitz wrote an unsympathetic "History of the Jewish People's Fraternal Order." The JPFO was the building block of the IWO, which was created, Davidowitz wrote, after leftists within the Circle lost out to a more right-wing Socialist faction.[10] Debates within the Jewish Fraction of

---

8. LC, Reel 162/1, Delo 2161, minutes, South Slavic Bureau meeting, October 1, 1930; Reel 154, Delo 2017, letter, November 3, 1930, secretary, Language Department, to Secretariat, CPUSA.

9. Ibid., Reel 154, Delo 2018, "The Work of the Communist Fractions in Fraternal Organizations," "excerpt from Com. Marcus Jenks' Report to Our Last Party Convention" (1930)

10. New York University, Robert F. Wagner/Tamiment Labor Archives, International Workers Order collection, Folder 8, typescript, "The History

the CP's Actions Committee and the party's Language Department confirm the IWO was created by party members dissatisfied with the pace of its work trying to get the Workmen's Circle to become a more forceful advocate for social insurance and relief.[11] But while Davidowitz, writing at the height of the Cold War, cast the IWO as an organization solely dedicated to furthering a Communist revolution, the minutes of these meetings reveal a more nuanced story. When it was decided to form an independent IWO, founders such as Max Bedacht and Rubin Saltzman were clear it was only by persuading potential members of the Order's benefits that it would grow.

To be sure, in setting out the benefits of joining the IWO, M.J. Olgin explained in a 1931 Yiddish pamphlet "it is already clear that the I.W.O. must look upon the Communist Party as the only labor party in the United States." While members were welcome from all political persuasions – save those who had scabbed on strikes – Olgin and others assured newcomers, "The members of the International Workers Order are not Communists. They are not subject to Communist discipline nor do they belong to Communist nuclei. They do not have to accept every point in the Communist program. They may disagree here and there with a certain action of the Communists." Yet Olgin seems to have gone back and forth on the Communists' centrality to the Order, writing that "The International Workers Order…recognizes the Communist Party as the leading organization of the working-class, the brain, the will, and the fighting force of the working-class."[12]

Of course many IWO officers such as General Secretary Bedacht, JPFO General Secretary Saltzman, Gebert of the IWO's Polish section and Vice President Louise Thompson Patterson were active in the

---

of the Jewish People's Fraternal Order of the International Workers Order," Lucy Davidowitz (November 1950).

11. LC, Reel 87, Delo 1180, minutes of Actions Committee of the Jewish Fraction of the Workers (Communist) Party, January 12, 1927, January 28, 1927, February 2, 1927, February 10, 1927, March 23, 1927; Reel 129, Delo 1674, "The Workmen's Circle Policy and the Renegade Trio" by Moissaye J. Olgin; Reel 129, Delo 1680, minutes of Language Department meeting, October 29, 1929; Reel 129, Delo 1683, letter, September 9, 1929, H.I. Costrell to P. Smith of Language Department; Reel 154, Delo 2014, minutes, Language Department meetings, January 8, 1930, September 18, 1930; Reel 154, Delo 2015, "Minutes of the Meeting Held on the Amalgamation of the Sick Benefit Organizations Held on September 18, 1930;" Reel 154, Delo 2016, "Report of the Language Department C.C. – Unite to fight for full insurance for the entire working class" (September 1930).

12. NYU, Folder 8, "The History of the Jewish People's Fraternal Order."

Communist Party,[13] and there was in many lodges a concerted effort to get members to contribute to collections for causes such as the *Daily Worker*. A policy of endeavoring to lead individual members to endorse the party and its causes, via advocacy and persuasion, not strict control, seems to have been followed. Here the IWO anticipated the Popular Front policy of working in cooperation with as broad a progressive coalition as possible to further economic and civil rights goals.[14]

The politically ecumenical nature of the IWO may have been a necessity. Its founders were determined to reach as broad a membership as possible in order to give it an effective lobbying base on social insurance and other issues. And as the Order grew by amalgamating preexisting ethnic fraternal societies such as the Slovak Workers Society and the Hungarian Workingmen's Sick Benefit and Education Association, IWO proponents were instructed to answer honestly any reservations members of those societies had about the Order. In letters in Hungarian and Slovak newspapers, as well as speaking tours to ethnic lodges, Saltzman, Emil Gardos, and other IWO proponents explained how a larger, pan-ethnic, interracial IWO would be in a better position to provide for members. Members would be won over for a larger IWO, however, not through guile, but only when facts and logic were used to explain the benefits of an amalgamated Order. "Faith in the masses, give leadership to the masses," Gardos lectured Earl Browder on his method of selling the IWO to potential Hungarian recruits. "But you got to do it, by working with them, guiding them, having patience with them, yes putting in a lot of time into every individual comrade or worker..." In 1932, Gardos' patience was rewarded, as the Hungarians voted to amalgamate with the IWO; in 1935 Slovak and Polish fraternals followed suit. Eventually 15 language sections, as well as an African American Douglass-Lincoln Society and a Spanish language Cervantes Society affiliated with the IWO. English-language lodges

---

13. Cornell, IWO, Box 5, Folder 1, letter, September 18, 1933, inviting recipient to a "Vote Communist Banquet," New York, lists Bedacht and Saltzman on the New York State Committee of the Communist Party. WS, Binkowski, Box 4, Folder 4-14, Gebert biography, April 15, 1932.

14. Cornell University, Kheel Center, IWO supplemental collection, Box 4, Box 4, "Digest of Testimony of Witnesses for the State in the I.W.O. Matter. January 29, 1951, to March 7, 1951," 100, testimony of Charles Baxter, 110, testimony of Simon Weber.

enrolled second-generation workers, but white-ethnic immigrant groups conducted meetings in their own languages.[15]

But in a move unusual for the Jim Crow 1930s and 1940s, interracial organizing allowed Black and white members to meet in English-language lodges when they desired. Cape Verdeans established New England lodges, while Black Muslims in New Haven and other locales also retained lodge autonomy. In the Detroit area, too, Arabic lodges were organized, while on the West Coast Asian and Mexican members worked side by side with Euro Americans.[16]

---

15. LC, Reel 214, Delo 2752, letter, June 29, 1932, Emil Gardos of Cleveland to Earl Browder. WS, Binkowski, Box 4, Folder 4-29, OSS/FNB report – FNB to the Director of Strategic Services. "Communist-Line IWO Reorganizes to Emphasize Nationality," July 11, 1944; Box 4, Folder 4-42, Part of FBI report on *Głos Ludowy*, May 17, 1941, 6. Reel 247, Delo 3175, letter, March 30, 1933, Emil Gardos of the Hungarian Bureau, Cleveland, to the General Fraction of the IWO. Reel 129, Delo 1681, "Four Months Program of Work – Language Department – Building and Organizing the Communist Fractions in the Language Mass Organizations" includes a section, "I.W.O." (No date, 1929.); Reel 154, Delo 2016, Report on the Language Papers of the Party, October 3, 1930; Reel 177, Delo 2334, Language Department report, January 6, 1931. "The Building of the Working Class Mutual Aid Organizations – A Plan for Immediate Action;" Reel 177, Delo 2334, Report from the Language Department on the Hungarian Workers Sick Benefit and Educational Federation and other fraternal societies the IWO (1931); Reel 177, Delo 2334, Report, April 15, 1931, by the Language Department, "Present Status of the IWO." See Cornell, IWO, Box 48, for multilingual editions of the *Fraternal Outlook* from 1939-1943. LC, Reel 177, Delo 2334, Language Department report, January 6, 1931, "The Building of the Working Class Mutual Aid Organizations – A Plan for Immediate Action;" Reel 155, Delo 2021, letter, November 12, 1930, H. Beck, Los Angeles, to Louis Kovess, Language Department; Cornell, IWO, Box 48, contains issues of the IWO's magazine, the *Fraternal Outlook*, November 1939 and December 1939, for example, that printed articles in English but also Carpatho-Russian, Croatian, Italian, Magyar (Hungarian), Romanian, Polish, Russian, Slovak, Spanish, Ukrainian, and Yiddish. By 1944, the *Fraternal Outlook* was published only in English.

16. LC, Reel 177, Delo 2334, report, April 15, 1931, by the Language Department. "Present Status of the IWO;" Reel 298, Delo 3002, letters, August 27, 1935, September 8, 1935, October 4, 1935, Alexander Wright, on organizing African American small businessmen, as well as Jewish members, in English-speaking branches in Norfolk and Portsmouth, Virginia. See, too, Reel 309, Delo 4110, reports on questionnaires from ethnic groups to Organization Department, including Japanese and Chinese efforts to build IWO lodges. Cornell, IWO, Box 4, Folder 5, Outline for Dave Greene JPFO speech, Brooklyn, June 19, 1950, notes the IWO's growth to 160,000 members came about because of growth in African American, Spanish, as

As early as 1938, too, more than 1,300 Spanish-language members enrolled in lodges not just in New York and Los Angeles, but also in smaller industrial places such as Mount Carmel, Pennsylvania, Lorain, Ohio, and Holden, West Virginia.[17] In an era when segregated lodges and insurance price gouging for minorities was the rule, the IWO was one of the few fraternal organizations that could honestly boast, "No Jim Crow in the IWO!"[18]

---

well as European ethnic lodges; Box 7, Folder 3, letter, February 7, 1945, Eleanor Broady of Detroit, Michigan State Committee, IWO, to Louise Thompson Patterson details recruitment of African Americans into the IWO; Box 9, Folder 8, report, "The Hispanic American Section from January 1940 to January 1944" (at 1944 IWO convention), 4-5. Box 48, *Fraternal Outlook*, October 1940, adds a Spanish section to the articles printed in various European languages. Cornell, IWO, Box 5, Folder 5, includes a report, "Notes on the Portuguese and Cape Verdeans" (no date); LC, Reel 246, Delo 3150, letter, December 19, 1933, Organizing Committee, C.C., to Jose Novo of New Bedford, Massachusetts. Reel 214, Delo 2753, letter, March 30, 1932, N. Economos of Chicago to Greek Bureau of Central Executive Committee, CP, notes building of IWO lodges in Illinois, Indiana, and Wisconsin. Cornell, IWO, Box 6, Folder 8, letter, April 6, 1945, Frank Gevize of Detroit to I.W.O. National Office; letter, April 23, 1945, Sam Milgrom to Gevize. WS, Binkowski, Box 16, Folder 16-36, FBI file, December 10, 1945, IWO Detroit section, page 16, "Arabic Section. For Cuban IWO members in Tampa, see LC, Reel 233, Delo 3017, letter, September 15, 1932, Homer Barton of the Florida Organization of the Young Communist League to the National Election Campaign Committee. For Cubans in Ybor City, Tampa, see Gary Mormino and George Pozzetta, The Immigrant World of *Ybor City: Italians and Their Latin Neighbors in Tampa, 1885-1985* (Urbana: University of Illinois Press, 1987); Ferdie Pacheco, *Ybor City Chronicles: A Memoir* (Gainesville: University Press of Florida, 1994.) Cornell, IWO, Box 8, Folder 2, letters, February 2, 1945, Harold Peters to Metropolitan Life Insurance Co.; February 12, 1945, Peters to IWO; February 19, 1945, Sam Milgrom to Peters; February 22, 1945, Peters to Milgrom; March 22, 1945, Peters to Milgrom; March 31, 1945, Milgrom to Peters; April 3, 1945, Peters to Milgrom; April 6, 1945, Milgrom to Peters; May 15, 1945, Peters to Dave Greene; October 5, 1945, Sol Vail to Milgrom. Cornell, IWO supplemental, Box 4, affidavit of Jumal Ahmad, Cleveland, April 1951.

17. Hunter College, Institute for Puerto Rican Studies, Jesús Colón Papers, Box 18, Folder 5, membership rolls, IWO Spanish Section, 1937 and first three months, 1938.

18. Cornell, IWO, Box 5, Folder 7, pamphlet, "Our Plan for Plenty" (no date, circa 1941); WS, Binkowski, Box 2, Folder 2-55, The *Sunday Worker*, Sunday, September 4, 1949, 7, ad, "Greetings to Labor by the IWO." Box 26, Folder 5, in synopses of SWS material from the FBI, Slovak-language copy of "Our Plan for Plenty;" Box 19, Folder 10, a resolution passed on "Negro

The booklet "Guiding Policy for the Communists in their Leadership and Work in the International Workers Order" reminded party members the Order was open to workers of all races – in the 1930s atypical for insurance fraternals – but also urged them to take their healthcare and benefits provision duties seriously.[19] Thus it was recognized the delivery of insurance, pensions, health care, and other benefits was the best way for Communists to be successful. By providing a needed service to victims of industrial America, it was perhaps no wonder the IWO attracted thousands. The leaders of the Order were indeed Communists who aspired to persuade other workers of the justness of their cause, but this was not some cabal. It was an organization serving its membership when employers and the private insurance market were lacking.

The Order publicized "low-cost insurance" offering "one low rate for all occupations (coal miner and shoe clerk pay same premium)," desirable in an era when many private insurers barred workers in noxious industries and most minorities from policies. The IWO's promise of "No Jim Crow" was a welcome, unusual practice.[20] An organizer in western Pennsylvania also explained to meetings of Slovak, Croatian and Carpatho-Russian members in Pittsburgh and Duquesne, Pennsylvania, that the IWO provided "the same protection at a lower cost" than commercial insurance policies.[21]

The severity of the Depression, combined with the tangible benefits the Order offered as it fought for workers' causes, led to a rapid expansion of the society. As the Federal Bureau of Investigation later noted, "a group photograph which appeared in the *Daily Worker* of November 20, 1936" was captioned "Like Jack's Beanstalk," and detailed the growth of the IWO under leaders such as Thompson Patterson, who recruited African American and white members into the IWO's English Section.[22]

Work in the IWO" at a conference of the IWO, April 8, 1941, stressed the relevance of the "Plan for Plenty" to African Americans. Box 4, Folder 5, outline for Dave Greene JPFO speech, Brooklyn, June 19, 1950, refers to dissemination of the Plan among JPFO lodges.

19. Ibid., Box 19, Folder 6, "Guiding Policy for the Communists in their Leadership and Work in the International Workers Order" (no date, but 1930s).

20. Ibid., Box 5, Folder 7, pamphlet, "Our Plan for Plenty."

21. Ibid., Box 8, Folder 12, letter, March 9, 1949, Mike Hanusiak to Sam Milgrom.

22. File Eleven, 21, FBI report, Louise Thompson Patterson, Supplementary Correlation Summary, July 19, 1955.

The IWO would also grow to include many non-ideological members and had officials from the country's mainstream political parties, such as its vice presidents Vito Marcantonio and Stanley Nowak. Marcantonio, who was the leader of the Order's Italian section (Garibaldi Society), was first elected as a Republican, albeit progressive, congressman from East Harlem, and Democrat Stanley Nowak represented a Detroit district in the Michigan state senate. While both Marcantonio and Nowak were accused of "un-American," leftwing activity during the course of their careers, neither was a Communist. The same could be said of many thousands of less prominent IWO members.[23]

During the Depression, a workers' insurance society pooling resources to bar the wolf from members' doors quickly grew. At a Communist-organized rally for Philadelphia's unemployed, "white and Negro workers" were reminded eight million were jobless and those working were still vulnerable. "Wage cuts in factory after factory! Speed-up undermining the health and life of the workers! Evictions for non-payment of rent taking place daily! And still the conditions grow worse!" The IWO offered practical relief but also a broader vision of something better than Herbert Hoover's neo-Dickensian free market nostrums.[24]

Low-cost medical care and insurance attracted many members. The FBI and Office of Strategic Services admitted the IWO provided superior, low-cost benefits to members. The FBI noted, the IWO began a 1941 membership drive promising "it protects the worker as an individual. It gives him funeral-insurance, sick-benefit, and medical care, all at a low cost." In recruiting Hungarians, Gardos highlighted the Order's provision of free medical and hospital care for needy members. Larger cities maintained IWO medical clinics, the only care many members could afford. New York's leader acknowledged most members joined because of "the general appeal we make, namely the benefits we offer to the workers in this country." These benefits, he noted, were "better and more attractive than most fraternal organizations." The New York Medical Department,

    23. Gerald Meyer, *Vito Marcantonio: Radical Politician, 1902-1954* (State University of New York Press, 1989); Annette Rubinstein, ed., *I Vote My Conscience: Debates, Speeches, and Writings of Vito Marcantonio* (New York: Calandra Institute, 2002, 1956); Margaret Collingwood Nowak, *Two Who Were There: A Biography of Stanley Nowak* (Wayne State University Press, 1989.)

    24. LC, Reel 165, Delo 2206, flyer, demonstration, "Organize Against Attacks on Foreign-Born Workers," Hungarian Hall, Philadelphia, November 2, 1930.

with its Specialists Department, Dental Department, day nursery, and arrangement with pharmacies for low-cost drugs, were also "well-paying source[s] of revenue for the City Central Committee," a boon, for while Communists, Order leaders still had to pay the bills.[25]

By 1937 the New York IWO's Medical Department was "operating a Birth Control Center in the interests of the membership of IWO and all of their friends." It was considered "one of the finest and best equipped in the City of New York." A veteran of the Margaret Sanger Clinic ran the Order's center, which stayed open evenings "to accommodate the working woman who is in no position to come to the Center during working hours." New York City's Education Committee conducted, with Spanish-speaking lodges, a health survey of Harlem and lobbied for the opening of "additional health facilities;" other cities operated IWO medical clinics, too, including birth-control facilities. While birth control information was into the 1950s criminalized as "pornography," the IWO aided working women.[26]

---

25. WS, Binkowski, Box 4, Folder 4-29, OSS/FNB report, FNB to Director of Strategic Services. "Communist-Line IWO Reorganizes to Emphasize Nationality," July 11, 1944; Box 4, Folder 4-42, Part of FBI report on *Głos Ludowy*, May 17, 1941, 6. LC, Reel 247, Delo 3175, letter, March 30, 1933, Emil Gardos of Hungarian Bureau, Cleveland, to General Fraction of IWO. Reel 294, Delo 3811, minutes of meeting, District 2 Bureau (New York), CPUSA, September 4, 1935, includes report on IWO by N. Shaffer to District 2 Bureau meeting. The Philadelphia IWO also maintained a Medical Department. New York Public Library, Vito Marcantonio Papers, Box 47, telegram, May 3, 1940, Max Bedacht to Marcantonio; LC, Reel 318, Delo 4243, *Daily Worker*, May 17, 1940, 5, "Court Allows I.W.O. to Inspect Seized Files." NYPL, Marcantonio, Marcantonio's "Copy of following telegram sent to Martin Dies, Chairman, Investigating Un-American Activities," from Bedacht (May 1940), Cornell, IWO supplemental, Box 3, affidavit, George Gombasy, Detroit, April 23, 1951.

26. Cornell University, Kheel Center, Zimmerman collection of the ILGWU, Mss. 5780/014, Box 17, Folder 4, letter, August 27, 1937, N. Shaffer to Charles (Sasha) Zimmerman; NYPL, Marcantonio, Box 44, letter, October 18, 1940, New York City Central Committee, International Workers Order, M. Horwitz, Educational Director, to Marcantonio, notes the Birth Control Center. LC, Reel 294, Delo 3811, minutes of meeting, District 2 Bureau (New York), CPUSA, September 4, 1935, includes report on IWO by N. Shaffer to District 2 Bureau meeting. The Philadelphia IWO also maintained a Medical Department. NYPL, Marcantonio, Box 47, telegram, May 3, 1940, from Bedacht to Marcantonio; LC, Reel 318, Delo 4243, *Daily Worker*, May 17, 1940, 5, "Court Allows I.W.O. to Inspect Seized Files." NYPL, Marcantonio, Marcantonio's "Copy of following telegram sent to Martin Dies, Chairman, Investigating Un-American Activities," from Bedacht (May 1940.) Cornell,

Even as the IWO later faced liquidation at the hands of red bait-ers, members from across the country expressed their gratitude for the vital medical care and financial support the Order provided in time of need. Members pooled resources to obtain affordable dental, medical and optometrist services, services gratefully acknowledged by members from Los Angeles to Boston. In deposing in defense of the Order, Emil Betley in 1951 said his Carpatho-Russian lodge "fur-nish[es] far more than insurance, we visit the sick in truly fraternal sprit."[27]

Italian members in Shickshinny, Pennsylvania, declared "the workers are entitled to better conditions, as for instance, better Social Security, medical help, hospitalization, and many other things." In 1950, the leader of the Italians' Garibaldi Society reminded his mem-bers, "We favor an extensive medical plan for the people. Is this a crime?" In smaller towns members gratefully knew the IWO often offered scarce, reliable medical care.[28]

The IWO's provision of medical care and low-cost insurance free of racial discrimination was praiseworthy policy during the 1930s and 1940s. But true to its initial pledge, the IWO didn't stop there; it militantly lobbied to force the government to provide humane unemployment and old-age provisions and campaigned for systemic improvements in the country's social programs. A 1932 memorandum on "The Activities of the I.W.O." pledged "to mobi-lize and organize its membership for the fight for social insurance."

IWO supplemental, Box 3, affidavit, George Gombasy, Detroit, April 23, 1951; NYPL, Marcantonio, Box 47, letter, August 9, 1940, Max Hurwitz of New York City Education Department, IWO, to Marcantonio. For Marga-ret Sanger and the criminalization of birth-control information, see Andrea Tone, "Contraceptive Consumers: Gender and Political Economy of Birth Control in the 1930s," *Journal of Social History* 29, no. 3 (Spring 1996): 485-506.

27. Cornell, IWO supplemental, Box 3, affidavits, Lewis Marks of Rox-bury, Boston, April 21, 1951; Emil Betley of New York, April 1951; Max Lange and John Uhrin of Los Angeles, April 24, 1951; Peter Gal of New York, April 24, 1951; Johanna Tykyra and John Shery of Cleveland, April 23, 1951. For appreciation of medical and insurance benefits of the IWO, see, too, Box 3, affidavits of Abraham Kaplan of Roxbury, Boston, April 24, 1951, and Lazarus Jacovides of Boston, April 20, 1951.

28. Cornell, IWO, Box 4, Folder 7, letter, August 27, 1953, Vuko Draskov-ich, Alton, Illinois, to IWO; letter, August 31, 1953, Draskovich to IWO; letter, September 9, 1953, Dave Greene, General Director of Organization, IWO, to Draskovich. Box 25, Folder 5, letter, July 20, 1949, Luigi Ciarafoni, Shickshinny, Pennsylvania, to Vito Magli; letter, July 22, 1949, C. Lippa to Ciarafoni; Box 10, Folder 10, letter, April 26, 1950, Lippa to "Dear Member."

While the Order was committed to instilling in members the need for government unemployment insurance and old-age pensions, the memorandum stressed, members must be convinced of the logic and necessity of these policies; no ideological browbeating was permitted, as such a policy was seen as counterproductive.[29]

The Order's Spanish (Cervantes) Section in 1940 recounted its success in fighting for enactment of Social Security, the Wagner Act, and other social programs, as well as in combating racial discrimination, but warned creeping conservatism and ballooning military budgets imperiled these gains. "You all know the struggles we have had endeavoring for a bigger health program, better housing, schools, relief and work with union wages," the Spanish Section's leader reported. "You all know our fight against race discrimination and for the recognition of our civil rights. We have fought against the anti-alien bills recently introduced in Congress and have supported union workers in their struggle for decent wages. All these efforts have helped in the introduction of new laws for the betterment and economic problems of the people of the United States..."

But already by 1940, the Order's officials warned reactionary forces were rolling back some of these gains:

At the present time all the social and economic advantages that we have obtained by means of our struggles, are in danger of being nullified by the present administration...and the reactionary forces known as 'The American Economic Royalists.' Today these forces are asking billions of dollars for armaments while nearly 200,000 [Works Progress Administration] workers have been dismissed. Millions are assigned for airplanes while better housing programs are slashed; millions are assigned for militarization of our young people...while our educational program is slashed. While $350,000 is spent in the construction of a warfare apparatus to murder people, they cannot provide $50,000 for the construction of a maternity clinic in 111th Street, New York City. All this is happening in the United States at the present time.[30]

Warnings of the fragility of social gains seem prescient in our own deregulatory times.

---

29. LC, Reel 234, Delo 3037, memorandum, "The Activities of the I.W.O." (1932.)

30. Colón, Box 18, Folder 7, "Report" (in English) on the Educational Work of the Spanish Section (1940.)

194   FAITH IN THE MASSES

An IWO pamphlet, "Why Not Social Insurance?" made the case for government relief by emphasizing the free market's shortcomings. "The worker has only wages as a source of livelihood. When disabled because of sickness, accident, childbirth, old age, etc,... [h]e and his dependents face privation. This privation is caused by the method of operation of present-day society. It is therefore the duty of society to relieve it." While committed to mutual aid, the IWO's author labeled "the problem of economic insecurity...much too big to permit a complete solution by mutual aid." Only the government had the means to redress the miseries of capitalism, the writer argued; moreover, he emphasized "Society must approach this problem not as one of charity, but as a duty of the government toward the working masses." At a time of 25 percent official unemployment in cities such as Detroit, the IWO drive for social insurance, Communist or not, drew many supporters.[31]

The author of "Why Not Social Insurance?," however, also rejected the demeaning terms on which minimal relief was granted. "It is a disgrace that an unemployed, destitute worker is treated as a miserable beggar," he declared.

He is adjudged a pauper. When he asks for relief, his antecedents are investigated, his morals are gone into, his religious beliefs are inquired into, his politics are checked up. A worker who for many years of his life has done useful work, has built houses, constructed railways, made the things society needs to live, is investigated just because he committed the 'crime' of being unable either to find or to fill a job. In very many cases he is investigated by a useless parasite who never in his life did any useful work and who holds a political sinecure.

Instead, the writer said the unemployed "are entitled to maintenance by society on the same level on which they did maintain themselves while working," coming close to calling for a guaranteed annual income. This IWO pamphleteer concluded taxing the profits of the wealthy and corporations, and reducing war spending, could lead to adequate relief for the jobless – without the shaming ritual that

---

31. LC, Reel 234, Delo 3037, IWO Flyer, "Why Not Social Insurance?" (1932.) Irving Bernstein, *The Lean Years: A History of the American Worker, 1920-1933* (Penguin Books, 1966), 254-259 316-317; Karen, Miller, *Managing Inequality: Northern Racial Liberalism in Interwar Detroit* (New York University Press, 2015), 124-125, 157-161.

Michael Katz and Piven and Cloward have written often has undergirded America's "welfare" system.[32]

Louis Kovess, secretary of the Communist Party's Language Department, wrote an editorial urging workers to join the Order, and spelled out the need for unemployment insurance:

There is the greatest number of workers unemployed (at present over 8 million) a large number of them permanently thrown out of industry...As a result of capitalist rationalization, terrific speed up, the 'human machinery' breaks down sooner and more often, than in the other capitalist countries. But there is no state insurance for sickness. About ¼ million workers are victims of industrial accidents yearly and in the average 22,000 of them die as a result of the accidents. But even in those states, where there is workmen's compensation law, it is very far from being satisfactory...[It]...is a promise of 'You'll get pie in the sky when you die.'[33]

Workers facing a 21st-century "gig" economy and automation might appreciate the IWO's call for a sustainable guaranteed income.

Similarly, the Slovak section in February 1934 planned a "United Front conference in New York for unemployed and social insurance." An earlier Slovak conference on social security was urged to "bring forward the necessity of the struggle for bread, for immediate relief and unemployment insurance. The participation of the Slovak workers in the local struggles is the only way to effectively fight against starvation, against wage cuts, against the collapse of the mutual organizations." Similar social insurance conferences were conducted by Croatian comrades, while by 1935 Cleveland organizers reported

---

32. Ibid., Reel 234, Delo 3037, IWO Flyer, "Why Not Social Insurance?" (1932.) On 1970s proposals for a guaranteed annual income, see Brian Steensland, *The Failed Welfare Revolution: America's Struggle Over Guaranteed Income Policy* (Princeton University Press, 2008.) Michael Katz, *In the Shadow of the Poorhouse: A Social History of Welfare in America* (Basic Books, 1996); Katz, *Improving Poor People: The Welfare State, the 'Underclass,' and Urban Schools as History* (Princeton University Press, 1995); Frances Fox Piven and Richard Cloward, *Poor People's Movements: Why They Succeed, How They Fail* (Vintage Books, 1979); Piven and Cloward, *Regulating the Poor: The Functions of Public Welfare* (Vintage Books, 1993.)

33. LC, Reel 177, Delo 2334, editorial, "Amalgamation of the Workers' Sick Benefit Organizations" (no date, 1931?) by Louis Kovess.

a "broad united front" among Bohemians, Lithuanians, Italians, Hungarians, and Ukrainians agitating "for insurance."[34]

Following enactment of minimum-wage, Social Security, and other federal measures, the IWO was not modest in taking credit for its lobbying pressure on the government and reminded members of its heroic role in the fight for a humane economy. Dave Greene noted in a Brooklyn speech celebrating the IWO's 20th anniversary, their "struggle for unemployment insurance and social security in the early '30s – now the law of the land."[35] Slovak Workers Society President Helen Vrábel likewise reminded members of the struggles they had engaged in to ensure enactment of the Wagner and Social Security acts even as the SWS continue to call for universal health care.[36] Even a witness for the prosecution in the New York state case against the IWO, former Communist George Powers, noted that around 1941, the Order's chief activities "included campaigns for relief of the unemployed and for unemployed insurance."[37]

Not every campaign ended in harmony. A 1932 Hunger March on Washington, like a similar event at the Ford plant in Dearborn, Michigan, was violently suppressed by the police. But the March was doubly a fiasco; an IWO organizer asked sympathizers in Jacksonville, Florida, to contribute in aid, and then urged them to donate a truck to get marchers to Washington. Comrades managed to pool $46 to rent a truck. A few weeks later, a letter came from the capital saying the truck had been abandoned by the IWO marchers, who declared "the truck will remain in Washington until hell freezes over, that it was a lousy truck anyway, that the gear case was

34. Ibid., Reel 273, Delo 3502, minutes, Czechoslovak Bureau meeting, February 23, 1934. See, too, Reel 213, Delo 2747, letter, September 2, 1932, Language Department to Czechoslovak Bureau; Reel 213, Delo 2749, letter, April 25, 1932, Language Department to Chicago South Slavs; Reel 213, Delo 2749, letter, April 27, 1932, Language Department to Chicago South Slavs; Reel 154, Delo 2016, "Report of the Language Department C.C." (September 1930); Reel 155, Delo 2021, letter, December 26, 1930, S.M. Loyen, Chicago, South Slavic Fraction, to Louis Kovess; Reel 295, Delo 3837, "Status of our Campaign for Unemployment Insurance" – "to give new life to our language movement" in Cleveland – part of Unemployment Council report (1935.)

35. Cornell IWO, Box 4, Folder 5, outline for speech by Dave Greene of the JPFO, Brooklyn, June 19, 1950.

36. NYU, IWO, Folder 12, minutes of General Council Meeting, September 15-16, 1945, Helen Vrábel, Slovak Workers Society report, 7.

37. Cornell IWO supplemental, Box 4, testimony digest, trial, January 29, 1951, testimony, George Powers, 27. LC, Reel 307, Delo 4091, "Notes on the Work of the CPUSA Among the National Groups," April 3, 1941.

wrecked…" An irate Jacksonville man named Berenhaut wrote the IWO's national office seeking restitution, exclaiming, "I wouldn't expect such a dirty deal even from Al Capone's men." He added, "I am long enough in the movement to swallow such slaps in my face but the young movement here in Jacksonville will not outlast this affair if it is not settled…We are willing to be used but not abused."[38]

The IWO's Bedacht lectured the Hunger March's truck-nappers, saying "such irresponsible behavior" had to end. "Some comrades seem to think that the taking serious of obligations we undertake is an anti-revolutionary bourgeois quality that a good revolutionary must get rid of," he wrote. "What this leads to can be seen here… When we started out, we had five friends, when we got through we have five embittered and antagonized former friends."[39]

If property was theft, such cavalier actions did nothing to build the movement. Still, the story of the threadbare truck suggests conservatives' fears of a tightly disciplined leftwing conspiracy were greatly exaggerated, in the 1930s and by historians examining the CP thereafter. The IWO, and other militant leftwing organizations, were often strapped for cash. In 1935, Sidney Bloomfield of Boston similarly harangued comrades for not paying their debts to his party district. "How do you comrades think we can pay for all this," he asked. "[D]o you actually believe the fairy stories of the Hearst press that we get a shipload of gold from Moscow every Saturday afternoon."[40] Such squabbles suggest anti-Communists mischaracterized a sometimes disorganized, often underfunded left as "a conspiracy so immense."[41]

Members also participated in anti-eviction campaigns, barring sheriff's deputies from throwing poor people out of their apartments. President Vrábel was proud of the SWS's anti-eviction campaigns, but other women participated in such demonstrations in aid of poor neighbors, even if this later branded them "criminal subversives." In 1951, Russian immigrant and IWO member Clara Dainoff faced deportation over her 1933 disorderly-person arrest stemming from "a mass arrest of persons watching an eviction." Fortunately, Dainoff

38. LC, Reel 234, Delo 3037, excerpt from letter, Comrade Berenhaut, Jacksonville, Florida, to IWO (no date, 1932.)

39. Ibid., Reel 234, Delo 3037, letter, December 24, 1932, Max Bedacht to Israel Amter, National Committee on Unemployed.

40. Ibid. Reel 294, Delo 3826, letter, August 20, 1935, Sidney Bloomfield, District Organizer of Boston, to "Dear Comrades."

41. David Oshinsky, *A Conspiracy So Immense: The World of Joe McCarthy* (Oxford University Press, 2005.)

was allowed to remain in the U.S., where she may have remained unrepentant for her actions on behalf of the "wretched refuse." [42] In any event, the IWO continued championing the cause of those facing eviction throughout its existence.[43]

During the Depression, some of these evictions hit uncomfortably close to home. In 1931, the Czecho-Slovak Workers' Savings and Loan Society, "Svepomoc," went bankrupt. Svepomoc, which was headquartered in the Slovak Workers' House owned by the SWS then in the process of amalgamating with the IWO, proposed a rescue "by taking out a second mortgage on the Workers' House." Other radical Slovaks, however, wanted to know why they should bail out the "Pussy-Foot Marxians" of Svepomoc, as party members had played no role in the "financial speculations of the Society." The collapse, "the Consequences of the Financial Orgies of American Capitalism," confirmed the party's predictions on the folly of relying on savings societies as a solution to workers' misery under capitalism. In turning down Svepomoc's request for help, they added "a probable undesirable effect upon some old lady, who may lose some money there" was a small price to pay for exposing the bankruptcy of capitalism. While a bit heartless, the SWS was itself desperately cash strapped.[44]

Even after Franklin Roosevelt's New Deal began offering some help to the destitute, the IWO kept up the pressure when relief measures were inadequate. The SWS's newspaper, *Denník Rovnost' ľudu*, condemned segregation within National Recovery Administration jobs. "N.R.A. does nothing for blacks," the paper declared, while also condemning lily-white union apprenticeship programs.[45] Earl

---

42. Cornell IWO, Box 2, Folder 2, "proceedings of the fourth national convention, IWO, April 30, 1938, Pittsburgh" for Thompson's election. Cornell IWO, Box 3, Folder 3, contains report to IWO Youth Conference by Vrábel as head of the Slovak Workers Society, IWO fifth national convention, June 8-14, 1940. Cornell, IWO supplemental, Box 1, Deportations Proceedings, December 11, 1951, In re: Clara Dainoff, or Kraina Dainoff or Rose Draina Dainoff. See, too, Cornell IWO supplemental, Box 1, letter, January 8, 1952, Arthur Kinoy to Thomas R. Jones Esq., Brooklyn.

43. Cornell, IWO, Box 22, Folder 22, letter, October 23, 1949, Jack Schacht, chairman, East Side Tenants Council, to "Shop Chairman, Office Staff, I.W.O."

44. LC, Reel 191, Delo 2533, Czecho-Slovak Obrana & Savings & Loan Society – "Sve Pomoc" (1931), "A Request for Immediate Action & Ruling on the situation arisen around the Czecho-Slovak *Obrana*."

45. *Denník Rovnost' ľudu*, April 7, 1934, 4.

Browder urged Slovak editors to continue hammering at the NRA, suggesting they run a *"Daily Worker* cartoon Evolution Eagle."[46] The Blue Eagle decal, symbol of the NRA, was pasted in factory windows proclaiming "We Do Our Part."[47] For radicals, the Blue Eagle offered "Very thin stew," as a cartoon in the *Delco Worker*, a Communist shop paper in Dayton, Ohio, termed it. A worker facing meager NRA pay warns Roosevelt's favorite bird, "Tomorrow I may have to make eagle soup. [48] Black tobacco workers similarly mocked the Blue Eagle, telling an investigator, "he ain't never fly no more money to me." Even Diego Rivera painted into his doomed Rockefeller Center mural protesters carrying signs, "We Can't Eat Blue Birds."[49]

The IWO also issued pamphlets exposing the NRA's flaws, highlighting the case of a member killed on an unsafe New Deal job site.[50] On behalf of the IWO's Polish Section, party member Gebert demanded inclusion of unemployment insurance in codes of industry fair competition established by the National Industrial Recovery Act; the IWO did what they could to make the New Deal more just to millions of forgotten men (and women).[51]

The party's Agitprop Committee, at one time chaired by Bedacht, distributed *NIRA Notes,* a newspaper cataloguing the high cost of living and miserly pay, long hours, speedups, and stretch-outs that the industrial codes still permitted in textile mills. Those who complained about the stretch-out had been fired, the paper alleged. The paper also cited "The *New York World-Telegram*, one of the strongest rooters for the Roosevelt program," which it said "admits editorially

46. LC, Reel 245, Delo 3143, telegram, August 23, 1933, from Earl Browder to *Rovnosť ľudu*.

47. For the CP's take on the National Recovery Administration, see LC, Reel 239, Delo 3097, pamphlet, "What Every Worker Should Know About the N.R.A." (September 3, 1933) by Earl Browder, in which Browder refers to the N.R.A. as, among other things, "the Blue Buzzard."

48. LC, Reel 283, Delo 3650, shop paper, *The Delco Worker*, Issued by the Delco Unit of the Communist Party. Vol. 1, no. 1, May 1934, Dayton, Ohio.

49. Robert Korstad, *Civil Rights Unionism: Tobacco Workers and the Struggle for Democracy in the Mid-Twentieth-Century South* (University of North Carolina Press, 2003), 128. A version of Rivera's mural completed in Mexico City is included in the Whitney Museum exhibit, February 2020.

50. LC, Reel 287, Delo 3709, "Crushed to Death!" (1934 flyer on National Recovery Administration and James Owens, member of IWO Branch 589 – Chicago.)

51. Ibid., Reel 246, Delo 3150, letter, December 20, 1933, Organizing Committee C.C., CP, to John Williamson, Cleveland.

that 'the cotton textile code does not establish Utopia for mill workers. The wages it provides are not enough for decent living.'" The
codes did nothing to end backbreaking speedups and seasonal layoffs. Nor did the codes include unemployment benefits for workers.[52]

Three years later the IWO's Slovak paper denounced racially
exclusionary lending practices of the Home Owners Loan Corporation, exposing denial of mortgages to Black Chicago families.
Redlining and other racially discriminatory practices undergirded
many New Deal programs. Redlining would continue as federal policy for another 30 years, and eventually earned the condemnation of
scholars such as George Lipsitz and Kenneth Jackson. The IWO beat
them to it by several decades.[53]

And yet, as some of the IWO's program was enacted during the
Second New Deal, the IWO began supporting the Roosevelt Administration as the best option to protect workers' gains. Still, the SWS
reminded members it was their own lobbying efforts that had led
to passage of the Social Security Act and urged further pressure to
expand this measure to encompass universal health care.[54] The Popular Front seemed to be yielding material gains.

But the IWO did not rest on its laurels. The Order unveiled its
proposed "Plan for Plenty" with pamphlets featuring a social democratic cornucopia. The Plan said America owed it to its citizens to
ensure everyone had a living wage, access to enjoyable, creative
employment, and universal healthcare. Should workers prove
unable to find gainful employment, the Plan said, the government
must guarantee them an annual income sufficient to live decently.
Generously funded health centers in every corner of America were
part of the Plan. All this went far beyond the meager dole that, even
under the Social Security Act, was dispensed only grudgingly.[55]

A Russian lodge in 1940 enthusiastically endorsed the Plan, as
well as an IWO petition sent to Congress "to make the minimum

---

52. Ibid., Reel 247, Delo 3155, *NIRA Notes*, August 1, 1933.

53. *Ľudový denník*, April 5, 1937, 5. George Lipsitz, *The Possessive Invest-
ment in Whiteness* (Temple University Press, 1998); Kenneth Jackson,
Crabgrass Frontier: The Suburbanization of the United States (Oxford University
Press, 1985.)

54. NYU, IWO, Folder 12, minutes, General Council Meeting, September
15-16, 1945.

55. Cornell, IWO, Box 5, Folder 7, *Our Plan for Plenty* (pamphlet from the
IWO, circa 1941.) See, too, *Promoting Security: Facts About the Role and Purpose
of the International Workers Order* (New York: National Educational Department, International Workers Order, October 1940.)

wage of the American worker $100 a month." "We will see if Mr. Roosevelt will keep his word and take care of the American workers as the American millionaire," a lodge speaker declared. The guaranteed annual wage was necessary, he added, "Because today no one can live on $300 a year like a human!" The IWO prodded the administration to be as progressive as possible.[56]

The "Plan for Plenty" was sold as beneficial to the Order's various ethnic and racial groups. In cooperation with the National Negro Congress, the IWO stressed its work on social welfare and how it benefited African Americans, noting the organization's "struggle for social security; the Plan for Plenty; old-age pensions; health; housing; increased educational facilities; and the fight against discrimination in education."[57] The "Plan" was translated into Slovak, and explained in *Głos Ludowy*, Polish Section newspaper. "The IWO protects the interests of the worker as a member of a great society – the American people," members read. "It stands for the workers' unceasing desire for peace, his battle for proper living conditions, his contributions to progressive culture, his plan for economic rebirth, the 'Plan of Plenty.'"[58]

A Brooklyn lodge of the Spanish Section, headed by Communist activist Jesús Colón, endorsed Congressman Marcantonio's introduction of a bill seeking to make the IWO's "Plan for Plenty" the law of the land. Marcantonio, an IWO vice president, was thanked for his defense of his East Harlem Latino constituents' rights and needs. Brooklynites noted their own efforts to combat malnutrition, unsanitary living conditions, and prostitution in Puerto Rican neighborhoods and were confident the Plan's guaranteed income, full-employment and health-care provisions would improve working-class neighborhoods throughout the nation. "Save our people from humiliation and poverty!" the Puerto Rican IWO lodges cried.[59]

---

56. WS, Binkowski, Box 16, Folder 16-37, FBI report, December 31, 1946, IWO, Detroit division, 253.

57. Cornell, IWO, Box 19, Folder 10, resolution passed on "Negro Work in the IWO" at a conference of the IWO, "National Commission of Negro Work," April 8, 1941.

58. Ibid., Box 26, Folder 5, synopses of Slovak Workers Society material; WS, Binkowski, Box 4, Folder 4-42, FBI report on *Głos Ludowy*, May 17, 1941, 6.

59. Colón, Box 17, Folder 5, flyer, "Socorro Pro-Desempleados en Puerto Rico," Lodges 4480 and 4797, IWO, Brooklyn (1941.)

Even then, budget cutters were lurking, ready to slash spending on human needs. In 1939, Puerto Rican lodges organized an East Harlem demonstration denouncing state educational cuts that closed kindergartens, night schools, and playgrounds. The austeritarians were always in the cross hairs of the IWO, defenders of the people's welfare.[60]

Members were grateful to Marcantonio for his attempts to get the "Plan for Plenty" and its guaranteed annual wage and health clinics enacted. They also appreciated Marcantonio's campaign for a mine-safety bill. Bedacht offered to testify before Marc's committee, noting a recent accident in Bellaire, Ohio, had killed 71 miners, of whom at least eight were IWO members. A lodge from Yukon, Pennsylvania, whose members were directly affected by mine cave-ins, contacted the congressman to thank him for pushing the mine-safety bill, and also urged Marc to continue combating Congressman Martin Dies' vicious House Un-American Activities Committee, which they were sure was designed to strangle union gains. IWO members from Yukon, Harlem and elsewhere linked Marcantonio's good work on behalf of labor with his opposition to HUAC.[61]

Members in industrial America remembered the hardships they faced in demanding adequate wages or a safer work environment and were grateful to the IWO for aiding their cause. From its founding the IWO sent organizers to support union drives throughout America. Thompson Patterson enrolled both Black and white workers in Congress of Industrial Organization unions, one of the few African American women in 1930s America leading such drives.[62] The IWO concentrated on auto, steel, mining, and longshore workers, reporting some success among miners and steel workers in Pennsylvania and West Virginia.[63] In Buffalo, the IWO attracted "steel workers, metal workers, and workers in other basic and important industries of Western New York," and undertook in particular a campaign to organize "Americanized" workers at Bethlehem Steel's Lackawanna

60. Ibid., Box 17, Folder 8, flyer, "! Gran Parada!" June 23, 1939.

61. NYPL, Marcantonio, Box 47, letter, March 21, 1940, Max Bedacht to Congressman Vito Marcantonio; letter, April 25, 1940, Victor Pöverk, Yukon, Pennsylvania, to Marcantonio.

62. Emory University, Louise Thompson Patterson papers, Box 20, Folder 5, Louise Thompson manuscript autobiography, chapter 6, page 25. For Southern union drives by the CP, Robin Kelley, *Hammer and Hoe* (University of North Carolina Press, 2015.)

63. LC, Reel 247, Delo 3175, Hungarian Bureau C.C., December 11, 1933, report on National Fraction Conference.

plant.[64] Other IWO lodges raised funds or sent food and clothes to aid union drives and strikes.[65]

Roger Keeran notes some of the most energetic and successful organizers for the CIO's United Auto Workers were members of the IWO.[66] The same story could be told of unionists in the Steel Workers Organizing Committee. Pittsburgh area IWO conferences were held to get steel workers into the union, and the CIO district president "expressed his appreciation for the support the I.W.O. is giving the steel drive, adding that the I.W.O. has earned the respect of all the workers." Thompson Patterson recruited Black steel workers to serve as SWOC speakers, but later noted Ukrainian men and women aided her work, too. So instrumental was the IWO in the steel drive that Steel Workers president Philip Murray wrote Bedacht thanking him for the Order's "patriotic" efforts, which he praised as essential to the union's success. The IWO published Murray's missals as a pamphlet, "Two Letters about One Cause."[67]

64. Ibid., Reel 294, Delo 3826, letter, July 16, 1935, Communist Party, District 4, Buffalo, New York, to "Dear Comrades."

65. Ibid., Reel 177, Delo 2334, letter, July 8, 1931, Brown, Language Department, "To All Language Bureaus of the C.C.;" Reel 193, Delo 2558, "Statement of Miners Relief of Williamsburg, Section 6. Submitted by Joseph Lapidus" (no date, 1931); Reel 177, Delo 2325, letter, May 15, 1931, Organization Department to Jewish Bureau C.C.; Reel 193, Delo 2558, letter, June 8, 1931, Pittsburgh to "Comrades." Reel 193 Delo 2561, flyer, "Workers of Newark!" for an IWO-sponsored picnic, August 14-15, 1931, to raise funds in support of striking National Miners Union coal miners.

66. Roger Keeran, *The Communist Party and the Auto Workers' Unions* (New York: International Publishers, 1980), Keeran, "National Groups and the Popular Front: The Case of the International Workers Order," *Journal of American Ethnic History*, 14, no. 3 (Spring 1995): 23-51; Keeran, "The International Workers Order and the Origins of the CIO," *Labor History*, 30, no. 3 (Summer 1989): 385-408.

67. NYU, IWO, Folder 43, *The New Order*, September 1936, "I.W.O. in the Steel Drive," Rebecca Grecht. "You May Not Know How Much I.W.O. Has Been Doing ... Read It Here;" WS, Binkowski, Box 4, Folder 4-14, *Daily Worker*, October 23, 1936, 3, "Fraternal Orders Backing Steel Drive to Meet Sunday. Pittsburgh Conference First of Series to Speed Campaign," *Sunday Worker*, November 1, 1936, 6. Emory, Thompson Patterson, Box 27, Folder 1, Thompson Patterson interview (no date, but 1950-51); Box 27, Folder 8, Thompson Patterson interview, June 2 and 9, 1987; Box 28, Folder 2, Thompson Patterson interview, April 20, 1989, interviewed by Margaret Wilkerson. NYU, IWO, Folder 43, "Steel," Philip Murray, *The New Order*, September 1936, 14; letter, Philip Murray, commending the IWO for its support. April 13, 1937; letter, April 20, 1937, Max Bedacht. "Two Letters About One Cause."

Slovaks in the Order read in their newspaper of interracial union meetings held in Chicago's packinghouse district, where Black and white unionists heard speeches in English and Polish. Slovaks also read praise for Pittsburgh Black churches' endorsement of SWOC's drive and Murray's pledge of racial equality in his union. As Murray wrote in praise of the IWO, it really was "helping the entire nation."[68]

Not everyone, however, was all that happy about this. The Detroit Police "Red" Squad scrupulously noted the "subversive" behavior at a December 1939 rally "For Peace and Civil Rights" sponsored by the Michigan State Committee of the IWO. Vice President Louise Thompson spoke, as did Michigan IWO Secretary Joseph Schiffer, who backed Chrysler strikers and pledged the IWO's cooperation. According to the police report, Schiffer also "attacked the strike-breaking methods of the Chrysler Corporation" and the reactionaries "leading the back to work movement." Schiffer denounced the Dies Committee's allegations the auto workers were plotting to sabotage industry, a charge that would be leveled at leftist unions following the war. Schiffer regarded the Dies Committee as "a smoke screen to discredit labor unions." The Michigan IWO passed a resolution supporting the strikers and took up a collection for them.[69]

Following the war, the IWO continued supporting embattled unions in a growing conservative climate. The Order published an ad in the *Sunday Worker* before Labor Day 1949 applauding "the men and women in the factories, mines and mills, who are the source of America's riches." The ad featured a photograph of Philadelphia members preparing donations of canned food for United Electrical Workers strikers. The ad lauded the IWO's work in building CIO unions, and pledged to continue fighting on labor's side "for the repeal of the Taft-Hartley Act and against the reactionary drive aimed at the civil liberties of progressive Americans," as well as "to help end discrimination against Negroes, to abolish segregation and Jim Crow, to achieve the full equality of the Negro people in every

---

68. *Ľudový denník*, February 17, 1937, 5; November 6, 1937, 4; February 11, 1937, 1. NYU, IWO, Folder 43, "Steel," Philip Murray, *The New Order*, September 1936, 14; letter, Murray to IWO, April 13, 1937; letter, April 20, 1937, Max Bedacht.

69. WS, Binkowski, Box 2, Folder 2-55, Detroit Police Department, Office of the Special Investigation Squad, report, December 2, 1939, Michigan State IWO Committee, rally for "Peace and Civil Rights."

sphere of life." As in so many of its campaigns the IWO linked the fight for workers' justice to racial equality.[70]

Canned food drives, though, were only stopgap measures, and throughout its existence the IWO called for government provision of healthcare. In 1938, the IWO pledged to continue working for universal healthcare. "Health insurance is still merely a dream," Bedacht said. "We must make it an imperative demand." The Order committed "to work out a detailed program for a fraternal campaign for public health and for health insurance."[71]

The IWO backed Senator James Murray of Montana, who between 1944 and 1947 introduced several plans to extend Social Security to provide federally funded health insurance. "Medical Care is one of the necessities of life which a democracy should provide to all members of the community," he told the IWO's Jewish section convention. Bedacht's support for the bill was publicized in venues such as *Národné noviny*, newspaper of the National Slovak Society. The SWS passed a resolution supporting the Murray-Dingell health bill.[72]

Bedacht more fully countered opposition to government health insurance in a January 1944 article in the IWO's magazine, *Fraternal Outlook*, refuting canards of "socialized medicine" that still impede the U.S. from enacting equitable health-care provisions. In an argument salient even in 2020, Bedacht pointed out in the alleged free market, millions of Americans were left with no choice if they could not afford private insurance. Instead, the IWO's leader wrote,

---

70. Cornell IWO, Box 46, *"Bombardier,"* Lodge 466 JPFO newsletter, 2014 N. 32nd Street, Philadelphia (Strawberry Mansion,) March 1946; Cornell IWO supplemental, Box 3, affidavits of Bice Diana, Detroit, and Jacob Balan, Highland Park, Michigan, both April 23, 1951; Box 4, Folder 5, Dave Greene JPFO speech, Brooklyn, June 19, 1950; WS, Binkowski, Box 2, Folder 2-55, *Sunday Worker*, Sunday, September 4, 1949, 7, full-page ad, "Greetings to Labor by the IWO."

71. Cornell IWO, Box 2, Folder 2, "Report to the General Executive Board IWO by the General Secretary (Max Bedacht)," September 1938, 14-15; Box 1, Folder 5, minutes of plenary session of General Executive Board of IWO, September 10 & 11, 1938; Box 1, Folder 6, March 1939 plenary, 19-20, 25-26.

72. Ibid., Box 27.1, Folder 2, speech, Senator James Murray of Montana, to sixth annual convention, Jewish American Section, IWO, July 4, 1944, pages 6-7 of convention program; *Národné noviny*, March 8, 1944, 5, "Gives His Views of Wagner Proposals;" Box 54, Slovak Workers Society meeting minutes, February 27, 1944.

extending Social Security to include healthcare would at last "accept government responsibility for the health of the people." [73]

At war's end the IWO produced a pamphlet, "Never Again!" by party member Joseph Starobin demanding "a National Health Insurance Fund to cover every man, woman and child in the United States. Out of this Fund, a man could call up any doctor he wanted…" The pamphlet urged passage of the Wagner-Murray-Dingell Bill to close the country's "medical gap." Starobin noted one of the measure's sponsors, New York Senator Robert Wagner, wondered why Great Britain, Venezuela, Uruguay, "even Canada!" could enact such plans, but not the U.S.[74]

Starobin noted the bill would enable the federal government to lend "$950,000,000 to the various states for the building of hospitals and starting public health services in all parts of the country." Such a policy was necessary, he argued, since already miners in Pennsylvania had gone out on strike, not for higher wages, but to demand access to healthcare. He cited findings in many rural areas a single doctor was available to serve 5,000 patients, a situation invariably causing preventable illnesses and a drain on the economy. Tying support for universal healthcare to the broader social-welfare planks of the "Plan for Plenty," Starobin again cited Wagner: "If we do not achieve full employment, it is all the more imperative that we have a complete and adequate social security program."[75]

Not all strikes were created equal, however. In 1944 the Philadelphia JPFO took out a full-page ad in newspapers condemning the hate strike by city trolley car drivers determined to prevent African Americans from acquiring jobs as motormen. The IWO disseminated flyers in Yiddish and English calling for "Negro and White! Christian and Jew" to oppose the hate strike. The IWO's action opposing this strike was in line with the interracial Order's consistent policy of championing African American civil rights and working to root out all traces of racism in Jim Crow America. Throughout its 24-year existence, anti-racist activism was a strong component of the interracial IWO's "Plan for Plenty."[76] Left-wing white ethnics worked with

73. Ibid., Box 48, *The Fraternal Outlook*, January 1944, "What About Socialized Medicine?," Max Bedacht, 16-17, 28 and 30.

74. Ibid., Box 49, Joseph Starobin, "Never Again!" (pamphlet by IWO, August 1945.)

75. Ibid.

76. Ibid., Box 45, Folder 1, *Philadelphia Daily News*, August 5, 1944, 5, ad, "Philadelphia on Guard;" leaflet, "On Guard! Against Hitler's Attack!;" news release, August 3, 1944, IWO of Philadelphia.

Blacks and Hispanics through the IWO to dismantle Jim Crow, end lynching and the poll tax, and foster racial equality. The IWO's campaigns to smash American apartheid represent the road not taken, the multicultural path to racial equality.[77]

In 1936 Slovaks in the IWO read in their newspaper of the lobbying efforts by a young Ella Baker backing a federal anti-lynching bill. The following year they were urged to join interracial rallies in Harlem and elsewhere to put pressure on Congress to break a Southern filibuster and make these racial torture-murders a federal crime. Although Congress never enacted such a law, the IWO kept up the pressure. Following an especially brutal Florida lynching, the SWS's *Ľudový denník* editorialized, "In Dixie...the big shots ignore the 13th, 14th and 15th Amendments...it's about time that the federal government end this Jim Crow justice." As radical Slavs – marginalized and racialized in the view of many conservative Southerners – readers likely worried, "Today they're lynching black people, but tomorrow they'll be lynching white people."[78]

Following World War II, the IWO continued participating in marches on Washington as part of the pilgrimage to end lynching, which was on the upswing again in the South. The "snakelike" actions of Attorney General Tom Clark, like President Truman a product of the Southern segregationist Democratic Party, were decried as he refused to intervene in a Georgia lynching case. As with local officials who exonerated lynchers, the IWO's Polish paper surmised, "Human corpses don't mean much to him as evidence." The paper publicized the IWO's telegram campaign, which tried in vain to get federal charges brought against the Georgia lynchers. *Głos Ludowy* published a cartoon showing "1,000,000 U.S. Negroes who fought fascism" facing the "KKK Lynchings" and wanted to know, "Have we Really Defeated Fascism?"[79]

The IWO also vigorously lobbied to make the wartime Fair Employment Practices Committee a permanent civil-rights agency ensuring racial equality for all Americans. The Order's Slovaks in 1942 read articles quoting the FEPC's chairman on the necessity of

---

77. For white-ethnic resistance to black equality, see Robert Zecker, *Race and America's Immigrant Press: How the Slovaks Were Taught to Think Like White People* (New York: Continuum, 2011.)

78. *Ľudový denník*, March 6, 1936, 6; February 26, 1937, 6; April 5, 1937, 2; April 17, 1937; July 24, 1937, 2.

79. *Głos Ludowy*, August 3, 1946, 4; August 10, 1946, 1; August 10, 1946, 7; August 10, 1946, 1, second section; September 21, 1946, 4, "Pilgrimage to Capitol to Protest Lynchings."

fair treatment of African Americans, so that the talents of all citizens could be harnessed to speed Allied victory. Near war's end, though, the IWO took up the cause of the FEPC as a matter of justice, not expediency. An IWO delegation including the Slovaks' Charles Musil traveled to Washington to lobby officials. "Stating that the battle for the F.E.P.C. has become the acid test of honest patriotism, a delegation representing the International Workers Order, an interracial fraternal society, was in Washington today to urge that funds be restored to the Committee," Slovaks read.[80]

When Josephine Picolo, a Brooklyn member of the IWO's Garibaldi Society, wrote to segregationist Mississippi Senator Theodore Bilbo urging enactment of a permanent FEPC, he replied in a sneering letter addressed to "Dear Dago." The Garibaldi Society president, Congressman Marcantonio, called for Bilbo's expulsion from the Senate, a campaign joined by Order members throughout the nation. The IWO called for racial equality, while "respectable" politicians like Bilbo warned of the dangers of "race amalgamation."[81]

In such an atmosphere, the IWO kept up a forceful campaign to end racial discrimination. Polish members joined African Americans in celebrating "Negro History Week," and while such occasions offered

---

80. *Ľudový denník*, March 12, 1942, 6; July 13, 1945, 6, "I.W.O. Delegation in Washington for F.E.P.C."

81. NYPL, Marcantonio, Box 46, letters, July 1, 1945, Senator Theodore Bilbo to Josephine Picolo; July 18, 1945, Picolo to Vito Marcantonio; July 21, 1945, Marcantonio to Bilbo; *New York Daily News*, July 24, 1945, "Vito Demands Apology on 'Dago' Note;" letters, July 24, 1945, Bilbo to Marcantonio; July 24, 1945, Marcantonio to Picolo; July 25, 1945, Marcantonio to Bilbo. Cornell, IWO, Box 46, Civil Rights Congress pamphlet, "Oust Bilbo, you Can Do It Now …" (no date, 1945 or 1946); WS, Binkowski, Box 2, Folder 2-15, letter, September 13, 1946, Civil Rights Congress to Bessie Hillman; NYU, IWO, Folder 13, "Report of Max Bedacht, General Secretary, to the General Council Meeting of the International Workers Order, September 7-8, 1946;" Folder 12, minutes of General Council meeting, September 15-16, 1945, 7-8; Cornell, IWO, Box 30, Folder 6, letter, November 12, 1945, National Committee to Combat Anti-Semitism and the JPFO, with petition on Bilbo; Box 30, Folder 7, letter, November 18, 1946, George Starr, JPFO, to "Dear Brothers and Sisters;" NYPL, Marcantonio, Box 48, letter, August 30, 1945, Nathan Shaffer, New York County JPFO, IWO, to Marcantonio; Cornell, IWO, Box 8, Folder 10, letter, December 6, 1945, Sol Rotenberg to Sam Milgrom; WS, Binkowski, Box 16, Folder 16-36, FBI report, December 10, 1945, on the Detroit IWO, 126. *Głos Ludowy*, August 11, 1945, 5; August 18, 1945, 3; September 8, 1945, 4; September 8, 1945, 1, second section; October 6, 1945, 2; October 13, 1945, 1.

festive entertainment, they were twinned with renewed commitment to fight for a federal anti-lynching bill, permanent FEPC, civil-rights law, and an end to HUAC.[82] Sadly, these campaigns remained necessary throughout the IWO's life, as the virulence of racist assaults on African Americans did not abate in midcentury America. Some of the Order's first campaigns had been mass demonstrations in 1931 and for years thereafter to save the Scottsboro Nine, African American youths facing the death penalty on spurious allegations they had raped two white women on a freight train traveling through Alabama.[83] More than 20 years later, the fire-bombing murder of Florida NAACP leader Harry Moore and his wife was denounced as terror, and the IWO, already facing dismemberment as a suspected subversive organization, lobbied Truman to act on the murders, "a shame and blot against America." "The prevalent anti-Negro violence has the earmarks of genocide," the unrepentant IWO added.[84]

The IWO worked to eradicate racism not just in the broader American society, but in its own white ethnic members, too. The SWS's newspaper ran articles debunking the myth "blacks are the lowest race of people," detailing for immigrant readers the advanced development of African and East Asian civilizations at a time when "the Germans were half-savage tribes" and even "the Slavs obviously lived in a savage way." *L'udový denník* a few years later decried race prejudice among Slovaks, refuting a conservative Slovak newspaper's smearing of Blacks by noting the many African American contributions to the war effort. "Prejudice against blacks is just as un-American and undemocratic as Hitler's racism and cannibalism against the Jews," *L'udový denník* averred. While other, more conservative white ethnics worked hard to solidify their part in the white man's republic by shunning African Americans, within the Order members eschewed white privilege.[85]

---

82. *Głos Ludowy*, February 8, 1947, 6, "Tydźień Historji Murzynów;" January 19, 1946, 1, "Fight for Democracy … Negro History Week;" February 9, 1946, 3, IWO ad, IWO, "Prepare to Celebrate Negro History Week."

83. LC, Reel 177, Delo 2332, minutes, Language Department meeting, May 11, 1931; Reel 177, Delo 2336, letters, May 6, 1931, Charles Dliba, Lettish Bureau, to Language Department; May 7, 1931, Czecho Slovakian Bureau to John Mackovich; Reel 195, Delo 2584, *The Spark*, July 1931, 30. For the Scottsboro case, see Dan Carter, *Scottsboro: A Tragedy of the American South* (Baton Rouge: Louisiana State University Press, 2007, originally 1969.)

84. *Głos Ludowy*, January 12, 1952, 1, second section.

85. *L'udový denník*, June 26, 1935, 4; January 3, 1942, 4; June 25, 1942, 2; July 6, 1944, 5. The January 3, 1942, article refers to Hitler's "židožrútstvo" (cannibalism of the Jews.)

Discrimination was also combated closer to urban members' homes. In 1934, the IWO Spanish section of Brooklyn joined in El Frente Unido Contra la Descriminacion to combat anti-Puerto Rican discrimination endemic to New York. The Order demanded equity in relief for all Latinos suffering through the Depression and that welfare agencies act to end the misery of the Hoovervilles plaguing Brooklyn.[86] On its 10th anniversary, Lodge 4840, Luchadores del Porvenir Puertorriqueño, celebrated its work unifying Hispanics across the color line and hailed the IWO for combating racial prejudice.[87]

Segregated recreational facilities were targeted by Blacks and whites in Chicago's IWO lodges when an interracial beach parade and swim-in was held at Jackson Park. The SWS's newspaper proclaimed, "The IWO Stands for Racial Equality!" and urged members to turn out to overturn segregated swimming on Lake Michigan. Blacks had frequently been attacked for venturing too near "whites-only" beaches, the paper noted. Indeed, the city's infamous 1919 "red summer" of race riots began when whites assaulted a Black youth for inadvertently drifting too near the "whites-only" side of the lake. As a result of continuing racism in recreation, the IWO mobilized a parade of trucks decorated with anti-Jim Crow slogans and headed to Jackson Park for an integrated swim-in. This interracial action anticipated by three decades the kinds of demonstrations that finally integrated northern beaches and amusement parks.[88]

More vicious white attacks occurred when African American war workers tried to move into Detroit's Sojourner Truth Housing Project, which white Detroiters perceived as an invasion of "their" neighborhood. The IWO was one of the only organizations to defend the Black would-be residents; while "mainstream" Polish newspapers cheered the white rioters as modern day Paul Reveres defending their racially defined liberty, the IWO denounced a Polish American congressman who supported the segregationists and worked for his defeat at the polls. Segregated public housing in nearby Hamtramck was similarly denounced by the Order. The following year IWO members were instrumental in shutting down a hate strike by white workers who objected to working with newly hired Blacks at the Packard auto plant. And when Detroit erupted in white-initiated

---

86. Colón, Box 16, Folder 14, "Manifesto a la Colonia Hispana en General" (1934.)

87. Ibid., Box 17, Folder 6, program book, 10th anniversary of Lodge 4840, Luchadores del Porvenir Puertorriqueño, Sociedad Fraternal Cervantes IWO, Brooklyn (1950.)

88. *Denník Rovnosť ľudu*, July 27, 1934, 4.

race riots against Blacks, the Polish IWO newspaper, *Głos Ludowy*, was the only city journal unequivocally to call for federal punishment of white rioters.[89]

The rights of Asian and Mexican Americans were defended, too. Only months after Pearl Harbor, *L'udový denník* cautioned, "Color is not the Issue" and "We must guard against falling into the Nazi trap of describing the war in the Pacific as a clash between 'white' America and 'yellow' Japan." When the government established relocation camps for Japanese Americans, IWO members denounced the policy. Ethel Stevens of Oakland, California, addressed a national conference of the IWO on the Japanese Americans in her lodge. Stevens denounced "the persecution the Japanese Americans had been subjected to." Stevens stressed "in the main, these people were loyal, hard-working Americans, and that this persecution was eminently unfair to them."[90] When Mexican youth were falsely arrested on murder charges, Mexican members of the Order attempted to hold a charity boxing match in Los Angeles to raise money for the Sleepy Lagoon Defense Committee. The newspaper of the Hidalgo Lodge, however, noted the management of Olympic Auditorium proved too greedy, so the match wasn't held. The proposed interracial audience for the match likely also alarmed management.[91]

Members of the IWO were instrumental, too, in testing segregation at New York's Stuyvesant Town housing development. A white IWO college teacher who lived there allowed a Black friend to use his apartment, and the managers sought to evict them. The IWO joined in a petition campaign and lawsuit to integrate the development. "The petition to admit Negro families to Stuyvesant Town continues to circulate and when a majority have signed it, the mandate will go to the Mayor, the Board of Estimate, and the Metropolitan Life Insurance Company," the Order's *Fraternal Outlook* reported. "The IWO General Council has wholeheartedly endorsed the fight of the tenants committee." Perhaps overoptimistically, the magazine predicted, "Walls of prejudice in other projects and cities will surely

89. *L'udový denník*, March 3, 1942, 6; *Głos Ludowy*, April 11, 1942, 5; June 13, 1942, 5; July 18, 1942, 6; August 1, 1942, 5; June 12, 1943, 1; June 26, 1943, 1; June 26, 1943, 1 of 2nd section; July 3, 1943, 1; July 3, 1943, 1 of 2nd section. Cornell, IWO, Box 2, Folder 7, "The IWO and its Tasks," report by Max Bedacht, IWO Functionaries Meeting, August 24, 1942.
90. *L'udový denník*, January 22, 1942, 3; Cornell, IWO, Box 9, Folder 1, minutes, National Conference of General Lodges of IWO, July 4, 1944.
91. Colón, Box 19, Folder 6, "Acion Social, Organo Oficial de la Sociedad Beneficia Hidalgo IWO," July 1944.

tremble when the good people of Stuyvesant Town tear down the sign that reads: 'For Whites Only.'"[92] Although *de facto* segregation long continued in the urban North, so, too, the IWO's commitment to racial equality endured.

While the IWO stressed the need to educate workers on interracial solidarity and the justness of the campaigns for social insurance, comrades nevertheless also recognized the need to build esprit de corps through recreational activities. The IWO took its cues from such Communist-affiliated organizations as the National Textile Workers Union, which asserted, "Educational activity must not be of a dry-as-dust manner," and use of movies, theatricals, dances, and sports was urged to enhance the effectiveness of recruiting meetings.[93]

IWO meetings were anything but "dry-as-dust." In discussing the "Plan for Plenty" and the "Nationality Problem," the Cervantes Society proposed the creation of a drama group, saying "The main tasks of such a drama group should be to present the Puerto Rican problems to the North American in the English language, and to interpret the U.S. to the Puerto Rican and other Hispanic American groups by presenting in Spanish translations, the problems and the life and culture of the United States." They also announced the formation of nine baseball teams, male and female softball, and basketball, as well as a cornet band. Cervantes amply provided for the cultural needs of its members, often tying entertainment to social-justice campaigns. In 1948 the Society noted "In Lodge 4834 in the Bronx, a Junior Dramatic Group has been organized. Their first 'play' they are going to stage is 'Snow White and the Seven Union Dwarfs,' for which a translation has been made into the Spanish."[94]

Other ethnic groups likewise offered plays to build amusement and camaraderie. The IWO's musical "Let's Get Together" toured various lodges, harmoniously making the case for racial justice and social democracy. At performances of the play by the Freedom Theatre Players, audience members signed petitions against the Mundt Bill, which proposed punitive measures for those deemed

92. Ibid., Box 19, Folder 14, *Fraternal Outlook*, January 1949, "Stuyvesant Town – For Whites Only," Alex Leith.

93. LC, Reel 114, Delo 1507, "Socials and Entertainments," in minutes, national convention, New York, September 22-23, 1928, National Textile Workers Union.

94. Colón, Box 20, Folder 5, "Plan General Para La:" "La IWO y el Problema Nacional" (1943); Box 19, Folder 9, "Factual Report from July 1947 to March 1948 of the Cervantes Fraternal Society of the International Workers Order," 5.

"subversive." Vera Nickoloff of the Polyanka Group of the American Russian Fraternal Society toured with the troupe, offering folk songs of various ethnic groups as well as "the Negro people."[95] Not all plays were as class-conscious. Slovaks in Garfield, New Jersey, offered the comedy, "Kopaničiarov" ("Hillbilly") at the city's swanky Paradise Ball Room, with comrades from Singac, Linden, Garfield, Passaic, and Lodi attending.[96]

The wartime OSS noted the array of entertainment venues the Order provided its members. A Foreign Nationalities Branch officer in 1944 wrote, "In fulfillment of one of its announced aims the IWO pursues a diversified program of social-cultural activities," listing song, dance, drama festivals, sports, and summer camps as some of its offerings. The IWO's National Film Division, a concert bureau, and dancers and singers in Ukrainian, Russian, Polish, and African American troupes helped the IWO "spread its message and gained new adherents to its viewpoints," the agent wrote. He also quoted a *Daily Worker* article that asserted of its cultural program, "When you give people a chance at self-expression…you are doing a valuable thing for them, a thing they appreciate. Whether they participate as actors or as audience, sharing a cultural experience creates a bond and makes them willing to listen to what you have to say."[97]

The IWO's recreational facilities were also some of the only integrated venues, even in the North. Louis Hernandez's 1949 obituary noted aside from founding the "Mutualista Hispano-Americano I.W.O.," co-founding "the 'Puerto Rican Anti-Imperialist League' to defend the small Puerto Rican community against police brutality, evictions and for jobs to the unemployed," and running as Communist candidate for the New York Assembly, he ran Villa Buena Vista, an interracial summer camp. His obituary hailed Hernandez for "his progressive activities in South Brooklyn in the fight for better living condition for the Puerto Rican and Italian people in the community." Villa Buena Vista offered recreation and fun to Latinos in an era of otherwise segregated summer camps. It advertised "special rates for Cervantes Society members" and promised "a wonderful vacation in the Catskills" at an "interracial resort" where "everyone is invited." Swimming, hiking, table tennis, baseball, dancing, and badminton were prominently featured in flyers. But what really

---

95. *Głos Ludowy*, April 22, 1950, 3.

96. *Denník Rovnosť ľudu*, April 23, 1935, 2, ad, "Kopaničiarov."

97. WS, Binkowski, Box 4 Folder 4-29, OSS/FNB report, July 11, 1944, FNB to Director of Strategic Services, "Communist-Line IWO Reorganizes to Emphasize Nationality."

was special about Villa Buena Vista was Hernandez's assurance that Hispanic, Black, or white New Yorkers seeking "a happy holiday" would also get a break from the racial discrimination endemic to 1940s New York. "If you have in mind taking a break in a village of respect and in a family atmosphere," his brochures said, "visit Villa Buena Vista in the Catskill Mountains where the water, air, fruit and vegetables are all fresh and will give you all the vitality necessary to return to work with more energy."[98]

Vitality and energy were on display at Cervantes Society lodges. Many lodges sponsored children's bands, while in 1940 Cervantes happily noted, "Our Junior Section has 1,195 members and under the expert guidance of our Sister Dora López, and others, this section has successfully engaged in activities, such as excursions and the teaching of home economics, music, drama, painting, dancing, languages, etc." The Central Bronx District sponsored many elaborate social events, such as a 1947 Gala Evening and Ball. Lodge 4834 hosted the ball and "invited its members, their relatives and the entire Hispanic colony" to attend. The gala culminated in a presentation by the Society's "united artists" of "a colossal drama in three acts."[99]

On the Spanish Section's 10th anniversary, leader Jesús Colón noted the popular "annual contest in which a young queen is crowned by the Spanish section as the most popular girl of all the lodges. The crowning of the most popular girl as the queen has been serving as an instrument of unity and the annual social gathering of all our members is very helpful to build the I.W.O. spirit." While perhaps smacking of 1940 male chauvinism, such ceremonies, in which queens and attendees wore grand regalia, served to lend dignity and stature to IWO members who on other days were denigrated as racialized, "lower-class" workers. While 1940s racialized beauty standards dictated only blonde, blue-eyed applicants could aspire to be Miss America, elaborate Cervantes Society galas in Brooklyn and

98. Colón, Box 17, Folder 8, obituary, Louis Hernandez, November 1, 1949; Box 20, Folder 1, flyer "Villa Buena Vista – La Villa auspiciada per la Sociedad Fraternal Cervantes, Cornwallville, N.Y." (no date, 1940s); Box 17, Folder 8, brochure, Villa Buena Vista, Cornwallville, N.Y. (no date, 1940s.)

99. Ibid., Box 17, Folder 7, photo, Lodge 4788, Mutualista Obrera Lodge 4788, IWO, Puertorriqueña children's band (no date, 1930s-1940s?); Box 18, Folder 7, "Report" (in English) on Educational Work of Spanish Section, 1940; Box 15, Folder 7, invitation, Centro Fraternal Hispano del Bronx, Lodge 4834, S.F.C. (Cervantes) IWO, Gran Velada y Baile, 1947.

the Bronx ensured working-class women could be crowned Queen Lydia I or Brunhilda, Queen of Cervantes.[100]

On its first anniversary, the Spanish Section prominently high-lighted the wide array of interracial sports and entertainment provided, as well as noting the medical services provided to the men, women, and children of Harlem.[101] The following year the Section's second anniversary memorial book noted the "Los Amigos" basket-ball and softball teams fielded by Lodge 4790, as well as the annual festival of the IWO's New York City Central Committee held at Brandt's Farm in Yonkers. There the IWO's "Golden Gloves" boxers put on exhibitions. Also on offer were jitterbug and rumba dancing, choirs, mandolin orchestras, and cornet and tamburitza orchestras. A chorus interpreting Earl Robinson's songs also performed.[102]

The *Fraternal Outlook* noted the success the Order had in extending valorizing cultural programs to the many ethnic groups stigmatized in nativist America. Counter to the narrow "America First" ideology of its era, the IWO proclaimed:

It is the rich democratic traditions created by the many nation-alities which contributed their culture to America that enabled the I.W.O. to develop many new cultural groups. The many colorful dramatic and dance groups, choruses and orchestras, junior drum and bugle corps, sports teams with their national competitions, arts and crafts groups, spread the ideals of our brotherhood in scores of American communities, reaching thousands of American people.

The Russian Society's Radischev Dancers, the Harlem Suitcase The-atre organized by Louise Thompson Patterson, and other Black

100. Ibid., Box 18, Folder 7, "Report" (in English) on Educational Work of Spanish Section (1940); Box 19, Folder 17, program, coronation of First Queen of the Children's Spanish Section of the IWO. Crowned at the fifth anniversary celebration of Spanish Section (1941); Box 32, Folder 23, photo "Lydia Primera" ("La Srta. Lydia Romero, coronada Lydia Primera, Reina de la Victoria de la Sociedad Fraternal Cervantes, Sección hispana de la I.W.O. en un grandioso Baile de Coronación, el sábado 26 de Mayo del 1945, en los salones del Hunt Point Palace."

101. Ibid., Box 19, Folder 3, "Memoria del Primer Aniversario de la Secion Hispana Orden Internacionales de Trabajadores," December 4, 1937.

102. Ibid., Box 19, Folder 3, Memorial book, second anniversary, Spanish Section of IWO (1938.)

members, and the American People's Chorus were singled out for
their "nation-wide fame and prestige."[103]

Even after government persecutors proclaimed the Order
"un-American," a broad array of cultural activities enhanced the
development of members young and old. In 1949, the *Fraternal Outlook* detailed nine children's folk festivals planned for New York,
Newark, Philadelphia, Chicago, Detroit, and Pittsburgh. Children's
groups from Jewish, "Negro," Carpatho-Russian, Russian, Puerto
Rican, Croatian, Finnish, Italian, Greek, Hungarian, Polish, Slovak,
Ukrainian, and Chinese lodges demonstrated their talents in performances valorizing the cultures of these communities, still denigrated
as non-Anglo-Saxon (hence "inferior") in 1940s America. The very
act of expressing one's culture in such a milieu was recognized as
an act of defiance. Carnival games, folk dancing, choruses, dramatic
plays, puppet shows, and exhibits of arts and crafts guaranteed
defiance was also fun. The following month, Croatian lodges of San
Pedro, California, and Akron performed plays, songs, and tamburitza numbers to overflow crowds.[104]

Such activities continued even as red-baiting attacks increasingly
occupied the IWO's time. Foreign-born members faced deportation proceedings or harassment from the INS, as when South Slavic
members in Farrell, Pennsylvania, were interrogated on membership in "subversive" organizations such as the Croatian Fraternal
Union, the IWO, and the Aria Singing Society. Even during World
War II, the FBI reported that Katherine Elovich of Gary was "active
in IWO-Croatian lodge...and was a member of the Croatian Glee
Club, which is believed to be a Communist front organization."[105]
Don't mourn, harmonize.

In the face of such attacks, progressives continued to use social
occasions as opportunities to entertain targeted fellow workers,
celebrating their achievements and also sometimes mocking their
dilemma. In 1954, Clark Foreman of the Emergency Civil Liberties
Committee sent a letter to supporters, including members of the

103. Ibid., Box 27, Folder 8, *Fraternal Outlook*, June-July 1940 (Tenth Anniversary edition.)

104. Ibid., Box 19, Folder 14, *Fraternal Outlook*, January 1949, "IWO Children's Festival," 18; Box 20, Folder 1, *Fraternal Outlook*, February 1949, 11.

105. NYU, IWO, Folder 31, press release, April 25, 1947, "IWO Urges
Investigation of Immigration Office in Youngstown, Ohio;" FBI report on
American Slav Congress made at Indianapolis, January 26, 1944, by Agent
Douglas Williams. Contained in FBI file on American Slav Congress, in
author's possession. Thanks to John Enyeart.

recently disbanded IWO, urging attendance at a fundraising performance of George Bellak's play, "The Troublemakers." The play enacted the tale of "a student organizer for the 1948 third-party presidential campaign killed on campus." Many members of the IWO had campaigned for Henry Wallace's Progressive Party, and while few had been murdered, many had indeed suffered red baiting as a result.[106]

Miraculously, the IWO looked after the cultural needs and spirit of its members, not just their insurance policies, right up to its demise. The Order ran a Concert and Lecture Bureau providing "Entertainment and Speakers for Your Lodge Meetings and Affairs." Believing that "interesting meetings make for good attendance" at lodges, plays by groups such as the Harlem Suitcase Theatre, films and musical combos traveled to raise members' spirits. To be sure, not all entertainment was necessarily high-minded or class-conscious. "The Yiddish Ventriloquists and Puppeteers, Ben Yano and Horowitz," were touted by the IWO. Compared to "The Troublemakers" or "Snow White and the Seven Union Dwarfs," a Yiddish-speaking ventriloquist seems to have been a less politically engaged act. Although maybe not: Did Yano the dummy name names?[107]

If a fraternal insurance society that cared about members' health, lobbied to enact humane legislation, militantly campaigned for racial justice, and enriched the cultural life and recreation of its members seems too good to be true, anti-communists thought so, too. In 1938 the Massachusetts Department of Insurance refused to renew the Order's license due to its "Communistic activities." Bedacht accurately noted "reaction threatens our Order."[108] Fortunately, the Order's general counsel, Joseph Brodsky, was able to convince a judge none of the IWO's corporate funds were used for political purposes, but that members voluntarily engaged in lobbying on issues germane to the organization's social-welfare purposes.

---

106. Cornell, IWO supplemental, Box 1, letter, December 21, 1954, from Clark Foreman, Emergency Civil Liberties Committee.

107. Colón, Box 27, Folder 11, "Entertainment and Speakers for Your Lodge Meetings and Affairs" by IWO Concert and Lecture Bureau (no date, 1940s?)

108. Cornell, IWO, Box 1, Folder 5, Joseph Brodsky, General Counsel of the Order, report to General Executive Board, IWO, plenary session, September 10-11, 1938, 19-24; Max Bedacht's report to GEB, plenary session, September 10-11, 1938, 10, "Reaction Threatens Our Order." See, too, Lewiston Evening Journal (Maine), July 23, 1938, 4, "International Workers Can't Issue Insurance. Mass. Commissioner Finds Purported Fraternal Order is Communistic" for an Associated Press story.

The IWO dodged a bullet, but Brodsky stressed the Order had to be careful. He counseled, "We must realize that we are attacked because we are the organization that we are…[I]t becomes equally clear that we must learn to carry on in a manner least harmful to ourselves." The Communist lawyer cautioned, "Our organization, like Caesar's wife, must be above all suspicion."[109]

The IWO soon faced an even graver assault. Martin Dies' House Un-American Activities Committee also in 1938 launched an investigation of "alien" groups he deemed subversive, the IWO among them.[110] HUAC argued in January 1939 that the IWO was "possibly one of the most effective and closely knitted organizations among the Communist 'front' organizations." Support for Communist candidates for office, participation in "left-wing strikes," and Bedacht's Communist Party offices were offered as proof of the IWO's evil purposes.[111]

Defenders of "Americanism" conveniently forgot about the Bill of Rights and HUAC's agents raided the IWO's Philadelphia regional headquarters, seizing financial records, medical files, as well as "subversive" material such as a lantern slide lecture on the life of Lincoln. As the IWO fought the raid, securing an injunction returning its property, HUAC's supporters wanted to know why the IWO didn't voluntarily turn over such material if it had nothing to hide. Bedacht countered that for 10 years the IWO had acted as nothing but a fraternal benefit society, dispersing more than $4 million in benefits, and its conscience was clear. "But we will never help you to persecute, to hound and to blacklist innocent people by volunteering to turn over names to your committee."[112]

While the IWO was heartened when a court ordered HUAC to return its material, on the local level anti-communist investigations took a toll, even if snooping bordered on the surreal. In spring 1941 Dies demanded a list of members of the Cooperative Bookshop in Washington because he objected to some of the speakers who

---

109. Cornell, IWO, Box 1, Folder 5, Brodsky, report to GEB, IWO, September 10-11, 1938, 19-24.

110. *Milwaukee Sentinel*, November 28, 1938, 3, "Dies Demands 'Alien' Groups be Prosecuted. Note to Hull Claims Registration Law Violated."

111. WS, Binkowski, Box 16, Folder 16-37, FBI report, Detroit division IWO, December 31, 1946, citing report of Special Sub-Committee on un-American Activities, January 3, 1939.

112. NYPL, Marcantonio, Box 47, from Bedacht to Marcantonio, "Copy of following telegram sent to Martin Dies, Chairman, Investigating Un-American Activities" (no date, May 1940.)

had appeared there, including Eleanor Roosevelt, poet Langston Hughes, and the artist and IWO member Rockwell Kent, later the Order's president. "The Dies Committee's roundabout methods of securing a list of the Cooperative Bookshop's members are dime-novel detective nonsense," the bookstore's manager charged, noting Dies "express[ed] himself as suspicious of such Bookshop programs as 'From Bach to Boogie-Woogie.'" The manager wondered "what such censorship will mean to the future of democracy in America."[113]

The wartime years of Soviet-U.S. alliance gained the IWO some respite from government persecution, although the FBI and OSS continued closely monitoring the Order. With the Cold War's onset, however, harassment was ratcheted up. In 1947 Attorney General Tom Clark placed the IWO, its foreign-language societies, and the Douglass-Lincoln Society for African Americans on his Attorney General's List of Subversive Organizations. Although ostensibly only requiring government employees to take a loyalty oath, the list opened the door to all levels of government to begin attacks on members of organizations branded political pariahs. The New York Board of Education barred the Jewish Peoples Fraternal Order and other IWO societies from using the public schools for their night schools. Erie, Pennsylvania, and Jacksonville, Florida, both passed ordinances restraining members of designated organizations living in their cities. Although these ordinances were struck down by the courts, in the latter city a distraught IWO member attempted to commit suicide.[114]

---

113. NYPL, Marcantonio, Box 47, statement, Cooperative Bookshop, Washington, D.C., Jules Yanover, executive secretary, May 17, 1941.

114. NYU, IWO, Folder 30, Flyer, reprinted from the *New York Star*, January 19, 1949. "To Mayor O'Dwyer and the New York Board of Education;" Cornell, IWO, Box 8, Folder 11, letter, December 27, 1949, Sol Rotenberg to Sam Milgrom and Rubin Saltzman, about a JPFO school evicted from a Philadelphia shul. Cornell, IWO, Box 25, Folder 1, letter, September 20, 1950, Daniel Kasustchik to Ya. Peters, N. Daneyko and M. Burenko, Lodge 3018, Erie, Pennsylvania; Box 26, Folder 3, letter, September 26, 1950, S. Nowacki, assistant secretary, Polonia Society, IWO; Box 25, Folder 1, letters, October 9, 1950, Ossip Blachnic, Erie, to Kasustchik, and October 11, 1950, Kasustchik to Blachnic; Box 10, Folder 10, monthly letter, Garibaldi Society IWO, November 1950; *Milwaukee Journal*, October 27, 1950, 6, "Anti-Red Law Effect Halted." Cornell, IWO, Box 32, Folder 11, letters, September 14, 1950, B. Klein, secretary, JPFO Lodge 644, Atlantic Beach, Florida, to George Starr, JPFO, and September 22, 1950, Starr to Klein. Klein's letter was accompanied by September 13, 1950, clippings from the *Florida Times-Union*, "Stab

Government employees in the IWO, especially Post Office employees, were fired. Many had been union activists and fighters for racial justice for Black postal employees. Such firings led other postal employees to resign.[115] As a Bronx mailman noted, members fearful of the repercussions of belonging to an organization the federal government officially labeled subversive resigned within days of publication of the Attorney General's List.[116] Others, such as an IWO member who delivered mail in Hammond, Indiana, was apologetic when resigning, but noted he had to feed his family. "I don't want you to think that I have given up on my convictions or beliefs," he reassured headquarters. "I have not." In a sad commentary on the suppression of free thought, this mailman ruefully added, "One of these days the hysteria will die down and light will appear again."[117]

The IWO filed a lawsuit to force Clark to remove the designation. The *Michigan Edition – The Worker* appealed for contributions to its legal defense fund while noting our "membership is of diverse political beliefs. There are Republicans, Democrats, Communists, Socialists, Labor Party members and others in the IWO. We do not ask anybody what political beliefs he holds and we do not discriminate against anyone because of his political beliefs. Naturally there are Communists in our organization..." In 1948, while some national officers such as Rubin Saltzman and Louise Thompson Patterson made no secret of their party membership, others such as Rockwell Kent and Vito Marcantonio were never party members. Only a small minority of the IWO's overall 180,000 members were Communists. But in 1948 an organization with even a minority of its members in the party was anathema to the Justice Department. In June 1948, the Polonia Society's newspaper, *Głos Ludowy*, reported rallies in 10 cities to "defend people's right of freedom of association," but also to protest the Treasury Department's withdrawal of the IWO's tax-exempt status. This move came soon after publication of the

Wound, Fall Imperil Life of Red" and from a second, unidentified newspaper, "Trainor Still Reported on Critical List."

115. Cornell, IWO, Box 4, Folder 4, letter, December 6, 1947, N. Gish, Brooklyn, to "Dear Brother Dave Greene;" letter, December 8, 1947, Greene to Gish.

116. Ibid., Box 4, Folder 4, letters, December 30, 1947, Dave Greene to Nathan Reiser, the Bronx; December 30, 1947, Greene to Dr. Louis Roberts, the Bronx. Cornell, IWO supplemental, Box 1, letter, January 16, 1950, Abraham Chapman to Lee Pressman; draft *Fraternal Outlook* article, "Arthur L. Drayton Fights 'Loyalty' Suspension."

117. Cornell, IWO, Box 32, Folder 24, letter, January 10, 1950, Seymour Press, Hammond, Indiana, to Sylvia Rigel, Chicago.

Attorney General's List, and like that action, the burdensome change was announced with no explanation or evidence of any wrongdoing on the Order's part. Indeed, as the IWO would point out in its battles with the federal government and the state of New York, its record as a financially sound insurance organization had been consistently rated spotless; now that its politics were unpopular, it was condemned.[118]

The IWO demanded a hearing to show they were not subversive and impel Clark to show evidence why they were so designated. But Clark denied any of his actions had substantively harmed any IWO members. If the INS had subsequently begun denaturalization or deportation proceedings against foreign-born IWO members, or Treasury stripped the IWO of its tax-exempt status, Clark claimed these actions were merely incidental, not a direct result of his list. An outraged IWO Treasurer Peter Shipka wrote an "atomic chain reaction of an irresponsible smear" had led to these actions.[119]

The IWO cited earlier assurances from the INS membership in the Order did not prevent naturalization,[120] but as the Cold War continued, harassment of members was unrelenting. Brodsky intervened in Chicago, where Nicholas Athanos Seoeff had been investigated by the police at the behest of the INS pursuant to his naturalization application. Although the police admitted they could find no criminal record for Seoeff, they wrote to the INS he was a member of the IWO and ARFS, which they labeled "Communist" organizations." Brodsky objected to such characterization as likely to sink Seoeff's chances of winning citizenship. He cited a 1943 case in which an alien successfully appealed his denial of permanent residence, but the epithet "Communist" may have scuttled Seoef's chances of naturalizing.[121]

More bluntly, INS agents in Cleveland told a Serbian woman she could not be granted citizenship until she quit the IWO. Lee Pressman reported on a similar case in Sacramento, where a dentist from

118. WS, Binkowski, Box 16, Folder 16-38, FBI report on IWO Detroit division, November 20, 1953, cites *Michigan Edition – The Worker*, June 6, 1940, 9, and *Głos Ludowy*, June 19, 1948.
119. Cornell, IWO, Box 46, "Department of Justice Evades Justice" by Peter Shipka, *The Jewish Fraternalist*, November 1948, 3-4.
120. NYU, IWO, Folder 31, press release, April 25, 1947, "IWO Urges Investigation of Immigration Office in Youngstown, Ohio."
121. Cornell, IWO, Box 9, Folder 5, letter, April 13, 1947, Joseph Brodsky to John Prendergast, Commissioner of Police, Chicago. Re: Nicholas Athanos Seoeff.

222 FAITH IN THE MASSES

India was being denied citizenship due to past membership in the Order. The Justice Department said they were prepared to offer witnesses in the dentist's case that the IWO "advocates the overthrow of the Government by force and violence." Pressman told the JPFO's national board, "It might be interesting for us to note that the witnesses who were going to testify were Kornfedder [sic] or alias Zack from Detroit and a man named Crouch from California – two professional stoolpigeons." Two years later, Joseph Kornfeder and Sylvia Crouch (wife of professional anti-communist witness Paul Crouch) indeed were two of the witnesses against the IWO in its liquidation trial.[122]

The IWO offered constant, and accurate, denunciations of state "terrorization." To defend its non-naturalized members, the IWO mobilized "stop deportation drive" rallies.[123] The necessity of such rallies was evident, for even non-citizen members who had been in the U.S. for decades were facing deportation orders for allegedly concealing their radical, "subversive" beliefs. Peter Harisiades, head of the Order's Hellenic American Brotherhood, was deported due to his brief membership in the Communist Party, even though he had come to the U.S. as a child of nine. The IWO joined a campaign to save Harisiades, distributing flyers picturing another undesirable alien, the Statue of Liberty. "Should Miss Liberty Be Deported?" the flyers asked, arguing "If Peter Harisiades is deported, the Statue of Liberty will be in the boat with him." Fearing his life would be in peril were he deported to the U.S.-backed Greek military dictatorship, Harisiades opted to relocate to Poland, even though he spoke not a word of Polish.[124] Even a naturalized, former elected official such as Stanley Nowak, Polish American IWO officer, faced multiple deportation attempts, the first begun when he was a sitting state senator. Unlike Harisiades, Nowak successfully fought his deportation

122. Ibid., Box 4, Folder 4, letter, August 30, 1948, Nick Baltich to Dave Greene, re: Sister Ljubice Pribicevich of Lodge 4014, Cleveland; Box 27, Folder 2, National Board, JPFO, meeting minutes, November 19, 1949, report by Lee Pressman on "the legal problems we have faced in the past few years;" Arthur Sabin, *Red Scare in Court: New York Versus the International Workers Order* (University of Pennsylvania Press, 1993), 136-146.

123. Cornell, IWO, Box 48, news releases, October 21, and November 1, 1949. Rallies were listed in Indiana, Ohio and Pennsylvania towns. See, too, Box 48, news release, July 22, 1949, "IWO Condemns Deportation Arrests in Detroit; Refutes Press Slanders."

124. NYPL, Marcantonio, Box 46, flyer, "Should Miss Liberty Be Deported? The Case of Peter Harisiades" (1950.)

order, the Supreme Court in 1957 declaring his political beliefs could not be held against him.[125]

Other officials of the IWO and American Slav Congress were not as fortunate as Nowak, in many cases forcibly expelled from the country for their political beliefs. George Pirinsky, executive secretary of the Slav Congress, was in 1948 arrested and detained at Ellis Island pending his removal from the land of the free. The president of the IWO's Russian society wrote to the group's New Haven lodge, urging members to attend Pirinsky's hearing and demonstrate solidarity with him. "You know that the Secretary of the American Slav Congress has been held, for 69 days, on Ellis Island, or, as it is commonly called, the Island of Tears," he wrote. Pirinsky shared a cell "behind double barbed wire" with the National Maritime Union's Ferdinand Smith, soon to be deported to Jamaica for militant advocacy on behalf of his multi-racial membership. Pirinsky was briefly freed on bail ("It's nice to be out of Ellis Island," he wrote to Nowak. "My advice to you is to try to keep out of there."). He went on a speaking tour to defend those targeted for deportation. But he was soon back behind bars. Pirinsky's appeal was denied and he was shipped to Bulgaria.[126]

In the end, the government deployed Insurance Department regulations and compliant courts to destroy the IWO. New York state's Insurance Department declared the actuarial term "hazard" – a

125. WS, Binkowski, Box 7, Folder 7-48, pamphlet, "An American Family Faces Separation or Exile," Stanley Nowak Defense Committee (April 1956.) See, too, Box 7, Folder 7-49, FBI report, Stanley Nowak Defense Committee (1953), citing defenses of Nowak in *Głos Ludowy*, January 17 and 31, 1953; WS, Nowak, Box 9, Folder 9-9, letter, May 28, 1957, Ernest Goodman of Goodman, Crockett, Eden & Robb, to Victor Perlo of Flushing, New York; Rachel Buff, *Against the Deportation Terror* (Philadelphia: Temple University Press, 2018.)

126. *Chicago Daily Tribune*, September 24, 1948; WS, Binkowski, Box 1, Folder 1-18, *Washington Star*, September 25, 1948, "Slav Congress Leader Is Seized on Charge Of Communist Ties;" WS, Binkowski, Box 1, Folder 1-19, telegram, January 17, 1949, George Pirinsky Defense Rally, to President Truman; *Národné noviny*, July 13, 1949, 4; Cornell, IWO, Box 25, Folder 1, letter, September 13, 1949, S. Nikolauk to Executive Committee, American Russian Fraternal Society Lodge #3171, New Haven, Connecticut; Gerald Horne, *Red Seas: Ferdinand Smith and Radical Black Sailors in the United States and Jamaica* (New York: New York University Press, 2005), 203; WS, Nowak, Box 4, Folder 4-16, letter, October 10, 1949, Pirinsky to Stanley Nowak; WS, Nowak, Box 4, Folder 4-2, "Statement of the American Slav Congress on the Arrest of George Pirinsky," October 23, 1950.

financially unsound insurance society – to encompass the novel idea the IWO was a moral and political hazard for advocating unpalatable ideas, even though its finances were impeccable. A judge agreed, and the IWO was ordered liquidated, even though both the Insurance Department and court agreed the Order's finances were excellent and all insurance-policy business actuarially sound. In a Kafkaesque twist, the state alleged the IWO was too solvent, hence funds might easily be transferred to Moscow. No proof any such action had ever occurred or been contemplated was offered; the Communist affiliation of some IWO officers was "hazard" enough. As the *New York World-Telegram and Sun* jeered, "Their Books Balanced, But Politics Were in the Red."[127]

The IWO organized a Policyholders Protective Committee to fight the state diktat, and raise funds for judicial appeals.[128] Lodges, however, were now severely restricted in their activities. In Detroit, FBI agents noted "the funds of the IWO had been frozen and that this action could not be hidden from the IWO members." Some officers hoped the Order's members could be aroused to "cause a lot of trouble." More constructively, an officer noted, while "IWO lodges could meet only for the purpose of defending the Order and no other business could be transacted," protests and letters should nevertheless be sent to New York Governor Thomas Dewey. "The main thing," he added, "was to keep the people advised and to hold on to members."[129]

Policyholders appealed to the Constitution's right of free association in asking Judge Henry Clay Greenberg to lift the liquidation order. When he upheld the ban, rallying IWO members declared N.Y. Insurance Superintendent Alfred Bohlinger the real moral hazard,

---

127. Cornell, IWO supplemental, Box 2, *New York World-Telegram and Sun*, January 23, 1951, "Their Books Balanced, But Politics Were in Red." The writer called Bedacht "a procurer for the Soviet government's espionage network in this country. Box 2, *New York World-Telegram and Sun*, January 20, 1951, "Among Reddest Red Nests." Box 3, reprint from *American Legion Magazine*, March 1951, "IWO – Red Bulwark: The Inside Story of an Outfit That Works Hand in Glove with the Communist Party and Which Now Faces a Crackdown That is Long Overdue" by Louis Budenz.

128. Cornell, IWO, Box 5, Folder 16, letter, December 28, 1950, Peter Shipka to "Lodge Financial Secretaries;" Box 16, Folder 13, news release, December 28, 1950, "IWO Policyholders Form Protective Committee, Plan Albany Gathering and Visit to Gov. Dewey."

129. WS, Binkowski, Box 16, Folder 16-38, FBI report on IWO Detroit division, November 20, 1953, citing Detroit meetings on December 17 and 21, 1950.

decrying the liquidation as "Hitlerism with an insurance twist." A Boston man wrote the Policyholders Protective Committee with simple advice: Tell the Insurance Department to go away.[130]

The woes of IWO members were compounded after the ruling. In 1952 the Gwinn Amendment was added to the United States Housing Law, excluding from public housing any member of a "subversive" organization. The case testing use of the Attorney General's List to bar tenants with stigmatized beliefs involved IWO members living in Brooklyn's Williamsburg Houses. In January 1953, the IWO won a temporary injunction prohibiting enforcement of the loyalty oath, by which tenants affirmed they did not belong to a designated "subversive" organization. While the American Civil Liberties Union sought to make the temporary injunction permanent, IWO official Dave Greene coaxed public-housing tenants who had quit the Order to rejoin. The IWO had to continue fighting in court, with *Głos Ludowy* celebrating legal victories to "halt evictions." The IWO also supported a federal case seeking to throw out the loyalty oath in Newark's housing projects. This case involved a war veteran who had lost his legs in World War II. James Kutcher, however, belonged to the Socialist Workers Party, and his Trotskyist beliefs led Newark to seek his eviction from Seth Boyden Terrace. (Newark's Housing Authority required tenants to affirm they did not belong to 200 listed "subversive" organizations.) In time of government suppression, the IWO forgot its earlier animus toward Trotskyists. In July 1953, the Order won a victory forbidding the New York Housing Authority to require tenants to take a loyalty oath, but the victory was short-lived. A federal court overturned the decision, ruling "In the present-day context of world crisis after crisis…the danger the Congress is seeking to avoid (i.e., infiltration of government housing by subversive elements) justifies the requirement that tenants herein choose between government housing and membership in an organization that they know to have been found subversive…" The court pointed to the recently created Subversive Activities Control Board to argue "subversive" organizations now had an opportunity to challenge their listing. Although the U.S. Supreme Court later threw

---

130. Cornell, IWO, Box 23, Folder 4, "Answer to Superintendent of Insurance Bohlinger Adopted at Membership Meeting of the International Workers Order – Saint Nicholas Arena, March 7, 1951;" Box 25, Folder 1, letter, January 24, 1951, translation from Russian, D. Fedonik, Boston, "to the Plenum of the IWO Committee."

out the Gwinn Amendment, this victory for freedom of association and thought came too late for the IWO.[131]

In the Order's appeals of its liquidation, lawyers argued the liquidation was censorship by government decree, a violation of the Fourteenth Amendment and an unparalleled twisting of the concept of "hazard" in insurance law.[132] All appeals, though, were unsuccessful as jurists ruled the "present-day…crisis after crisis" outweighed members' free-association rights. Defense counsel Arthur Kinoy wrote to the IWO, the court "here in a conscious manner brushed aside all previous existing law in its efforts to uphold a political result."[133]

In demanding a rehearing, lawyers argued the concept "moral hazard" had no basis in insurance law, and the liquidation order amounted to a state seizure of millions of dollars of policyholders' assets. New York once again insisted the Order posed a moral and political hazard. The state's move to liquidate, it argued, was brought because of "Communist and hence seditious activity" by the IWO. In the state's petition, the economic hazard of a potential funneling of IWO funds to Communists abroad – again no evidence of such a scheme was presented – was conflated with a broad moral hazard.[134]

---

131. Ibid., Box 4, Folder 6, letter, January 14, 1953, Dave Greene to Rockwell Kent; Box 17, Folder 14, letter, January 22, 1953, Greene to "Dear Brother or Sister;" Box 4, Folder 8, letter, January 29, 1953, Greene to "Dear Brother or Sister;" Box 4, Folder 6, letter, January 30, 1953, Kent to Greene; Cornell, IWO supplemental, Box 2, *Morgen Freiheit*, January 30, 1953, 1, "The Order Obtains Temporary Injunction;" Box 2, *New York Times*, February 3, 1953, "Newark Housing Authority Called to Court on Tenant's Loyalty Oath;" Cornell, IWO, Box 4, Folder 8, letter, February 10, 1953, Greene to "Dear Brothers and Sisters;" Box 17, Folder 14, news release, July 9, 1953, "State Supreme Court Rules Against Tenant Oath;" Cornell, IWO supplemental, Box 3, *New York Times*, March 9, 1954, 19, "Loyalty Question to Tenant Upheld;" WS, Binkowski, Box 5, Folder 5-29, *National Republic*, March 1953, "Turning Searchlight on Reds," in FBI file on Polonia Society of IWO. *Głos Ludowy*, February 7, 1953, 4 of 2nd section, "IWO Secures Injunction to Halt Evictions Under Gwinn Law;" February 28, 1953, 1 of 2nd section, "IWO Wins Halt to Evictions."

132. Sabin, *Red Scare in Court*, 325-330.

133. Cornell, IWO supplemental, Box 1, July 8, 1952, Arthur Kinoy, preliminary notes on N.Y. State Appellate Court case, re: Liquidation of the I.W.O., to Sam Milgrom, Rubin Saltzman, Dave Greene, Peter Shipka.

134. Ibid., Box 3, petition, September 11, 1952, for rehearing, filed by Philip McCook for IWO; memorandum, September 16, 1952, to Supreme Court of N.Y. State from Paul Williams & James Henry, special assistant attorneys general of N.Y. State.

In a political milieu in which Ethel and Julius Rosenberg, alleged Soviet spies, had been unmasked at their trial as IWO members, it was difficult for the Order to prevail, and in April 1953 the appellate court let the liquidation order stand.[135] As lawyers petitioned the U.S. Supreme Court to consider their appeal of the decision, the Policy-holders Protective Committee issued a pamphlet stating its case: "A Fraternal Order Sentenced to Death!"[136] Indeed, by September 1954, as the Supreme Court refused the Order's final appeal, and the SACB ruled former IWO officials had no standing to testify before it, the Order was declared both subversive and liquidated, its assets scattered to for-profit insurance corporations, its members stripped of their fraternal "big family."[137]

Not all IWO members went so gently into the night. The Yiddish Communist *Morgen Freiheit* reprinted a letter to "Saint Bohlinger" in which "G.M." demanded, "Who gave you the right to tell me where I should belong? Do you imagine yourself riding high on Hitler's

135. Sabin, *Red Scare in Court*, 212-215; Cornell, IWO, Box 23, Folder 5, "Court of Appeals Opinion – I.W.O. v. Bohlinger, April 23, 1953;" *New Yorský denník*, April 25, 1953, 1, "Rozpustenie Medzinárod. Rob. Spolku" ("Liquidation of the International Workers Order.")

136. Cornell, IWO, Box 16, Folder 13, pamphlet, "A Fraternal Organization Sentenced to Death! The Strange Case of the IWO Now Before the U.S. Supreme Court" (1953.)

137. Ibid., Box 16, Folder 13, news release, October 20, 1953, "Statement of the Policyholders Committee on U.S. Supreme Court Denial of Review of IWO Case;" Box 23, Folder 7, news release, "IWO Demands Re-Hearing of Supreme Court Denial to Hear Its Case" (1953); Cornell, IWO supplemental, Box 4, IWO petitions, October 23, and November 4, 1953; Box 2, *Morgen Freiheit*, December 5, 1953, 1, "Supreme Court Rejects Second Appeal of Order to Consider Appeal Against Liquidation Order" and December 9, 1953, 4, editorial, "The Answer of the Members of the Order to the Dewey Brownell Pogrom;" Cornell, IWO, Box 23, Folder 3, letter, to all policyholders, November 18, 1953; Cornell, IWO supplemental, Box 2, letter, September 1, 1954, Alfred Bohlinger to "All Policyholders and Certificate Holders of the International Workers Order." See, too, Cornell, IWO, Box 53, clipping, *Daily Worker* (no date, but 1953), "Right to Belong to Fraternal Group Strangled by Gov't. Attack on IWO." Cornell, IWO supplemental, Box 1, transcript, December 16, 1953, Subversive Activities Control Board, hearing for the IWO; Order and Report of the Subversive Activities Control Board, re: IWO. January 14, 1954; Box 2, letter, November 30, 1953, Insurance Superintendent of New York to Kinoy; *Morgen Freiheit*, January 16, 1954, 2, "Statement of the Former Officers of the Order Concerning the Order of the McCarran Board." Cornell, IWO supplemental, Box 3, letter, October 23, 1953, Joseph Petercsak, secretary, Lodge 1007, to U.S. Supreme Court.

white horse, controlling my thoughts and my right of association. Do you really want to push yourself, with your stormtrooper's paws, into my head and my mind?"[138]

Months after the IWO's liquidation, an appeals court ruled the SACB had illegally declared the organization "subversive" and that its decision that former IWO members still had to register as "subversives" was void. Perhaps cold comfort to members who lost the fraternal bonds of the IWO, the decision was nevertheless hailed by *Głos Ludowy*, which took the opportunity to celebrate the Order's accomplishments. "IWO Helped Blaze Trail in Fight for Democracy," the paper declared. Perhaps this is the final verdict on the International Workers Order.[139]

---

138. Cornell, IWO supplemental, Box 2, *Morgen Freiheit*, February 4, 1954, 3, "A Reply to 'Saint Bohlinger'."
139. *Głos Ludowy*, March 12, 1955, 16.

Chapter 7

"Has White Supremacy Ended Your Pain": Beulah Richardson and art in the struggle against racism

By Denise Lynn

In the social and political milieu of the Cold War, Beulah Richardson stood out for her poetry and presence. Richardson wrote and performed to audiences that shared her political vision for the future, a socialist America where race and gender oppression would be demolished and the future secure. This commitment could be seen in her creative work, including her 1951 poem "A Black Woman Speaks...of White Womanhood, of White Supremacy, of Peace" where Richardson declared that white supremacy was the enemy of Black people and white people and that it perpetuated divisions that prevented much needed unity against American capitalist interests. Her art and politics existed in tandem with political activism at a time when advocating socialism was linked to treason and engaging in civil rights was believed to be a Communist plot. But in the face of Cold War oppression and racist policy, Richardson used her art to advocate socialism, the destruction of racist and sexist institutions, and a classless society where equity reigned. For Richardson and her cohort, socialism offered the only way to end racist and sexist oppression, militarism, and capitalist exploitation, and achieve economic justice. She also recognized that womanhood and Blackness were not defining categories of identification and that differences had to be accounted for in calls for justice.

Richardson's politics can best be seen in her most famous written work including her 1951 poem on white supremacy and white women's role in it. That same year, Richardson wrote a lengthy poem that she and others would perform titled "Genocide." The poem was written to support the Civil Rights Congress's petition to the United Nations charging the United States with the willful genocide of Black Americans. In these works, Richardson's political commitments are on full display. Though confident that equality was not possible under capitalism, Richardson believed that race and gender differences were a barrier to the collective that was needed to create a socialist America. Using her art, Richardson tried to convince white audiences that white supremacy and capitalism was their enemy too.

Beulah Richardson, known to many as the actress Beah Richards, was born in Vicksburg, Mississippi in 1925. Richardson attended Dillard University in New Orleans graduating in 1948. Tired of the Jim Crow south and seeking to break into acting, she made her way to San Diego and later to Los Angeles. It was in California that Richardson met prominent activists linked to the Communist Party, USA, including Louise Thompson Patterson and her husband William L. Patterson. Dayo Gore argues that Richardson met progressive activists in both cities in California, but the Patterson's would become future allies and would introduce her to CPUSA politics and campaigns.[1]

One of those campaigns captured the attention of CPUSA activists throughout the United States and would inspire Richardson's poem "A Black Woman Speaks...of White Womanhood, of White Supremacy, of Peace." On November 4, 1945, World War II veteran Willie McGee was arrested in Laurel, Mississippi for the rape of a white woman named Wiletta Hawkins. Hawkins reported that two days before, McGee broke into her home and raped her while her husband was asleep in an adjoining room. McGee claimed that he and Hawkins had a consensual affair, but in the Jim Crow south, sexual relations between a Black man and a white woman were an affront to white supremacy and the racial caste system that convinced white men it was their duty to protect white womanhood at all costs. McGee later claimed that the police forced a confession out of him. In a two day trial, the first day devoted almost entirely to jury selection, McGee was found guilty and sentenced to death, the sentence to be carried out one month later on January 7, 1946.[2]

---

1. Erick McDuffie, *Sojourning for Truth and Justice: Black Women, American Communism, and the Making of Black Left Feminism* (Duke University Press, 2011), 171 and Dayo Gore, "A Black Woman Speaks: Beah Richards Life of Protest and Poetry," in Howard Brick, Robbie Lieberman, and Paula Rabinowitz, eds., *Lineages of the Literary Left: Essays in Honor of Alan M. Wald.* (Michigan Publishing Services, 2015)

2. Leandra Zarnow, "Braving Jim Crow to Save Willie McGee: Bella Abzug, the Legal Left, and Civil Rights Innovation, 1948-1951," *Law & Social Inquiry*, Vol. 33 No. 4, (Fall 2008), 1006-1007

The NAACP's Legal Defense Fund passed on the case, partly because it did not have a presence in that part of Mississippi and the state was too dangerous for Black lawyers, but also interracial sex cases were highly inflammatory, tended to alienate local sympathy, and inflamed the white community. Instead the Communist adjacent organization the Civil Rights Congress took up the case. William Patterson was a CRC co-founder in 1946. The organization was created to defend the working classes against state abuses and interracial rape cases exposed the most "brutal elements" of the justice system. The CRC focus was not just on defending its clients in the courtroom, it brought the defense to the public to publicize the injustices in American courts, particularly against Black Americans. "Lynch law" was a phrase used by Communists to describe the use of the justice system to lynch Black defendants; Willie McGee's forced confession, expedited trial, and sentence exemplified lynch law. The CRC created an entire movement around McGee's defense and drew in people like Beulah Richardson to speak on his behalf.[3]

The CRC used the "mass defense" technique common in many Communist linked organizations; it described legal defense in the courtroom and mobilization of activists to apply pressure to local, state, and national authorities to force a fair reconsideration of legal cases. These tactics made the CRC highly unpopular among organizations like the NAACP, which believed that agitation and calling attention to unfair legal tactics in the South persuaded local juries and residents against defendants. Though these concerns were probably true, what it did accomplish was to bring the defendants, in this case Willie McGee, enough press attention to prevent an easy execution outside the national spotlights gaze. It also meant that the defendant's case would have to be reconsidered so that Mississippi could claim it gave McGee a fair hearing. Over the next six years, McGee's case regularly made headlines in Communist and fellow traveler newspapers. His original sentence was overturned, but a second trial led to another conviction and death sentence. This second conviction was overturned because of a lack of Black jury members, so once again McGee stood trial, this time with future Congresswoman Bella Abzug working on his defense. The case dragged on for three more years, until midnight May 8, 1951, when McGee was electrocuted. This was an enormous loss for left-wing activists who saw the

---

3. Danielle McGuire, *At the Dark End of the Street: Black Women, Rape, and Resistance – A New History of the Civil Rights Movement from Rosa Parks to the Rise of Black Power* (Vintage Books, 2010) and Zarnow, "Braving Jim Crow to Save Willie McGee," Ibid, 1010

McGee case as evidence that the U.S. government's indifference to egregiously racist cases amounted to Black genocide.[4]

Beulah Richardson was inspired by the McGee execution and conversations with Louise Patterson and Willie McGee's widow, Rosalie, to write her poem "A Black Woman Speaks...of White Womanhood, of White Supremacy, of Peace." This poem, as Dayo Gore argues, made Richardson a well-known artistic figure in the Cold War Black left. Erik McDuffie argues that the poem was one inspiration for the creation of the Sojourners for Truth and Justice, a short-lived Black women's group that organized against war and racism. The poem was an "indictment of white supremacy" and echoed Richardson's preoccupation with shattering the barriers that prevented substantive change for women and Black Americans.[5]

Richardson read the poem at a women's workshop at the American People's Peace Congress in Chicago at the end of June 1951. It begins by declaring "It is right that I, a woman black, should speak of white womanhood." Because as she continues, Black men are being killed by lynchers and by the hangman's noose, "legally" and extralegally, for the white supremacists' "mad desire for profit." In the poem's first stanza, Richardson describes racist violence and legal lynching as mechanisms used to maximize white profits at the expense of Black life. She linked white supremacy to economic gain, and anti-Black brutality to white people securing their economic fortunes. Party member or not, Richardson opened her poem with the accusation that white supremacy was fueled by capitalism.[6]

She continued by rejecting the assumptions that womanhood is a universal descriptor that encompasses Black and white womanhood in a bonded sisterhood. Instead, she accused white women of wearing a "bloodied skirt" and living in "willing slavery," where white women chose their oppression to seek comfort and solace in their whiteness. Richardson acknowledged the slavery inherent in women's oppression but noted that white woman's oppression is different "by degree" than Black women's. While she indicted white women for their complicity in Black women's oppression, Richardson

---

4. Zarnow, "Braving Jim Crow to Save Willie McGee," 1010 and 1031 and Shirley Graham, "Oh No Brother, No One is Going to Forget About Willie McGee," *Freedom*, June 1951, 1

5. McDuffie, *Sojourning for Truth and Justice...*, Ibid, 11, Gore, "A Black Woman Speaks: Beah Richards Life of Protest and Poetry," and Beulah Richardson, "A Black Woman Speaks...of White Womanhood, of White Supremacy, of Peace" (New York: American Women for Peace, 1951), 2

6. Richardson, Ibid, 2

simultaneously struck a note of unity by comparing women's sale into marriage to that of Black women into bondage. But that degree of difference is significant because the white woman consented to Black women's oppression with their silence to their own oppression. Black women were trapped with "chain and gun" and white women with "lying tongue" but white supremacy convinced white women that all was well because "white skin is supreme." The white woman, Richardson accused, was complicit in Black oppression and their own oppression by linking their fortunes to whiteness.[7]

White womanhood failed to protest Black slavery and instead "cuddled down" into its own "pink slavery," assuming safety, but Richardson argued, there was no safety; jewelry was just shackles, and a husband's fidelity was just an illusion. As white women bore their husband's sons, so did Black women; white women were purchased with bobbles and silent endurance from their husband's, while Black women were raped. It is here where Richardson begins to speak about the unspeakable, the sex at the heart of American racism. She suggested that marriage made white women sexual and emotional slaves purchased by white men, but Black women endured rape at the hands of white men with white women's consent. Their silence was their consent; as white women chose whiteness, they also chose silence, the inability to challenge white male power, and the choice to accept second class status. For Richardson, white women could use their racial power as a positive good to challenge and undermine the authority of men. Instead, they chose the safety of whiteness.[8]

With white supremacy came economic security, which is why white women failed to speak out for Black women. Richardson notes that some white women fought against slavery, but too many were invested in their own whiteness to join hands with others to usurp the power of men. And many actively deployed white supremacy to cover their own sins. Richardson accused Hawkins, McGee's accuser of covering her own adulterous affair with her rape accusation. When McGee said no to Hawkins to end their affair, she knew she could use her whiteness to destroy him. But all of it was a trade for freedom and equality. Whiteness offered women some benefits, but not freedom. Richardson ends the poem with a cry for unity against the forces that kept all women everywhere oppressed, noting that white supremacy would never free white women.[9] This

---

7. Richardson, Ibid, 3-4
8. Richardson, Ibid, 5-6
9. Richardson, Ibid, 8-10

is an important indictment because white women's sexuality was so often weaponized against Black men, like McGee, in upholding lynch law. Richardson sought to appeal to women to reclaim their own sexuality, take it out of the hands of white supremacy, and challenge the racist claims made against Black men. It was an important political statement because Richardson was highlighting a primary division between white and Black women; the value of the white body over the Black body sexually and politically. Both were policed and only through unity and rejecting white supremacy could all women secure real freedom.

Richardson's poem reflects the difference "feminism" that radical women activists deployed at mid-century, though they would have rejected the use of feminism since it was linked to bourgeois claims for generic equality without acknowledging race and class. Communists and other radical women acknowledged for decades before contemporary feminists described intersectionality, that women's difference was a fundamental part of oppression, that women did not share the same experience under patriarchy simply because of gender, and that white womanhood was/is complicit in white supremacy. Richardson also argued throughout the poem that white supremacy offered no benefits to white women who lived in a gilded cage. Economic and sexual independence were impossible for white women, but they confused racial power for power, when they too were subordinated to the white man. The poem was a powerful reminder that there was no real safety in whiteness for women, only the illusion of control while sacrificing true freedom.

The poem was powerful and resonated with audiences, so the American Women for Peace published it in a pamphlet. In the September 1951 issue of Paul Robeson's newspaper *Freedom*, a paper Richardson frequently wrote for, a glowing review of the poem appeared in a description of Richardson's arrival to New York. The author, Yvonne Gregory, described how a contingent of women arrived at the airport to pick up the poet, all of whom were eagerly awaiting her arrival, because her poem spoke to them personally. The poem made them all feel "grief, and anger, and outrage" at the understanding of how things were. It was "wrenched out of the 300-year old hunger and passion" of Black women for justice, and Gregory noted, it already won over some white women to the understanding that white supremacy was a "choking poison" that hurt them as well.[10]

---

10. Yvonne Gregory, "Poet Demands Equality for Negro Womanhood," *Freedom*, September 1951, 8

Activist John Hudson Jones described in the Communist *Daily Worker* Richardson's reception in New York, where she moved the same time her poem was released. Richardson told Jones that her poems were meant to be heard, not just read and that she anticipated a new Black renaissance in art. She also suggested that the new renaissance would be centered in the south, her birthplace. The *Daily Worker* reprinted a short stanza from the poem, but one that got Richardson's message across. In it she states clearly, "White supremacy is your enemy and mine," and that white women had to begin to see their own investment in white supremacy. Richardson's goal was "full equality" and that required unity. Interracial unity was a central goal for the Cold War Communist Party in hopes to swell their ranks, but also to demonstrate the power of a unified working class. But just as the party became more appealing to some Black Americans, it came under assault from the American legal system making appeals to interracial unity more difficult.[11]

According to Erik McDuffie, Richardson's poem became a "smash hit" among the Communist left in the summer of 1951 and was also an inspiration for the founding of the Sojourners for Truth and Justice. After Richardson moved to New York City she was immediately enveloped in the radical circles her friends the Patterson's were in. She and Louise Thompson Patterson decided to put out a call for an organization of Black women. They issued "A Call for Negro Women," to organize a meeting in September 1951 in Washington D.C. to create the organization. The organization sought to call attention to the dangerous American foreign policy that committed the country to contain communism at the expense of addressing racism and sexism in the United States.[12]

The call that initiated the organization's founding laid out the fundamental problems facing Black America, racist policy, programs, and the indifference of a federal government that ignored the needs of Black Americans. It demanded "absolute, immediate, and unconditional" redress of grievances. Hate, the document argued, was a weapon deployed by all levels of government and law enforcement as well as individuals, and its expression was obvious in the violence meted out in cases like that of Willie McGee. Lynch law was inherently violent because it degraded Black lives, made a farce of the

11. John Hudson Jones, "New Negro People's Poet Talks of Art and Liberation," *Daily Worker*, 14 October 1951, 7

12. Erik McDuffie, "A 'New Freedom Movement of Negro Women:' Sojourning for Truth, Justice, and Human Rights during the Cold War," *Radical History Review*, Issue 101, Spring, 2008, 86

justice system, and left Black America with no recourse or safety. The Sojourners argued that it was not just the legal system that destroyed the Black community, poverty destroyed communities and led to "drudgery and disease." The call included extralegal violence like lynching of Black men and sexual violence against Black women. They invoked Harriet Tubman and Sojourner Truth and called on Black women to "ARISE" and join them in Washington to confront the President, Harry Truman.[13]

Writing for the *Daily Worker*, Charlotta Bass, editor of the famous Black newspaper *The California Eagle*, and an important activist in her own right, described the founding meeting of the Sojourners. She noted that Beulah Richardson initiated the "Call for Negro Women" along with a committee that included leading Black left activists of the time including Louise Thompson Patterson, Eslanda Robeson, Marvel Cooke, Alice Childress, and others. Bass described Richardson as the inspiration behind the call describing her with eyes like two "red hot coals," and her voice that "burn her words" into the minds of her listeners as she read the call to an audience in Harlem. She likened Richardson to Harriet Tubman, who also called her people out of oppression toward a new light and toward freedom.[14]

Bass described the new organizations goal in traveling to Washington, D.C. The women hoped to meet with the president, to call attention to the plight of "15 million" Black men, women, and children in the United States. She noted that while there might be some Black leaders in the halls of Washington, that power was only interested in securing and maintaining power, thus these leaders had their own self-interest in mind. The Sojourners were also deeply concerned about America's involvement in the Korean War and included this concern in their call to Black women. They believed that the Cold War containment policy only exported American racist policies to other nations and that the United States sought not to contain communism, but to contain non-white aspirations abroad. While the United States pursued a policy of endless war via containment, it ignored poverty and persecution at home. Additionally, they saw war as a means to enrich capitalists and make working Americans cannon fodder for the U.S.'s imperialist ambitions. Bass noted that the women had every intention of registering their concerns about

---

13. "A Call to Negro Women," Louise Thomson Patterson Papers, box 15, folder 26, Emory University Archives, Atlanta, GA

14. Charlotta Bass, "Why We're Going to Washington," *Daily Worker*, 27 September 1951, 2

the war to Harry Truman and insist that Black men should not be fighting and dying for a country that did not treat them as citizens.[15]

Bass's article was a call to action inviting like-minded women to join the Sojourners in Washington. Lorraine Hansberry, playwright, and participant in the Sojourners, described the Washington meeting in Paul Robeson's newspaper *Freedom*. The meeting held in a Washington church featured Black women whose lives were directly touched by legal lynching, including a Mrs. Westry whose son was killed by police officers while he was in the hospital being treated, and Mrs. Josephine Grayson, whose husband was part of the Martinsville Seven, a group of men accused of raping a white woman. Hansberry noted that the group left empty seats for those unable to make it to the meeting, those who were imprisoned, those who had been killed, and those unable to afford to travel. The gathering declared "In the spirit of Harriet Tubman and Sojourner Truth – we demand the death of Jim Crow!" [16]

The Sojourners survived only one year, but in that year, the group managed to address a number of campaigns that brought the plight of Black Americans to a national and international audience. Perhaps the most important, and one that Beulah Richardson became deeply involved in was the CRC *We Charge Genocide* petition to the United Nations. After the United Nations was created in the wake of World War II, one of its mandates was to prevent the wholesale slaughter of national, racial, and religious groups like what occurred during the Jewish Holocaust. At the same time, with growing tensions between the two big superpowers in the Cold War, American racism became a focus for other countries, particularly the Soviet Union. American activists saw an opportunity to bring racial injustice to a global audience and try to force the United States to address inequalities, and more importantly racist violence.

Between 1946 and 1951, three separate civil rights organizations presented petitions to the United Nations accusing the federal government of genocide against Black Americans. The Communist affiliate, the National Negro Congress tried first in 1946. It presented its petition to the secretary of the UN Human Rights Commission asking the organization to assist in ending racial discrimination in the United States. The NNC asked the UN to conduct studies on "political, economic, and social discrimination" and to make recommendations to end "human rights abuses" within the U.S.

---

15. Bass, Ibid, 2
16. Lorraine Hansberry, "Women Voice Demands in Capital Sojourner, *Freedom*, October 1951, 6

Communist and historian Herbert Aptheker created a seven page appendix to accompany the petition outlining racial discrimination. Though the NNC printed 100,000 copies and distributed them nationwide, it failed to receive much attention. The NNC eventually merged with the Civil Rights Congress.[17]

W.E.B. DuBois suggested to the NAACP leader Walter White that the organization should present its own petition. Rather than a short petition with an appendix, DuBois recommended putting together a detailed study of over 100 pages documenting human rights abuses aimed at Black Americans. DuBois had a draft in a year that included essays on discriminatory laws and the rights of minorities, particularly regarding the UN's stated purpose of ensuring human rights. In October 1947 DuBois presented it to UN officials, one of whom informed him that the UN was not prepared to handle complaints, but that the document would help in "drafting a covenant on universal human rights." Unlike the NNC petition, the NAACP document gained the attention of the foreign press, was widely circulated in the Black press, while the mainstream press reported on it with "mixed feelings." The primary concern was an international organization becoming involved in domestic issues, particularly during the Cold War when the Soviet Union gleefully exploited America's racial issues in its propaganda.[18]

The NAACP printed the 95 page document and distributed it to UN ambassadors, but it became a casualty of Cold War politics. Because it was highly inflammatory and "tattled" on the United States, DuBois believed that American leaders silenced it. At the same time, as anti-communist hysteria increased in the United States, criticism of American policy, both domestic and foreign, was akin to treason in the eyes of some in the American public and intelligence agencies. The NAACP began to silence its own criticism on American foreign policy focusing instead on internal campaigns for integration and equality. DuBois and Walter White disagreed over the organization's policy of acquiescence. In 1948, DuBois was ousted from the NAACP and efforts to gain UN support for the petition ended.[19]

<hr/>

17. Charles H. Martin, "Internationalizing 'The American Dilemma': The Civil Rights Congress and the 1951 Genocide Petition to the United Nations," *Journal of American Ethnic History*, Vol. 16, No. 4, Summer 1997, 37-38 and Carol Anderson, *Eyes off the Prize: The United Nations and the African-American Struggle for Human Rights, 1944-1955* (Cambridge University Press, 2003)

18. Martin, "Internationalizing 'The American Dilemma'," 38-40

19. Martin, Ibid, 41-42

William Patterson, Beulah Richardson's friend and colleague, would take up a petition to the UN under the banner of the CRC, of which Patterson was leader. The CRC was created to defend "victims of racial persecution," Patterson took over as the national executive secretary in 1949. He wrote that he believed the United Nations charter to secure global peace and prevent mass slaughter had to be "made the property" of Americans and in particular Black Americans. In 1947, the UN issued the "Universal Declaration of Human Rights," without the United States endorsement. Patterson saw an opportunity to use the declaration to accuse the United States of genocide. Patterson acknowledged the previous attempts to draw international attention to the plight of Black Americans in the NNC and NAACP petitions. But he noted a major difference, the CRC petition would accuse the racist United States government of fomenting war abroad to secure its power because no government invested in racist violence would seek peace. In other words, Patterson's petition would attack Cold War policy as imperialist and nothing more than an effort to secure global white supremacy.[20]

The petition, titled *We Charge Genocide*, was created from research and surveys of legal and historical scholars. It accused the federal government of genocide via its policy of indifference in allowing local and state governments to issue their own brand of justice as they saw fit, advocating oppressive laws, and using law enforcement to maintain Black oppression. The CRC also included the federal government's endorsement of Jim Crow in federal policy, and the perpetuation of Black poverty from segregation and violence. The document came in at over 200 pages and covered cases of police brutality, judicial misdeeds, rape, and legal lynching between the years 1946 and 1951. It was signed by several prominent activists and academics including Charlotta Bass, W.E.B. DuBois, and Alphaeus Hunton.[21]

Patterson was a fan of Beulah Richardson's poem and wrote her a glowing letter about its importance to the movement. He noted that criticism about white womanhood was needed, as was remembering the cause and push for unity, and the poem encapsulated both for him. In the letter, he noted that one thing he wanted to see was Richardson more directly attacking the federal government, because it was the government that was perpetuating racism, while blaming it on individual actions. But he claimed that this criticism could come

---

20. William Patterson, *The Man who Cried Genocide: An Autobiography of William L. Patterson*. (New York: International Publishers, 1971), 156, 174-175

21. Patterson, *The Man who Cried Genocide*, 179-181

in another "marching song" that she should write for the future. That "marching song" would come in the form of a performance poem titled "Genocide" that dramatized the *We Charge Genocide* petition.[22]

In November 1951, William Patterson traveled Europe to publicize the petition and Paul Robeson introduced it in the United States. Richardson's poem was debuted at its American release. The 12 page poem was performed with a cast that included a chorus to dramatize the hundreds of cases included in the petition. The goal was for the performers, which included children, to give voice to murdered, raped, and oppressed Black Americans. The three part poem's opening, titled "Mood: Urgent and Angry," was read by a Black woman and was accompanied by the children's chorus. It set the tone for the dark and dramatic rendition of the petition.

The opening is focused on the mood of Black America, personified by the Black woman narrator. She described her "furrowed brow... scarred hands" her "gaunt body" and "bursting veins," all from the pain inscribed on the Black body by "three hundred and thirty-three years" of oppression, abuse, violence, and murder. The pain, Richardson argued, was "unended" because the government's policy toward Black America was "ever changing, but unchanged." Invoking the constitution, Richardson linked the protection of slavery in the nation's founding document and the perpetuation of slavery in the treatment of Black American's nearly 100 years after emancipation. The slaves may have been emancipated, but their kin were liable to laws and unspoken policies that perpetuated their oppression under a false banner of freedom. Richardson's point was that slavery might have ended, but its legacy of oppression and violence remained.[23]

Richardson continued by describing African culture and the African people kidnapped from the continent – taken from its people, its religion, its geography, and its history and then taken to the cotton fields of the old south. The chorus meanwhile echoed the fear and darkness in these descriptions by shouting "Beware" and describing slave treatment as "unpaid" and "unamended" labor. It moved on to directly attack the farce of American democracy as the Black woman narrator noted that she was the "constitution unamended" and the "citizen undefended." The narrator introduced the audience to the case against the United States government and in particular she

---

22. William Patterson to Beulah Richardson, 24 July 1951, Box 61 Folder 114, Civil Rights Congress Papers, Gale Cengage

23. Beulah Richardson, "Genocide," 1-2, Box 27 Folder 9, Civil Rights Congress Papers, Gale Cengage

called out the hypocrisy of American democracy and the continued abuse and violence against the Black community. It is a powerful and personal indictment and would have been impressive as a live event to bring America's sins to the public.[24]

But Richardson did not wholly abandon the message of unity among working people, she forwarded the idea that white supremacy injures and kills the Black community, and leaves the white community, maimed, battered, and less than itself. It is a powerful invitation for white America to imagine itself not only a part of the regular abuse of Black Americans, but victims of that same abuse and violence. White America has often claimed to be victims of racism, when non-white, non-gender conforming, and non-males speak out for rights, the repeated retort has been discrimination and reverse racism. In the poem, Richardson frames it as a victimization of their own making, racism benefits no one. The Black community is harmed mentally and physically, the white community, psychically.

Richardson explained it as racism robbing white America of its humanity. In an interesting turn of phrase with more meaning to contemporary audiences than to 1950s America, Richardson likens it to an abortion of humankind. A different kind of pro-life idea that advances the rights of all living people to be free not only from racist violence and policies, but free from the damaging effects that hatred has on those doing the hating. Racism aborts white America's soul, because most people do not want to see their "hands stained" in other's blood and destruction. Racism has made Blackness evil and whiteness pure, creating racist hate that transforms white people into killers. But in an appeal to humanity Richardson noted that not all white people are invested in the slaughter, but that it nevertheless robbed all white people of their humanness, even those that rejected racism were stained by the actions and feelings of their fellows. There are those "white-folk" who knew that what robs them of their humanity kills Black people "utterly." It is a shared pain, but it's a shared pain among those who have come to that awareness and the petition and the poem were working to raise that awareness among white Americans.[25]

The poem described how the white person was corrupted, starting as an innocent baby with pink cheeks and an unknowing smile, who grows up to be a child afraid of Black people, but not sure of what exactly to be afraid of. The infant grows to be a child taught to use the "n" word and the teenager learning to use violence to react to

24. Richardson, "Genocide," 2
25. Richardson, "Genocide," 3-5

Blackness. But this teenager will grow to hate his poverty and looks for someone to blame it on. Here Richardson offers up a socialist analysis in art form, insisting that poverty leads to displaced hate, and that hate for white America leads directly to the arms of the Ku Klux Klan. The old adage that children learn hate, included that children learn that poverty is shameful, and poverty is like Blackness. White people learn to hate the people that suffer at the hands of capitalism, much to the delight of capitalist interests who employ white supremacy to ensure their stranglehold on power. The infant in Richardson's poem grows up to be a judge, a police officer, a businessman with a learned hate that served no one but those in power.[26]

Once again the now dead Willie McGee makes an appearance in Richardson's work. Executed in May of that year, his death figured prominently in the minds of CRC activists who felt defeated by the failure to save McGee's life. Richardson noted that though his accuser was a white woman, other white women stepped in to advocate for him and try to save his life. A white woman narrator takes over at this point to appeal to other white people and urge them to stand up for the rights of their Black compatriots. The narrator asked a compelling question, "has white supremacy ended your poverty, your pain, your misery?" She then asks what is to be gained by white supremacy, and the chorus answers "Injustice and death for us, money for our rulers." This passage is particularly poignant because while the CRC and the Communist Party tried to invoke cross-racial unity, Richardson's poem asks the hard questions, does whiteness secure your wealth? Does whiteness ensure safety from war, poverty, and pain? Does whiteness protect white children from prison, violence, and hatred? Richardson asks white America to confront what racism has really done for it. Her answer is that white America loses its humanity with every racist act. Her goal was to put these fundamental questions before white America and to get it to consider deeply what real benefits it gained from racism.[27] Though Richardson was aware that white supremacy and capitalism worked in tandem, she was appealing to working class whites whose grasp on the benefits of their race was contrary to their economic interests. This was a fundamental question for American Communists who tried desperately to convince working people that unity was the only way to achieve economic security and social justice.

Part two, titled "The Dirge," focused on dead Black Americans whose bodies could "bridge the continents" if they were laid end to

---

26. Richardson, "Genocide," 5-6
27. Richardson, "Genocide," 5-6

end. Richardson described the violence of these deaths, and included the violence of poverty, starvation, and neglect. This is an important point because the petition was directly accusing the federal government of complicity because of its inaction. Allowing the states to operate on their own under the guise of state's rights, led to death, unfair arrests, prosecution, and sentencing, and continued segregation, economic disenfranchisement, and a general assault on Black America's well-being. Lynching and execution were not the only forms of genocide, and Richardson made this clear to the audience.[28]

Richardson lists names of those who were in the petition and the manner of the crime committed against them. She lamented the lost potential of each of the men and women who were denied their rights while alive, and brutally murdered, raped or executed. The narrators discussed the 2,000 Black Americans killed since 1945 whose murderers or executioners went unpunished. Therefore, the poem warned there were 2,000 killers still on the loose, still able to prey on Black Americans, knowing that they could escape punishment and condemnation. Their actions were endorsed by the federal, state, and local governments and law enforcement evidenced by the lack of arrests and prosecutions of the killers of Black America.

We Charge Genocide listed a disturbing number of murders, false imprisonments, and incidents of harassment. One particular crime that figured prominently in the petition was the unprosecuted rape of Black women. It included the case of Recy Taylor in Abbeville, Alabama. Taylor was abducted by a group of six white men, taken to a remote location, and repeatedly raped. Danielle McGuire has written at length about this case, and it was invoked by Oprah Winfrey at a 2018 Golden Globes award show. A documentary on the case has also been released that discussed the case and the history of sexually abusing Black women. As *We Charge Genocide* demonstrated, Taylor's case was unfortunately not unusual as white men were rarely ever arrested for raping Black women, unless a local judge was particularly offended by the men willing to soil themselves with interracial sex. Taylor's rape was notable for a number of reasons, a young NAACP field worker named Rosa Parks tried to investigate the case until she was run out of town. The men were also arrested but were not prosecuted and faced no real punishment.[29]

Taylor's rape occurred in 1944, but the petition included it because the case dragged into 1945 and 1946 as local authorities, despite a confession, refused to indict the men. The petition mentioned Parks,

28. Richardson, "Genocide," 7
29. McGuire, *At the Dark End of the Street…*, Ibid

though not by name, simply as an executive secretary of the Committee for Equal Justice for Recy Taylor and included her attempt to visit Taylor's home. Parks was "manhandled" by the local sheriff and ordered out of town. The case garnered so much attention that the Alabama Governor called a special grand jury. It failed to indict the rapists.[30]

Richardson's poem did not mention the Recy Taylor case, but she did include Lilla Bell Carter. Carter, 16 years old, was abducted, raped, and murdered in Pine Island, South Carolina. The man who abducted and raped her was an insurance agent, just a regular guy who knew he would not face real legal consequences. The man broke Carter's neck and put her face down in a mud puddle to try and make it look like she drowned. Richardson asked her audience to consider what Carter could have become if given the chance to live, an explorer, architect, or inventor? Richardson highlighted these cases, particularly Carter's, to demonstrate the horrors of Black life, and particularly Black women's lives, in the United States. The crime of genocide was not only in the rape and murder, but in the failure of local law enforcement to arrest and prosecute men for their crimes. Black women remained vulnerable and white men were able to act without fear of consequences.[31]

Richardson closes part two by likening the American genocide against Black America with the Nazi holocaust. *We Charge Genocide* tried to appeal to the global horror at the Nazi atrocities against Europe's Jews and the fear that it could happen again if developed nations remained indifferent. But Richardson suggests, and historians have confirmed, that Hitler was partly inspired by white supremacists in the United States. An admirer of U.S. restrictive immigration and eugenic laws, Hitler could and did turn to America's example for inspiration and Richardson noted that the genocide that inspired the UN's commitment to human rights was mirrored in America's actions against Black citizens. Not only was the United States guilty in standing by while Hitler and his lackey's murdered millions, it was also guilty because it allowed racist violence from state politicians and law enforcement to go unchecked even while its own policies upheld segregation and perpetuated poverty.[32]

---

30. William L. Patterson, ed. *We Charge Genocide: The Crime of Government Against the Negro People.* (New York: International Publishers, 1951), 80

31. McGuire, *At the Dark End of the Street…*, 34 and Richardson, "Genocide," 8

32. James Q. Whitman, *Hitler's American Model: The United States and the Making of Nazi Race law* (Princeton University Press, 2017)

Part three, titled "Angry and Challenging," takes up the perpetrators of racist violence. Richardson opens with the "clear and present danger" that rapists and murderers run free, free to "mob and lynch and burn." It seems like an obvious point, but to white America, racist violence was also so naturalized that racist criminals were no criminals at all. The government allowed rapists and murderers to roam free in the streets of the United States; and many of those rapists and murderers were the very people who were meant to keep the streets safe. Richardson does not allow white women off the hook accusing them of lying against Black men to save themselves, the very same message from her poem on white womanhood. She wrote that law enforcement and racist whites were "so base" that they were a disgrace to the "whole human race." This part of the poem strikes a shockingly different tone than her poem about white womanhood, but it reflects the anger in the title of part three. She let her feelings of anger rise to the surface as the remainder of the poem described the brutality of racist white America and laid the charge of genocide at its feet.[33]

White America's "eager hands" cut out hearts, and gouged out eyes, and its feet "stamp out life." White Americans burned Black flesh without disgust at its smell and watched "gleefully" as its victims died. The illusion to the Jewish holocaust at the end of part two is brought to life in part three. Richardson, however, flips the narrative to put the brutality of white America into familiar terms and asks the question, who are Americans to condemn the Nazi holocaust, while a genocide was perpetrated in its own house. The difference was that the United States did not need a gestapo because white America "gleefully" participated in Black America's murder. She indicts all of white America in Black genocide.[34]

She continued to describe what today would be labeled the "social construction" of white supremacy. The pink child she described at the beginning was not conceived and born a racist, it was influenced by a culture that valued white lives over all others. The federal government was certainly to blame, but Richardson pointed the finger at movies, schools, radio, and the church. These institutions and outlets were where young naïve babes learned hate and murder. White parents trained their children to be "arsonist[s], rapist[s], murderers, and thieves." This is a damning indictment that put the blame

33. Richardson, "Genocide," 8
34. Richardson, "Genocide," 10

on white America and the institutions it controlled, and Richardson does not offer excuses for Americans who claimed to reject racism.[35]

She linked Black genocide to the American Indian genocide writing that the "red men are dead and dying" while white America clings to innocence. White supremacy drank the blood of "two whole nations," Black and Native. Richardson's use of "nations" to describe Black Americans and American Indians invoked the CPUSA's 1928 Black Belt Thesis that recognized Black Americans as an oppressed nation. She also likened the Black nation to America's imperialist ambitions in Korea where the United States exported "armies across the sea" to spill the blood of "still another colored nation." This colonial analysis was a central point of the CPUSA's anti-Cold War platform. The treatment of people of color at home was mirrored in the imperialist ambitions to secure global capital's resources via neo-colonialism. The U.S. extracted land, labor, and resources from its own national minorities, but capitalist thirst could not be quenched and required even more.[36] This investment in whiteness was an investment in wealth and capitalism; therefore, the answer was to destroy capitalism.

The chorus meanwhile shouts throughout the third act "THIS IS A CLEAR AND PRESENT DANGER." This is a reference to the 1919 *Schenck* decision that ruled first amendment rights were not unlimited if the speech could pose a danger. Richardson was deploying federal legal decisions against the United States arguing that racism, and racist violence, even if committed under the "law" were dangerous and genocidal. She described the base inhumanity and violence in "dismembering" the Black body, cutting out its heart, beating out brains, burning the living and the dead, and dragging bodies through the streets. How could speech be more dangerous than that? This violence was made by "government policy" and it shaped white America into "merciless killers." Richardson asked whether the "pink child" wanted to be a killer, but it hardly mattered when the government fed him white supremacy.[37]

Though the poem's tone changes in part three, Richardson continued her appeal to white America. She asked white citizens if they wanted to remain neutral even while their sons and daughters were being shaped into "beasts, arsonists, rapists, murderers, thieves." It's an interesting question because while Richardson appeals to humanity by asking it to reject the brutality inflicted on Black America, she

---

35. Richardson, "Genocide," 10-11
36. Richardson, "Genocide," 11
37. Richardson, "Genocide," 11

eventually suggests that if white America cannot be made to care, perhaps it can at least care that its own children will be destroyed too. If white America cannot care about saving their fellow Black Americans, they might care about preventing their children from becoming monsters. Any white American reading or listening to the poem should have been appalled at the violence of their own indifference and silence on racism. That is part of the point. It was not enough for whites to condemn racism, white America had to stop it, as actively and aggressively as it participated in it.[38]

Richardson closed the poem by encouraging her listeners to turn to William Patterson and his petition. It was Patterson that was challenging white supremacy and seeking justice and equality for all, including white America. Securing justice for Black America would benefit all Americans because lifting up the oppressed would lift everyone up. The poem ends on a positive note exhorting listeners to engage, not to ignore their government's policies, and to seek justice for themselves by rejecting racism against others.[39] "Genocide," much like Richardson's "A Black Woman Speaks...of White Womanhood, of White Supremacy, of Peace," sought to condemn, but also to encourage, to highlight the dangers of whiteness, and to encourage unity. They are both works of art that are deeply uncomfortable to white listeners, but also encouraging and enlightening. It is art at its greatest, personal, political, terrifying, and loving.

We Charge Genocide did not arouse much interest among the American public, and both the CRC and William Patterson would become ensconced in legal battles against government harassment that effectively destroyed the petition. The CRC and Patterson promoted it throughout 1952, but with an indifferent American public and a federal government actively pursuing Communist and Communist affiliated organizations, the petition was doomed to failure. The CRC disbanded in 1956. Other countries took notice of the document, particularly the Soviet Union, and often called the United States out on its hypocrisy. America's Cold War containment policy was a banner program in anti-democracy as the United States actively silenced domestic critics, suppressed national and anti-colonial movements overseas, and ensured American capitalist investments in non-white nations, all the while securing its place as a global police force willing to destroy democratic governments in its anti-communist zeal. It seemed only to be lost on political figures that anti-communism

---

38. Richardson, "Genocide," 11
39. Richardson, "Genocide," 13

was as un-democratic as the government was accusing communism of being.[40]

Richardson herself would go on to have a remarkable career. In 1959, she took a role in the film adaptation of the play "Take A Giant Step," about a young Black teenager coming of age in white America. While television was becoming the medium of choice for many Americans, Black American actors found little work in the field until the 1960s. Richardson, who used the screen name Beah Richards, would work in film and on stage until landing some television roles. She would continue to work in film and television appearing in major motion pictures like *Beloved* and popular television shows like *The Cosby Show* and *ER*. She was nominated for an academy award and won an Emmy. Richardson is remembered for her acting work, while her political art is largely ignored by anyone aside from scholars. Her writing was not only deeply poignant and popular among an embattled left during the Cold War, but it inspired her comrades to take action, as demonstrated by the Sojourners for Truth and Justice. Her poetry also remains relevant.[41]

Richardson's poetry holds important lessons for a contemporary audience. She makes it clear in her art that white America is guilty, it is guilty of being racist, and it is guilty of choosing its own economic comfort and siding with capitalism, rather than actively challenging the violence of poverty and neglect. Today Americans confront the question of what capitalism has done for it, how voting choices around so-called economic questions further disenfranchise people of color and women, and how appealing fascism and racism become when trying to find the culprit behind white America's economic misery. As Richardson would ask, look past the benefits of whiteness, are they benefits at all? Can securing temporary comfort lead to justice and freedom? Can dwelling in a place of hatred liberate you? In the end, Richardson would likely argue that whiteness can be a shelter, but it too suffers from impermanence. Without seeking racial and economic justice, white America can only find succor in hatred, and that hardly seems an answer to anyone's problems.

---

40. Martin, "Internationalizing 'The American Dilemma'," 54
41. Brian Baxter, "Beah Richards," *The Guardian*, 25 October 2000

Chapter *8*

A Culture of Human Liberation: U.S. Communist Writers in the 20th Century

By Joel Wendland-Liu

"Not to die, but slowly to validate our lives..."
(Muriel Rukeyser, "The Blood is Justified,"
Theory of Flight, 1935)

As many as 4,000 enthusiastic activist-writers jammed the Mecca Temple in New York City in May 1935 to attend the inaugural convention of the League of American Writers. The League had been launched by Communist Party activist-writers to promote unity across the left and center against fascism and reaction. Its membership and leadership would include well-known writers and artists such as Orson Welles, John Steinbeck, Meridel Le Sueur, and Richard Wright. Its members participated in the Unemployed Councils, the John Reed Clubs, the labor schools, the anti-fascist movement supporting Spain and Ethiopia, and the organizing drives of the Congress of Industrial Organizations. They wrote for such magazines and newspapers as the *Daily Worker*, *New Masses*, *Art Front*, *Negro Digest*, *The New Tide*, *Rebel Poet*, *Science & Society*, *Marxist Quarterly*, as well as mainstream publications like *New Republic*, *Harper's Bazaar*, *Town & Country*, *The Nation*, *New Yorker*, and myriad local magazines and community newsletters.[1]

---

1. Michael Denning, *The Cultural Front: The Laboring of American Culture In The Twentieth Century* (Verso, 2011), 434-445. Other more recent useful accounts of this period include T.V. Reed, *Robert Cantwell and the Literary Left: A Northwest Writer Reworks American Fiction* (University of Washington Press, 2014) and Mary Washington, *The Other Blacklist: The African American Literary and Cultural Left of the 1950s* (Columbia University Press, 2015)

In preparation for the convention, organizers shared ideas about the function of revolutionary art and literature. They heard Kenneth Burke, the future president of the American Writers' Congress, organized out of the convention, argue for a "popular front" strategy for left and revolutionary artists. In a speech titled "Revolutionary Symbolism in America," Burke reasoned that in the struggle against capitalism a broad unity of classes could be shaped around artistic symbols related to "the people," rather than the exclusive concept of "the worker." A Marxist critique of capitalism that centers a critique of worker exploitation is pivotal, but art that makes an argument for a mass revolutionary movement must focus on more than a "critique." Rather it must create a positive image of the Communist ideal embodied in the beyond class persona of "the people."[2]

In other words, Burke believed in an organized revolutionary cultural practice that imagined the "widest possible frame of acceptance," or the kind of language and naming systems that could assemble the broadest possible class and democratic forces in that struggle. While Burke specifically named for inclusion other subjectivities closely related to social class (petty bourgeoisie, peasants/tenant farmers, intellectuals, and unemployed workers), I argue that his approach creates an opening for a revolutionary insurgence of what scholar Cheryl Higashida calls "multiply situated, coalitional subjects who adopt historically contingent strategies of resistance." Higashida refers here specifically to people and communities who struggle against special forms of oppression, demand radical social organizing, and craft revolutionary cultural responses (e.g., people who face racism, exploitation due to their citizenship status, oppression as religious minorities, gender or sexual discrimination, disadvantage based on physical or mental [dis]ability). In other words, Popular Front politics resisted the submersion of all into a singularity of a class relation.[3]

Burke's paper produced a flurry of creative discussions about the role of art in society and of ideas in social movements. After the dust settled, the Congress oriented itself toward the Popular Front

---

2. Kenneth Burke, "Revolutionary Symbolism in America" (League of American Writers, 26 April 1935). Burke was elected to lead the American Writers' Congress in 1937 and 1939. His 1935 speech was reprinted in the volume of papers and reports given at the League convention, which included pieces by James T. Farrell, John Dos Passos, Langston Hughes, Meridel Le Sueur, Eugene Clay Holmes, and John Howard Lawson.

3. Cheryl Higashida, *Black Internationalist Feminism: Women Writers of the Black Left, 1945-1995* (University of Illinois Press, 2013), 8

concept, and symbolic representations of both the working class and a progressive people's front flourished. In the first six decades of the Communist Party's existence, novelists, artists, musicians, photographers, playwrights, filmmakers, poets, journalists, educators, scholars, and critics affiliated or sympathetic with it produced a body of lasting influential cultural products, scholarship, and critical theory. This essay is an analysis of a narrow slice of that big picture with its focus on the theories of scholar activists such as W.E.B. Du Bois, Alain Locke, Kenneth Burke, and Claudia Jones, and a synthesis of the common themes of novelists Claude McKay, Agnes Smedley, H.T. Tsiang, Arna Bontemps, Carlos Bulosan, Muriel Rukeyser, Alexander Saxton, Lloyd Brown, and Alfred Maund.[4] These authors made conscious artistic efforts to foreground the specific values of the exploited and oppressed and their revolutionary actions in attempting to build a new world. And, to their understanding of social conditions and theories of liberation, they used groundbreaking concepts of systemic intersectionality that flex and expand Marxian concepts.

Symbols of Authority

Radical cultural theory and practice were especially essential for Marxist rhetorician and critic Kenneth Burke. Perhaps it was the unique combination of the revolutionary spirit of his cohort of writers, his enthusiasm for creative and intellectual work, and the blending of thought with activism that prompted a burst of theoretical creativity. The 1930s saw a proliferation of his writing. In that decade, he published one novel, a collection of poems, and by the time he published a collection of essays with the Louisiana State University Press in 1941, he had written a total of four other nonfiction books of literary and social criticism.[5]

---

4. My choice to include two novels published before the Popular Front policy in 1935 complicates these matters. But, as Mark Solomon has argued in *The Cry Was Unity: Communists and African Americans, 1917-1936* (University Press of Mississippi, 1998), the requirements of real-life promoted Popular Front strategies in advance of the adoption of the Popular Front as Party policy (258-284). I argue that when invoking broader concepts of political struggle for liberation, radical writers imaginatively rendered a multidimensional representation of reality that resists economistic formulas.

5. For the later editions of these books, republished in the 1950s through the 1980s, in submission to red-baiting discipline, Burke deleted some of his more partisan thoughts and, in addenda, downplayed his affiliation with

As cultural historian Michael Denning has argued, "Kenneth Burke remains a starting point for reconstructing the cultural theory of the Popular Front." Today, many graduate students in rhetoric and composition studies, communication studies, and English Departments will recognize his difficult *Motives* texts published in 1945 and 1950. As vital as those books have been to shaping those academic fields, according to Denning, they remain a minor part of Burke's overall contribution to cultural studies and reflect only a sliver of his most creative ideas.[6]

Burke's best theoretical contributions appear in his earlier books and in contributions to the *New Masses* and *Science & Society.* One important idea he developed is the concept of "symbolic authority." In *Attitude Toward History* (1937), he defines it as the ideological hegemony of ideas, institutions, biases, knowledge, and rules of right behavior manipulated by the dominant classes of society. In a concrete social formation "a vast symbolic synthesis, a rationale of imaginative and conceptual imagery that 'locates' the various aspects of experience" is produced and flexibly altered by contending class and social forces. The structure and function of this symbolic field is closely related to the needs of the dominant class (and its allied forces). The symbolic field mobilizes what Antonio Gramsci would characterize as a "constellation of historic forces," and aims to extract loyalty from the mass of people and workers to the status quo.[7] Indeed, Burke argues, this symbolic field is most effective when it succeeds in producing a desire on the part of the oppressed and exploited to participate in their subjugation.[8] For example, in Arna Bontemps's novel, *Black Thunder* (1936), the elderly slave Ben Woodfolk is deeply pleased when his white masters call

---

and leading role as a Communist Party cultural theoretician. For a discussion of how Burke edited his books and memories of the 1930s, see: Denning, *The Cultural Front...*, Ibid, 434-445.

6. Denning, *The Cultural Front...*, Ibid, 435

7. On Gramsci, see: E. San Juan Jr., *Hegemony and Strategies of Transgression: Essays in Cultural Studies and Comparative Literature* (SUNY Press, 1995), 54. Denning notes strong similarities between Burke's and Gramsci's ideas, 435. I contend that Burke, Du Bois, Locke, and Jones developed an understanding of the complexities of "historic forces" well in advance of the circulation of Gramsci's work in the U.S.

8. Kenneth Burke, *Attitudes Toward History* (University of California Press, 1984), 179. On the participation of the oppressed or exploited in their own and the general subjugation of the exploited and oppressed, see, for example, 36 or 156. Burke's shows how a powerful minority can control a social system.

him "a good boy," partially motivating his decision to betray the slave insurrection.[9]

In a revolutionary setting, however, a mass of people may threaten to shift their loyalties from one set of symbols of authority to another; for example, they may start to discuss the value of socialist ideas or throw their support to a socialist candidate or reject the legitimacy of the exploitation of nature for profit. In this situation, the symbols of capitalist authority, the rhetoric of what DuBois calls the "American Assumption" – individual hard work makes success, "America, love it or leave it," "there is no alternative," investors create jobs – don't seem reasonable anymore. Sometimes the symbols of authority are layered with complicating falsehoods: white people are obviously superior to people of color, immigrants (of color) steal jobs, Muslims are dangerous, political correctness represses religious freedom, etc.

Burke's model of symbolic conflict doesn't reduce class struggle to a mere skirmish over words, ideas, or abstractions, however. Instead, critical ideas should reveal levels of power in a capitalist system in a particular national and international framework.[10] All symbols, critical or dominant, are closely linked to economic and political contradictions and historical developments. Symbols of authority, however, work to shape individuals to beliefs and actions that express support for a vested interest in the capitalist controlled state, in dominant racial, social, and gender identities, and existing social institutions. As these symbols make claims about the nature of the world, they work to baffle us about objective social relations of capitalist society. In *Daughter of Earth*, for example, Marie Rogers encounters a college professor who convinces his students of the justice of super-exploitation of Black Brazilian plantation workers because it keeps rubber prices low for American consumers and because those workers *enjoyed* exploitation. Thus, an argument about low prices and the apparent normalcy of white supremacy elicit support for imperialism and brutal work conditions.[11]

Because, for many people, symbols of authority seem to explain social experience, however inadequately, they feel natural and given. Symbols of authority work because they make the status quo seem normal and even *just*; alternatives too radical, change impossible or

---

9. Arna Bontemps, *Black Thunder*, 11

10. Kenneth Burke, "Twelve Propositions on the Relation Between Economics and Psychology," *Science and Society* 2(2), 1938, 242-253. Burke's critical essays from this period are collected in the 1941 book *Philosophy of Literary Form*.

11. Agnes Smedley, *Daughter of Earth*, 287

utopian. Sometimes social movements pressure elites to extend or flex those symbols of authority. Perhaps overtly racist laws or words become unacceptable. But impassioned defenses of racist police brutality continue to dominate debates on public safety and crime. Often, defenses of immigrant rights center on their adjustment or assimilation of American values and culture rather than on a right of the free movement and fair treatment of labor.

The general acceptance of symbols of authority can be made vulnerable by economic or political crisis or effective social movement organizing, engendering a large scale popular realization of capitalism's failures and various linked oppressions and abuses. But the process of such an unsettling shouldn't be limited merely to critique, and the process isn't automatic. Radical cultural production promises to connect "our spiritual values to external necessities." Artistic work that assembles an imaginative social organism stitched together by threads of cooperation and socialization – communism – offers the best hope for establishing a clearer relation between thought, language, and social practices rooted in and supplementing the democratization of resources and relations. Such a process calls for a common or public ownership of symbols, ideas, words, and authority. A culture that values new symbols of authority that stress these values provides an essential resource for human liberation.[12]

The secret lies in the non-rational[13] psychological process by which a reader naturally and almost unconsciously identifies with the "hero" of a novel, the speaker of a poem, the subject of a painting, the protagonist of a movie. (Or, the psychological process could be reversed or unsettled wherein a reader explicitly refuses identification with authority or learns to identify in fresh ways with a character that holds unfamiliar social identities.) What makes that cultural artifact "good," is its production of meaning through identification with the broadest experiences. This latter element is related to what Marxist scholar Sidney Finkelstein calls "typicality," or the "revelation of a response to a challenge raised by life which can be found in others because they share the same world."[14] The emotional experience of engaging with reality through an imaginary experience

---

12. Kenneth Burke, "My Approach to Communism," 16-20

13. Burke identifies the pairing of rational and irrational as incomplete; instead, he links rational, irrational, and non-rational to human psychology. *Attitudes Toward History*, 171n

14. Finkelstein, *Existentialism and Alienation in American Literature* (New York: International Publishers, 1965), 9; San Juan Jr., *Hegemony and Strategies of Transgression*, 58-60. San Juan Jr. traces the development of and different

produces pleasure (or pain) in questioning common sense notions about social relations or the nature of perceived reality.

Four Revolutionary Concepts

Revolutionary writers, Burke argued, experiment with this non-rational process of identification in order to challenge accepted symbols of authority within the capitalist frame and to promote a shift in values that favor human connections to other people, the democratization of resources and power, the power inherent in cooperation, or the strategic value of cultural diversity and collective self-determination of the oppressed. Four dialectically constellated concepts emerge that sum up the cultural theory of the times: (1) humanization, (2) collective action, (3) "the widest possible frame of acceptance," and (4) an awareness of the role of non-class systems (like racism/white supremacy or gender relations) in creating oppression and determining the social forces for change.[15]

Capitalist symbols of authority normalize dehumanization through the process of an imaginary invisible hand of the market. What appears as a brutal or immoral system of exploitation to the Marxist critic, capitalist ideology regards as mandated action based in the sole imperative of realizing a profit. The only choice available is whether or not to submit to that imperative, for it will operate regardless of our choices. Dehumanization works through the suspension of human agency and choice against this imperative. It is also constituted by the necessary expansion of markets, the excess of commodities, proliferation of technology, which seem to lie outside of human control and serve as measures of progress, strength, growth, success, and even racial hierarchy. When making and selling more things serves as the measure of the quality of a society, and the collection of more commodities around us signify status or social progress, we experience more intense degrees of dehumanization, the particularities of which reveal relations of power hierarchies.

Agnes Smedley dramatizes class dynamics of dehumanization in her novel *Daughter of Earth* (1929; republished in 1973, 1987, and again in 2019). The protagonist/narrator Marie Rogers describes a conflict

---

positions staked out in Marxist cultural theory from Lenin, Gramsci, through Brecht and Lukacs.

15. For a broader discussion of how U.S. multi-ethnic, working-class culture deployed radical versions of these concepts see Wendland, *The Collectivity of Life: Spaces of Social Mobility and the Individualism Myth* (Lexington Books, 2016)

over payment between her father and the operator of a nearby coal mine. John Rogers believes that he has been unfairly treated by the owner, Mr. Turner, who refuses to pay him despite having hauled tons of coal. Rogers first appeals to reason and morality, arguing that he worked long hours every day to bring Turner's coal from the mines. As if he was powerless to comply with this explanation, "Mr. Turner said, 'Look at the contract, Mr. Rogers. Look at the contract.'" The capitalist Turner deflects Rogers' entreaties, deferring to abstract legality beyond his power which forces him to render the contract void and the promise of payment withdrawn. Indeed, once signed, the contract itself holds sole authority over the two men, supposedly in equal force, is morally as well as legally binding, and thus can't be broken. Turner's imperative for increasing his profit margin justifies his dismissal of Rogers' moral claim to payment. In frustration, Rogers threatens to reclaim his humanity by assaulting Turner but realizes that the power of the law would be on the owners' side and resigns himself to this alienated power.[16]

The scene contextualizes human power within class forces shaped by a concrete social formation and diminishes the ideology of individualism as an illusion of personal sovereignty. The men in this scene turn out to be "powerless" to act in the face of power supposedly beyond themselves. If Turner chooses to do the right thing and pay Rogers for his work, he would violate the imperative of profit making and position himself at a relative disadvantage to other coal operators. Turner's position within a network of institutional class power shapes the achievement of his goals through market imperatives, legal discourse, and state coercive might. Roger's lack of affiliation with a parallel set of class forces puts him in the position of fending for himself without any luck. His inability to reconnect with a larger class collectivity to enhance his individualized humanity or to sustain his resistance to exploitation proves a continuing source of frustration, driving him to excessive alcoholism, gambling, abuse, and ultimately a path of personal self-destruction.

The interaction of these two men produces the possibility of imaginatively reversing the social process of alienation. By recognizing the absurdity of Turner's claim of powerlessness, the scene reveals how carefully the capitalist used his knowledge of legal symbols and his class affiliation with social institutions to squeeze a little bit more out of John Rogers. It opens up the necessity of the cooperative connections with other humans that people like Rogers need to improve their relative position in society, for it is only an alignment

---

16. Smedley, *Daughter of Earth*, 68-70

of sympathetic forces on a collective scale that will alter the balance of power with the Turners of the world. Thus, it offers a revealing critique and points to the strategic mechanisms for radically altering capitalist relations.

Alienation of human power as part of the imperative of capitalist profit taking finds itself mirrored in heteronormative patriarchal relations that organize the working class family. Rogers remains committed to a system that allocates to him violent control over his wife and children. Despite his powerlessness in class relations, Rogers can use his physical power to control the labor, emotions, actions, and life choices of his wife and daughters. His wife's sister turns to prostitution to earn her living independently of a husband, father, or brother-in-law. Marie Rogers, the narrator, daughter, and protagonist of the novel, learns that women face only two choices in life: financial security through the acceptance of subjugation through marriage (never guaranteed for a working class woman) and prostitution and be deemed "fallen." Her discovery of radical politics, anti-imperialist, and collective struggle enables her to defy this trap created through an intersection of capitalist class relations and patriarchal gender relations. Disruption of dehumanization occurs with the realization that "human beings can now begin to solve their problems realistically," that they can intervene in social processes that seem alien to them.[17]

Cooperative human connections serve as a common theme among most of the working class and progressive culture of the era under consideration in this essay. For example, Claude McKay, the bisexual African American poet and novelist, who helped shape the Communist International's political positions on racism, national self-determination, and anti-imperialism, approaches cultural theory with racism at the center of his worldview.[18] In his second novel *Banjo: A Story Without a Plot* (1928; republished in the 1970s), a small group of Black sailors from the African diaspora meet in the bustling port city of Marseilles, France and build a collectivity to ensure their survival and which also sustains them politically and

---

17. Finkelstein, *Existentialism and Alienation in American Literature*, Ibid, 41; Burke, *Attitudes Toward History*, 150

18. In 1922 and 1923, McKay attended the Fourth Congress of the Third Communist International at which he wrote a slim volume of essays on aspects of African American life published as *Negroes in America* (Associated Faculty Pr. Inc.), not translated into English until the 1970s. See also, McKay, "The Situation of Blacks," 250-257; David Levering Lewis, *When Harlem was in Vogue* (Penguin Book, 1997), 56-58; McKay, *Negroes in America*, 1979 [1923].

culturally. Together they encounter and resist racism, colonialism, and exploitation.

Instead of centering the class relations of forces wherein the working class characters confront the exploitative capitalist class characters, McKay's work explores the misalignment of these forces in particular places and situations due to racism and imperialism. Banjo is the name of one of the two main characters, whose real name is Lincoln Agrippa Daily. He takes the nickname because he owns and plays the banjo, with a dream of forming a band in the city of Marseilles (or "Europe's back door") to earn some money and entertain the inhabitants of the Ditch. The Ditch is the section of the city to which Black, working class migrants from all over the world flock.[19]

As the novel progresses, we discover that Banjo's life philosophy is to resist capitalist imperatives of work and industrial discipline, patriarchy, racism and imperialism, individualist ideology, and the hierarchies of authority embedded in modern society. Thus, Banjo serves as a magnet for several other Black, African, and Arab working class men and women who share this philosophy, forming a small collective that share resources, develop a political analysis of local and global events, and work together to build a shared, life sustaining cultural identity. This collectivity simultaneously nurtures group identity and survival while allowing space for individual choices and autonomy.[20] Part of Banjo's group launches a jazz band to earn some money. But innovative collaboration and free artistic expression supplant even their material goals. Instead, their collective work promotes joy and fosters a collective identity through the exploration of Black musical forms, exchanging jokes and storytelling, and vibrant political discussion. Theirs is a celebration of Black diasporic culture that displaces the dominant white claim that Black culture is inherently degraded and backward.

One member of the group, Goosey, who expresses political views affiliated with the Garveyite movement, criticizes Banjo for taking that nickname and playing the instrument. "Banjo is bondage," he opines, claiming that white people pay to be entertained by Black banjo players and that Banjo is merely performing a stereotype of the happy Black entertainer playing "coon" music. Goosey prefers more highly cultured music of the classical variety to what he characterizes as backward African music, enunciating a discourse of racial uplift

---

19. McKay, *Banjo*, 69
20. See: A.B. Christa Schwarz, *Gay Voices of the Harlem Renaissance* (Indiana university Press, 2003), 115

through the assimilation of acceptable cultural values. Banjo replies, asserting personal as well as Black cultural autonomy: "I play that theah instrument becaz I like it. I don't play no Black Joe hymns, I play lively tunes."[21] While this discussion reveals an ongoing tension within the group about their relation to white cultural dominance, it accentuates Black autonomy and creativity as their primary motive.

Banjo's evocative declaration of cultural self-determination aligns him with proletarian internationalism but resists a Eurocentric frame that prioritizes a proletarian standpoint at the expense of cultural affiliations forged through resistance to imperialism and racism. Banjo's friend Ray, whose biography mirrors McKay's (West Indian born, a writer with a radical leftist outlook and a searing critique of racism and imperialism), witnesses and comments on life and events in the Ditch. As a member of Banjo's collective, he views Banjo's philosophy as an expression of a "real" version of Black life, authentically African in origin. He links Banjo's declaration of artistic autonomy to the "self-mastery" and "self-assurance" of African sculpture.[22] While this assertion of autonomy is essential, both Banjo and Ray recognize that it doesn't automatically free the Black artists from the puzzle of white racism and cultural dominance.

Ray expresses a Marxist critique of capitalism in a conversation with a white friend, recognizing the value of multiracial alliances. Ultimately, however, when urged to move away from the Ditch, Ray rejects the idea of staying in a "respectable" (white) proletarian neighborhood. Frequent racist interactions with working class whites have caused Ray to feel "an inside-boiling mood," which his white friend fails to understand. "His white face and the privileges of his white inheritance in a white universe" limit his ability to connect with Ray's experiences and to prioritize the special oppression of Black people.[23] While the cultural differences between the two men do not bother Ray, the limit of the white man's political consciousness and his idealistic radicalism does. Ray is tired of whites who fail to account for their role in the perpetuation of racism, which cannot be overcome through easy platitudes about proletarian politics. Racism can be observed in radical movements in which white activists regard anti-racist or anti-colonialist formations as challenges to the supremacy of class-based action.

Banjo offers insight into whiteness, especially its radical, progressive form. By comparison, we see that Marie Rogers, in *Daughter of*

21. McKay, *Banjo*, 90
22. McKay, *Banjo*, 130
23. McKay, *Banjo*, 272

Earth, regards racism primarily as an intellectual, abstract term. But, when her work and emotional life involves her in the Indian anti-colonial struggle and the specific experiences of Indian comrades with white supremacy, she attains a new understanding.[24] In *Banjo*, white intellectualizations of racism drive Ray to seek spatial distance from them. As a remedy to for this alienation, he pursues stronger bonds of diasporic collectivity and more profound anti-imperialist politics. These symbolic renderings of barriers to effective multira-cial alliance substantialize Burke's call for the humanization of social relations, cooperative human collectivity, and a more comprehensive "frame of acceptance" of the political field of resistance.

Class, Race, and Anti-colonialism

My thematic comparison of *Daughter of Earth* and *Banjo* points to the-matic issues that form vital refrains in the theoretical contributions of W.E.B. DuBois and radical philosopher Alain Locke. During the Great Depression, both men gravitated (if critically) to the radical politics of the Communist Party and contributed to the ideas that sustained its cultural movement. In 1935, DuBois published what still stands as one of the most important nonfiction works of the 20th century: *Black Reconstruction in America* (republished in 1992).[25] That same year, Alain Locke taught as the only professional Black phi-losopher in the U.S., and had been a founding figure of the Harlem Renaissance in the 1920s, mentoring many artists and writers affil-iated with that cultural movement. By the 1930s, Locke had grown "supportive of the new thrust of proletarian literature," aligning with the Marxist left and the Popular Front. He regarded himself as an economic democrat, an internationalist, and an anti-colonialist.[26] His intellectual efforts centered on the emergent field of cultural

---

24. *Daughter of Earth* could be read constructively in conjunction with Gerald Horne, *The End of Empires: African Americans and India* (Temple Uni-versity Press, 2009), and Vijay Prashad, *Everybody was Kung Fu Fighting: Afro-Asian Connections and the Myth of Cultural Purity* (Beacon Press, 2002), and *The Karma of Brown Folk* (University of Minnesota Press, 2001)

25. For more on Du Bois, see: Gerald Horne, *W.E.B Du Bois: A Biography* (Greenwood Press, 2009), *Black and Red: W.E.B. Du Bois and the Afro-American Response to the Cold War* (SUNY Press, 1985) and *Race Woman: The Lives of Shirley Graham Du Bois* (NYU Press, 2008) for additional details on Du Bois's political development, activities, influences, and perspectives.

26. Leonard Harris, "Introduction," *The Philosophy of Alain Locke: Harlem Renaissance and Beyond* (Temple University Press, 1991), 7-8

relativism that had begun to challenge dominant concepts of biological and scientific racism. Rather than the product of nature, social
identities (like race and ethnicity), he showed, are historically conditioned by how people organize social systems. Further, through
self-activity, people resisted and reshaped those systems over time.

The profound influence of DuBois and Locke on the creative minds
and intellectual ferment of the period is worth careful attention, particularly on DuBois's *Black Reconstruction* and Locke's essay titled
"Values and Imperatives." As noted earlier, DuBois had adopted the
phrase "American Assumption" to name the ubiquitous ideology
of classlessness and social mobility. Essentially, American workers
accept the myth that anyone could become a capitalist through hard
work, intelligent decision making, and a commitment to Christi-
anity, individualism, and competition. Social mobility by will. Of
course, DuBois also notes, this ideology entailed a racist and gendered component in that it applied to white men alone, excluding
Native Americans, African-descended people, and other people of
color from its swath of influence.[27] Indeed, the frenzied and violent
reaction to Black social mobility through collective political and economic activity during Reconstruction, proved how well guarded
were the racial borders of the American Assumption.

In close conjunction with the American Assumption, there lurked
what DuBois called the "American Blindspot." This feature of white
American self-delusion explained why whites refused to recognize or
meaningfully address the special racial oppression of African Americans. This "blindspot," at best, worked to allow whites to pretend
that the American Assumption was racially neutral or color blind,
and that failure to accomplish social mobility proved the biological
or cultural inferiority of Black people. At worst, white indifference to
racism resulted from racist hate.[28]

Even radical whites are susceptible to this "blindspot."[29] They
sometimes create a formula of class struggle that envisions two
contending class forces, the bourgeoisie and the proletariat (as
abstractions), competing for social power. This recipe – concealing
differences constituted by cultural experiences, racism, gender ideologies, detaching class struggle from global contexts – ignores real

---

27. Du Bois, *Black Reconstruction in America*, 183
28. Du Bois, *Black Reconstruction in America*, 376-377
29. Du Bois's metaphor of blindness suggests the indifference of whites
to Black suffering depends on a privilege of sight that regards blindness as
a weakness or shortcoming rather than another way of experiencing and
knowing the world.

262   FAITH IN THE MASSES

historical data that demands more complexity. Indeed, for DuBois, Black initiative in the form of a "general strike" (in alliance with and not led by abolition-democracy forces) produced the conditions that Frederick Douglass had described as "[e]vents more mighty than man" and forced abolition, voting rights, and equality onto the democratic agenda. This movement, which DuBois acknowledges as spontaneous and disorganized in most places, set in motion, events that foreshadowed and conditioned the major social revolutions and global conflicts of the early 20th century.[30]

DuBois's study of the Civil War and Reconstruction reveals that class alignments were not as simple as theory would have them. He shows how contending class forces sought allies in competition for power in ways that proved that abstraction untenable. What he calls "a new doctrine of race hatred" or "racial propaganda" served to divide the U.S. proletariat along the lines of section, race, and nationality, often pitting them against each other in a bid to realize the American Assumption.[31] Meanwhile, Northern capital and the Southern planter class – both capitalist classes – fought to control the U.S. government after the Civil War, and made concessions to sections of the working class in temporary alliances to gain the upper hand over their rivals. The result was never inevitable; racism did not necessarily have to work out as a source of division in the working class. Working class whites chose to accept that alignment in exchange for a "psychological wage" of superiority and for social benefits at the expense of their Black neighbors and their collective class power.[32]

DuBois's analysis moves from economistic abstractions to concrete, historical reality. It is a materialist concept of history that emphasizes the social construction of non-class forces that mutually constitute the level of consciousness of class positionality and struggle, that shape the nature of that struggle. White supremacy subverted a genuinely revolutionary program (the radical Reconstruction of the South and the U.S. after the Civil War) and abetted "the counter-revolution of property" in the post-Reconstruction reactionary period that established Jim Crow apartheid. Instead of radical change, what emerged from the Reconstruction period, DuBois argues, was a united capitalist class led by Northern finance capital and a divided working class, fractured by racism, xenophobia, and the acceptance of whiteness as a social property and privilege.

---

30. Douglass quoted in Du Bois, *Black Reconstruction in America*, 101
31. Du Bois, *Black Reconstruction in America*, 670
32. Du Bois, *Black Reconstruction in America*, 700-701

Social status for whites, even the minuscule privilege distributed to poor white people, was accompanied by institutionalized insult, harm, and degradation for African Americans. Many whites had come to believe that if Black people (or people of another nationality or non-white ethnic group) realized some economic gains or political power, it would diminish the status of white workers. Indeed, DuBois observes that many white workers preferred poverty and subjugation to the capitalist class over alliances with workers of color that could result in a collective revolutionary change.[33] This produced a balance of forces that allowed capitalists to dominate political parties with a conservative and imperialist agenda that would never be seriously challenged until the Great Depression realigned those forces. DuBois, thus, regards theories of class struggle as incomplete if they fail to submit a working class strategy to an analysis of non-class[34] and extra-national systems, forces, and ideologies such as racism and imperialism.

Locke extends this argument into the field of philosophy. The essay, "Values and Imperatives," if read as a critique of contemporary interpretations of Marxism with which Locke was sympathetically engaged, reveals a similar complexity. Locke criticizes what he calls "monism" and "absolutism" in philosophy, or the construction of a closed system of thought that explains human social and psychological life as universal without consideration of how the cultural biases intrinsic to the philosopher's experience, ideas, language, and perspectives shape the construction of that system. Manufacturing an ethical system of values and imperatives based on a culturally biased system of thought, when elevated to the level of universality and objectivity, produces social hierarchies or ethnocentrism, or the delusional belief in one's cultural superiority over other values

---

33. Du Bois, *Black Reconstruction in America*, 700-701

34. I do not wish to imply that racism is a wholly non-class social relation. It is shaped by and shapes class relations within a social totality of capitalist forces and relations of production. However, it remains semi-autonomous of class forces. Racism is inherent within the totality of social relations of production but contradictorily also outside of that totality, revealing the necessity for a horizon of revolutionary politics. While working-class people should use the specific tools of power related to class struggle to alter racist relations, the presence of racisms outside of the particular relation of capital to labor ensures they will have to adapt non-class strategic goals and forms of struggle. See Wendland, "Class, Community, and Working-class Consciousness," and "Race, Gender and Structural Inequalities in the Great Recession and the Recovery." See a discussion of a "horizon" of politics in Jodi Dean, *The Communist Horizon* (Verso, 2018).

systems. This problem has plagued Western philosophy for centuries and afflicts Western Marxism as well.

He offers a path away from this problem but reframing the central ethical problem of the transition to socialism: "how to ground some normative principle or criteria of objective validity for values without resort to dogmatism and absolutism on the intellectual plane, and without falling into their corollaries, on the plane of social behavior and mass coercion."[35] In other words, demobilizing Western delusions of economic, ethical, ethno-cultural, political superiority leaves us with the difficult but liberating problem of working out what system of values could replace it that doesn't reinstall a new coercive dogma.

Here, his version of cultural relativism serves as a healthy substitute for bigotry. Cultural bias, when combined with the "American Assumption" and the "American Blindspot," produces circular reasoning. The worldview of white supremacy, of support for capitalism, of an uncritical belief that American society is ethically and culturally superior to all others, justifies war, intervention, imperialism. This imperialist agenda is hidden behind the lie of helping others who are incapable of governing themselves while extracting their resources and labor for profit that support an excessive life that prolongs the delusion of American cultural superiority. It is a vicious and deadly tautology that subverts the ideals of humanistic democracy. Cultural relativism, however, unlocks the recognition that "our varied absolutes are revealed largely as a rationalization of our preferred values and their imperatives" rather than universal, objective truths. People in different places and social systems may value other things. Values "are rooted in attitudes, not in reality, and pertain to ourselves, not the world."[36] Acknowledging the gap between our experience and global realities, combined with what Locked calls "social reciprocity," can reduce value bigotry and introduce "value pluralism."[37] By way of example, we might regard Marie Rogers' enthusiasm for work in the anti-colonial struggle with her Indian comrades as a form of social reciprocity. Locke's system establishes cultural and national self-determinism as pillars of the anti-imperialist movement.

To buttress this point, Locke notes that during the transition to socialism, the ascendancy of the global working class would propel a revolutionary alteration in the power and alignment of class forces.

---

35. Locke, "Values and Imperatives," 36
36. Locke, "Values and Imperatives," 46
37. Locke, "Values and Imperatives," 48

But such revolutionary focus would not alone end "psychological tribes," his term for racial, cultural, or other political collectivities that often nurture hierarchical, ethnocentric values. In other words, a Marxist revolution will not by itself end racism (or other systems of oppression). A revolution of values aimed at producing social reciprocity and value pluralism against dogmatism and absolutism – even Marxist ones – would aid the dialectical transformation of those specific non-class conflicts.

Thus, DuBois and Locke flex and bend Marxism to incorporate a "wider frame of acceptance," a larger terrain of analysis that positions revolutionary agency outside of the major colonial centers, links people of color in a systematic anti-colonialism and global anti-racism, and emphasizes the agency, self-activity, and self-determination of the oppressed as the catalyst for revolutionary change. But DuBois's work also serves as something of a warning. Despite scholar Bill Mullen's overly simplistic claim that *Black Reconstruction* submits a "typology" of international revolution naively linked to a "Stalinized" bureaucracy,[38] DuBois's work situates the industrial working class insurgency he observed within a broader historical context. Its roots lay in the fertile soil of the revolutionary-democratic promise of Reconstruction led by an activated Black proletariat emergent from slavery, demanding political, economic, and social power. When the working class had the opportunity through inter-racial alliance to remake fundamentally American values and society shaped by a revolutionary, multi-racial proletarian leadership, white workers chose instead a chimerical racial affiliation with white supremacy and the white capitalist class, leaving Black people to suffer the consequences of Jim Crow racial apartheid. Sixty years later, DuBois is saying, American Blacks have a more prominent international ally in the global anti-imperialist left. If white American workers want to come along, they are welcome.

Individual, Society, World

H.T. Tsiang's *And China Has Hands* (self-published in 1937; republished in 2003 and 2016), Arna Bontemps' *Black Thunder* (1936; republished in 1968 and 1991), Muriel Rukeyser's *Savage Coast* (rejected for publication in 1938; published in 2011); and Carlos Bulosan's *The Cry and the Dedication* (unpublished in the 1950s; published in the U.S.

---

38. Bill V. Mullen, *Un-American: W.E.B. Du Bois and the Century of World Revolution* (Temple University Press, 2015). Mullen expresses doubt about the "general strike" concept, hinting that it Du Bois exaggerated the strike.

in 1995) explore radical connections among individuals, localized social relations of production, and transnational anti-imperialism. Each develops the four theoretical concepts associated with the Popular Front cultural paradigm: 1) the humanization of the oppressed, 2) collective, cooperative action for revolutionary change, 3) promoting the broadest possible alignment of class forces in the struggle, and 4) recognition of non-class systems of oppression. Following the logic of the anti-imperialist Popular Front, each locates the content of political struggle in overlapping local, national, and international contexts.

The Popular Front cultural ethos influenced the literary works of the Louisiana born Arna Bontemps significantly. Raised in Los Angeles, Bontemps migrated to New York City to join the Harlem Renaissance. There he published poems and a mostly ignored novel while teaching in a parochial school. He befriended the poet Langston Hughes and in 1931 co-authored with him the children's book *Popo and Fina*. Bontemps moved to Huntsville, Alabama shortly after that with his wife to teach at Oakwood Junior College. His radical affiliations were exposed, and in three short years, he was forced out of that job and to return to his parents' home in Los Angeles. There, he wrote *Black Thunder*, which earned him some critical praise. He published other children's books (with radical writer Jack Conroy), a play, anthologies of African American poetry and folklore, and one other novel.[39]

The plot centers on the historical 1800 conspiracy and the short lived revolt led by Gabriel involving over 1,100 enslaved and free Blacks in and around Richmond, Virginia. The plan included the creation of three columns of several hundred insurgents to capture an armory, the seats of civil authority, and to secure the highways to other major cities to which the conspirators expected the rebellion to spread. Armed with a handful of guns, clubs, and homemade swords, the insurrectionists began to march toward their objectives, when an unprecedented rainstorm flooded the local rivers and streams preventing their quick passage across the countryside. Reluctantly the rebels returned to their homes expecting to put their plan into effect a couple of days later. Fearful participants in the plot, however, confessed the deed to local white authorities, and widespread panic and a mass killing of suspected rebels ensued, until Gabriel and his lieutenants were hunted down and assassinated.

Bontemps explores the relationships of the insurrectionists to white radicals affiliated with the Jacobin current in the French

---

39. Rampersad, "Introduction to the 1992 Edition," *Black Thunder*, vii-xx.

revolution, to the slave revolt that overthrew French rule in Haiti, and to the individual consciousness of both supporters and opponents of the rebellion. In line with DuBois's "general strike" thesis, *Black Thunder* emphasizes that Black liberation centers mainly on the actions and choices of Black people, not on the leadership or values of radical white people. While abolitionist whites play a crucial role, it is Gabriel's obsession with freedom, the strategic thinking of the leadership of the insurrection, the willingness of the collective to work to dismantle the authority of the slave system through work and sacrifice that will bring freedom. Additionally, the story attributes value to both Western and African cultural resources for sustaining a shared belief in their humanity, the necessity of their struggle for freedom, and the worth of their sacrifice. Similar to DuBois's internationalism, the novel deploys inspirational relations to the Haitian rebellion, and the strategic goal of material connections with the Black Jacobins in the Caribbean maps the possibility of making permanent their revolution.

The narrative strategy of "interior monologue" reveals these motives, inspirations, and goals as mental processes during which his characters comment on their own and others' actions. This form enacts the decisive relation of thought, language, individual choice, and action with historical transformation. For example, Ben, the older enslaved man who ultimately betrays the rebellion, reveals a conflicted consciousness that craves freedom but has so internalized white supremacy that he accepts the racial hierarchy. While his friendship with another enslaved man trigger his involvement with the rebellion, his fear and his love for his white oppressors prove disastrous. At one point, Ben carries his aging master, "Marse Sheppard," to bed after a fainting spell. Ben reverses the relation between the two men by comforting Sheppard, saying, "you got so much mo' to think about. That's howcome I don't have no spells like you. I got *you* looking out after me, but who's got you?" Later, while preparing the house for bedtime, Ben thinks about feeling "the warmth and security of Mr. Mosley Sheppard's supper table." Indeed, these scenes hint that Ben's relation to Sheppard mimics that which an old married couple might share.[40]

This mystifying reversal of dependency, power, and care within the racist and exploitative relation of slavery inflicts Ben's consciousness, distorting his perception of the necessity of freedom and the nature of his humanity. Though he briefly supports the insurrection, Ben constantly worries about the harm renegade slaves would inflict

---

40. Bontemps, *Black Thunder*, 51, 71, 93

on whites and their threat to the supposed security of the slave system. He wonders to himself, "Oh, it was hard to love freedom. Of
course, it was the self-respecting thing to do. Everything that was
equal to a groundhog wanted to be free. But it was so expensive, this
love; it was such a disagreeable compulsion, such a bondage." [41] In
this state of mind, Ben turns freedom into its opposite, "bondage,"
marking a conscious, if confused, choice to accept white racial superiority. By dramatizing Ben's consciousness and decision to betray
the revolt, Bontemps makes explicit the links between individual
thought and actions to the success or failure of a revolutionary
movement.

This thematic dialectic of the individual and the social recur in the
fiction of H.T. Tsiang (Jiang Xizeng). Born in 1899 in eastern China,
Tsiang fled repression for his pro-democratic activism. He migrated
as a student to California, briefly attending Stanford University.
Because of activism in the "Hands off China" movement, he was
expelled from Stanford and moved to New York where he enrolled
at Columbia University. There, Tsiang strove to launch his career as
a writer in the late 1920s. The *Daily Worker* published several of his
poems in 1928, and he self-published a collection of poems the following year. With a positive endorsement from Communist Party
cultural leader Waldo Frank and an encouraging statement from
novelist Upton Sinclair, Tsiang followed up with a novel in 1935
titled *The Hanging in Union Square* (republished in 2013). In 1937,
he self-published his best work as *And China Has Hands*. Unable to
make a living at writing, Tsiang returned to California and acted bit
parts in Hollywood during the war years.[42]

The main protagonist in *And China Has Hands*, Wong Wan-Lee,
is a believer in the "American Assumption," although he suspects
that as a Chinese person, he will be able to do it better and faster
than native born Americans. He migrates to the U.S. apparently as a
"paper son" with citizenship rights, spending almost $2,000 in legal
fees to avoid extensive detention or deportation. He settles in New
York City with a dream of opening his own business, making a pile
of money, and returning to China triumphantly. Upon his arrival, he
works briefly as a dishwasher where he befriends his African American co-worker. After purchasing his laundry business, Wong quits
and fantasizes that he will return to the restaurant, throw his money

---

41. Bontemps, *Black Thunder*, 93
42. Wendland, "Illegal Noise: The Sound of Change in H.T. Tsiang's *And
China Has Hands*," 425-427

around, and prove to his co-workers how well he had succeeded in America.

His dreams of success are short lived, however, as he is exposed to American racism, encountering harassment from white children, unemployed white men who blame Chinese immigrants for the economic crash, and corrupt white municipal officials who demand bribes to keep his business open. Initially, he maintains his belief in the possibility of success, identifying his interests with the business elite of the Chinese community and even unwisely buying things to promote a successful appearance. One day a Chinese coat salesman arrives at the shop offering his wares. He sympathizes with Wong's experience with racism and offers him a solution. "It was unfortunate...being Chinese in this country... No matter how much money you had, you could not change your face, but with money you could change your manner. The overcoat was the very thing to show outsiders what you were, and what you had in your pocket, and what you had in your head." [43] Wong accepts the argument and purchases the coat on a payment plan, only to discover later that he can't afford to appear well off. Along with bribes to local officials, extortion payments for "protection," and interest rates to loan sharks, payments on the coat force him to give up the business. Instead of triumph, financial disaster leads Wong into wage labor, where he joins the union movement and reconnects to the working class Chinese migrant community which links the struggle against exploitation with the anti-imperialist struggle against Japanese atrocities in China.

Significantly, Wong's plight – his realistic experience with American racism and its failure to live up to its promise of social mobility – is placed in relation with that of African descended peoples through his romantic relationship with Pearl Chang. Born of Black and Chinese parentage, Pearl is a migrant from the U.S. South. This Great Migration background locates her, along with Wong, at the intersection of two significant migration flows: the enslaved-cum-freed people of African descent and Chinese migrant laborers seeking economic opportunities employed by Southern planters or capitalists as alternatives to discontented Black labor.[44]

Having internalized white supremacy, Pearl holds stereotypical views of Chinese men, and fantasizes about becoming a movie star, even wishing she could appear to be whiter. But Wong's stories of Chinese history and language, cause a shift in her consciousness. She

---

43. Tsiang, *And China Has Hands*, 40

44. Ronald Takaki, *Strangers from a Different Shore: A History of Asian Americans* (Little Brown and Company, 1998), 94

throws away a picture of a Hollywood star that she carries as an emblem of her ambition, and tells Wong, "I am glad I am Chinese!" [45] The text indicates the importance of the intersection of the streams of human migration that brought those two people together. Following DuBois's argument in *Black Reconstruction*, Tsiang's work explicitly links individual consciousness and actions into the larger global movements of people of color and their struggles for liberation.

U.S. imperialism also places Filipino migrant workers into relation with the U.S.-based working class. Carlos Bulosan, the child of Filipino tenant farmers, exemplified this relation in his fiction and non-fiction writing. After arriving in the U.S. in 1930, he immediately went to work under super-exploited conditions in an Alaska cannery, then other Seattle area factories, in the farms all along the Pacific Coast. Most of his jobs placed him among the highly vulnerable and racially oppressed migrants from Asia. In that workforce, Bulosan lunged into the labor movement, organizing for the CIO affiliated cannery workers union and writing for its monthly newsletter. Later, he worked for ILWU Local 37, a cannery workers union in Seattle.

In 1936, Bulosan was hospitalized in Los Angeles for two years due to an extended battle with tuberculosis. During his hospital stay, his life's work turned in new directions. He read works of fiction and philosophy and wrote copiously original poems, stories, memoirs, letters, and novels. His labor movement experiences, and his writing talent led to friendships with Communist Party activists and radical writers such as Sanora Babb (who later married Chinese American cinematographer James Wong Howe), Richard Wright, and Carey McWilliams. Bulosan is most well-known for his popular memoir *America is in the Heart*, but the discovery of dozens of unpublished poems, short stories, and novel manuscripts in his personal papers in the 1970s by scholar E. San Juan Jr. has since established his reputation as a poet and a writer of fiction. Bulosan probably never held official membership in the Communist Party, but his dedicated support for a radical vision of socialism, for the Communist-led anti-colonial struggle in the Philippines, and his relationships with American Communists ensured constant FBI harassment in his final painful years. He died in Seattle in 1956.[46]

---

45. Tsiang, *And China Has Hands*, 53. *And China Has Hands* could be read constructively in conjunction with Gerald Horne, *The End of Empires* and Vijay Prashad, *Everybody was Kung Fu Fighting* and *The Karma of Brown Folk*.

46. San Juan Jr., *Bulosan and the Imagination of the Class Struggle* (University of Philippines Press, 1972), 1-6; "Excavating the Bulosan Ruins," 162;

San Juan Jr. argues that Bulosan modeled his manuscript of *The Cry and the Dedication* on the autobiography of Luis Taruc's *Born of the People* (1953). Taruc was one of the founders of the Communist-led, anti-Japanese underground movement known as *Hukbong Bayan Laban sa Hapon* or Hukbalahap during World War II. He guided the movement in the late 1940s first into the electoral arena, competing for seats in the national elections, and then into armed struggle when elected Communist Party members were denied their seats in the national legislature and faced a wave of violent U.S.-backed repression.[47] Taruc's account described the post-war era thus: "American imperialism had deliberately perpetuated the backward, feudal agrarian system which had been used by Spain." Further, he specified precise relations of the Filipino people to American workers, thus: U.S. military, political, and business leaders had perpetuated this colonial order to maintain control of the islands, to extract its wealth, and to create the "opportunity" that people in the U.S. identified as the "American Dream."[48] In other words, Filipino exploitation served the material needs of the U.S. capitalist class as well as the ideological purposes of the American Assumption and the American Blindspot in extracting working class consent for capitalist rule. Bulosan's relation to Taruc ensures a reading of *The Cry and the Dedication* as fundamentally "a long argument about the right of national self-determination," bearing a specific relation to the U.S. working class.[49]

In addition to this literary influence, Bulosan's manuscript bears a strong resemblance to McKay's *Banjo*. Both operate as stories without much plot, where the action of the characters works to move through subaltern or colonized spaces seeking liberation. McKay's acknowledgment of the missing plot is a deliberate function of his novel; while Bulosan's narrative ends before the planned arc is achieved. For each, the importance of the story lies in the formation of collectivity, the mapping of space for rebellious or insurrectionist purposes,[50] and the articulation of insurgency against racism in the

"History, Class Consciousness, Imperialism," 2; "Introduction," *Selected Writings*, 1-44

47. For a history of these events and San Juan Jr.'s argument about Bulosan's inspiration, see San Juan Jr., "An American Witness," 55ff.

48. Luis Taruc, *Born of the People* (New York: International Publishers, 1953), 266-267

49. San Juan Jr., "History, Class Consciousness, Imperialism," 11

50. San Juan Jr., "Introduction." In Carlos Bulosan, *The Cry and the Dedication* (Temple University Press), xix.

former and colonization in the latter. The uncertainty of the narrative arc mirrors the uncertainty in the reader's perception of the actual world, a consciousness of urgency for the problem (of racism and colonialism).

Both novels develop the cohesion of a small group of protagonists who form a collective identity and consciousness through their experiences of objective conditions, their subjective choices and, significantly, the production of narratives about themselves. In *Banjo*, the characters tell jokes and stories that produce a shared existential and psychological experience of both the historical African diaspora, their local and national cultures, and their direct experiences of Marseilles. Similarly, jokes and stories in *The Cry and the Dedication* form essential aspects of relationships among the characters, joining them into tight-knit personal relationships, and establishing their subjective relationships to the movement for liberation. Both rely on stories and modes of expression rooted in non-Western folkloric traditions and cultures that instantiate a destabilization of white supremacy, Eurocentrism, and legitimacy of Western or U.S.-originating economic or political dominance. For both McKay and Bulosan, each narrative depends on the absence of finality or totality indicated by traditional narrative arc. There remains in each an unarticulated utopian "political unconscious,"[51] a "better world in birth."

Bulosan's work, however, develops a more profound experience of the relationships among subjective identities, objective conditions, and the historical urgency of each to a process of revolutionary transformation. *Banjo*'s collectivity resists self-actualization through political action, preferring instead the "infrapolitics" of everyday resistance to labor regimes, racism and colonization, and colonial hierarchies imposed on the African diaspora.[52] In *The Cry*, by con-

---

51. To borrow from Marxist literary critic Frederic Jameson, *The Political Unconscious: Narrative as a Socially Symbolic Act* (Cornell University Press)

52. For a discussion of "infrapolitics" as "everyday forms of resistance" outside of the organized frame of a social movement, see Kelley, *Race Rebels: Culture, Politics, and the Black Working Class* (Free Press, 1996), 8-10. Likewise, Cedric Robinson uses the phrase "petty resistances" to describe the basic building blocks of "collective intelligence" of oppressed communities built up over time as a resource for revolutionary action (quoted in Burden-Stelly, "Cold War Culturalism," 217). Also note that recent "Communist" philosophical discourse has recently revived discussions of "infrapolitics," apparently without reference to Kelley's 1994 work, which acknowledges its intellectual debt to the 1980s work of anthropologist James C. Scott in his important book *Domination and the Art of Resistance: Hidden Transcripts* (Yale

trast, the goal of completing the mission as a single, but decisive step in the national liberation struggle motivates the thoughts, choices, morality, and relationships of the characters. As Hassim, the leader of the mission, reflects, "their collective fate will be crystallized beyond doubt, beyond all reasoning and reckoning, and the destiny of the whole peasantry would be shaped irrevocably, unalterably, in success or in defeat."[53] Indeed, a narrative effect of the novel is a recognition that the mission's objective lies in an compulsive resistance to dehumanization created by colonization and capitalist imperatives. One of the characters thinks, "Man is loneliness...He made the world and yet does not own it. He conceived the idea and yet it eludes him."[54] As San Juan Jr. writes, Bulosan developed an artistic objective "[t]o overthrow the competitive, dehumanizing set-up of a society based on commodity-exchange" and instead "elevates the ideal of an organic community represented in native folklore and folk art."[55]

This dramatization of the relationships of workers across national borders and the urgent necessity of collective human intervention in exploitation and oppression drives the taut narrative of Muriel Rukeyser's *Savage Coast*. Her direct experience of the Spanish Civil War permanently impacted her political consciousness. She had just published an award winning collection of poems for Yale University Press, covered the case of the Scottsboro Nine for the Communist press, and had been intimately involved with a miner's strike – all before the age of 22. She traveled to Europe to write about the People's Olympics to be held in the summer of 1936 in Spain as a protest of the Berlin games. Upon arrival in Moncada, Spain, news of a fascist coup that had begun in the Spanish colonies in Morocco and had spread to the metropole threatened to undermine the elected Republican government led by left-center coalition of political parties. Rukeyser's novelization of these experiences in *Savage Coast* was rejected by her publisher in 1937 as much for the novel's open "communist sympathies," as for its progressive interracial and same sex content, and its experimental modernism. Rukeyser edited the manuscript a few more times over the next few years but ultimately moved on to other projects. The manuscript

University Press, 1992). Philosopher Bruno Bosteels insists the concept was invented in 2006. See Bosteels, *The Actuality of Communism* (Verso, 2014), 108.
53. Bulosan, *The Cry and the Dedication*, 8
54. Bulosan, *The Cry and the Dedication*, 34
55. San Juan, Jr., *Bulosan and the Imagination of the Class Struggle*, 15

was misfiled in the Library of Congress archives and lost until the early 2000s.[56]

Interest in and solidarity with the anti-fascist struggles in Ethiopia and Spain in the late 1930s played a vital radicalizing role for many American women. Emergent African American leaders of the Communist Party such as Claudia Jones and Esther Cooper became activists through anti-fascist work. Anti-fascist politics also opened up space for politics specifically oriented toward women's equality. Party publications, women leaders in the party, and party affiliated mass organizations delved deeply into analysis of right-wing and fascist family values that supported women's repression. In so doing, women militants developed what is now, unfortunately, a largely forgotten body of theory and a record of political organizing that, according to scholar Denise Lynn, "expanded the Marxist class analysis to include women."[57] Thus, Popular Front politics signaled new ways for theoretical and cultural work to link democratic struggles to class politics that envisioned what Burke had called "the widest possible frame of acceptance." Rukeyser's *Savage Coast* participates in this mass reconfiguration of symbols of authority aligned with patriarchal dominance.

Each of the authors studied here argues that there can be no guarantee of freedom without human action or labor. Rukeyser, a decade after her manuscript for *Savage Coast* was rejected, wrote an extended essay on *The Life of Poetry* (1949), in which she argued that art "gives you imaginings," but this doesn't produce on its own a new reality. "You are going to have to use that imagining as best you can, by building it into yourself, or you will be left with nothing but illusion." Distinct from the faddish project of "self-improvement" or its corollary in the "American Assumption," for Rukeyser, a refashioning of self is only a piece of a larger social project of humanization and democratization. She adds, "Dead power is everywhere among us – in the forest, chopping down the songs, at night in the industrial landscape, wasting and stiffening the new life; in the street of the city, throwing away the day. We wanted something different for our people: not to find ourselves an old, reactionary republic, full of ghost fears, the fears of death and the fears of birth. We want something else."[58] The labor

---

56. On the background of the novel, see Kennedy-Epstein, "Introduction," *Savage Coast*, vii-xxxvii.

57. Lynn, "Fascism and the Family," 185, 190

58. Muriel Rukeyser, *The Life of Poetry* (Wesleyan University Press, 1996), 23-24, 89. Well in advance of most social critics, Rukeyser warns against

of reconstructing the self and society against destructive, mind numbing capitalism stands at the center of another of the modes of proletarian fiction: the trade union story.

Trade Union Stories and Revolutionary Intersections

The concept of a "triple oppression paradigm"[59] originated with African American women activists and writers such as Claudia Jones who talked about the intersection of oppressions by gender, race, and class. Contemporary sociologists who use an intersectionality framework occasionally mention Claudia Jones' writings but usually ignore her leading role in the Communist Party.[60] When historians and literary scholars discuss details of her party role, they tend to present her primarily as a critical outsider who addresses flaws in the party. While the theoretical construct christened the "triple oppression paradigm" emerged from articulations of Black working class women's experiences (including Black women party leaders), those experiences were rooted in capitalist social relations of production that relied on the super-exploitation of workers of color, in colonialism, and in the oppression of women as linked systems.

Jones's analysis and articulation of this paradigm were not merely individual ideas she happened to express. Most of Jones's theoretical work was published by the Communist Party's journal *Political Affairs*, originated as reports to various party collectives, and likely were revised based on discussions there. Given the policy of democratic centralism, these circumstances show an official and collective quality in Jones's contribution to the party's official policies on peace and anti-imperialism, super-exploitation and class struggle, the Black freedom movement, and women's equality between World

---

ecological destruction, opens a discussion on the cultural influences and worth of Native and African American songs and poetry, and advances some grounded speculation into the Walt Whitman's non-conforming gender identity and its influence on his worldview.

59. This term is coined by historian Erik S. McDuffie, *Sojourning for Freedom: Black Women, American Communism, and the Making of Black Left Feminism* (Duke University Press, 2011), 91

60. For example, sociologist Vivian May comes close to pointing to Jones's political orientation by labeling her a feminist and a Marxist but limits her discussion to that imprecise information. See, May, *Pursuing Intersectionality: Unsettling Dominant Imaginaries* (Routledge, 2015), 132

War II and her ultimate arrest, conviction, imprisonment, and deportation on political grounds in 1955.[61]

The "triple oppression paradigm" extends and flexes the DuBoisian concept of the "American Blindspot" to an analysis of the systematic form of racism that intersects with systems of patriarchy, national chauvinism and imperialism, as well as with class exploitation. Jones describes multiple positions of Black women this way: "The super exploitation of the Negro woman worker is thus revealed not only in that she receives, as a woman, less than equal pay for equal work with men, but also in that the majority of Negro women get less than half the pay of white women."[62] Triple oppression is not, however, confined to economic expressions. Jones details the intense racism Black women face due to housing segregation, unequal educational access, insufficient healthcare resources, racist depictions of Black women in media and everyday language, and racist discrimination in the criminal justice system. In other words, intersecting

---

61. McDuffie provides terrific details about (and photos of) Jones's experience in the Young Communist League and the Communist Party but describes her theoretical contribution as merely critical rather than as policy-making, 141. See also: Robin D.G. Kelley, *Freedom Dreams: The Black Radical Imagination* (Beacon Press, 2003), 55, 57, 136; Washington, *The Other Blacklist…*, Ibid, 28-29, 143-144, 180; Angela Jones, *Modern African American Political Thought* (Routledge, 2012), 297-300; Dayo F. Gore, *Radicalism at the Crossroads: African American Women Activists In The Cold War* (NYU Press, 2011), 68-72; Higashida, *Black Internationalist Feminism…*, Ibid, 20-22, 46-48; Carol Boyce Davies, *Left of Karl Marx: The Political Life of Black Communist Claudia Jones* (Duke University Press, 2008), chapter 1; Kate Weigand, *Red Feminism: American Communism and the Making of Women's Liberation* (Johns Hopkins University Press, 2002), 102-113. Each of these scholars develop excellent analyses and readings of Jones and the political situation in which she wrote. However, as far as I am able to discover, no scholar has recognized Claudia Jones's role in *making* official Party policy. The closest may be Carol Boyce Davies' description of Jones as "a major theoretician" and "prime organizer" and whose "particular ranking position" in the Communist Party provided her with a platform and "considerable power of persuasion," Davies, *Left of Karl Marx*, 30. Additionally, Weigand argues that "Communists broadened their theoretical approach to the woman question by adopting a black feminist perspective and extended their women's work to include writing an popularizing black women's history, appointing Communist women of color to local leadership positions, and lending support to black women's efforts to improve conditions for themselves and their families" (112-113).

62. Claudia Jones, "An End to the Neglect of the Problem of the Negro Woman!," *Political Affairs*, June 1949, 52

systems of oppression combine to subjugate Black women on multiple levels and in various sites of social existence, and these have to be addressed in particular as well as economic experiences.

The depth and breadth of change depends on how much the democratic and working class movements themselves are motivated to make internal changes and to resist existing symbols of authority. Despite a record of Black women's effective militancy in social movements, even some of the most progressive labor unions denied leadership roles to Black women, and acquiescence to racist conventions could also be found in Communist Party collectives, Jones' reports assert. Meanwhile, many white radicals seemed to believe that socialism would cure all ills automatically, seemingly making specific measures to address racism unnecessary. Nevertheless, "The growing militancy among Negro women has profound meaning both for the Negro liberation movement and for the emerging anti-fascist, anti-imperialist coalition."[63]

Like DuBois, Jones believes that ending class exploitation through an insurgent anti-racist and working class centered movement embedded in an internationalist struggle against war and colonialism would produce a new stage, a deeper political class struggle with the object of socialism. Movement to such a stage depends on how meaningfully progressive white workers, men, and women, successfully aligned their interests with the "growing militancy" of African American women, an urgent necessity shaped by racism and super-exploitation. The new Black women-led militancy carries on regardless, however, and it will impact the shapes and outcomes of the Black Freedom struggle and its partner in the peace movement as strategic anti-imperialism.[64]

This intersectional theory and practice of radical working class politics and the struggle for democracy had a significant influence on the cultural practices of writers of the post-World War II period. For example, Alexander Saxton incorporated themes about working class unity and anti-racism in all of his fiction. Saxton had been born into a well-to-do white, New England family, had attended Harvard but had grown politically radical by the late 1930s. He moved to Chicago to become a writer, to join the working class and its social movements, and alter the trajectory of his life. He worked in several industrial jobs, including railroads and construction in Chicago and San Francisco from the 1940s through the late 1950s. In Chicago, he

---

63. Jones, "An End to the Neglect of the Problem of the Negro Woman!," Ibid, 51-67

64. See: Weigand, *Red Feminism…*, Ibid, 105-106

joined the Communist Party and would adopt many of the working class themes of the cultural Popular Front in his three novels: *Grand Crossing* (1941),[65] *The Great Midland* (1948; republished in 1999), and *Bright Web in the Darkness* (1958; republished in 1997).

Saxton's final novel, *Bright Web in the Darkness*, reveals a growing concern about the labor movement and the working class during the McCarthy era. While the novel was published after many Communist Party members had been expelled from labor union leadership, and when even openly resisting racism could draw attention as an indication of one's sympathies with communism,[66] the story is set in the West Coast shipyards during World War II. At that time, many women had gotten industrial jobs due to the shortage of male workers drafted for military service, and the themes of racism and gender discrimination in the workplace are centered in the narrative. The novel's juxtaposition of the two major protagonists, Joyce, an African American woman, and Tom O'Regan, a white skilled worker and an up-and-comer in the racially segregated local, foregrounds the theoretical approaches developed by Claudia Jones.

Joyce's first appearance in the novel occurs in a literal fog, reflecting her timid, quiet personality informed by alienation and an acute sense of powerlessness in a hostile, white, and male dominated workforce. One evening, as she prepares for a date, she sees herself in her mirror and imagines the presence of two people: "The watcher and the watched; the one so often lonely and frightened, the other cool and smiling, untouched and untouchable." [67] Due to the "triple oppression paradigm," she frequently experiences life in disembodied states, alienated from her capabilities and agency.

One friendly mentor named Brooks, the president of the Jim Crow-style Black "auxiliary" local, urges her to sign up for a welding class to improve her pay, her skill and knowledge of the work, and to increase the representation of skilled Black workers in the shipyard. After reluctantly doing so, Joyce's self-confidence grows, and the world she had viewed as in a fog seemed more brightly lit. In the early stages of the story, she is distrustful of her perceptions of herself. As the story proceeds, however, and she discovers her knowledge and power as a skilled worker and her role as a leader of dissident unionists fighting racism and class collaboration, she comes out of the fog. She returns to the piano lessons she had given up as a child and discovers a renewed desire to be a good musician

---

65. Wendland, "Becoming Working Class."
66. Burden-Stelly, "Constructing Deportable Subjectivity," 342-358
67. Alexander Saxton, *Bright Web in the Darkness*, 47

and to create music. Ultimately, she leads her co-workers in a wildcat strike in protest of the company's threat (with official union acquiescence) to lay-off African American workers who refuse to pay dues in protest of racial segregation. The action sees her transformed from a quiet, scared person to a skilled, creative leader of workers. At the same time, her political commitment to democratic equality and working class power put at risk her job, her resources, and the time and space she has secured to develop creatively; it threatens her new identity as a leader. Despite this threat, the fight is urgent and compelling.

The fight against racism is less urgent, perhaps even odious, for Tom O'Regan, who typifies the consequence of the loss of political focus following the expulsion of Leftists from the labor movement. After political repression of the Left, white industrial labors, once able to recognize the power of class unity, seemed less inclined to resist racial and gender inequality in the workplace. This regressive turn of events echoes the events of the post-Civil War period addressed by DuBois in *Black Reconstruction*. The dramatic shift from democratic insurgency to a fragmented and racist movement disunited by race baiting and red baiting mars working class politics.

At one union meeting, Tom's wife, Sally, who also works in the shipyard, urges adoption of a resolution calling for the desegregation of the union. In addition to a charge of being a Communist, other workers accuse her of sleeping with Black men. An anonymous voice in the crowd cries out, "Hey sister you like layin' that black meat?" A fight ensues, and Tom, who arrives at the union meeting to pick up Sally and her friends, manages to break up the melee targeting the resolution's supporters. Tom, too, suspects that Sally's sexual loyalties lie somewhere with her politics.[68] He mentally reduces the democratic demand for racial equality to a racially charged sexual politics, revealing just how powerfully discourses of race, gender, and sexuality intersected in the politics of white supremacy. He also suspects that an anti-racist intervention could jeopardize his ability to get support from the leadership for a law school scholarship and a future leadership role in the union.

By contrast to Joyce's development toward the Communist ideal of the liberated human, Tom's hesitation about white male supremacy jeopardizes Joyce's new life and also likely ensures a prolonging of working class subjugation, even if he secures an improved personal status. Tom will have to obey the authority of the union leadership and its acceptance of the racist status quo if he wants their support.

---

68. Saxton, *Bright Web in the Darkness*, 234-240

Though there remains some hope that Tom can learn to empathize with people who do not share his racial or cultural heritage and to value their desires to achieve their potential, the outcome remains uncertain.[69]

Uncertainty about the direction of the U.S. working class during the Cold War also found expression in the fiction of African American editor and novelist, Lloyd L. Brown. Brown was born in Minnesota in 1913, and, at the age of 16, joined the Young Communist League and was an avid reader of African American history. He visited the Soviet Union in 1933, worked as a YCL and CIO organizer in Connecticut, Ohio, and Pennsylvania, and edited the YCL newspaper. In 1940, Brown, along with 17 other Communists, was jailed for political activities. During his four month detention, Brown taught a class on African American working class history and led an ultimately unsuccessful campaign on behalf of William Jones, an African American man sentenced to death. During the war, Brown served three years in a segregated Air Force unit and returned to labor organizing in the late 1940s. Brown also continued to write for and edit Communist Party journals, writing extensively on radical aesthetics, especially from an African American perspective.[70]

Experimenting with modernist techniques such as documentary and drama, Brown's 1951 novel *Iron City* imagines a complex topography of African American working class life, politics, social and geographic origins and mobilities, cultural customs and habits, and economic positions and goals. Published by *Masses & Mainstream*, *Iron City* asserts a commonality among Black people in the fight against racism and capitalism. It chronicles the experiences of three African American Communists jailed for Smith Act "violations" who launch a political movement within the prison to save the life of an unfairly convicted Black death row inmate. In the #BlackLivesMatter era, Brown's spatial equation of the "Iron City"/Pittsburgh as a prison/racialized urban space disciplined by a racist law enforcement regime remains as relevant as ever. As the plot unfolds, the three men recite their life stories and the different avenues by which they came to join the Communist Party. In so doing, they divulge diverse views on what the party can and ought to do, as well as their sometimes competing views of Black history, economics, culture, religion, among other things.

For Isaac Zachary, a railroad worker forced out of his job by white workers who claimed it was a "white job," joined the party because

---

69. See, Wendland, "'A Prelude to Some Finale.'"
70. Wald, "Foreword," xxiv-xvii; Washington, *The Other Blacklist*, 45

it echoed his objections to racism and pointed to the possibility of ending it. "Zach" had been enamored by a poster depicting William Z. Foster and James W. Ford, candidates for president and vice president during the 1932 election. The party's illustration of Foster and Ford on the poster sent a message that broke through the rigidity of racist apartheid by allowing viewers to imagine a Black-white alliance in a struggle for the highest echelons of power. For Zachary, a recent Southern migrant, this image of a Black man and white man, both industrial workers and labor union leaders, "was something that belonged to the world of fantasy," like a Hollywood movie. The dominant belief in the fallacious division between whites and Black workers seemed to collapse in the embodiment of two workers, one white and one Black, claiming a right to contest for the most powerful offices. Zach had come to believe in this vision and had worked for the next two decades to realize it.[71]

The closing sections of *Iron City* revisit a world of human liberation that compels the urgency of action and commitment in a reality rife with uncertainty and contingency. In her discussion of the novel, scholar Mary Helen Washington argues, this section of the book depicts a "state of suspension between uncertainty and hope" that "betrays Brown's underlying anxieties."[72] While this assessment speaks much truth, it does not fully capture the significance of what Brown is attempting. He aims to sketch the contours of a new reality, doubly abstract, for it is a dream within a fictional tale. In this imaginary, we are asked to envision something that is both racially unlike the one they presently inhabit and the intensity of commitment to collective action need to materialize and substantialize that new reality. He wants us to believe in the shared humanity and capability of Black and white working class people, and to recognize the duty to reject the symbols of authority embedded in systems of racist inequality, exploitative labor and capital relations, and oppressive dominant social institutions. Brown's story offers us mental and emotional pleasure in imagining specific acts of rejection and the possibility for social transformation we could make with them. In providing pleasure in potential racial insurrection, the story mobilizes individual subjectivity as a collective force to change objective social conditions.

Iron City presents in detail the ironies and contradictions of the racist capitalist system. The racist criminal justice system had convicted, imprisoned, and is set to kill Lonnie James for a crime he

---

71. Lloyd Brown, *Iron City*, 168-169
72. Washington, *The Other Blacklist*, 64-65

didn't commit. Because of rules about segregation, prison officials put in the same prison with James three African American Communists, convicted for thinking about and working toward ending capitalism. From there, they launch a campaign to save James' life by exposing the racism in the system and appealing to the world to pressure the government to halt the execution. Prosecutors and government officials blame the bad publicity on "Red propaganda," attempting to derail the campaign, but promoting the Communist Party-led cause more and strengthening the alignment of anti-racism with the working class. Without the logic of segregation, there would be no campaign to save James, no unjust criminal trial, and fewer divisions to prevent working class power in effectively fighting back against its subjugation. Thus, Brown dramatizes a racist capitalist system that produces the tools of its overthrow, requiring only that people recognize the utility and justice in using those tools, act on those contradictions, and work toward that unrealized fantasy.[73] The spectral possibility of revolt haunts the material reality constituted under modern racial capitalism.

The twin problems of racism and class collaboration in the labor movement surface in Alfred Maund's fiction also. He had begun writing as a teenager and then had studied English at Tulane University during World War II. Subsequently, he worked as a journalist and editor for several local Southern newspapers, the monthly bulletin of the Southern Conference Education Fund,[74] and for labor union publications. He was fascinated by the life of John Brown, and early on devoted his literary skills to dramatizing U.S. racism and the role of the working class in fighting it. He wrote articles on the Montgomery Bus Boycott for the *Daily Worker*, on John Brown for *Monthly Review*, and for the *American Socialist* on his friends and Communist Party leaders Anne and Carl Braden who were charged with "inciting insurrection" for their role in attempting to desegregate housing in Louisville, Kentucky. Maund's first book, *The Big Boxcar* (1957; republished in 1999) earned praise from reviewers at the *Daily Worker*, the *Saturday Evening Post*, and the *New York Times*, as well as denunciations from some Southern reviewers. By the late 1950s, as his literary career blossomed, Maund directed public relations for

73. Brown, *Iron City*, 201
74. Maund, "The Untouchables: The Meaning of Segregation in Hospitals." For the pro-civil rights organization, Maund investigated racial apartheid in healthcare, writing, "the only humane and democratic way to meet the situation is to share what there is according to need and not on the basis of racial fiat."

the International Chemical Workers' Union and later overseas as a university professor.[75]

The International (1961) was far less successful than his first novel and remains out of print. But it stands as a solid literary effort that reminds one of the strike novels[76] of the 1930s but with a gritty political thriller quality. It is also fun to read Maund's use of mid-20th century regional slang and idioms such as "the flivver jolted off like a salted dog" and "stump pine didn't breed pecan trees."[77] It tells the story of Wick Simmons, a former organizer and current Vice President of "the International" who defies the racism and class collaborationism of the Cold War era labor movement through a challenge for the presidency of the international. While, the novel's main protagonist frequently uses racist anti-Chinese and anti-Semitic expressions, spews sexist and homophobic slurs, and struggles to humanize African Americans, he puts into motion events that make fundamental changes to institutional white and male supremacy.[78] How is this possible?

While it is worthwhile to be critical of the backwardness of Wick Simmons' consciousness and attitudes, as scholar E. San Juan Jr. has argued, "it is not wise to fuse the narrative persona, the invented character, with the author."[79] Instead, it is crucial to look at how this retrograde consciousness works to underline how working class individuals confront *or* comply with dominant social values. This consciousness provokes the reader with sexist, homophobic, and racist attitudes and actions that demand address. They place the protagonist in the position of having to act against dominant values (which he may have accepted) to win gains for his union's members and to give meaning to his life. Like Tom O'Regan in *Bright Web in the Darkness*, to hold onto his dignity and ethical principles, Simmons must choose to thwart the union leadership's class collaborationist trend and act against white racism –both material expressions

75. Wald, "Introduction," vii-xvi
    76. Robert Cantwell's *Land of Plenty* may be considered exemplary of this type. See, Reed, *Robert Cantwell and the Literary Left*, 64ff.
    77. Alfred Maund, *The International*, 67, 170
    78. For example, when Simmons encounters new characters, the narrator provides detailed physical descriptions of those characters that link bodily attributes to personality or emotional characteristics – except when those new characters are Black people. His portraits are superficial, sometimes confined to the word "Negro," applied collectively, and are combined with Simmons' admission that he has difficulty understanding the inner life of African American individuals.
    79. San Juan Jr., "Internationalizing the US Ethnic Canon," 133

of Cold War versions of the American Assumption and American Blindspot. Otherwise, he would have to submit to a regime of leadership that rejects democracy and conforms to corporate needs for profit and worker exploitation. Instead of being a fighter for the working class, he would have to accept serving as a tool of white supremacy and the class power of corporations. Such a path of least resistance is nothing more than a complete betrayal of the ideals that had led him to labor movement in the first place. In seeking a strategic path to reclaim his personal values, Simmons is forced to recognize both the intersections of systems of oppressions enacted through race, gender, and class, as well as to construct institutional solutions to overcome them to make possible working class unity.

For instance, in exchange for their support Black union members convince Simmons to include Blacks on the negotiating committee and to force the company to integrate the "Negro" division of the plant in training programs and better job assignments, instead of confining them to lower paid, lower skilled "Black" jobs.[80] To preserve the unity of the union membership, Simmons is even required to physically challenge white workers (drawing on masculinist and ablest privilege) who are angry about the disruption of the white supremacist status quo. In such situations, Maund dramatizes what was in the post-war period a wave of anti-Black racism where white workers walked off the job to protest gains made by their Black co-workers in the workforce. As George Lipsitz documents, in the late war period in cities such as Detroit, Toledo, Philadelphia, and Cincinnati, white workers walked off the job to protest gains made by Black and progressive white workers against discrimination.[81] For Simmons, the recognition of necessity overcomes the subjective consciousness or "psychological wage" of white and male supremacy among working class people who have no other means but their unity, will to act, and relation to production to claim new power.

Along the way, Simmons glimpses fundamental flaws in the relation of capital to labor and of class collaborationist trade unionism, opening a desire for more fundamental and revolutionary transformations. For example, in one conversation between Simmons and the main female protagonist, she tells Simmons that she

---

80. Maund, *The International*, 142, 277-278

81. George Lipsitz, *Rainbow at Midnight: Labor and Culture in the 1940s* (University of Illinois Press, 1994), 78. See also: Joshua Freeman, *In Transit: The Transport Workers Union in New York, 1933-1966* (Temple University Press, 2001)

resists societal pressure to act the way a good Southern white girl is expected to act. "I'm not built to be happy by making other people happy – maybe I'm not a *fit* little mother or woman even, but to hell with them." She adds that she finds some affinity with her African American friends because "They *have* to do a lot of things, of course, and I do what I *have* to do, too. But they don't like it, and I don't like it." This distinction between willingly fulfilling expectations and doing what one "has to" to survive suggests a significance to the social differences defined by the relation of identity to power: for a white, working class man, the nature of expectation and the *"have* to" are experienced differently revealing layers of systemic complicity and agency. The character hints that white working class men conform to a politics of class collaboration, patriarchy, and white supremacy not because they *have* to but rather out of a willing fulfillment of the expectation that they will play that role, thus preserving systemic inequalities and the sources of working class subjugation.[82] This space between willing fulfillment and *"have* to" suggests an opening through which white working class men could challenge to racial capitalist sexist symbols of authority, seeking multi-racial, multi-gendered, and intersectional political alliances.

The positioning of this exchange early in the novel seems to establish the political orientation of the events that unfold in the narrative and the novel's general argument. Class collaborationist unionism seeks to maintain existing social relations of capital to labor by offering white male workers a smidgen of decision making power at contract time, some economic benefits related to racial and gendered divisions of labor, while maintaining the hegemony of capital through an offer of a continued belief in the "American Assumption" and structural motives to preserve the "American Blindspot." This ideological and material formation is disciplined as well by the Cold War anti-communist and anti-radical affiliation with U.S. national identity and regimes of repression. Simmons' challenge to the class collaborationists and business unionism bureaucrats requires a readjustment of the class forces and divisions of labor along democratic lines that take into account the specific experiences of sexism and racism by women and people of color in order to succeed. Maund asks us to consider the revolutionary potential of this readjustment and the inherent democratic possibility in thinking of class struggle in intersectional terms.

---

82. Maund, *The International*, 74

Continuity and Change

Though each of the authors discussed in this essay has been recognized as making a vital contribution to American letters, the works presented here remained marginal to the popular market or went unpublished during the authors' lifetimes. More recently, those works have earned sizable reading publics, critical reception, and established (if minor) places in the (internationalized) American literary canon. Since the 1990s, the authors and their works discussed here received a new wave of attention through republication, engaging a new audience of readers with their revolutionary ideas. Each inscribe relations of language and symbols, individual consciousness and action, and the broader systemic and international dynamics, dramatizing localized political struggles within the global, naming and sketching international balances of power, imperialism, and the necessity of alliances of working class and anti-colonial forces.

Explorations of the continuing influence of the cultural Popular Front movement on the academic, intellectual, political, and aesthetic life on the U.S. would unearth myriad permutations of impact. Theories and themes uncovered in this essay might be used to explore the development of socialist consciousness in contemporary cultural expressions. Likewise, differences in modern cultural practices would help elicit new developments within the democratic struggles beyond those which predominated a century ago.

These authors have produced an account of a historical ancestry of reaction, offered cultural resources to sustain a common, collective humanity in the necessary transformation of the world, created striking narratives of conflict and liberation, and shaped a consciousness of resistance to the symbols of capitalist ruling class authority. At least four themes resound: 1) the urgency of revolutionary change, 2) the necessity of collective human power to resist oppression, 3) the human capacity to imagine and construct a democratic world, 4) and the need to continue to view a larger frame of struggle that includes non-class democratic forms beyond the speculative abstraction that confines revolutionary change on a class against class basis.

Each of these point to Burke's urge for a strategic policy of association democratization with an insurgent public ownership of the symbols of "the people." This idea remains on the radical democratic socialistic and communist agenda of the present. As the Tunisian activist Sadri Khiari writes, a decolonial and anti-racist process in Western countries requires "a revamped definition of popular sovereignty, the redistribution of economic and social powers, and *the redistribution of cultural and symbolic powers*." Heavily influenced in his thinking by the African American freedom movement, Khiari alludes to a tradition of Popular Front cultural thought that rejects narrow and singular conceptualizations of people or class as revolutionary subjects. Rather, a decolonial plurality, emergent in the intersectional theories of African American Marxists discussed here, a more adequate basis for a democratic popular politics positioned against imperialism, capitalism, and oppression, in his view.[83]

In the last two decades, in the U.S. alone, the anti-globalization movement/World Social Forum, the Occupy Movement, the #BlackLivesMatter movements and insurrections, and #NoDAPL/Standing Rock water protectors' resistance, the struggle against global climate change, local movements for alternative economic development, the massive peace movement against endless war, the Great Recession and its attendant uneven global crises for working class people of color and women, all and each expose the contradictions of capitalism, the limits on its capacity for democratic development, and the necessity for building a socially just system in the interest of human survival. While the theorists and writers of the early and mid-20th century Communist cultural movement did not create this wider, intersectional frame of analysis and political struggle, they did give it life and showed how it coupled human imagination and action against encumbering social systems within social movements for human liberation.

83. Sadi Khiari, "The People and the Third People," 99 (emphasis added).

Chapter 9

The Cartoons of Ollie Harrington, the Black Left, and the African American Press During the Jim Crow Era*

By Rachel Rubin & James Smethurst

"Stark tragedy and humor are separated by a mere hair's breadth. That is why there is so much in Harlem," dryly commented cartoonist Ollie Harrington in an introduction to his role in the Harlem *People's Voice,* a significant oppositional African American newspaper.[1] This remark immediately demonstrates what many African American cultural figures – including Virginia Liston (1923), Lead Belly (1935), Langston Hughes (1952), Lester Young (1958), the Isley Brothers (1963), Mississippi Joe Callicott (1967), Son Seals (1980), and Tyler Perry (2011) – have called "laughing to keep from crying." But it also powerfully and efficiently presents comedy as a serious portrayal of social injustices.

The comic works of Ollie Harrington appeared regularly in a variety of publications, but part of the purpose of this essay is to reaffirm the cartoonist and visual artist Ollie Harrington as an important artist of the Black radical tradition in the United States and to extend the work that Brian Dolinar has already done in resituating Harrington's work in the Left milieu that shaped it. In addition, another goal here is to look at how his cartoons, which were more widely circulated among Black readers than any others during the 1930s and 1940s, themselves serve as a sort of metonym for the large

---

* This chapter originally appeared in *American Studies,* Volume 59, No. 3 (2020), and is republished with permission.

1. Llewelyn Ransom, "PV's Art Editor Ollie Harrington, Creator of 'Bootsie' and "Pee Wee,' Enjoyed Life, Despite Setbacks," Harlem *People's Voice,* August 8, 1942, 4. Over the years, Harrington signed his work as "Oliver," "Ol," and "Ollie." For the purposes of this essay, unless we are quoting someone else, we will use "Ollie," which seems to be the most common.

and changing influence of the Black Left on the press with significant consequences for African American politics and culture during Jim Crow; one way we conduct this is through close textual analysis of several examples.

In thinking about the influence of the organized Left, especially the Communist Party, USA, on politics and culture in the United States, one crucial, if often under considered, arena of such influence is the Black press. With a few exceptions, notably Brian Dolinar's *The Black Cultural Front*, Bill Mullen's *Popular Fronts*, and Fred Carroll's *Race News*, most considerations of the African American press give short shrift to the influence of the organized Left. Similarly, histories of the Communist Left in the United States and its impact on the African American community often pay little attention to Black newspapers. For example, Vernon Pedersen's *The Communist Party of Maryland, 1919-1957* concludes that the CPUSA made relatively little headway in Baltimore's African American community, but does not examine the profound CPUSA influence on the *Baltimore Afro-American*, both a major local and national Black institution and for decades the most consistently leftwing major Black paper in the United States. In part, this is due to the fact that the apogee of leftwing influence on Black newspapers (and most African American communities, including Harlem) was in the 1940s not the 1930s, the so-called "Red Decade." After all, the 1940s in Harlem saw the election of local CPUSA leader Benjamin Davis, Jr., to the New York City Council and the flourishing of the *People's Voice*, the chief editors of which were Communists. This timeline conflicts the still common declension narrative following the German-Soviet Non-Aggression Pact of 1939 in most histories of the Communist Left in the U.S.

During the extended Popular Front era from roughly 1935 to 1948 (and beyond, in some cases, notably the *Baltimore Afro-American*), the Black Left, through publishers, editors, reporters, cartoonists, and columnists, deeply shaped the trajectory of such major African American newspapers as the *Chicago Defender*, *Baltimore Afro-American*, *Michigan Chronicle* (Detroit), *California Eagle* (Los Angeles), *Pittsburgh Courier*, *Amsterdam News*, *Sun-Reporter* (San Francisco), *People's Voice* (New York), and *Boston Chronicle*. The Cold War quashed the open expression of this Black Left strain, as these reporters, editors, columnists, and (in the case of Charlotta Bass of the *California Eagle*) even publishers were driven from their posts by anti-Communism. (The major exceptions were the *Baltimore Afro-American* and the *Sun-Reporter*, where leftist publishers George Murphy and his family and Carlton Goodlett could not be dislodged; neither would the African

American communities of Baltimore and Washington, D.C. and the San Francisco Bay abandon them.) Nevertheless, the legacies of the radical Black journalism of the Popular Front could not be entirely erased from the Black press, African American politics, and culture. These legacies continued, often (but not always) sub rosa, in major Black papers. More open reminders of the Popular Front impact on the Black press and through that press, Black politics and culture, appeared in radical African American newspapers and journals, such as *Freedom*, *Freedomways*, *Muhammad Speaks*, and *Liberator*, increasingly revised and repurposed by the Black Power and the Black Arts Movement at the end of the Jim Crow era, as well in other less-specifically Black journals and papers, mostly associated with the Communist Left, such as *People's World*, *The Worker*, the *Daily World*, and the *National Guardian*.

Harrington's career began in the mass Black press and migrated to more openly radical venues, much as Harrington moved to Paris (where he was close friends with Richard Wright) and then the German Democratic Republic under the pressures of Jim Crow and the Cold War. His *Dark Laughter* (later *Bootsie*) comic in the *Amsterdam News* (and later the *Pittsburgh Courier* and finally the *Chicago Defender* and syndicated throughout the Black press) was perhaps the most popular strip among African American during the 1930s and 1940s. *Bootsie*, featuring a portly Black "everyman" in Harlem – basically a forerunner to Langston Hughes's character Simple – won over its audience through its humor, recognizable landscapes and personalities, and sharp social criticism. Hughes, in an introduction to a 1958 collection of Harrington's Bootsie cartoons, called Harrington "Negro America's favorite cartoonist."[2] Harrington also produced comics and drawings in a wide range of genres, including illustrations, editorial comics, a Black adventure strip *Jive Gray*, a brief run of what we would now think of as a serialized graphic novel adaptation of Richard Wright's *Native Son* (in the *People's Voice* during the 1940s), and paintings. His cartoons became increasingly and often harshly pointed, as the Cold War and Jim Crow forced him into exile. His cartoons, like the work of such other Black radical artists of the extended Popular Front era as Elizabeth Catlett, Langston Hughes, Max Roach, Alice Childress, Lorraine Hansberry, Harry Belafonte, Jackie Ormes, Hazel Scott, and

---

2. Langston Hughes, "Introduction," in Oliver W. Harrington, *Bootsie and Others: A Selection of Cartoons* (New York: Dodd, Mead, 1958), n.p.

Brumsic Brandon, can be examined as a bridge between different periods of Black cultural radicalism.

Before proceeding a few general comments about terms and periodization in this essay are in order. While it basically covers Harrington's career during the Jim Crow era, like most periods, Jim Crow's start and end dates are variable. One might begin it in 1881 with the passage of the first state law segregating transportation in Tennessee; or pick the Plessy v. Ferguson decision in 1896 as the beginning; or Williams v. Mississippi in 1898 when the Supreme Court rules that the various devices used to disenfranchise Black voters were legal; or Woodrow Wilson's segregation of Federal employment in 1913. Similarly, the conclusion of Jim Crow is also mutable – if it can be said to have ever completely ended. Is it with Brown v. the Board of Education decision? The passage of the Voting Rights Act? This essay takes a long view of the ending of Jim Crow. While undoubtedly the legal underpinnings for segregation had been severely challenged and the infrastructure of the system eroded in many respects during the 1960s, it was not until the 1970s, for example, when school desegregation was seriously undertaken in many school systems from Jacksonville to Boston. So, for the purposes of this article, the Jim Crow era will be considered as running to about 1970 or so, basically ending about the same time as the high Cold War.

Born in 1912, Harrington grew up in a sort of pocket ghetto in the South Bronx and came of age during the Great Depression when he moved across the river to the cultural, political, and social center of Black life in New York – and, according to some, the world: Harlem. As Michael Denning points out, one of the fundamental motors of the growth of what he calls the "cultural front" of Left influence in art and culture was the tremendous expansion of the mass culture industries in the 1920s and 1930s and the employment of "plebian" "ethnic" Americans in those industries. While African Americans were substantially excluded from many of those industries, such as film, radio, advertising, and music, except as performers in often very constrained modalities, the Jim Crow system Northern-style did provide work for Black writers, editors, visual artists, and other sorts of cultural workers as the Black press burgeoned. It is hard to overstate the importance of this press and its reach into the Black community. It needs to be remembered that the so-called "mainstream" press virtually ignored the Black communities of the United States except to report on sensationalized incidents of crime and violence. If you wanted to know what was going on in Harlem, for example, who was getting married, who died, what the Masons and Elks were doing, what civil rights demonstrations occurred, what musicians had played or were going to play in local halls and clubs, and so on, as well as national and international news of particular interest to Black people, you read the *Amsterdam News* and, later, the *People's Voice*.

The ideological slant and the intensity of the focus on political issues of these papers and journals varied considerably, but all of them were anti-Jim Crow, pro-civil rights, anti-fascist, and anticolonial – and, as noted above, quite a few had a marked leftwing cast. The Black press provided employment not only to those whom we might consider professional journalists, such as the editor Marvel Cooke at the *Amsterdam News* and the *People's Voice*, but also writers, actors, visual artists, and so on, such as Langston Hughes, Melvin Tolson, Ann Petry, Fredi Washington, and Ollie Harrington, who produced columns, sketches, short stories and comic strips and line illustrations. Some, of course, like the poet Frank Marshall Davis, were both fulltime journalists and creative artists. One of the key supports of the Black press was the growth of other African American oriented genres and media of popular culture (recorded music, film, theater, and, eventually, radio) that advertised in Black papers and journals.

Harrington's Harlem was a vital nexus of Black radicalism in which the Black Left, particularly with the advent of the Popular Front in 1935 (the year that *Dark Laughter* first appeared), intersected with Black nationalism, primarily Garveyites and what could be thought of as post-Garveyites, in ways that might seem surprising. While the Black Popular Front (or Black cultural front, if one prefers) was a national phenomenon, reaching North and South, active in every city (and many towns and rural areas) with a significant Black population, Harlem was one of the two most prominent epicenters, surpassed only, perhaps, by Chicago's South Side.

Brian Dolinar suggests that the Black cultural front in Harlem was substantially brought into being by the organization of the *Amsterdam News* by the Committee for Industrial Organization affiliated Newspaper Guild and a subsequent strike in 1935 in which the support of Communists and leftists was crucial, resulting in the radicalization of much of the staff.[3] This is a bit of an exaggeration since a network of Left cultural and political institutions had already begun to coalesce in Harlem during the early Depression, but Dolinar makes the valuable point that the Black press in Harlem, as elsewhere,

---

3. Brian Dolinar, *The Black Cultural Front: Black Writers and Artists of the Depression Generation* (University Press of Mississippi, 2014), 176

was a particularly important node of Black Left cultural activity, both because the press employed cultural workers in a wide range of genres and media and because it reached a mass Black audience. With the rise of the Popular Front in 1935-36 and the emergence of such groups and institutions as the National Negro Congress, the various Federal Arts Projects of the WPA that employed many Black artists, the Harlem Arts Center led by Augusta Savage and then Gwendolyn Bennett, and the 306 group of artists that met at painter Charles Alston's studio on 143rd Street, this "black cultural front" in Harlem really took shape, directly touching the lives of tens of thousands, if not hundreds of thousands, of Harlemites buffeted by Jim Crow Northern-style, overpriced and substandard housing, unemployment and severe job discrimination, inadequate access to medical services, and extreme and frequent police brutality.

However, contrary to many accounts of the influence of the Communist Left on Black politics and culture, the real heyday of the CPUSA in Harlem (and other Black communities) was the 1940s. In part, this failure to accurately assess the Black Left in the 1940s has to do with the still powerful narrative of Communist betrayal and decline after the "Hitler-Stalin Pact" of 1939. Also, the alienation of Richard Wright and Ralph Ellison (though Ellison was not a particularly prominent writer at the time) from the CPUSA due to what was seen as a retreat from support of "Negro" liberation in an attempt to build anti-Nazi solidarity during World War II (in contrast to the Double V campaign of victory over Jim Crow at home and over Fascism abroad, which basically emerged from the Black press, that the Communists formally opposed – though often less publicly supported on the local level) has sometimes been taken to be a larger trend than it was. The fact is that the early and middle 1940s were the years in which Adam Clayton Powell, Jr., whose early political career was very much a product of the Popular Front, was elected to the New York City Council and then to the U.S. House of Representatives. When Powell left the City Council for Congress, he was replaced by the Harlem CPUSA leader Benjamin Davis, Jr., who was elected with Powell's support in 1942. The expansion of CIO unions with significant Black membership, particularly the National Maritime Union, in the 1940s left a big mark on the Black community in New York, the most important port in the U.S. The NMU's First Vice President, Ferdinand Smith, was a familiar figure of the streets (and the newspaper columns) of Harlem. The 1940s were a period of intense Left cultural and educational activity in Harlem with schools, theaters, reading series, rallies, exhibitions, bookstores, galleries, and so on. It was also the decade of Paul Robeson's greatest success as performer and a political figure as well as when he was most prominently associated with Harlem after spending much of the 1930s in the United Kingdom. Harrington was a close friend of Robeson, who was a key influence on Harrington's ideological journey.

One of the most important Left initiatives of the 1940s was the founding of the *People's Voice* newspaper in 1942 by Powell and what was essentially the Harlem Popular Front, largely out of a dissatisfaction with the failure of the *Amsterdam News* to adequately cover the issues facing the Harlem community and Black people generally as well as its largely anti-labor management. The *People's Voice* had a decidedly leftwing profile with Powell as the publisher, Doxey Wilkerson, a Communist, as editor-in-chief, and Marvel Cooke, another Communist, as essentially managing editor. (Cooke's title was officially "Assistant Managing Editor," but there was no "Managing Editor" for nearly all of her tenure at the paper.) Most of the staff, including writer Ann Petry and actress Fredi Washington, were leftists of one stripe or another. Benjamin Davis was a major, if unofficial, advisor to the paper's editorial direction. In fact, until the unfriendly takeover of the paper a by then decidedly anti-Communist Max Yergan in 1947 as the Cold War began to ramp up, no other major Black paper in the United States, not even the *California Eagle* or the *Baltimore Afro-American*, presented such an openly leftwing profile as the *People's Voice*. Indeed, part of the paper's front page masthead are the words, "A Militant Paper."

Harrington served as the editorial cartoonist to *People's Voice* within this Black Left milieu even as he continued to produce *Bootsie* for the *Pittsburgh Courier*. Shortly after Harrington joined the *People's Voice*, in 1942 the paper ran a detailed introduction of him by Llewelyn Ransom – an introduction that is quite telling because, like Harrington's cartoons, at some points the author demonstrates the utter seriousness of humor. For instance, he noted that the fact that Harrington was biracial should "help to send the silly adolf to the early grave he faces on the Russian front."[4] Tellingly, the author does not capitalize "adolf" or "hitler" at any point – a strategy for conveying disrespect – and notes that because Hitler's paintings were recognized as bad, he'd be especially furious about the talented Harrington. The reference to the "Russian front" in conjunction with the inferred linkage of Nazism and racism at home and abroad, recalling Langston Hughes's poem "Good Morning, Stalingrad," is

---

4. Llewelyn Ransom, *People's Voice*, August 8, 1942, 4

also a significant reference to the Black Left stance of both Harrington and the paper generally.

At some point in the 1930s or early 1940s Harrington joined the CPUSA. Ellen Perlo, a central and prominent member of the Party's Arts Club in New York, confirms that he was a member, noting, "He had an intense, dark look about him, and his artwork was always full, finished in appearance, never sketchy."[5] Leaving aside the irony of Harrington's work being "never sketchy," Perlo's testimony is evidence of Harrington's organizational commitment to the Left as well as his sentiments, a commitment that is important to recall in terms of Harrington's artistic and personal trajectory. After all, there is no reason that Harrington had to actually join the CPUSA. Many artists and intellectuals lent their support to the Popular Front and its initiatives without doing so. To join the Party and sit through its club meetings (and even in an artists club, discussions of *Daily Worker* distributions, leaflets, so on), involved a sort of drudgery that only a practical commitment to social change would warrant.

Harrington's engagement with the organized Left and the CPUSA's artists club also reminds us that he was a part of a vital web of Black (and white and Latinx and Asian American) Left visual artists and arts activists that in Harlem included Romare Bearden, Charles Alston (Bearden's cousin by marriage), Augusta Savage, Gwendolyn Bennett, Jacob Lawrence (a student of Alston's), and Georgette Seabrooke Powell. It is striking how important cartooning and graphic art were to this group of Left Black artists. Like the German Expressionists, Alston, Bennett, Lawrence, Bearden, Charles White, and Elizabeth Catlett were all so-called fine artists who had a deep interest in cartoons and the sort of graphic art that could reach a mass audience. This is to say that Harrington's cartooning did not stand outside of "serious" Black visual art; instead, his work formed a vital part of it. Conversely, the work of Catlett, White, Lawrence, et al, cannot be clearly distinguished from the cartoons of Harrington, Jackie Ormes, Brumsic Brandon, and later Tom Feelings (a frequent contributor the journal *Freedomways* in the 1960s and 1970s). This can be seen in the use of Charles White's work as essentially editorial cartooning in *Freedom*, a Black Left journal founded by Paul Robeson and Louis Burnham (a Black Communist who was later one of the primary initiators of *Freedomways,* too). Harrington served as Art Director of *Freedom* at the invitation of his old friend and mentor

5. John Pietaro, "Ellen Perlo and the Bold Shade of Red," *The Cultural Worker*, May 27, 2018, http://theculturalworker.blogspot.com/2016/05/essay-ellen-perlo-and-bold-shades-of-red.html

Robeson and was no doubt largely responsible for the appearance of White's work in the newspaper.

With the rise of the high Cold War, Harrington (like many radical Black artists) fled the United States in 1951, settling first in Paris, where he joined a circle of expatriate Black artists and activists, including Richard Wright (who became a close friend of Harrington's). With Wright's death (which Harrington believed to be a murder by the U.S. government due to Wright's renewed radicalism and sympathies with the Left), he applied for and received political asylum in the GDR in 1961, remaining in Berlin for the last four decades of his life. His fellow artist Elton Fax asserted that Harrington's physical distance from the United States gave him a useful vision. As Fax noted, "Because he has put distance between himself and America Ollie is able to clearly see the oppressors in his native land as partners of other oppressors elsewhere. He therefore links his thrusts at the Nixon policies, the C.I.A., and domestic racism to fascism in Europe and Asia and apartheid in Africa."[6]

The CPUSA's major newspaper, the *Daily Worker*, stopped publishing in 1958 under the pressures of the Cold War and internal battles caused by the fallout from Nikita Khrushchev's "secret speech" about Stalin's crimes and the Soviet invasion of Hungary in 1956. When the CPUSA revived its daily newspaper (the *Daily World*) again a decade later, it chose as editor the Black Communist journalist John Pittman. Pittman knew Harrington and his work through the both the Left and the Black press. Pittman hired Harrington as an editorial cartoonist for the new Communist daily.

Pittman's move clearly provided Harrington with much needed income since his *Bootsie* strip was dropped by the *Chicago Defender* in the early 1960s under the pressure, Harrington suspected, of the U.S. government. Contrary to some assessments, Harrington's work for the Communist press allowed him to develop certain aspects of his art that he had only been able to do to any significant extent during his time with the short-lived *People's Voice* and *Freedom*. While Harrington was clearly a part of the cultural and political circles of the Communist Left in Harlem from at least the mid-1930s, his artistic career from his time with the *People's Voice* on marked a new phase in his cartooning, one in which he was operating in a clearly leftwing context and consequently felt free to be as pointed as he wished to be with a tone that was at least as savage as Goya and George Grosz

---

6. Elton C. Fax, "Foreword to Oliver Harrington's Portfolio," *Soul Shots: Political Cartoons by Ollie Harrington* (Longview Publishing Company [printed in the GDR], 1972)

and other German Expressionist graphic artists – not to mention Charles White, Charles Alston, and Elizabeth Catlett. (Earlier, in an interview in *Life*, he had noted the influence on his own work of El Greco and Thomas Hart Benton, both of who rejected simple realism and pleasantness.[7]) In that sense, Harrington's later days as a contributor to the Communist press in the U.S., especially the *Daily World* and *People's World*, while living in the German Democratic Republic was more liberating than constraining.

Harrington first developed the character he is most known for, Bootsie, in the *Amsterdam News*, one of the very earliest Black newspapers. Starting in 1935, Harrington contributed a comic strip that was ultimately named for that character but was at first called *Dark Laughter*. The strip's original name is quite striking because of the tradition it places Harrington in; "Dark Laughter," along with the title of a book (explicitly for white people illustrated by Harrington's cartoons), *Laughing on the Outside*, lines Harrington up with a significant historical sweep of writing and naming that refer to laughing as a social and cultural strategy of concealment and misdirection by African Americans. A few examples are Paul Laurence Dunbar's 1896 "We Wear the Mask," which opens with the line, "We wear the mask that grins and lies" and two answer poems, by Maya Angelou (1987) and Tolbert Jones Small (n.d.);[8] the previously mentioned Langston Hughes collection *Laughing on the Outside*; at least two Smokey Robinson songs ("Tears of a Clown," and "Tracks of my Tears"); Amiri Baraka's "Masked Angel Costume: The Sayings of Mantan Moreland" (1996); numerous hip hop songs (a particularly powerful example is the Fugees "The Mask," in which they rap about needing a mask because "Feds be hawkin' me"); and so forth.[9] (The subtitle of *Laughing on the Outside*, which is edited by Philip Sterling, is *The Intelligent White Reader's Guide to Negro Tales and Humor*; this directly invokes George Bernard Shaw's 1928 book *The Intelligent Women's Guide to Socialism and Capitalism*, which similarly picked up by Tony Kushner in the title of his 2009 play confronting gay characters and communism, *The Intelligent Homosexual's Guide to Capitalism and Socialism with a Key to the Scriptures*.) It is, then, quite significant

---

7. "Tradition and Technique Are Watchwords at Yale's School of Fine Arts," *Life*, 8 (February 12, 1940), 46

8. Paul Laurence Dunbar, "We Wear the Mask," *American Negro Poetry*, Arna Bontemps (ed.) (Hill and Wang, 1963), 14

9. A few more examples are Future's "Mask Off" and "Lil One," 2Pac's "Under Pressure," and Nicki Minaj's "Feeling Myself"

that in his introduction to a 1958 collection of Harrington's work, called *Bootsie and Others*, Langston Hughes writes that Harrington's cartoons have the quality of the blues, that "behind their humor lurks the sadness of 'when you see me laughin', I'm laughin' to keep from cryin'."[10]

Langston Hughes also notes that sometimes Harrington's work is "too bitter" for "many whites," but the character of Bootsie became quite familiar in the Black press, and ran for more than 20 years in the *Pittsburgh Courier*, which had a range of regional versions and was one of the most significant Black papers – in terms of both size and influence.[11] Harrington published his first cartoon in the *Courier* in 1938, and would later become a war correspondent for the paper, writing more than 50 articles. (He noted quite precisely that this solved an ethical dilemma for him: he was deeply anti-fascist but balked at the notion of serving in a segregated military.)

A useful way to explore the overlap between Harrington's artistic and activist role is the response he invoked. This sometimes took the form of letters to the editor, including one declaring, "Sirs, I think Ol Harrington's 'spots' are one of the best parts of your paper. And as for Blues in the News – Harrington's cartoon take on a news story – I'd like to stand up and cheer every time the paper comes out. More power to PV and to Ol Harrington's pencil."[12] However, many readers worried that his cartoons would encourage racist responses. For instance, another letter to the editor opens with how much the writer loves the paper. The only disturbing element, she comments, is Harrington's cartoons, whose characters ("pimps, cowards, and other such characters") contribute to the belittling of African Americans that so many white cartoonists already take up.[13] Indeed, the paper received so much feedback early in its printing of Wright's *Native Son* – illustrated in a pull-no-punches way by Harrington – that the editors asked readers to send in postcards with their opinions about the printing, and in response, the paper stopped the series very early. Tellingly, most of the respondents who didn't want the series to continue were worried about what white Americans would think because of the novel's rough language. A sort of delightful "wink" about this is included in the editorial

---

10. Langston Hughes, "Introduction"
11. Ibid
12. *People's Voice*, Letters to the Editor, May 2, 1942, 21
13. Ibid

IMAGE 1: *People's Voice*, 1943

response, which says that in response to feedback, they were pulling the series, because readers found it to be "too damn profane."[14]

One of the most instructive aspects of Harrington's work is the way he tips his hand – emphasizing what culture is *for* – by repeatedly presenting culture as a potential "shelter," which he makes literal in this space-filler cartoon, from the *Amsterdam News* (IMAGE 1).

Here, a fashion choice that Harrington repeatedly focused on, the zoot suit, provides literal safety in World War II – a war against a political party that, among other things, sought to establish Black inferiority. In fact, it must be noted that the establishment of this racial hierarchy happened on both sides: at this time, the U.S. military was still segregated, which was something Harrington spoke out about, and culture's function as a shelter is particularly true, he instructed, of African Americans involved in the vexed Double V moment.

<hr/>

14. "Native Son: Requiescat in Pace," *People's Voice*, April 18, 1942, 5. It is worth noting that while some readers were worrying about what white people thought of the *Native Son* cartoon in a newspaper read almost exclusively by Black people, the book the strip was based on had become a bestseller and was a Book of the Month Club selection.

IMAGE 2: *People's Voice*, February 28, 1942 (p. 20)

These images – for instance, the one above (IMAGE 2) that equates racialized murder by Nazis to racialized lynching – were both emblems and strategies of Harrington's broad anti-racist agenda; a central focus of Harrington's was the intersection of police brutality and African American veterans of WWII.

This comparison is something Harrington – and, indeed, the *People's Voice* overall – often took up. Not only did he repeat this side-by-side structure and commentary in another cartoon in this paper, but the comparison is directly visible in Harrington's cartoon of a veteran in a wheelchair being threatened by a policeman wielding a club. The veteran is asking, "Officer, what Alabama bar was you holed up in back in '44 when I was in Normandy protectin' your civil rights?"[15]

Harrington's attention to the Double-V campaign came together powerfully in the 1946 pamphlet he wrote about a Columbia, Tennessee riot perpetrated by the police against returning Black veterans while he was working for the NAACP Public Relations Council, having left daily cartooning to do so.[16] Harrington was subpoenaed to testify in front of a grand jury – with an unsympathetic judge – about what he wrote in the pamphlet, and was blamed for inflaming public sentiment. The NAACP pamphlet illustrates that

15. M. Thomas Inge (ed.), *Dark Laughter: The Satiric Art of Oliver W. Harrington* (University Press of Mississippi, 1993), 21

16. Oliver Harrington, "Terror in Tennessee: The Truth About the Columbia Outrages" (National Association for the Advancement of Colored People, 1946). The handwritten comments on the copy of that pamphlet used for this essay are telling: on the cover someone has penciled "Very exaggerated" and inside, "CRAP."

Harrington offered strikingly astute commentary in multiple forms: not just in his political cartoons, but also in pamphlets, in illustrations of news stories, in small space-fillers (such as the zoot suiter above), in cartoons accompanying subscription forms, and in remarkably astute and sly essays. Nonetheless, there is not nearly enough attention paid to Harrington's cartoons. The attention he does receive almost always focuses on Harrington's most mainstream (and famous) work. But his most biting political cartoons, his astute and uncompromising attacks on the structural racism in the United States, summarized well by his comment, "Black people are all refugees, unless they are African people living in Africa," have not received sufficient recognition.[17]

Of course, one thing that has kept Harrington from receiving recognition is his relationship with the American Left, particularly with the CPUSA, which some scholars (such as M. Thomas Inge, who has edited a collection of Harrington's work and a collection of his essays) try hard to gloss over. For instance, Inge works to expunge Harrington's political location by remarking with no evidence that people only read the *Daily World* for the pictures (including Harrington's cartoons), noting that "One or more of Harrington's cartoons would remain a mainstay of the paper which reached 72,000 readers, many of whom came to look mainly for the cartoons and had less interest in the political content."[18] In a collection of civil rights oriented political cartoons for high school students edited by Mary E. Williams, there is a list of the major places Harrington published that does not include the *Daily World* – but the Harrington cartoon included in the collection is from the *Daily World*.[19] Similarly, in Sheena C. Howard's *Encyclopedia of Black Comics*, she refers to the *"New York Daily World"* but does not identify it as the paper of the CPUSA (though she does address Harrington's closeness to Party members, followed by an unsupported assertion that he was not a member).[20]

In addition to such attempts to purge Harrington's political stances, it is striking how the few people who have usefully paid attention to his cartoons seldom look at them as art and examine them visually; instead, they are mostly captured by the captions.

17. Oliver Harrington, "Look Homeward Baby—Part II," *Freedomways*, Vol. 13, No. 3, 1973, 207

18. Inge, *Dark Laughter*, xxxviii

19. Mary E. Williams (ed.), *Civil Rights* (Greenhaven Press, 2002)

20. Sheena Howard, *Encyclopedia of Black Comics* (Fulcrum Publishing, 2017), 105

In short, while Harrington's artistic strategies are occasionally broadly described (for instance, Howard notes that "Harrington's use of rich pencil shading gave the comic a lush atmosphere and provided gravity to each cartoon"), his individual pieces of work are infrequently analyzed.[21] In particular, a category of Harrington's work that has received no attention is his "space-filler" drawings in *People's Voice* – likely because they are seen as unplanned and off-the-cuff, but as the illustration above of the zoot suiter indicates, they are actually quite profound.[22] Therefore, to explore his strategies and artistic/political priorities, we will examine Harrington's comics from the perspective of textual analysis. Roi Ottley, in his 1943 *New World A-Coming,* says that the inclusion of Harrington and other Black cartoonists was to "soften the blows dealt by a tough front page," but in fact Harrington's cartoons frequently both worsened the blow, and provided self-defense, which is different from softening.[23] Indeed, the number of Harrington's cartoons that have white men holding a noose cancels any notion of "softening." A 1973 collection of poster reproductions of Harrington's *Daily World* cartoons consists of 16 cartoons. One fourth of them have nooses or whips that visually double as nooses (connecting slavery and lynching), as Harrington establishes a range of new ways to "lynch" Black Americans: courtrooms, poverty, political corruption.

As we have mentioned above, Harrington was quite occupied with the Double-V campaign, referring, for instance, to the segregated South as a "huge concentration camp."[24] In a 1942 *People's Voice* comic (IMAGE 3), *Blues in the News,* he has four funny, joking panes, including jokes about zoot suiters, followed up by an upsetting image of Black soldiers in the trench, with the words, "We know that our country has been giving our boys a dirty deal but out where they are they need us...and our old pots and pans, discarded sewing machines, and irons will help them pull through. Then we'll all demand a fair share of this democracy they're all blowing off about!"

Strikingly, there is an artistic shift toward realism in the final panel, when he is confronting a reality facing the African American soldier:

21. Ibid, 103
22. For instance, Harrington frequently illustrates, in space-filler cartoons, the separation of blood donations from Black and white Americans, which continued until 1950.
23. Roi Ottley, *New World A-Coming* (Houghton Mifflin Company, 1943), 282
24. Oliver Harrington, "Terror Grips War Veterans in Georgia Lynching Center," *Los Angeles Sentinel,* August 29, 1946

IMAGE 3: *People's Voice*, October 10, 1942 (page 14)

IMAGE 4: *People's Voice*, September 5, 1942 (page 14)

both the irony of fighting against fascism abroad in a segregated military, but also the need for civil rights work when they come home.

In another cartoon (IMAGE 4) that addresses the contradiction implicit in fighting fascism abroad and maintaining it at home, Harrington tracks African American men trying hard to get jobs and being rejected repeatedly, even a handicapped man applying for a job particularly for handicapped men.

But the most striking panel shows industrialists with "fat war contracts drawing up plans for employing Negro labor," which Harrington represents with a blank panel. It is fascinating how striking this artistic emptiness is, especially compared to Harrington's usual dense style of drawing. And it is also important to note that the panel establishes art as labor, because of what is missing there.

In addition to World War II, Harrington uses the Cold War as a way to comment on how institutional racism permeates daily life. In one of the cartoons in the 1958 collection that Langston Hughes introduced, a woman is speaking to her pastor about the destruction of her home, in which she is pictured protectively holding a small child (IMAGE 5). The woman notes that she initially thought that the Russians had dropped a bomb on the house, but it turns out that in fact, it was "the white citizens council" (basically a front for the Ku Klux Klan) and it was not the first time. While the exact location of the cartoon is not specified, it appears to be in the South based on the layout of the house, perhaps in Birmingham, Alabama, which earned the nickname "Bombingham" for the number of explosions (forty plus) set off in the homes of Black families that moved into predominantly white neighborhoods between 1947 and 1965. The cartoon focuses on how the bombing put out the lights (literally and figuratively) by picturing multiple destroyed lamps. The destruction of art is also emphasized in the drawing. Overall, the grief on the pastor's face makes it impossible to find this cartoon funny at all. Of course, the political takeaway is that, in fact, Russia is not the immediate threatening enemy: American racism is far more dangerous. It must also be noted how muscular and strong the Black woman is drawn. Harrington's style here is full and fleshy, not sketchy, giving actual weight to what the characters are saying.

Another cartoon in this collection presents police as a threat to African Americans, a stance Harrington takes up multiple times in multiple contexts. A man is explaining to his wife why he has cut a hole in the floor right behind the front door because of how often the "ofay policemens" keep breaking down doors in the neighborhood (IMAGE 6). In a visually striking way, a framed picture of boxer Joe Louis – known as the "Brown Bomber" and a Black Popular Front hero – on the apartment wall has Louis's fists directed at the door, where the cops are threatening to come in. Further, in the picture Louis's posture is exactly the same as the hands on the nearby clock, which strongly suggests that the time for true resistance has come. Langston Hughes famously said of Louis:

Each time Joe Louis won a fight in those depression years, even before he became champion, thousands of black Americans on relief or WPA, and poor, would throng out into the streets all across the land to march and cheer and yell and cry because

"At first we thought the Russians had went an' dropped one on us. You can imagine how relieved we were when we found out it was only the white citizens' Council bombin' our house agin'!"

IMAGE 5: *Bootsie and Others* (n.p).

"Now look, Baby, don't come tellin' me I'm crazy. I'm just gettin' tired of the way these big fat ofay policemens is breakin' down folks's doors and jumping in all snarlin' and growlin'!"

IMAGE 6: *Bootsie and Others* (n.p.)

of Joe's one-man triumphs. No one else in the United States has ever had such an effect on Negro emotions – or on mine. I marched and cheered and yelled and cried too.[25]

_____

25. Langston Hughes, *I Wonder as I Wander*, in *Collected Works of Langston Hughes Vol. 16* (University of Missouri Press, 2001), 307

This symbolic role of Black boxers found its way into multiple cultural forms; for instance, there are numerous blues and R&B songs invoking and praising them. Harrington took up boxing's symbolic role of representing African American fighting for equality and justice multiple times.

For example, a 1951 *Freedom* cartoon titled "In This Corner" depicts Sugar Ray Robinson in the boxing ring. The cartoon, for Harrington, is rather stark and bare – it shows Robinson in the ring, and then only many rocks and bottles coming at him. But once again, he pulls no punches, so to speak, here: labels on what is being launched at him include "Negroes not allowed," "To Ray from KKK" – and swastikas, leveling American white supremacy with the racial ideology of Hitler. However, Harrington's cartoon invokes serious fightback.

While the fightback is inspiring, a more pessimistic May 1951 cartoon in *Freedom* is captioned, "Old Generals Never Die, They Just Fly Away." This refers to a British song that introduced a saying, "Old soldiers never die, they just fade away," which in turn grew out of a gospel song, "Kind Words Can Never Die." But the cartoon came out right after the "old soldiers" phrase was used in General Douglas MacArthur's famous final speech to Congress, on April 15, 1951. The cartoon (IMAGE 7) strikingly inverts the phrase MacArthur uses, because piles of dead and dying soldiers – both black and white – are pictured here as being abandoned by a plane flying away with more privileged military officers. Below the plane, the cartoon is quite bleak.

Image 7: *Freedom*, May 1951 (p. 4)

There is nothing hopeful, even in a "natural" way, here. For instance, the trees have no leaves, and there is a mound in the back that is either a pile of bodies or a dead or dying hill. But what is made visually clear by the stark backdrop are agonized faces of soldiers on the ground.

As noted above, Harrington frequently pictured nooses in his *Daily World* cartoons. In a 1970 publication, his drawing overlaps a noose and a whip (IMAGE 8). By picturing Richard Nixon as an auctioneer of slaves, the cartoon not only strikingly brings theft of African American labor into the present, it notes that the United States' history of slavery has, at the least, a direct economic descendant – but Harrington is asserting more directly that in many ways it just has a new name and new ways to perpetuate it. One of these ways is unequal access to education: a sign on the stage talks about how keeping the children uneducated allows their labor to be exploited more than if they did have access to schools. Nixon's lack of pants and hairy lower body indicates that he is either a satyr (known for lasciviousness and being only partially human) or the devil. His hand is parallel to his gun and being held the way children do when they are playing with pretend guns – but in this case, it connects the work of Nixon's hand to the murder of African Americans. Further, in a simultaneously striking and gloomy way, the hat on one of the auction buyers visually links slaveowners with Uncle Sam. The racists are pictured as the trunk of the tree, which has many branches – indicating that there are many ways that the racism of slavery has grown and spread. The kids' faces are both hurting and defiant – which offers a tiny bit of light. Their vulnerability, though, is increased visually through their very small size.

It should come as no surprise that Harrington's radical cartooning made it impossible for him to remain in the United States. When he learned he was being investigated by the FBI, Harrington felt the need to move to Europe – first to France, and later to Sweden and then to the G.D.R. He did not return to visit the United States for 21 years. Although the pattern of African American artists moving abroad is by now quite familiar, with Harrington the matter is still not settled. Why did he stay in East Germany? Different answers circulate. It was "self-imposed exile" (Elton Fax).[26] It was because he was being investigated by HUAC (Henry Louis Gates).[27] He felt "not

26. Elton C. Fax, "Forward to Ollie Harrington's Portfolio"
27. Henry Louis Gates, Jr, Introduction, *Encyclopedia of Black Comics*, ix.

"OKAY GENTLEMEN, NOW HOW MANY 1972 DIXIE VOTES DO YOU OFFER FOR THIS EXCEPTIONAL, FINE BRACE?"

IMAGE 8: *Daily World*, (April 1970)

absolutely safe" in France (his widow, Helma Harrington).[28] Because of "trouble with the American authorities," his close friend Richard Wright suggested he leave France for a "socialist country."[29]

---

28. Stephanie Brown, "'Bootsie' in Berlin: An Interview with Helma Harrington on Oliver Harrington's Life and Work in East Germany, 1961-1995," *African American Review*, 44.3 (Fall 2011), 355

29. Michael Fabre, *The Unfinished Quest of Richard Wright* (University of Illinois Press, 1993), 510-511

As noted above, after leaving for Europe, Harrington did not visit the U.S. for 21 years. He still thought of Harlem as home, though, in many ways – but this, too, was not without conflict. In fact, the first time he came back to the United States after many years abroad, someone called him a "God damned fuckin' dumb n——r ," and he thought, "Now I knew where I was…I was home Baby!" [30] This brief exchange confirms what the mainstream, advertising filled *Ebony* magazine said about Harrington, right after he died. The short memorial notes that his cartoons "tell it like it was – and is."[31] This comment also reminds us that Harrington's work is a bridge between different moments of Black radicalism responding to Jim Crow, racism, colonialism, and neo-colonialism from the Popular Front in the 1930s to Black Arts and Black Power movements of the 1960s and 1970s.

What we have tried to do here is to open a further discussion about Harrington and his art as a bridge, a discussion that does not detach Harrington from his particular ideological and organizational commitments and institutional locations. More attention needs to be paid to the actual qualities of Harrington's drawings as they interface with text rather than simply focus on captions, as is all too often the case. Harrington created with significant success a formally and thematically radical yet popular art drawing on lines of black "high," "mass," and "folk" culture (fashion, music, graphic art, dance, humor, literature, and so on) in ways that anticipated Black Arts and what came after.

30. Harrington, "Look Homeward Baby—Part II," *Freedomways*, Vol. 13, No. 3, 1973, 211

31. "The Last Laugh: Cartoons by the late Ollie Harrington tell it like it was—and is," *Ebony*, February 1996, 122

Chapter *10*

Gita, Betty, and the Women's International Democratic Federation: An Internationalist Love Story

By Elisabeth Armstrong

Love & Primitive Accumulation

By 1948 the central offices of the Women's International Democratic Federation had been running for over two years. Located in Paris, the post-war global city for antifascist organizing, WIDF staff enjoyed support from the pro-communist (PCF) government. By 1950, France's central government had changed, and the WIDF's welcome had worn thin. French police arrested Eugenie Cotton, the president of WIDF, for advocating that women should tear up their sons' enlistment papers to fight against the Vietnamese liberation movement. By January 1951, the WIDF offices moved to Berlin – the Berlin of the state-socialist German Democratic Republic, where WIDF stayed until 1991.

"It seems they are quite the aristocracy over there in Berlin," wrote Gita Bannerji on July 1, 1954.[1] Gita was a Communist Party member from India who worked at WIDF's central offices between 1948 and 1952. Gita wrote her letter to another staff member from these early years: Betty Millard, a Communist Party member from the United States, who worked alongside her in Paris from 1949 to 1951. "But we may be pleased to remember that we did the primitive accumulation part," Gita wrote. "Now we are again engaged in primitive accumulation."[2] Gita's primitive accumulation, along the grain of

---

1. Gita Bannerji, Letter to Betty Millard, July 1, 1954. Elizabeth Millard Collection, Sophia Smith Collection, Smith College, Northampton, US. Hereafter cited as Millard Collection, SSC
2. Ibid

Rosa Luxemburg's use of the term, described the process of creating value from something in its raw, unrealized form. In jest, Gita flipped the term on its head. Rather than referring to the profits capitalism requires from commodifying land, resources, and labor, Gita imagined a Communist primitive accumulation that built valuable revolutionary movements from peoples' scattered struggles against their oppression. Left feminist activism, that created movements in Paris, Kolkata, and New York, to name just a few locations, built the women's movement in these years.

Gita and Betty met at a WIDF conference in Budapest, Hungary, but they became close friends while working together in Paris. They shared a wry sense of humor and a keen eye for the absurd that emerges in Gita's letters to Betty, and in Betty's diary entries. They wrote to each other from 1950 until the 1980s. Their friendship, built from shared ethics and imaginary of what could be, reveals a largely unsung love story on the Communist left. The love story between comrades in struggle is one vital piece; but the more poignant aspect is less triumphant, perhaps less instrumental in its telling. They gave each other joy, with the intimacy of their friendship in Europe. Their affection for each other lasted decades after they returned to the politically hostile soil of their countries of citizenship. They were lucky enough to have both kinds of love that sustained their activism; that is, their primitive accumulation, through fierce headwinds and devastating losses.

While in Paris, Gita and Betty supported the activism of WIDF's member organizations, their 91 million members, as well as their organizations. Gita worked as part of WIDF's anticolonial International Preparatory Committee to build women's organizations in colonized regions of the world. She played a key role organizing the 1949 Asian Women's Conference, held in Beijing. Betty was the editor of the CPUSA journal *New Masses* for four years before arriving in Paris. For WIDF, she edited the English language edition of its *Information Bulletin* that publicized international, regional, and national campaigns for women's emancipation. Like Gita, Betty also created the scaffolding for WIDF's internationalism by collecting and sharing information about ongoing local campaigns of its member organizations for the *Bulletin* and their powerful solidarity campaigns. WIDF's primitive accumulation plumbed the soil of internationalism after the destruction of planetary war. Gita's and Betty's work for WIDF strengthened old values of common worth, not as a hidden ore below humanity's surface, but as an affirmed commonalty of vision and purpose. Even during the four years when WIDF was welcome in Paris, this work was hardscrabble in the wreckage that a fascist war left behind: of broken lives, destroyed communities, distrust, and ongoing colonial occupation.

In 1950, both Gita and Betty coordinated WIDF's first international campaign for peace in Korea. Gita attended campaign organizational meetings across Europe, and Betty wrote press releases and speeches. WIDF framed the campaign in two ways. First, WIDF described women's activism as it forged solidarity against U.S. led imperialist aggression; this activism was led by women from Korea, but also women from other colonized countries. Second, WIDF framed the campaign as a maternalist fight led by all women from imperialist and colonized nations against the use of their sons and husbands as cannon-fodder for war. The World Peace Council, co-founded in 1947 by Eugenie Cotton and other WIDF members, joined their campaign against the NATO forces and U.S. military attack on North Korea to demand peace, self-determination, and an end to American occupation of the region. Working alongside their allies and state socialist governments around the world, WIDF ultimately lost the campaign for a quick end to the assault. The occupation of South Korea remained in U.S. friendly governments and even to this day, with U.S. military bases in the country.

The first United Nations backed invasion began in April 1950 when the United States launched a military attack on North Korea that continued for the next three years. By the end of the conflict, over 3 million Koreans were killed. In North Korea, civilians were half of the 2 million people killed. Over these three years, American planes dropped 635,000 tons of bombs and 32,557 tons of napalm on the country.[3] By 1952, no military targets remained, but the onslaught continued until 1953. The WIDF campaign against the Korean War spanned women's activism around the world to frame peace as a women's issue. In the words of historian Suzy Kim, "socialist internationalism in the context of a global peace movement facilitated a productive understanding of *difference* – whether gendered, racial, ethnic, national or any other – toward a 'transversal' politics of solidarity as seen during the Korean War [*italic* in original]."[4] The creativity and care of this transversal politics of solidarity was not enough to convince the United Nations to end its support for the invasion, nor was it enough to prevent breaking Korea into two antagonistic countries, to the enduring loss of both nations.

_____

3. Suzy Kim, *Everyday Life in the North Korean Revolution, 1945-1950* (Cornell University Press, 2013), 244

4. Suzy Kim, "The Origins of Cold War Feminism During the Korean War," *Gender and History*, 31:2 (July 2019), 461

The campaign against the Korean War was in full swing when both women returned to their homes in 1951. Without breaking stride, they carried their internationalist commitments back to their Communist-led movements. Gita plunged into the activism of the Mahila Atmaraksha Samiti (MARS), the leftist women's organization in West Bengal, India; and Betty joined the American Women for Peace in the United States. Both returned to fiercely creative left feminist movements and hostile central governments. In India, leftist women and men overturned old feudal orders through demands for universal land reform. Peasant women in remote areas in the states of Telengana, Tamil Nadu, West Bengal and Maharashtra attacked patriarchal relations of power in their demands for equal rights to own property, fair wages, literacy, an end to dowry payments, and the right to control their sexual autonomy.[5] The Communist Party, USA, in 1945 had returned to its radicalism of earlier decades, with Black liberation, workers' movements, and women's emancipation again at center stage.[6] Charged with revisionism after he dissolved the CPUSA as a political party, Earl Browder was expelled in 1946. William Z. Foster returned to reconstitute the party. In 1947, Elizabeth Gurley Flynn and Claudia Jones headed the newly reconstituted Women's Commission. They fought Black women's triple oppression in racially segregated job markets. Jones in particular emphasized the development of Black women's leadership in all leftist struggles.[7]

Moneyed, powerful interests sought to muffle the revolutionary creativity of these movements in India and the U.S. As Gita Bannerji joked, their work of primitive accumulation in Paris gave organizational form to shared ideals and disparate contexts around the world. Organizing to build socialism, with women's equality and justice at the heart of this vision, simply continued after they returned to their homes of origin. Gita and Betty wrote letters to each other for decades after spending those two years in Paris building WIDF together. They lived far apart geographically, never meeting again, but shared common ideals through their very different struggles. Their affection for each other and sense of humor about

5. Renu Chakravartty, *Communists in Indian Women's Movement*. (New Delhi: People's Publishing House, 1980)

6. Kate Weigand, *Red Feminism: American Communism and the Making of Women's Liberation* (Johns Hopkins University Press, 2002)

7. Cristina Mislan, "Claudia Jones Speaks to 'Half the World': Gendering Cold War Politics in the *Daily Worker*, 1950-1953," *Feminist Media Studies*, 17:2 (2017), 281-296

their lives refused to dim, even in the face of the growing hardships of anti-communism. Their relationship reveals the beating heart of long-term activism; the love that crosses the significant differences of their lives and experiences. To fight another day requires more than shared ideals among activists.

Gita's letter to Betty written in 1954 spurs two questions for this essay. How do you build a feminist people's movement for revolution grounded in a nation-state that does not want you there? And how do you build this movement alongside someone who is halfway around the world? Movement building – or in Bannerji's terms, primitive accumulation – developed during the 1940s and 1950s through WIDF's centrifugal energy as an international organization. But the creativity and vitality came not from the central offices in Paris, but from the varied struggles waged in colonialized, postcolonial and imperial contexts. International organizations like WIDF meant little without the bullets taken by its members, and the campaigns launched by its affiliated women's groups – campaigns that were won and lost and won again.

Gita

In 1948, at the age of 26, Gita Bannerji left Kolkata for Budapest to attend WIDF's second world congress of women. In 1948, Kolkata was a city that seeded revolt spilling beyond the confines of independent India to revolutionary movements across Asia. The World Federation of Democratic Youth held their Asian convention in Kolkata in February 1948. Students from Indonesia, Vietnam, Myanmar and elsewhere demanded independence not just from colonial occupation, but from capitalism itself.[8] WIDF's plans to hold the Asian Women's Conference in Kolkata later that same year fell through. Nehru's Congress Party members agreed to cancel the gathering – another anti-colonial conference would be too disturbing to the status quo.[9] They believed the new government was too fragile to withstand a sustained contest of its leadership. In 1948, the Congress Party banned the Communist Party of India. Its leaders went

---

8. Larisa Efimova, "Did the Soviet Union Instruct Southeast Asian Communists to Revolt? New Russian Evidence on the Calcutta Youth Conference of February 1948," *Journal of Southeast Asian Studies*, 40:3 (2009), 449-469

9. Elisabeth Armstrong, "Before Bandung: The Anti-Imperialist Women's Movement in Asia and the Women's International Democratic Federation," *Signs*, 41:2 (2016), 305-331

underground but continued to meet. As in colonial times, jails became cells for organizing as much as for confinement.

Soon after, the leftist women's movement in West Bengal linked to the CPI, the Mahila Atmarakshi Samiti, or MARS, also moved into hiding. Regional and national leaders were imprisoned or driven underground, moving constantly from house to house to escape arrest.[10] The rural movement integral to MARS activism called Tebhaga was also on the watchlist. In the Tebhaga movement, waged farmworkers and small-landholding peasant women and men sought basic human rights: fair land practices, and an end to the feudal tributes of forced labor (*begar*) and the sexual control of rural women. Violent police repression, that included widespread rape of rural women, sought to crush the uprising that united peasants and agricultural workers of all backgrounds, Muslims, and Hindus, *adivasis* (indigenous) and Dalits (oppressed castes).

MARS, Gita's WIDF member organization, developed powerful strategies to organize the "*sarbahara*" – or 'those who've lost everything.' Members of MARS mobilized mass public protests of women seeking redress on their own behalf. They built leadership at local and regional levels among the most oppressed women. They developed a signature petition to represent the women who supported their demands and give heft to cross-class campaigns. Perhaps most revolutionary of all, they listened to dispossessed women.

Rural landless and urban women, resettled refugees from India's partition violent were two central bases for MARS' membership. Demands for affordable food, clothing and housing combined with a focus on women's economic independence to imagine women's future independence from need. MARS propaganda – its songs, plays, pamphlets and speeches, explained women's basic survival issues through an analysis of regional class conflict and capitalism's global imperial war.

The story of Pratibha Ganguly and her comrades has the contours of an archetype of struggle. One afternoon in April 1949 the members of MARS gathered with their children in Kolkata.[11] They used a technique they had mobilized during the famine in the early 1940s. A large group of women marched peacefully in public streets to government offices. Their demands were also common ones: the release of political prisoners, many of whom had been imprisoned

---

10. Manikuntala Sen, *In Search of Freedom: An Unfinished Journey* (Kolkata: Stree, 2001)

11. Sonali Satpathi, "Mobilizing Women: The Experience of the Left in West Bengal, 1947-1964," PhD, History, University of Calcutta, 2013

without charges, and basic amenities of food, clothing, and work. In 1942, they faced the British colonial government. In 1949, they addressed the Congress Party. This time, instead of being beaten, jailed, and roughly dispersed as happened in 1942, the police fired on the protest and killed five people: four women and one child. Pratibha was one of the women who died. The novelty of women's public protest shifted from a shocking sight of women filling the streets to a body count. Women protested their impoverished living conditions and demanded their rights. Women died. After this, MARS joined the CPI underground. For the next two years, the women of MARS blended into their surroundings to carry on organizing in secret.

As a member of MARS and the CPI, Gita also lowered her profile. She took a slightly different route from many of her comrades and traveled as one of two Indian delegates to WIDF's second congress in Budapest, Hungary, in 1948. She first met Betty here and did not return to Kolkata until 1952. With the support from her party, the CPI, Gita joined the central offices of WIDF in Paris in 1949. Gita, alongside the Secretary of WIDF, Lu Cui, shouldered the logistics, outreach and communication for WIDF's mandate to support women's anticolonial organizing. Lu Cui's work involved considerable travel to colonized regions of the world to develop WIDF's contacts with local organizers and support their activism. Between 1949 and 1952, Gita mostly traveled within Europe. As her letters attest, she, quite literally in some cases, represented the anticolonial struggles around the world to internationalist allies.

Betty

Betty Millard was an editor of the CPUSA journal *New Masses* for four years, between 1943 and 1947. She was from a wealthy, white, conservative family from Chicago. She graduated from Vassar College and first learned about Marxism while in London, England. After her return from England in 1940, she joined the CPUSA. She lived in New York City, with its active resurgence addressing civil rights issues, and to a lesser extent, women's issues. Spurred by the formation of WIDF in Paris in 1945, the Congress of American Women formed as its national affiliate in 1946. Millard attended the founding meeting of CAW, alongside many other CP members, including Claudia Jones and Elizabeth Gurley Flynn. Millard wrote articles for the CAW newsletter, developed letter campaigns, taught at party affiliated Marxist schools. and researched critical questions of women's emancipation. She fought for consultative status in the United

Nations for WIDF and for CAW. In the face of women's retrenchment from living wage jobs in factories, the struggle against male
chauvinism was one aspect of the struggle to secure women's equal
rights and pay. Leftist women's activism during the period after the
war was led by a theory of Black women's "triple oppression," first
developed by Louise Patterson in the 1930s.[12] Leadership by Black
women in leftist politics grew, with campaigns that linked anti-Black
racism, anti-Semitism, and anti-immigrant violence to male supremacy and violence against women.

Betty Millard worked closely with Jones, who pushed her to better theorize the relation of anti-racism to anti-male supremacy. In
her journal, Betty wrote about a public meeting where she described
WIDF's second international women's congress in Budapest that she
and Pearl Laws, a member of CAW and the National Negro Labor
Council, had attended. "Claudia had me on the carpet in a nice way
about the state and the Negro woman."[13]

Jones read a draft of Betty's influential article, "Woman Against
Myth" first published in two parts in *New Masses* in December 1947
and January 1948. The essays commemorated the 100th anniversary of the Seneca Falls declaration and *The Communist Manifesto*
published the same year in 1848. Jones' letter to Betty outlining her
critique before the articles' publication also had her on the carpet in
a nice way:

> Does not this inferior status [of women] stem now as in the past
> primarily from woman's relation to the means of production?
> Surely if this is granted, then such must be the base and prem-
> ise of your opening theme. Without this, the article is stilted,
> extremely feminist in outlook…My opinion is that you should
> be more assertive, not asking simply why the history of the
> woman's battle for equality no longer seems to have mean-
> ing for any of us, but rather, such a history has new meaning
> for today, because of what we fight, because of efforts to win
> women for reaction (against) fascist ideology, etc.[14]

---

12. Erik McDuffie, *Sojourning for Freedom: Black Women, American Communism, and the Making of Black Left Feminism* (Duke University Press, 2011), 1
and Carole Boyce Davies, *Left of Karl Marx: The Political Life of Black Communist Claudia Jones* (Duke University Press, 2007)

13. Betty Millard, Journal entry dated February 3, 1949, Millard Papers,
SSC

14. Claudia Jones, letter to Betty Millard, November 11, 1947, Millard Collection, SSC

Jones' comments situated leftist women's activism in the conservative atmosphere after the war – where in dominant ideology, women's equality seemed to have already been won. She stressed the internationalism necessary for women's activism in the struggle against fascism, at home in Jim Crow United States, and abroad with the retrenchment of colonialism. Millard did not take Jones' advice. Rather than begin with the anti-fascist challenge faced by women internationally, she addressed the conservative gender and race mores of the domestic moment.

Jones also pushed Millard to draw out her comparisons between anti-Black violence and systemic racism to women's oppression. She wrote, "your analogy to Negro oppression is overdone. An example of this is your reference #3 to 'a deadlier kind of lynching' to describe women's oppression. This is an oversimplification to say the least."[15] Jones' refusal to equate the deathly boredom of "thirty-eight million American housewives" to lynching pushed Millard to edit her article, though she did not drop lynching as a metaphor for women's oppression. Instead, these confined housewives faced "a quieter, more veiled kind of lynching" in the final article.[16] The addition of an orientalist metaphor of veiling to describe the hidden quality of women's oppression exacerbates the unspoken address to *white* middle and working class women. Lynching, as Millard knew well, was not a metaphor for all women in the United States during the 1940s; it was a white supremacist form of terror for Black women and Black men.

Additionally, Jones suggested another change in the articles. She identified the similarity of male supremacy to white supremacy: both shared a ubiquity under imperialism as the highest form of capitalism. For male supremacy, she wrote, women are "oppressed regardless of class (except for the top few) by imperialism."[17] Jones' internationalism in this formulation addressed women in the U.S. and outside of it. Imperialism, she argued, did not play favorites among women. It wrested profits from women's unpaid labor and underpaid work as part and parcel of the theft of primitive accumulation. Imperialism as a system exploited all women; that is, "except for the top few."

---

15. Ibid

16. Betty Millard, "Woman Against Myth," *New Masses*, December 30, 1947, 7

17. Jones, letter to Betty Millard, November 11, 194, Millard Collection, SSC

Millard added the issue of "rape as a form of violence practiced against women" to illustrate how women's oppression intersected with anti-Black racism – systemically and specifically:

> But it (rape) is a criminal act of a special kind – an anti-woman act – just as the other two (anti-Black and anti-Semitic attacks) are crimes of a special kind. The lynching of a Georgia Negro is the violent expression of a pattern of white supremacy; rape is a violent expression of a pattern of male supremacy, an out-growth of age-old economic, political and cultural exploitation of women by men. When a Negro woman is raped by a white man these two aspects of our society merge.[18]

In 1948, only a month after the publication of "Woman Against Myth," CAW joined an international campaign for Rosa Lee Ingram, a Black woman who killed a white man in self-defense in Americus, Georgia. The campaign included the vast web of WIDF's global outreach for the sharecropper Ingram and her two sons – to protest the all-white jury that determined her guilt in one day. The case, as historian Dayo Gore describes it, "pushed front and center black women's experiences with sexualized racial violence and provided an implicit and at times explicit validation of a black defendant's use of deadly force in defending her own life."[19]

One year later, Claudia Jones published a rebuttal to Millard's essay that defined Black women's triple oppression as the reason for their heightened importance to revolutionary movements.[20] Jones elaborated on Patterson's argument about the exploitation faced by Black women; as women, as African Americans, and as workers. She also drew on the return to Marxist theories of "Black self-determination" that saw the Black industrial proletariat as a site for special militancy.[21] Jones argued that these conditions sharpened Black women's revolutionary potential, since they lived on the cutting edge of American conditions of oppression.

---

18. Betty Millard, "Woman Against Myth," *New Masses*, December 30, 1947, 7

19. Dayo Gore, *Radicalism at the Crossroads: African American Women Activists in the Cold War* (New York University Press, 2011), 76

20. Claudia Jones, "An End to the Neglect of Negro Women!" *Political Affairs*, 28:6 (June 1949), 51-67

21. Claudia Jones, "On the Right to Self-Determination for the Negro People in the Black Belt," *Political Affairs*, 25:1 (January 1946), 67-77

Jones and Millard shared a commitment to systemic anti-racism and anti-sexism, a commonalty that animated their dialogue in letters, in public talks, and in pamphlets. In the archival records of their interactions, the tone of their comments are direct, respectful but not exactly warm or even friendly. Their clearly stated disagreement over Marxist theory did not require intimacy or love between Millard and Jones; but it did rely upon their shared political project of anti-capitalism.

Budapest, 1948 & Beijing, 1949

Gita and Betty first met in 1948 at WIDF's second international congress held in Budapest, Hungary. They also both attended the Asian Women's Conference held in Beijing in 1949. The congress in Budapest brought members to assess their activism since its founding three years earlier. The decision to focus on women's anticolonial activism in 1946 expanded their founding commitment to anti-fascism.[22] WIDF explicitly added anti-racism and anti-colonialism to its commitment to fighting fascism. Women from the U.S. delegation and women from the Indian, Vietnamese, and Chinese delegations sought this clarity from WIDF's inception. In this sense, they adhered to a definition of fascism articulated in the 1930s.

Marxist theorist Rajne Palme Dutt, a member of the Communist Party of Great Britain, defined fascism as an integral ideology of capitalism.[23] Fascism maintained capitalism in the face of revolutionary upheaval. It intensified the dictatorship of capitalism and the repression of the working class. Fascism also concentrated each imperialist block into a single economic and political unity. War only solidified the antagonisms and contradictions within imperialism. Dutt also characterized fascism as a movement through its actors: "Fascism, in short, is a movement of mixed elements dominantly petit bourgeois, but also slum proletarian and demoralized working class, financed

---

22. "The Situation of Women in Colonies, Discussions on Racial Discrimination," *Bulletin à information*, 9-10 (October November, 1946), 7, Vivian Carter Mason, the US representative to WIDF from the National Council of Negro Women (NCNW), Jeanne Merens, a communist and founder of the Algerian Women's Union and Jai Kishore Handoo, member of the Women's Commnittee of India League in London developed early materials for the WIDF executive committee meeting focused on anti-colonialism and anti-racism.

23. Rajne Palme Dutt, *Fascism and Social Revolution*, (Proletarian Publisher, 1934), 92

and directed by finance capital, by the big industrialists, landlords and financiers, to defeat the working class revolution and smash the working class organization."[24] What made fascism specific, in Dutt's analysis, was the willingness to use violence and illegal methods for capitalist ends.

WIDF members from around the world sharpened a gendered analysis of fascism during these heady years from 1945 to the mid-1950s. They mobilized women's socially-dominant role as mothers and maternalist rhetoric to attack fascism. But anti-fascism in their publications also emphasized women's willingness to fight, physically and militarily, against fascist violence. WIDF's public materials used the terms of maternalism not as a biological destiny, but as a social role that anti-fascist, anti-racist, and anti-colonial women shaped rather than simply inhabited. The campaigns WIDF led, for example, in Netherlands against loading weapons shipments to arm the Dutch counterinsurgency in Indonesia, placed women on the frontlines of violent police repression.

Both Gita and Betty gave reports about the conditions of women in their countries. In addition, Gita contributed to the central document presented at the Budapest gathering, "The Women of Asia and Africa."[25] The report began with a quotation from the United Nations Charter, Article 73 about "non-self-governing territories" that affirmed "that the interests of the inhabitants of these territories are paramount, and accept as a sacred trust the obligation to promote to the utmost, within the system of international peace and security established by the present Charter, the well-being of the inhabitants of these territories," with cultural rights and self-government upheld. The photo after this declaration showed the severed heads of anticolonial insurgents on stakes. Underneath was the caption, "Here is how the colonialist countries respect the charter of the United Nations which they signed."[26]

The report mentioned the invitation from MARS to hold the Asian Women's Conference in Kolkata, India. It included the negative responses from Sarojini Naidu and other Congress Party members but announced that the conference planning was still active. Not until early 1949, when the leaders of the All China Democratic Women's Federation and the Chinese Communist Party, assured of their impending victory against the Guomindang, invited WIDF to hold

---

24. Ibid, 102
25. WIDF Preparatory Committee for the Conference of the Women of Asia, *The Women of Asia and Africa*. (Budapest: WIDF, 1948)
26. Ibid, 5

the Asian Women's Conference in Beijing. Held in December 1949, both Gita and Betty attended. Betty attended as a fraternal delegate from the U.S., alongside Eslanda Robeson and Ada Jackson. She also participated in her capacity as secretary of WIDF central offices. Gita was on the Asian Women's Conference organizing committee, spending over a month in China beforehand to prepare for the gathering. She also attended as a delegate. Due to the hostile political climate in India, she used a pseudonym, Mira Mitra, for her speech about children's conditions in India.

Notably, the Asian Women's Conference consolidated a transversal strategy for women's internationalism in the fight against fascism.[27] The conference resolutions drafted two parts to this strategy, one for women from colonized (and recently independent) countries, and one for women from imperialist nations. In Asia, Africa and parts of Latin America and the Caribbean, women fought imperialism and feudalism with renewed unity in their struggles. To do so, they should organize "the masses of women, help to educate them and defend their basic rights!"[28] For women in imperialist countries, the internationalist strategy developed in the Asian Women's Conference was related, but not identical. These women's activism should be rooted in an ethical and personal refusal to be accomplices in murder: "Do not permit our sons to kill each other! Stop colonial wars! Insist that your governments recall the troops from Vietnam, Indonesia, Malaya, Korea."[29] This linked strategy mobilized rather than ignoring or universalizing the differences in women's activism around the world. Internationalist women shared general commitments to anti-fascism, anti-white supremacy, and anti-colonialism; but their conditions of struggle were specific. This strategy dispensed with allies in struggle to create accomplices in the fight against colonialism, fascism, and racism.

In her diary about the Asian Women's Conference, Betty jotted notes about the film shot during the six days of the conference. On December 17, 1949, Millard described a "…chilly film taken to replace those burned up. Will falsify history considerably – will convey impression the Presidium listened to speakers which was seldom the case. Will also seem the very gay conference since we found

---

27. Elisabeth Armstrong, "Peace and the Barrel of the Gun in the Internationalist Women's Movement, 1945-1949," *Meridians: feminism, race, transnationalism*, 18:2 (2019), 261-177

28. "To Our Sisters, the Women of the Countries of Asia," *Information Bulletin*, 4:7 (1950), 9

29. Ibid

our own histrionics amusing..."[30] Two films were created about the conference: one by the Chinese and one by the Russians. However, the footage taken over the six days of the conference burned. The day after the conference ended, it was hastily reshot. A letter by Gita to Betty provided a more light-hearted assessment of the two films. She described watching the Russian version in Budapest, Hungary almost a year after the conference. "Yesterday I went to a movie to find you in various moods – mostly laughing. It was the Soviet version of the Asian Women's Conference...on the whole it was better than the Chinese version and the particular attraction was the Iranian and Indian delegates shouting 'Van Sui' which I recognized very much."[31]

International conferences, like the one held in Budapest, allowed local leaders from around the world to discover for themselves the complex linkages between women's struggles around the world. Each meeting was filled with women's conjunctural analyses of their countries. These reports developed a shared language of how to understand the events of the day. Regional gatherings, like the one held in Beijing, also allowed WIDF to build allied women's organizations where they barely existed, such as in Thailand and Malaysia. In other cases, it fostered the consolidation of myriad women's groups from different localities into a national organization, such as in Indonesia and Vietnam. But the simple enjoyment of each other's company, of finding the languages to communicate was also political.

Paris, 1949-1951

While working in the central offices of WIDF in Paris, both Gita and Betty began their correspondence with each other. Gita and Betty attended the WIDF executive committee meetings in Berlin, held in February 1951. They shared in WIDF's decision to send an investigative team to Korea to report on the military onslaught and the effects on North and South Koreans. After the meeting, Betty returned back to Paris and Gita stayed for a few more weeks in Berlin. On March 5, 1951 Gita wrote to Betty about her train journey with the East German WIDF contingent to Warsaw, Poland to attend a WIDF-sponsored rally for peace, as part of the "Hands Off Korea" campaign. Gita wrote that she was sure her adventure would make Betty "green with envy" as she sat in Paris editing WIDF's *Bulletin Anglais*:

---

30. Millard papers, SSC
31. Gita Bannerji, letter to Betty Millard, Budapest, September 4, 1950, Millard papers, SSC

I never knew the German women possessed as loud voices as the Bengalis and Americans or could speed up their speech like the French. Four of those German women – extremely friendly and delightful – four among the 91 million front ranks, kept up a non-stop conversation for 4 hours while the rather bewildered Bengali – also a front member of a more colonial order tried to catch a bit of sleep…At the stroke of twelve, suddenly the noise increased a thousand fold and in spite of the gradually developing deafness of the Bengali type, her eardrums seemed to be on the bursting point!

Gita's inability to rest on the overnight journey was compounded when five other men carrying bottles of vodka entered the compartment to jumpstart a party.

Peeping through a buttonhole, I beheld the following spectacle: in front of me (the compartment by the way, was 6 x 3 feet in size) a pug-nosed, bald-headed, perpetually smiling man; next to him one of the 91 million (members of WIDF), squeezed like a tomato in a sandwich; next, another stub-nosed, toothbrush-moustache, bald-headed Pole holding a vodka bottle near Elli's unwilling mouth...[32] They pushed me and thrust the vodka bottle to my horrified mouth, making me reflect a little bit on the inferiority of the European civilization!! I shouted 'Dormir' in pure French because I couldn't really remember any other language and shut my eyes as tightly as possible. In a little while the room became dead quiet and a load fell on my side. 'Hai ah' I shouted and found this giant, bald-head sleeping comfortably on my side smelling of vodka and on hearing me shout punched me affectionately!

The train journey ended with Gita's glasses broken after wrestling to avoid a hug.

On arriving, one of the toothbrush types thought of making up with an Asiatic type by asking for my Mao Tse Tung [Mao Zedong] badge, which I immediately gave him, fearing being vodka sprinkled. With the greatest passion he threw his arms around me and in the process of his trying to launch a toothbrush kiss and me trying to avoid it, a 'crack' was heard leaving

---

32. Elli Schmidt, President of the Democratic Union of German Women

my spectacles a little damaged which resulted in the blindness of my right eye…Well, Bettuska, would you ever again travel by plane? I would never. Life would be much uninteresting in contrast in such 12 hours – wouldn't it?!!

Bannerji's racialization of her journey multiplied and refracted through her telling: to be a "Bengali type" sent up ethnic codes of regionalized India. These regional types are colonial, since they were constructed and mobilized in the divide and conquer techniques honed by the British, as well as national, since they continued to have characteristic typecasting within India after independence. The "Asiatic type" she references carries a racism that crosses the globe and does not rely on overt colonialism for its violence. "European civilization," while intrinsic to the colonial rationalization of manifest destiny, in Bannerji's story is synonymous with alcoholic sexual harassment endemic to colonizing countries. The cacophony of languages with exclamations in French and Hindi, embedded in German, Polish, and English, adds yet another layer of discomfort through humor. Her final riposte, of always traveling by train, never plane, embeds a class analysis in her tale. The bourgeois manners of plane travel would have shut down the possibility of mayhem altogether. The humor of Bannerji's storytelling to Millard relied upon a shared critique of colonialism and male supremacism, without a doubt. But her humorous indirection also relied on a deeper level of intimacy; one of shared sensibility and knowledge that the humor in its complexity would be understood.

Hands Off Korea campaign, 1950-1953

With Gita's vision blurred in her right eye and a perpetual wink to gain some vision in her left eye, the Congress for Peace gathering began in Warsaw, Poland. The international peace movement against the bombing of Korea by U.S. and NATO forces was the central topic. Gita described her role as one "of a more colonial order" through the parochial but deeply felt solidarity of WIDF's Polish delegates.

> In the meantime, all the Polish women present at the Congress wanted me to be a Korean. This led to many tears and embraces, very touching, but it left me a bit shy on account of taking all the courageous fight of the Koreans on me.

This form of parochial solidarity was not Gita's first experience with it. A year earlier Gita added a personal note to Betty that she attached to a WIDF report she wrote from Budapest, Hungary. The "Asiatic type" that Gita references becomes quite literally her type, since she is interchangeable with a Korean woman.

> You may call me an imposter or whatever you like but the fact is that the Hungarians insist on my being a Korean and I like it or not I am a Korean in Budapest. But thanks to the People's government I have not yet encountered the inevitable questions in regard to jungles – snakes and tigers. It is wonderful to see how much they are propagating for Korea. Everywhere, in streets, in colleges, in cinemas one would find "HANDS OFF KOREA" posters. I wish Pak Den Ai [Pak Chong-ae] and the other Korean comrades could see all of this. (September 6, 1950)

Betty wrote to her mother about meeting Pak Chong-ae, a committed anti-colonial leader in North Korea who was the chair of the Democratic Women's Union of Korea and served on the WIDF Executive Council since 1948. "I have a Korean friend, Pak Den Ai, when I first met her in Budapest we could only smile and shake hands and talk sign language – by the time we met in Peking I had learned a few words of Russian and she of English – now in Helsinki we know a little more and we're old friends."[33] They first met in Budapest at WIDF's second international congress, then renewed their friendship on the train from Moscow on their way to the Asian Women's Conference in Beijing the following year.

By 1951, these interpersonal linkages proved pivotal in the campaign to oppose the NATO and American military campaign against Korea. At the invitation of Pak Chong-ae and the Korean Women's Democratic Union in January 1951 to witness the carpet bombing and ground troop assault, a WIDF fact finding delegation of 21 women from 18 countries traveled to North Korea in May 1951. They filmed what they saw and the women they met. Their report, *We Accuse!* was issued in five languages, English, French, Russian, Chinese, and Korean. As the campaign rippled outward, it was translated into 20 languages.[34] *We Accuse!* galvanized women's organizations around the world to oppose the US military occupation of Korea.

In Beijing at the Asian Women's Conference in December 1949, Pak Chong-ae described South Korea as a site of occupation with

---

33. Betty Millard, letter to her mother (copy), April 2, 1950, Millard collection, SSC

34. *We Accuse! Report of the Commission of the Women's International Democratic Federation in Korea, May 16 to 27, 1951.* (Berlin: WIDF, 1951)

its American backed strongman, Syngman Rhee. She explained the imperial significance of Korea for U.S. domination of the Asian region beyond Japan. Korea's importance intensified after the Communist Party of China defeated the Guomindang in China's civil war. Her report described the U.S. occupation by proxy:

> Our partisan units (in South Korea), fully supported by the people have won brilliant victories in battle. That is not all. The inner organization of Syngman Rhee's puppet army has begun to disintegrate. Opposing the traitorous policy of SYNGMANN RHEE [sic], soldiers have courageously revolted, and joined the people, fighting with the guerillas.[35]

North Korea and South Korea became separate states in 1948. Border skirmishes began with the formation of a border between them along the 38th parallel north. Women and men joined the self-defense units in North Korea that fought off cross border skirmishes, as well as looting and arson of food supplies.[36] Suzy Kim described the frustration of people living along the border. "One peasant woman in her late forties complained that the guard units had no countermeasure despite the kidnapping, claiming she would join them 'if they would be willing to go kill 'em.'"[37] WIDF's multiple international conferences, the meetings that delegates held with local clubs after they returned home, and the publication of WIDF's conference reports allowed internationalist women to frame their knowledge of the world from the perspective of leftist women's struggles.

Korea as a theater of war was not a conflict of Soviet aggression, nor of North Korean intractability as U.S. media portrayed it. Pak Chong-ae's, as a North Korean Communist feminist, provided a very different analysis. Beginning in 1945, U.S. forces occupied Korea against their own independence declaration. The U.S.-NATO forces did not act in self-defense to repel an attack from North Korea. Pak Chong-ae reminded her audiences that the war began with imperialist attack on an independent nation. North Koreans, and some South Koreans fought an anti-imperialist war that sought to end the neo-colonial occupation of the region by the United States.

---

35. Pak Chong-ae, "With the total support of the peoples…We are fighting to unify our entire land under the People's Republic of Korea," *Information Bulletin, Special Issue,* (April 1950), 37,47

36. Kim, *Everyday Life in the North Korean Revolution, 1945-1950* (Cornell University Press, 2013), 243

37. Ibid

We Accuse!, WIDF's report, detailed with devastating specificity how American and UN forces tortured 11 year-old girls, buried the people of entire villages alive, and raped women until they died.[38] They submitted their report, with its graphic and well documented testimony of chemical and biological warfare, to the United Nations. As a result of their opposition to the Korean War, they lost their consultative status to the UN, a status not returned until 1967.[39] The women who visited war sites, spoke to women and wrote the report lost their jobs, faced other retribution such as imprisonment, but no one recanted the truth of their findings. *We Accuse!* fueled the global peace campaign to rally against the war crimes committed in Korea in contravention of the Hague and Geneva conventions.

"Hands Off Korea!" read the posters on the streets of Hungary and Poland. "Germany No Second Korea!" was one slogan in East Germany. Another poster was more visceral: "Vermin Infestation. Korea is a warning! Fight for peace against the criminals of humanity."[40] Giant fleas with the faces of Harry Truman, Winston Churchill and Konrad Adenauer, the first chancellor of the Federal Republic of Germany, crawled toward the poster's viewer. The name of the campaign in the Soviet Union was "Struggle for Peace!" Millions of signatures were collected on petitions against the Korean War around the world. American women launched a letter writing campaign to President Truman demanding the release of WIDF's report to the American public.

International Women's Day became the touchpoint for anti-imperialism in the women's movement beginning in the late 1940s. Claudia Jones, close comrade of Betty Millard, wrote numerous articles against the bombardment of Korea in her column "Half the World" in the *Daily Worker*. The U.S. government arrested her three times between 1950 and 1951; under the Smith Act (the Alien Registration Act) and the McCarren Act, that required Communist organizations to register with the U.S. Attorney General.[41] She

---

38. *We Accuse!* (Berlin: WIDF, 1951)

39. Taewoo Kim, "Frustrated Peace: Investigatory Activities by the Commission of the Women's International Democratic Federation (WIDF) in North Korea During the Korean War," *Singkyun Journal of East Asian Studies*, 20:1 (April 2020), 84

40. Young-Sun Hong, *Cold War Germany, the Third World, and the Global Humanitarian Regime* (Cambridge University Press, 2015), 54

41. Denise Lynn, "Claudia Jones Against the Korean War," *Black Perspectives*, September 23, 2019, https://www.aaihs.org/claudia-jones-against-the-korean-war/

credited her speech (published soon after) written for International Women's Day titled "International Women's Day and the Struggle for Peace" as the reason for her first arrest.[42] In 1953, Claudia Jones contested her imprisonment to the U.S. Court:

> Will you measure, for example, as worthy of one year's sentence, my passionate adherence to the idea of fighting for full unequivocal equality for my people, the Negro people, which as a Communist I believe can only be achieved allied to the cause of the working class? A year for another vital Communist belief that the bestial Korean war is an unjust war? Or my belief that peaceful coexistence can be achieved and peace won if struggled for? [43]

Betty

Betty returned to the maelstrom of U.S. anti-communism in April 1951. Immediately upon her return, the government revoked her passport. In 1950, the United States government banned the Congress of American Women as a subversive organization and it disbanded. Two internationalist women's organizations emerged in its place – one was the interracial American Women for Peace and the other was led and organized by African American women, Sojourners for Peace and Justice.[44] In her first letter to Gita after she returned, Betty described her dispiriting observations of U.S. complacency, "...it's indisputable that the American people are being bought off by the relatively much higher standing of living resulting from the impoverishment of the rest of the world...People don't like the war but they're not doing much of anything to stop it. After all, they think, if there weren't a war there would be a depression, and they like a depression even less. They have no idea what American troops have done in Korea and simply don't believe it when told."[45]

42. Claudia Jones, "International Women's Day and the Struggle for Peace," *Political Affairs*, 29:3 (1950), 32-45

43. Claudia Jones, "Speech to the Court, February 1953," Thirteen Communists Speak in Court, (New York: New Century Publishers, 1953), 121

44. Gore, *Radicalism at the Crossroads...*, Ibid, 85-87

45. Betty Millard, letter to Gita Bannerji, May 30, 1951, Millard collection, SSC

Betty's analysis fueled her activism. She fought for the reinstatement of WIDF's consultative status in the United Nations.[46] She sought to launch a women's magazine in support of left feminist movements, building on the range of contacts with feminist editors around the world linked to WIDF. That effort failed, but she began editing another journal called *Latin America Today* in 1953, a position she held until 1956. She also wrote the press release for *We Accuse!* for the American Peace Council. In it, she mobilized the strategy solidified in the Asian Women's Conference held in Beijing in 1949. She demanded that ordinary Americans must take responsibility for U.S. militarism and oppose the war from their opposition to their nation's crimes. "The report is an indictment of U.S. brutality and sadism towards the Korean population without precedent in history. Everywhere the Commission went they were surrounded by people who wanted to tell them their personal experiences of families tortured, buried and burnt alive, beaten to death, children bayonetted. They repeatedly asked witnesses: 'Are you sure it was U.S. rather than Syngman Rhee troops who committed these acts?' The answer came again and again: 'There were only Americans in this district. They did it.'"[47]

Years later, Betty Millard reminisced about the importance of her years in France to her own acceptance of her sexuality as a lesbian. She wrote about her years in the 1930s and 1940s when she worked with a therapist in New York to change her sexual attraction to women.[48] The therapy did not erase her desire for women, and her diary mentioned "boring" dates with men.[49] Her time in France and her travels around the world provided knowledge about alternate social fabrics that celebrated homosexuality for women and for men. In one short journal entry from Beijing in 1949 she notes the ubiquity of men's physical contact with each other, particularly holding each other's hands.[50] She stopped the therapy after she returned to New York. She was not open about her relationships with women, however, until many years later.

---

46. Betty Millard, letter to Marie Claude Valliant-Courtier, May 15, 1951, Millard collection, SSC

47. "APC Bulletin," handwritten notes, Elizabeth Millard collection, SSC

48. Lisa Springer and Betty Millard, "Why Aren't You Angrier about Homophobia?" in Lisa Springer, Anna Bondoc and Meg Daly (eds.), *Letters of Intent: Women Cross the Generation to Talk about Family, Work, Sex, Love and the Future of Feminism* (New York: Free Press, 1999), 130-137

49. Betty Millard, 1949 Diary, Elizabeth Millard collection, SSC

50. Ibid

Gita

When Gita returned to India in 1951, MARS and the CPI were legal, but still targeted by the government. Tebhaga as a revolutionary peasants' movement had been largely crushed, but MARS remained vibrant in rural and urban areas across West Bengal. They continued to organize rural people from across West Bengal in cross-caste, cross-community, and cross-religious leftist movement. Gita moved to the rural heartland of militant jute mill workers, an area called Budge Budge in 24 Parganas. Her brave comrade Pratibha Ganguly had been a beloved Communist organizer in Budge Budge, trudging daily through the marshy ground of rural localities during monsoon rains to talk with peasant women. Between 1947 and 1951, 11,000 peasants and activists had been arrested in 24 South Parganas alone.[51] When Ganguly died in the women's march for peace and rights in 1950, she left tracks and networks that Bannerji followed.

Alongside women from 24 South Parganas, Bannerji opened a school for women and girls in Pratibha Ganguly's name. At first the school failed, since both the Muslim and Hindu women in the area said they were too busy to attend. They did not think that the school met their needs. Even after scouring the region, only two women joined the school. In response, MARS organizers developed specialized outreach methods for women of different ages: literacy for girls and young women, skilled work like midwifery, sewing and handicrafts for women, and organizing training for older women whose children had grown.

By 1953, the school gained the enthusiasm of women, young and old, who enrolled their daughters. Older women used their organizing skills to open new MARS chapters across the region. Middle-aged women opened women's work cooperatives, and schools. Young women created groups for teen girls (*Kishore bahinis*). The membership of MARS burgeoned in West Bengal, through its proliferation of schools, job-training sites, and self-help initiatives. They still fought for women's right to live free from violence. They still confronted the state for its neglect. But they also built the strength of women to live independently, a strength taught locally. Bannerji's school in Budge Budge became a model for radical women's education and proliferated. Survival could foster collectivity and local women's leadership. The schools used survival to develop women's structural

---

51. Statistics are from the CPI newspaper Swadhinata Patrika cited in Satpathi "Mobilizing Women: The experience of the Left in West Bengal, 1947-61," PhD. Dissertation, Calcutta University, 2013, 202

analyses of poverty and capitalism. They gave local roots to internationalist answers of peace and anti-imperialism.

Gita and Betty

In the 30 years of correspondence between Gita and Betty that followed after they left WIDF's central offices they celebrated Gita's four adopted children, they shared radical publications, they sent medicine for malaria, and voiced their heart break over the execution of the Rosenbergs.

The train journey from Berlin to Warsaw returned in Gita's mention, this time through the lens of nostalgia. In her first letter to Betty after landing in Kolkata, she announced her sudden marriage to a well-known revolutionary poet and Communist Subhas Mukhyopadhyay. "I am so anxious to know your reactions on this. Subhas (my husband) felt a bit jealous of you when I told him how all of you kissed me on all occasions and even men with moustaches embraced me." [52] The love within the movement, and its showering of affection stayed uppermost in Gita's memories of this time.

She also returned to what she calls the glamour of WIDF. Like Betty, Gita's passport was seized by the government as soon as she returned. In 1953 she wrote to Betty during WIDF's third international congress held in Copenhagen, Denmark. Neither could attend, but each of their national delegations were large and enthusiastic:

I feel a pang near my heart remembering the good old days. Remember being photographed in Berlin every two minutes? Imagine the Congress in Denmark. Click, click – click, click – the cameras go. I am here in this remote jungle in a hut beside a ditch. You are somewhere in Latin America maybe.[53]

Love is part of the story of women's anti-imperialist solidarity. Under the hawk-eyed watch of their anti-communist governments, both Communist feminist activists continued their fight to demand all the rights necessary to thrive. Both women continued to aspire to a world without imperialism, one built by solidarity, love, hard work, and revolutionary patience. Both women fought for socialism through the 1940s and into the 1950s as "whole-timers" (in the

---

52. Gita Bannerji, Letter to Betty Millard, October 24, 1951, Millard Collection, SSC
53. Gita Bannerji, Letter to Betty Millard, June 6, 1953. Millard collection, SSC

lingo of the CPI). They were full time activists who worked for their respective Communist Parties. This period, whether in India, in the United States or in France did not have to be an anti-communist era. The glamour of this period, as we look back, was its revolutionary potential: landlordism *could* have been abolished with the uprising of peasant women and men in the Tebhaga movement. The eradication of white supremacy and its noxious lived effects was not a lost cause. Marxist feminists like Gita and Betty organized together and apart for a socialist future, refusing to hand over history's arc of justice without a fight.

Chapter *11*

Far From Marginal: The CPUSA in the 1960s and early 1970s

By Tony Pecinovsky

1962: "The tide has turned..."

It was February 12, 1962. Communist Party, USA general secretary Gus Hall was in the midst of a West Coast speaking tour. On this particular evening, police on horseback nervously observed in the backfield while cheerleaders ushered attendees to their seats as more than 12,000 students packed the University of Oregon football field. Later that night, Hall spoke to an additional 3,000 students at Oregon College in Monmouth. On February 13, he spoke with 1,000 students at Lewis and Clark College and then on the 14th to "only 800" at Reed College, as Portland officials refused to let Hall speak at the city auditorium, which could have accommodated the additional 1,000 students who "stood around trying to get in." According to Philip Bart, onetime chair of the CPUSA's history commission, Hall spoke in front of a cumulative 19,000 students on five campuses between February 10-15, 1962,[1] including the University of California, where "a spontaneously organized gathering of hundreds" met with Hall after he concluded his remarks. Hall told students,

---

1. Gus Hall, "Talks With Students," *Political Affairs*, April, 1962, 5-18, Mike Davidow, "12,000 Listen to Gus Hall In Oregon Football Field," *The Worker*, February 18, 1962, 3, 11, Mike Davidow, "Gus Hall's 37 Speeches Stir the West Coast," *The Worker*, March 11, 1962, 6, 7, Rob Royer, "Gus Hall Rides a Golf Cart Into Eugene and the Demise of the Commonwealth Federation," *The Cascadia Courier*, April 9, 2012, http://www.thecascadiacourier.com/2012/04/gus-hall-invades-eugene-and-demise-of.html, Joseph North, James Jackson, George Meyers, *Gus Hall: The Man and the Message* (New Outlook Publishers, 1970), 31, and Philip Bart, ed., *Highlights Of A Fighting History: 60 Years of the Communist Party, USA* (New York: International Publishers, 1969), 329

"Anti-communism is just a smoke-screen, the real aim is to destroy the Bill of Rights."[2] This was a sentiment supported by over a decade of ramified political repression directed at the CPUSA and the broader movements for social and economic justice; the result was a constraining of domestic political discourse.

Just days later, Hall spoke at Stanford University in front of 1,500 students,[3] while his comrade Arnold Johnson jammed the 700 person capacity auditorium at Hamilton College. According to the *Utica Daily Press*, "There were people sitting in the organ loft and on stairs, the floor and window ledges" to hear the party stalwart.[4] Also in February, 350 students heard Bart at Bowdoin College in Maine and hundreds more heard Marxist historian Herbert Aptheker in St. Paul, Minnesota.[5] Aptheker also addressed 250 students at the University of Pennsylvania in early April,[6] while the onetime Communist Councilman from Harlem, Benjamin Davis, Jr., addressed 600 students at Harvard.[7] And African American party leader, James E. Jackson, editor of the *Worker*, spoke with 1,400 students at Colby College in May.[8]

It was reported in early March 1962 that Hall gave 37 separate speeches in just 12 days.[9] In April, he told 400 students at City College-New York that if the McCarran Act prosecutors succeed in jailing him and Benjamin Davis, Jr., "no American...will be free."[10] Unlike the political inquisitors, his sights were centered on domestic civil liberties. This was a recurring theme for the steelworker turned union organizer turned Communist. Fortunately, for Hall and his comrades, the political winds were shifting. Later that month nearly

---

2. Mike Davidow, "Gus Hall's Coast Visit Helps Deliver Blow to Ultra Right," *The Worker*, Sunday, February 11, 1962, 3, 10

3. "College Students Hear Hall, Bart and Aptheker," *The Worker*, Sunday, February 25, 1962, 2

4. "Hamilton College Hears Communist," *The Worker*, April 24, 1962

5. "College Students Hear Hall, Bart and Aptheker," *The Worker*, February 25, 1962, 2

6. "250 at Pennsylvania U. Hear Aptheker on McCarran Act," *The Worker*, April 3, 1962, 4

7. Mike Davidow, "Ben Davis at Harvard, His Alma Mater, Speaks on CP and the Constitution," *The Worker*, April 29, 2

8. James E. Jackson, *The Philosophy Of Communism* (New Century Publishers, 1963)

9. Davidow, *Gus Hall's 37 Speeches...*, Ibid

10. "Gus Hall at CCNY Warns His trial Is Meant As Wedge," *The Worker*, April 10, 1962, 1, 7

1,000 students turned out at Swarthmore College to hear Hall.[11] On May 1, Hall addressed 7,000 people at the Union Square May Day rally.[12] Days later, he spoke with 400 students at Hunter College,[13] 700 students at the University of Chicago[14] and 1,800 more at the University of Wisconsin, where another 1,500 students were turned away due to a lack of seating.[15] By mid-June 1962 Hall declared, "During the past six months I have spoken to some 50,000 students and youth directly...The tide has turned."[16] Communist speaking engagements continued into the fall. For example, in late November, Michigan party leader Carl Winter spoke with 900 students at Kalamazoo College,[17] a campus traditionally thought of as a conservative stronghold. Communists had every reason to believe it was time to go on the offensive.

That spring Hall noted, "In the mass movements, the most important and most active contingent are the youth." Jubilantly, he added, the "student demand" to hear Communists was "completely without precedent." "It is of such magnitude that no force is able to ignore it," including the FBI. "It has become a point of discussion on all levels of political life," he continued. "We are so close to it that we do not fully appreciate it." This is an important point, as many today seem unable to fully appreciate it as well. Hall called the growing demand for Communist speakers "a mass break-out from the conformist strait-jacket of McCarthyism" and a "rejection of anti-Communism," a bewildering defeat for the ruling class. Though many of the emerging student groups were "loose and even temporary in nature," Hall was optimistic. He saw the potential for a "spark that can fundamentally change" and challenge the contours of U.S. anti-communism, a spark spearheaded by youth. Additionally, he noted the array of self-published journals students were then

11. Arnold Johnson, "1,000 Swarthmore Students Hear Gus Hall," *The Worker*, May 6, 1962, 2

12. Art Shield, "7,000 in Biggest May Day Rally in Years," *The Worker*, May 6, 1962, 16

13. "400 at Hunter Hear Gus Hall," *The Worker*, May 12, 1962, 2

14. Sam Kuchner, "Gus Hall in Chicago, Ben Davis in Minneapolis Heard on McCarran Act," *The Worker*, May 13, 1962, 2

15. "Midwest Campuses To Hear Gus Hall," *The Worker*, May 6, 1962, 4 and "Wisconsin Hears Gus Hall In College, on Air, in Press," *The Worker*, May 20, 1962, 2

16. Art Shields, "Tide Turning, Hall Tells Anti-McCarran Rally," *The Worker*, June 17, 1962, 1

17. "Carl Winter Explains CP Views to Campus," *The Worker*, December 9, 1962, 4

printing. "Isn't it fantastic that in a number of colleges, there are two, three or four monthly magazines and newspapers," Hall continued, many with a Marxist outlook. That Communists "must be a factor in finding forms through which this tremendous energy can best express itself," was a given to Hall. That "We must not be mere observers," was also a given. Hall's perspective, that Communists "must be a force in helping to initiate forms of united action in this upsurge and help give it cohesion and direction,"[18] wasn't rhetorical. Party-led youth formations like the Advance Youth Organization, the publication *New Horizons for Youth,* the Progressive Youth Organizing Committee, and later the W.E.B. DuBois Clubs were emerging. In this regard, Hall viewed the string of Communist speaking engagements in the early 1960s as not just "victories for free speech and democratic rights, won in the face of a powerful campaign organized by the ultra-right,"[19] a campaign that was being defiantly challenged by youth and students. He also saw these engagements as an opportunity to introduce students to Marxism-Leninism and rebuild the CPUSA.

The substance of Hall's campus presentations often focused on free speech, democracy, the defeat of the ultra-right, and peace. Speaking to students in New York, Hall hailed freedom of speech as vital. "It's a weapon," he added. It must be preserved if we hope to collectively "thrash out the very complicated problems [youth] face." He connected the fight for free speech generally to the fight to hear Communists specifically. "There is a very deep feeling that if you can preserve the right of Communists to speak, then you can preserve the right of all to speak. That's true. But it's more than just a fight for the right of Communists to speak. The fact is that they [youth and students] want to hear a Communist speak…They are sick and tired of hearing the so-called Communist viewpoint from anti-Communists." To Hall, a shift in consciousness was taking place. The "fascist-like assault" designed to "transform the American people into a hysterical anti-Communist mob" had failed. Senator Joseph McCarthy had been silenced. The Smith and McCarran Acts would both be declared unconstitutional. Communists were now on the offensive, regularly speaking to thousands of students across the country. The "squirming of politicians," the "fanatical fascist-like fringe of the ultra-right" was being "pushed back into its lair," Hall

---

18. Gus Hall, *Main Street to Wall Street: End The Cold War* (New Century Publishers, 1962), 31-32
19. Davidow, *12,000 Listen to Gus Hall…*, Ibid

concluded.[20] This was partly due to the courage of student activists who spearheaded the right of Communists to speak on college and university campuses across the country, a strategic relationship Hall would not soon forget and one that would become a prominent feature of the general secretary's work for many years to come.

As noted above, J. Edgar Hoover's FBI unsurprisingly took note of this shift, too. They saw the tide turning as well. Cartha D. De Loach, assistant director of the FBI, speaking at an American Bar Association conference in January 1962, told reporters, "the Communists have grown increasingly ambitious in their designs upon youth." He noted that the Communist-led Progressive Youth Organizing Committee, which was founded on December 30, 1960-January 2, 1961, was created "to pave the way for greater Communist influence" among "broad segments of our college students." De Loach also credited Hall with the party's "renewed emphasis on youth."[21] Communists and their successful speaking engagements were getting under Hoover's skin. Uniformed and undercover police watched Hall's every move. For example, it was reported in the *New York Times* that 22 uniformed police and 15 detectives attended Hall's early May Hunter College speaking engagement.[22] That same month, *Time* magazine reported that "some 100 campuses" had extended invitations to Communist speakers.[23] It did not, however, report on the number of colleges and universities that had denied Hall, and other Communists, their First Amendment right – which was likely also a considerable number. Arnold Johnson spoke to an audience of 800 students at Washington University in St. Louis in May, as well.[24]

In September 1962, the party's Lecture and Information Bureau sent a series of letters to various professors, college papers, student councils and organizations requesting that "you invite representatives of the Communist Party to speak." This was a deliberate, systematic approach to reach students. In "the past year Communist

---

20. Hall, *Talks With Students*, Ibid, 5-18

21. Donald Janson, "Red Drive Found In U.S. Colleges," *The New York Times*, January 27, 1962

22. "Gus Hall at Hunter," *The New York Times*, May 3, 1962

23. Gerald Horne, *Black Liberation / Red Scare: Ben Davis and the Communist Party* (University of Delaware Press, 1994), 314

24. NYU, Tam 137, Box 3, Folder 3: Walter E. Orthwein, "On Washington U. Campus: Communism Debate Draws Yawns, Boos," *St. Louis Globe Democrat*, No date and "Hear Arnold Johnson In Collage in Midwest," *The Worker*, May 27, 1962

spokesmen addressed more than thirty colleges and universities" where "approximately 75,000 students and townspeople" attended. "It is clear from this," the letter concluded, "that students wish to hear the Communist viewpoint from bona fide spokesmen. Students in their search for knowledge apparently are not satisfied to learn about communism from anti-Communists."[25] Those hoping to stunt the youth and student movement and its welcoming of Communists were likely dismayed. After over a decade of political repression, Communists seemed poised to make a comeback.

Daniel Rubin, the party's youth coordinator, spoke on about 40 university and college campuses in the early 1960s; he boasted in fall 1962 that the PYOC had grown. Its growth suggested that "many students consider the CP a legitimate and necessary participant in the great debate on communism and our country's objectives." To Rubin, Communists were "taking a number of steps to increase their influence among youth." The party's support of the PYOC, the numerous college speaking engagements, and the considerable mobilization for the 8th World Festival of Youth and Students in Helsinki, in which 450 young people from the U.S. attended,[26] was his proof.

Communists were far from satisfied, though. They saw "that improving drastically the size and quality of the Communist youth is essential for influencing the mass democratic youth movement in a progressive direction." The party needed to do more, Hall and Rubin argued. To that end, they emphasized the creation of "an extraordinary organizational form, a Communist Youth Division" designed to "give proper emphasis, push and scope to youth activity." Coupled with their successful university and college speaking engagements, Communists also experimented with new and even "spontaneous forms" of youth organization.[27]

1963: "Audiences were not only large…"

Roughly one year after Hall's appearance at the University of Oregon, in February 1963, more than 1,000 students from the University

---

25. NYU, TAM 137, Box 3, Folder 19: Lecture & Information Bureau – To Editors of College Papers, To Student Councils, September 1962

26. Daniel Rubin, "Youth and America's Future," *Political Affairs*, October 1962, 1-12 and *Communist Party Oral Histories (Danny Rubin: Part 7*, Ibid, https://wp.nyu.edu/tamimentcpusa/collections/tamoh/danny-rubin/part7/

27. Rubin, "Youth and America's Future…," Ibid

of Virginia packed Cabell Auditorium to hear the party leader. Students came "in droves," the *Worker* reported. The auditorium was already at capacity when an additional 1,000 students were turned away. The overflow crowd was proof, according to Hall, "that the probing minds of youth" know no political boundaries – that they would not acquiesce to anti-communism. Hall viewed their eagerness to learn about Marxism-Leninism "as a reassertion," a commitment "to defend your right to hear whomsoever you choose,"[28] including Communists. Later that month Hall spoke with 500 students at Yale. He challenged the assertion that there was no freedom of expression in the Soviet Union, a popular theme among cold warriors, and added, "I won't slander the Soviet Union to win my place and my right to fight for socialism here." That Hall had spent most of the 1950s in hiding or in jail due to his political beliefs soured his faith in the elasticity of domestic free speech.[29] By mid-March, Hall was at Brandeis University where more than one-third of the student body filled Schwartz Hall. This was "the biggest meeting of the year on a campus of 1,200," it was noted. The visit, sponsored by the Student Political Education and Action Committee, was a huge success. Every seat was taken, and the doors were closed a half hour before Hall's appearance. Arnold Johnson, reported, "more [people] were turned away than were able to get in."[30]

The success of Hall's 1962-1963 speaking engagements were not an aberration. Communists continued to speak on college and university campuses in front of large and enthusiastic audiences all across the country. Aptheker addressed 250 students at Michigan State University in January 1963. That March, he spoke with 400 students at the University of Michigan, 1,200 students at Howard University, and about 125 students at Roosevelt University.[31] In June, Aptheker spoke to a packed hall at Bard College; that December he also spoke

---

28. Mike Davidow, "Gus Hall Speaks to Overflow Crowd At University of Virginia," *The Worker*, Sunday, February 12, 1963, 8, 11

29. Mike Davidow, "Gus Hall at Yale and Benjamin Davis at Brown Present Communist Views on Main Issues," *The Worker*, Sunday, February 24, 1963, 2, 11

30. Arnold Johnson, "Boston Areas Get an Earful on Communist Ideas, Goals," *The Worker*, Sunday, March 17, 1963, 2 and Arnold Johnson, "Brandeis Students Overflow Auditorium to Hear Gus Hall," *The Worker*, Sunday, March 26, 1963, 4

31. "Aptheker at Michigan State," The Worker, Sunday, January 27, 1963, 4, "Michigan Parleys Hear Dr. Aptheker," *The Worker*, March 26, 1963, 6, "More Colleges Hear Aptheker," *The Worker*, April 2, 1963, 7

at Harvard University.[32] Benjamin Davis, Jr., addressed 500 students at Brown University in February. He told curious students, "I joined the Communist Party as a result of my experience as a Negro...looking for freedom and first-class citizenship." He emphasized that his Communist beliefs were "made in the U.S.A."[33] In an interview with the *Detroit Free Press* Davis expanded upon his reasons for joining. "I am discriminated against by virtue of being a black man and I am a Communist by virtue of the fact that I want to fight against that discrimination."[34] That the Communist Party had "unquestionably been a powerful factor" in the advancement of African American equality, as CPUSA leader William Z. Foster wrote,[35] led thousands of Blacks, like Davis, to align with reds, and thereby help dismantle Jim Crow, spark the civil rights movement, and dramatically reshape U.S. politics. Further, Communists were now embarking on successful college and university speaking engagements, helping to spur a student-led revolt against the political straitjacket of McCarthyism.

In April 1963, 1,500 students heard party leader Hyman Lumer at Rhode Island College[36] and 2,500 heard Daniel Rubin at Colorado State College. Rubin defiantly said, "the world [is] heading toward socialism and eventually communism." According to him, this "is both desirable for mankind and inevitable."[37] In June, Carl Winter told 150 students at the University of Michigan, "Peaceful coexistence cannot mean merely the absence of war." This theme seemed to resonate with students "since the cold war – so long as it continues – prepares the conditions for the outbreak of an atomic holocaust." To Communists, Winter added, "peaceful co-existence cannot mean the preservation of the status quo but, rather, a new system of international relations."[38] With world socialism then ascending, this was a reasonable conclusion. That November, more than 2,000 students filled "every inch of space" in the Student Union Grand Ballroom "and adjoining lounges" at UCLA to hear southern

32. "Hear Aptheker," *The Worker*, June 30, 1963, 8 and "Cambridge Memorial for Dr. DuBois," *The Worker*, December 3, 1963, 3

33. Davidow, "Gus Hall at Yale and Benjamin Davis at Brown...," Ibid

34. Harry Golden, Jr., "The Ben Davis Interview," *Detroit Free Press*, May 3

35. William Z. Foster, *History of the Communist Party of the United States* (New York: International Publishers, 1952), 562

36. "1,500 Rhode Island College Students Hear Hyman Lumer on 'Capitalism and Socialism,'" *The Worker*, April 14, 1963, 2,11

37. "2,500 at Colorado State College Hear Communist Youth Leader," *The Worker*, April 23, 1963, 3

38. "Michigan U. Students Hear Carl Winter," *The Worker*, Sunday, June 9, 1963, 4

California party leader, Dorothy Healey. Earlier that year Healy spoke at Riverside, Cal-Tech and Occidental College, among others. She told students, "I became a Communist because I despised a system in which human beings could be degraded and oppressed while property rights were exalted. I remain a Communist, despite harassment and persecution, because I believe in man's capacity to build a society where all mem are free and where, therefore, each individual can freely develop."[39] In July, Albert Lima, another California party leader, helped break "the 12-year ban against Communist speakers" on the Berkeley campus.[40] Less than a year later, he spoke in front of 2,500 students at San Mateo College, though a so-called Taxpayers Committee to Oppose Communist Speakers on Campus tried to bar his appearance.[41]

In fall 1963, Aptheker – who was considered by Hoover "The Most Dangerous Communist in the United States" – spoke at Los Angeles State College, the University of California, San Jose State College, Oakland City College, San Francisco State College, the University of California (Berkley), University of the Pacific, and the University of Oregon. As Aptheker put it, "Audiences were not only large – that is not new; they were genuinely interested...*Anti-Communism, as an intellectual weapon, is losing its effectiveness* [italic in original]," he added.[42]

Hall agreed and he urged his comrades to see this upsurge as an opportunity to "put our house in order" with an "emphasis on party building" among youth. Self-critically, he told his comrades that the party needed to "correct the damage done [in the 1950s] through excesses in the name of security" and "take a fresh look at the problems and the tasks of party building." "We must find the way, in spite of, and in defiance of, harassment to build the party and the press, to increase our public activity." Though the party's "public activity" was at a high level, recruitment lagged. Membership hovered around

---

39. "UCLA Students Hear Dorothy Healey," *The Worker*, November 10, 1963, 3 and "A Communist Talks To Students," Communist Party of SO. California, October 1963, 5

40. "Ban Against Communists to End," *The Worker*, July 16, 1963, 8

41. Wallace Turner, "Red Speaks on Coast Campus Despite Protests," *The New York Times*, May 1, 1964

42. See: Gary Murrell, *'The Most Dangerous Communist in the United States: A biography of Herbert Aptheker* (University of Massachusetts Press, 2015), Herbert Aptheker, "Is the Soviet Union A Progressive Society," *Political Affairs*, April 1963, 45 and Herbert Aptheker, "Though Crushed, It Rises Again," *Political Affairs*, December 1963, 40

12,000, hardly the increase in dues payments the party had hoped for. Regardless, Hall continued, "The political needs of today make a breakthrough a real possibility. We must guarantee it," he added. "We had to fight to break the isolation of our party," after years of concerted political repression, "and we still need to do so," he continued. Hall was not willing to let the party rest on recent successes. "The task ahead is a big one. We need simultaneously to mobilize the party and to strengthen ourselves – organizationally, politically and ideologically. And we must do this while doing ever more in the field of mass work." Hall called for "a 3- or 4-month intensive period of Party renewal, a period of rejuvenation, refreshment and revitalization." We "must get with these historic times" and "make history," he added, which required "more alertness, more boldness, more determination."[43] If the reception reds were then receiving on college and university campuses was any indication – of which, the above is just a small sampling – Hall had every reason to expect a surge in influence and membership.

Party youth formations: Advance, *New Horizons*, and the PYOC

After nearly a decade in hiding, in jail, or on conditional release, Hall returned as a fulltime revolutionary in 1959 and at the party's 17th National Convention was elected general secretary. He quickly initiated "an intense period of intellectual and organizational activity."[44] He appointed Danial Rubin the party's youth secretary.[45] College and university speaking tours, which put Communists in front of tens of thousands of students across the country, were right around the corner. Reflecting on the recent wave of lunch counter sit-ins in Greensboro, NC, which led to the creation of the Student Non-Violent Coordinating Committee, Benjamin Davis, Jr., echoed Hall's energy and excitement. At a spring 1960 National Committee meeting Davis said, "our Party [must] give special attention to

43. Gus Hall, "For a Campaign Of Party Renewal," *The Worker,* Sunday, November 17, 1963, 5, 9

44. Harry Schwartz, "New Strain Seen Dividing U.S. Reds," *The New York Times*, December 15, 1959, Hall, *Working Class USA: The Power and the Movement* (New York: International Publishers, 1987), 48

45. *Communist Party Oral Histories (Danny Rubin: Part 3)*, part of the oral histories collection, Tamiment Library, NYU, https://wp.nyu.edu/tamimentcpusa/collections/tamoh/danny-rubin/part3/

youth, particularly Negro and student youth with a view to solidarity actions on all campuses."[46]

On and off the campus, Communists were involved in civil rights. For example, the young African American Communist Debbie Bell attended SNCC's founding conference in 1960. By summer 1963, she was working for SNCC in Atlanta, where she regularly dined with the Reverend Ralph D. Abernathy,[47] who roughly a decade later noted that it was an honor to work with Communists, such as Angela Davis.[48] Bell wasn't the only Communist to work for or with SNCC. Due to the lingering effects of McCarthyism, Communists helped build the movement for civil rights through a wide array of grassroots organizations, including SNCC and the Southern Student Organizing Committee,[49] among others. While the Greensboro sit-ins added urgency to Hall and Davis' desire to build the party among youth, CPUSA leaders had actually began discussions much earlier – prior to Hall's return.

In fact, in fall 1958 Communists held an East Coast conference to assess their status among youth and to discuss recommendations for growth. It was noted confidently at the conference that the party "has emerged from its internal crisis."[50] The cause of this crisis was multifaceted; domestic political repression, the Khrushchev revelations, the suppression of the Hungarian Revolution, sectarianism, factionalism, and damaging internal security measures. The party was bruised and battered, but not broken. It was ready to focus on youth and student recruitment.

Robert 'Bob' Thompson, a distinguished World War II veteran – later denied his pension and burial rights at Arlington Nation Cemetery[51] – was direct and to the point in his report on the conference. "Loss of ties with youth" was highlighted as a major concern.

---

46. Benjamin J. Davis, *Upsurge In The South: The Negro People Fight For Freedom* (New Century Publishers, 1960)

47. Holsaert, Noonan, Richardson, Robinson, Young and Zellner, ed., *Hands On The Freedom Plow: Personal Accounts By Women In SNCC* (University of Illinois Press, 2012), 55-61

48. NYU, TAM 132, Box 110, Folder 13: 10,000 March On North Carolina – "Unity is Our Weapon," NAARPR, 1974

49. See: Gregg L. Michael, *Struggle For A Better South: The Southern Student Organizing Committee, 1964-1969* (Palgrave, 2004)

50. Niebyl-Proctor Marxist Library: Bob Thompson, *Eastern Seaboard Conference Of Communist Youth*, October 1958

51. Mike Davidow, "Robert Thompson War Hero, Is Still McCarthyism Victim," *The Worker*, May 5, 1963, 12 and Fred P. Graham, "Communist Denied Burial in Arlington," *The New York Times*, January 28, 1966

The "small number of youth comrades and their relative isolation" was acknowledged. However, optimistically it was added, the party "has the capacity to re-establish these ties and to re-acquire an intimate knowledge of youth activities and problems and needs," which proved to be the case. Though the party had "not developed a definitive approach towards a youth organization yet," Thompson continued, "there has been much thinking and discussion" on the subject. It was urged that a "Party thesis" be adopted "within the next few months."

Numerous proposals came out of the conference. Some attendees envisioned "a Marxist-Leninist youth organization, to serve as a guiding force among youth to consolidate and give direction in the various aspects of youth activity towards socialism." Other comrades favored "some sort of Marxist youth organization," perhaps something "similar to the L.Y.L. [Labor Youth League]," which had been disbanded in 1957. Still others argued for "Party youth clubs" and saw the creation of a youth organization with a "broad progressive pro-labor, pro-peace character" as an initial first step in the right direction.

It was suggested that a "National Party Youth Conference" be held in early 1959.[52] In short, 1958 marked an important turning point for the CPUSA. Soon Communists would initiate youth and student formations, such as Advance, *New Horizons for Youth,* and the Progressive Youth Organizing Committee.

The party-led Advance Youth Organization (which included future Communist leaders such as Bettina Aptheker, Angela Davis, and Margaret Burnham),[53] founded in 1959, as well as the publication, *New Horizons for Youth*, proved to be moderately successful organizing tools,[54] despite ongoing government harassment. Youth Publications, Inc., publisher of *New Horizons,* was subpoenaed to appear before the McCarran Act Grand Jury. According to Lionel Libson, the publication's editor, *New Horizons* was "born out of the growing need for young people to have a periodical which reflects their interests and answers the burning questions" such as "peace, employment and desegregation." That the youth publication "answers these questions" with an eye towards "our own democratic traditions, and scientific socialism" meant it had to be

---

52. Niebyl-Proctor Marxist Library: *Eastern Seaboard Conference…*, Ibid

53. Re Aptheker, Davis and Burnham: Bettina Aptheker, author interview, 1/29/2018

54. *Communist Party Oral Histories (Danny Rubin: Part 4)*, Ibid, https://wp.nyu.edu/tamimentcpusa/collections/tamoh/danny-rubin/part4/

silenced through the McCarran Act's labeling provision. However, it was noted that "If this attack succeeds, all other youth publications of social concern"[55] would soon face the inquisitors, too.

Advance faced similar attacks. The Citizen's Committee for Constitutional Liberties and the National Student Association responded to this assault with solidarity and collaborated with Advance on a McCarran Act information kit, which was distributed to student leaders across the country in spring 1963. Included in the information kit was a letter from Miriam Friedlander, Advance's executive secretary, and future New York City Councilwoman. "It is clear that the action against Advance is calculated to suppress the voice of democratic youth which has broken through the pail of the McCarthy era." The McCarran Act was a "dangerous invasion" on civil liberties, she added. Also included in the kit was a sample NSA resolution against the Act,[56] which youth and students could use on their college and university campuses. In March, NSA would also partner with Advance and help organize a CCNY debate on the McCarran Act, featuring former Assemblyman Mark Lane who said, "The defense in this country of Advance…[is] the front line of defense of the rights of America's people and youth." According to the *Worker,* Lane's comments received "Thundering applause" from the assembled students.[57] That September, Mike Stein, Advance's president, sent a letter to "several hundred national and international youth and student organizations," indicating that the McCarran Act "endangers the rights and freedoms of all youth and student organizations." Advance, which had been scheduled to appear before the Subversive Activities Control Board on September 9, called for protesters to picket the hearing.[58] Students for a Democratic Society and Campus Americans for Democracy sponsored actions in support of Advance in October, while SNCC encouraged individual members to show support. The *Worker* captured the level of

---

55. "Gus Hall and Ben Davis Face Arraignment," *The Worker*, April 1, 1962, 1, 10

56. "McCarran Act Information Kit Sent to Student Leaders," *The Worker,* March 17, 1963, 3, "Woman Here Is Ordered To Register as Communist," *The New York Times*, November 6, 1962 and Sewell Chan, "Miriam Friedlander, Former Councilwoman, Dies at 95," *The New York Times*, October 8, 2009, https://cityroom.blogs.nytimes.com/2009/10/08/friedlander-former-councilwoman-dies-at-95/

57. "Debate on McCarran Act Heard by CCNY Students," *The Worker*, March 12, 1963, 8

58. "Advance Youth Group Asks Unity Against Persecution," *The Worker*, September 8, 1963, 9

unity in its headline, "Student Groups Unite To Picket Witchhunters [sic]."[59] Support for Advance was growing. Later that month, over 300 people rallied in support of Advance outside of the SACB hearings, a courageous show of support. SNCC leader Jim Monsonis, said, "Advance is being interrogated under the McCarran Act not because of the possible political associations of some of its members but because of positions which it has taken and argued for." Stein noted, "it was Halloween night," and declared that Attorney General Robert Kennedy "was witch-hunting in the wrong places."[60] In short, Communist-led youth organizations worked with the NSA and SNCC, among others, and in return received support from these same groups.

Despite the ongoing witch hunt, the party was optimistic. Advance, *New Horizons*, and the PYOC brought young Communists and their allies together to fight against political repression. In a press statement, the PYOC said it was "dedicated to the examination and advancement of the democratic labor and Socialist traditions and aspirations of the American people." At the PYOC's founding convention, greetings were sent by Harry Bridges, president of the International Longshore and Warehousemen's Union and W.E.B. DuBois, among others. Alva Buxenbaum, the future chair of the party's women's commission, told reporters, "American youth ar [sic] apart [sic] of the worldwide movement (for progress)" and they "demand [a] life that measures up to today's possibilities." Like Benjamin Davis, she also reflected on the lunch counter sit-ins, and added, "A year ago there were only occasional rumblings among youth. But since the first sit-ins…an ever growing number of youth, Negro and white, have been raising their voices, [and] demanding a brighter future." Emboldened by the upsurge, the youth group also adopted a Youth Bill of Rights. It said in part: Youth have the "right to plan our own lives free from the threat of nuclear annihilation and the burden of military service," the right to "organize freely; to examine all ideas," the right "to an education based on ability to learn, but not on ability to pay," and the right to "job training and full employment."[61]

---

59. "Student Groups Unite To Picket Witchhunters," *The Worker*, September 29, 1963, 2

60. "300 at Rally Defend Advance Youth Group," *The Worker*, November 5, 1963, 3

61. Sam Kushner, "Not Intimidated: Youth Organizing Conference Vows Convention within Year," *The Worker* (Midwest Edition), January 8, 1961, 1

Praising student leaders, like Buxenbaum, Hall remarked that the PYOC "constitute[s] an important step in filling the organizational vacuum that has existed. This vacuum has always been a weakness, but in the light of the rise in the movements [among] the youth, it has become a serious political question. The Party," Hall concluded, "must give higher priority for the work among youth."[62] Concomitantly, as noted above, Hall also "confronted the urgent job of rebuilding and unifying the Communist Party."[63] The two were interconnected.

Organizing speaking engagements and youth formations, like Advance and the PYOC – in alliances with NSA, SDS, and SNCC – were not the only ways in which Communists engaged youth. They urged students to take a more active role in campus administration, too[64] – which, obviously, did not curry favor among campus administrators. And they also encouraged students to conduct polls designed to challenge McCarran Act thought control,[65] which many were inclined to do. The results, usually in favor of free speech, were often published in campus papers, thereby bringing more attention to state sanctioned repression of Communists.

1960-1961: "All the gold in Moscow..."

In November 1960, African American party leader William L. Patterson, spoke with 500 students at Simmons College.[66] He and Benjamin Davis, who spoke at City College-New York in spring 1961, pulled on similar threads in their conversations. As Davis put it, "The growing strength of the socialist world has weakened the hold of the imperialist powers on Africa and Asia."[67] Soviet solidarity with national liberation movements, through ideological, economic,

---

and "Youth Bill of Rights," *The Worker* (Midwest Edition), January 8, 1961, MW 4

62. Fulton Lewis, Jr., "Washington Report," *Reading Eagle*, August 23, 1961, 12

63. Hall, *Working Class USA...*, Ibid

64. "Bigger Role Urged For CCNY Student," *The New York Times*, December 2, 1966

65. "Swarthmore Campus Poll Hits McCarran Act," *The Worker*, May 22, 1962, 1 and Andrea London, "Jersey College Poll Opposes Ban on Gus Hall," *The Worker*, April 2, 1963, 3

66. "500 at College Hear Patterson in Debate on Africa," *The Worker*, Sunday, November 27, 1960, 10

67. "Kennedy Can End Bias, Davis Tells CCNY Students," *The Worker*, Sunday, May 14, 1961, 12

and material aid wasn't lost on youth and students. And many –
especially, African Americans – looked East for allies.[68] Internationalizing the struggle for Black civil rights was a Communist goal,
a hallmark of the party-led defense of the Scottsboro Nine three
decades earlier, as well as the historic Civil Rights Congress petition
We Charge Genocide, among other examples. Black liberation aided
by Soviet socialism fueled world historic changes and forced an ago-
nizing retreat away from colonial subjugation, imperialism, and Jim
Crow, as historian Gerald Horne has written about extensively.[69]

Regardless, by 1960-1961 the "objective situation was becoming
more advantageous" for the party. After more than ten years of playing defense, "no longer were they virtually isolated in protest."[70]
While speaking to 450 students at Columbia University in November 1961, Davis mockingly joked, "All the publicity I have received
couldn't be bought by all the gold in Moscow," though his Soviet
comrades were likely pleased by the reception Communists were
then receiving. "Telephones are constantly ringing at Communist
party headquarters," he added triumphantly. That 1,000 CCNY students rallied the next day and called for a strike in support of free
speech served to highlight the failure of the campus speakers ban
on Communists. At CCNY Samuel Hendel, chairman of the political
science department, told assembled students, the ban was "a gross
violation of academic freedom unsupported by law." CCNY students did get to hear Davis' voice though, as a tape recorded speech
was played at a rally highlighting the ridiculous nature of the ban.
Apparently, students could hear, but not see a Communist speak
(a scenario that would be replayed on numerous campuses across
the country). On the recording Davis said, "if this ban is allowed
to stand, academic freedom will go out the window."[71] By mid-
November, 3,000 students were on strike and boycotting classes at
Queens College; 1,500 protested the ban on Communist speakers;
they held signs that said, "Ban the Ban!"[72] Just weeks later, PYOC
chair Alva Buxenbaum wrote to President Kennedy demanding the

---

68. Taj Fraizier Robeson, *The East Is Black: Cold War China in the Black Radical Imagination* (Duke University Press, 2015)

69. Gerald Horne, *Black Revolutionary: William Patterson and the Globalization of the African American Freedom Struggle* (University of Illinois Press,
2013), among other examples

70. Horne, *Black Liberation / Red Scare…*, Ibid, 311

71. "Red Ban Decried At City College," *The New York Times*, November
3, 1961

72. Horne, *Black Liberation / Red Scare…*, Ibid, 313

creation of a National Youth Act, which should include "apprentice-ship and skilled job training for 200,000 additional youth providing jobs with union conditions."[73] On and off the campuses, Communists were ambitiously making demands. By mid-December, the ban was lifted; two days later Davis was again invited to speak at CCNY, an engagement which he regarded as a "fitting tribute to the 170th anniversary of the Bill of Rights."[74]

Foreshadowing years of successful college speaking engagements, in a June 1961 television interview Hall blasted HUAC thought police. He advocated for a democratic free flow of ideas. He told reporters, "The attempt to jail ideas cannot succeed…Thought cannot be out-lawed." The party, he continued, will "struggle for every breath of legality."[75] That fall, Hall was speaking at Cornell University in front of nearly 2,000 students as an additional 2,000 were turned away.[76] His comrade, Herbert Aptheker, would speak at "more than two dozen colleges and universities" in 1961.[77] Other Communists did likewise.

On and off of the campuses, Hall increasingly framed the Cold War as a struggle between life and death. He attacked Cold War policies "at home and abroad" as undemocratic and even suicidal. He acknowledged that the domestic and international aspects of the Cold War differed tactically. However, he stressed that they were both geared towards the same strategic goal – the destruction of the domestic Communist left and the dismantling of international social-ism. He called the "policies that sacrifice the interests of the people and [the] nation to those of a few monopolies," a foundational con-cept of Cold War politics. That the Cold War is "self-defeating" was obvious, he told students. To Hall, these policies were of a "bankrupt and dead-end character." They were "suicidal policies of the ultra-right," designed to propel our nation down "a totally reckless" path towards nuclear war. He said, "Anti-Communism has truly become a big business," as weapons manufactures were living high off the government hog due to the increased military spending. Ominously,

73. "Urge Youth Committee 'Create Jobs,'" *The Worker,* December 3, 1961, 12

74. "Davis Hails Bid to Speak at City College," *The Worker,* December 24, 1961, 12

75. Art Shields, "Will Fight for Bill of Rights, CP Leaders Tell Newsmen," *The Worker,* Sunday, June 18, 1961

76. "Gus Hall Reviews Role Of Reds In U.S.," *The New York Times,* Decem-ber 8, 1961

77. Murrell, *'Most Dangerous Communist…,'* Ibid, 153

Hall added, the Cold War was "Political lunacy combined with nuclear power," an "unthinkable danger to all of mankind,"[78] especially youth and students who would bear the brunt of a new war. Fortunately, this same demographic was flocking to campus auditoriums and stadiums by the thousands to hear what Communists had to say. Al Richmond, editor of the West Coast *People's World* echoed Hall. He wrote, "The cold war is the malignant core of the social status quo." It was a cancerous growth then being excised by youth and student activists. "HUAC is among the monsters guarding it," he added. "'Anti-communism' is its weapon,"[79] a weapon then losing its effectiveness as youth and students by the thousands welcomed Communists to their campuses.

1964-1966: "An explicit program, banner and leadership..."

In her correspondence with CPUSA chairman Henry Winston, Elizabeth Gurley Flynn, the 'Rebel Girl,' boasted about the wave of wildly successful college and university speaking engagements. She told Winston, who was then in the Soviet Union, "Lots of news...Ben [Davis, Jr.] and Gus [Hall] are busy speaking at colleges."[80] She mentioned Hall's speech at the "football stadium in Eugene, Oregon," where 12,000 students attended, and that his speech would soon be printed as a pamphlet. "Gus spoke at City College and Hunter. Ben is going this weekend to Minneapolis and Chicago. They are really going places,"[81] she added, as reds continued to fill university and college stadiums with thousands of youth and students. "Gus had several fine college dates...Virginia, Brandeis and Yale. [Herbert] Aptheker went to Howard. Ben had a splendid trip to the Coast. Hy [Lumer] is leaving shortly for the mid-west and coast."[82] Jessica Smith, editor of *New World Review,* also shared with Winston the excitement surrounding the college speaking engagements. "The reports are that Gus had a most remarkable experience on the coast.

---

78. Hall, *Main Street to Wall Street...*, Ibid, 6, 23, 25
79. Al Richmond, *Campus Rebels* (Pacific Publishing Foundation, no date, circa 1960), 31
80. NYU, TAM 132, Box 150, Folder 13: Letter from Flynn to Winston, April 17, 1962
81. NYU, TAM 132, Box 150, Folder 13: Letter from Flynn to Winston, April 26, 1962
82. NYU, TAM 132, Box 150, Folder 13: Letter from Flynn to Winston, March 23, 1963

After his meetings first being banned, students, faculty and city officials insisted that they be held, and there were big crowds everywhere."[83] This was just a prelude, though.

James E. Jackson also wrote to Winston. Like Flynn and Smith, he saw the party's work among youth as essential and noted, by "early in '64 there will be born a real union of youth for socialism [the W.E.B. DuBois Clubs]," an organization "with an explicit program, banner and leadership." Jackson added. It "will carry forward in present times and circumstance" the work of comrades like Winston, Gil Green and Claude Lightfoot, Communists who "gave leadership" to the youth and student movement in the pre-war years. It "is gratifying to witness how people are emerging from the long night of McCarthyism,"[84] Jackson continued. The recent wave of successful speaking engagements as well as the 1963 March on Washington was fresh on his mind. Dawn brought tens of thousands of youth activists now packed into university stadiums fighting for the right to hear Communists speak.

Daniel Rubin would note in retrospect that the forming of the DBC was designed to attract young people to the party, "and it did to some extent,"[85] he added. DBC national chair, Philip Davis, articulated the youth organization's main goal: To become "a potent force on the American political scene,"[86] a goal young Communists strove toward.

Spur, the DBC's newsletter, echoed Jackson's excitement. The "new organization was born to fill a gap felt to exist by many young people who have been involved with the movements for peace, civil rights, and economic security for the American people." Youth across the country "agreed that an organization was needed which would stand for the goals of all these democratic movements, and at the same time go beyond them to point the way towards a socialist society." The newsletter's editors urged youth and students to "break out of the overstuffed [arm-]chair socialism which has become so comfortable for us." They criticized the "fireside discussion groups which analyze and reanalyze the movement – [a] searching of the line with which to 'guide' the movement, and of the proper book

83. NYU, TAM 132, Box 150, Folder 7: Letter from Smith to Winston, February 23, 1961
84. NYU, TAM 132, Box 150, Folder 13: Letter from Jackson to Winston, no date (circa fall 1963)
85. *Communist Party Oral Histories (Danny Rubin: Part 7)*, Ibid
86. Niebyl-Proctor Marxist Library: Phil Davis, *Memo From The National Office*, no date (circa summer 1964)

with which to establish our authority," as if "worship[ing] the printed word [was] an end in itself." The newsletter also briefly highlighted the work of nascent DBC chapters across the country, including the organizing of vigils in honor of James Chaney, Andrew Goodman and Michael Schwerner, civil rights activists murdered in Mississippi that spring.[87] That Schwerner was a Red Diaper Baby (his parents were New York party members)[88] brought the horrific murder too close to home for many Communists. Larry Rubin, Daniel Rubin's cousin and SNCC Mississippi field secretary, like other youth activists, noted in retrospect that he came to terms with the prospect of death while in the South.[89] That Phil Davis urged DBC members to "put our bodies on the line" for civil rights,[90] wasn't empty rhetoric. It was a terrifying reality. Black and white Communists saw the struggle for African American equality as central to the fight for democracy and did everything in their power build the movement and bolster unity.

In a September 1964 *New York Times* article, party leaders estimated that they spoke with "more than 100,000 students on 100 college campuses" between the fall of 1961 and summer of 1964.[91] Just a few months later the Berkeley Free Speech Movement emerged and propelled Communist Bettina Aptheker into the spotlight as a national leader of the youth and student upsurge.[92] To Aptheker, students were then "challeng[ing] the basic structure of power in the universities and in society." Inviting Communists to speak on their campuses was one way that they did this.

According to Aptheker, the youth and student upsurge began in spring 1960 and "reached its first plateau in the fall of 1964 with

---

87. Niebyl-Proctor Marxist Library: *Spur newsletter – w.e.b. dubois clubs of America*, October 16, 1964. For more on the murder of Chaney, Goodman and Schwerner, see: William Bradford Huie, *Three Lives for Mississippi* (University of Mississippi Press, 2000)

88. *Communist Party Oral Histories (Danny Rubin: Part 9)*, Ibid

89. Joe Atkins, "SNCC veterans and young activists testify to workers' rights as civil rights at Mississippi Freedom Summer 50th Anniversary Conference," *Facing South*, June 30, 2014, https://www.facingsouth.org/2014/06/sncc-veterans-and-young-activists-testify-to-worke.html

90. *Niebyl-Proctor* Marxist *Library*: Davis, *Memo From The National Office*, Ibid

91. Peter Kihss, "U.S. Reds Weigh New Command," *The New York Times*, September 26, 1964

92. Bettina Aptheker, *Intimate Politics: How I Grew Up Red, Fought for Free Speech, and Became A Feminist Rebel* (Seal Press, 2011)

the Berkeley Free Speech movement."[93] She articulated a cumulative, quantitative swell of activity. While the FSM "raised questions and challenged educational assumptions. It [also] offered a minimal program for and succeeded in gaining certain political rights for students" on and off the University of Berkeley campus. Additionally, and perhaps more importantly, it "lent direction and gave impetus to a student movement seeking redress of grievances on campuses throughout the nation." Though Aptheker saw the FSM as "the beginning of a long process of change," she credited her own activism in the FSM as a direct result of the 1959 party convention and the subsequent decision to focus on youth recruitment.

Aptheker had initially hid her CPUSA membership, which led some to see her attendance at the University of Berkeley "as part of an insidious Communist plot." To her, this was a ridiculous proposition. Instead, she argued, public knowledge of party membership "would have meant cooperation with a red-baiting attack on the FSM by helping to focus attention away from the issues raised by the FSM and onto the question of Communism." The Berkeley activist saw herself as a student, as an American and as a Communist, as someone participating "in common struggles for democratic liberties, for civil rights and for peace...I believed [these struggles] to be virtuous struggles commensurate with socialist aspirations. I am a member of the Communist Party because, as I see it, that Party upholds principles which combine a particularly enlightened view of society, with a sense of humanity and peace not to be found elsewhere. As a Communist I believe in the fullest expansion of the democratic liberties of the American people," she concluded. That at least 100,000 students had heard Communist speakers prior to the political quake that rocked the Berkeley campus, lent credence to the notion that Communists helped to lay the groundwork for a broad-based, cross-class assault on censorship, a free speech movement embraced by tens of thousands students – regardless of actual party membership. As Aptheker told party leaders in a report on youth work, "It is clear that when thousands demonstrate over a prolonged period dramatic change can be made."[94]

---

93. Bettina Aptheker, *Columbia, Inc.* (W.E.B. DuBois Clubs, 1968), Introduction

94. Bettina Aptheker, *Big Business And The American University* (New Outlook Publishers, 1966), 27-28, Aptheker, author interview, 1/29/2018 and *Niebyl-Proctor* Marxist *Library: Youth and the Communist Party* (National Youth Commission, CPUSA, no date, circa fall/winter 1965)

Though the political straitjacket of McCarthyism had been in retreat since at least the early 1960s, Communists were buoyed by the FSM and the various free speech organizations that emerged across the country in its wake. For example, Herbert Aptheker was invited to Ohio State University in May 1965 by a group calling itself the Free Speech Front. Some 2,500 students attended that event, where due to a speaker's ban, Aptheker sat in silence as FSF leaders read excerpts from his many books – books that were readily obtained from the campus library. Prior to the OSU engagement, Aptheker spoke with a crowd of 600 people at an off campus event.[95]

To party stalwart Arnold Johnson, Communist speaking engagements influenced students "far beyond the campus[,] through the radio, television and the press."[96] Johnson also noted in fall 1964 that 50,000 copies of Hall's pamphlet *The Eleventh Hour* had been printed and distributed, with an additional 50,000 on order; 100,000 copies of the party's *Economic Program*; 50,000 copies of a pamphlet titled *End the Ghetto*; and 30,000 copies of the *Appeal to Youth* had also been printed. "Thus, some 250,000 copies of our literature have been distributed within the past several months,"[97] he added excitedly. Many of the pamphlets were read by youth and student activists then gravitating around CPUSA speaking engagements and party-led youth formations.

With the deployment of U.S. combat troops to Vietnam in early 1965, Hall began to warn student audiences of a "New Fascist Danger!" He said, "The Republican Party is now transformed. It is now an instrument of extreme reaction. It can become the instrument of fascism." The Republican Party was now controlled by "fanatical fascist groups" and "virulent McCarthy[ists]," he added. Building on his earlier sentiments, Hall continued, the Republican party hoped "to provoke and to increase world tensions," though a Democrat, Lyndon B. Johnson, sat in the White House. They wanted to "put into practice a plan for a world-wide network of nuclear bombs to use as nuclear extortion. It is a policy of nuclear war – a policy of nuclear suicide,"[98] he concluded. To say Hall was worried would be an understatement. Nuclear annihilation was a very real possibility.

95. Murrell, '*The Most Dangerous Communist…*,' Ibid, 163
96. Arnold Johnson, "The American Peace Movement," *Political Affairs*, March 1963, 10
97. NYU, TAM 137, Box 4, Folder 5: Arnold Johnson, 1964 Elections (hand-written), 18, 19
98. Gus Hall, *The Eleventh Hour – Defeat The New Fascist Threat!* (New Century Publishers, 1964), 8, 9, 13

At Columbia University in 1965, he told 300 students that escalation in Vietnam could result in nuclear war. "It could be the war to end all wars," he said, "because it could end all human existence." Hall called American policy in Vietnam a "war of depopulation" and said the U.S. military was "putting the nation to the torch" with its indiscriminate use of napalm. With an eye towards the economic aspects of the war, Hall also noted that Chase Manhattan Bank and Bank of America had recently "announced the openings of their Vietnamese branches." He concluded, "This is what the war is about." Hall also called anti-communism a "demagogic appeal to utter falsehoods," an "ideological narcotic" designed to put students "under its spell."[99] Fortunately, however, youth and students seemed immune to this particular opiate.

That October a group of young Communists on the Harvard campus – like elsewhere – noted, reds "work in a large number of organizations other than their own. We seek to expand the membership, and to democratize the structure of these organizations." Though work within other organizations created both obstacles and opportunities for growth, young Communists undoubtedly bolstered youth and student activism. "We will be found in almost any organization for peace, jobs, or for freedom," the activists added.[100]

As one would expect from an internationalist organization, Communist activism was not confined domestically. For example, Herbert Aptheker – who led a delegation to Vietnam in December 1965 that included Tom Hayden, founding president of Students for a Democratic Society[101] – noted in *Political Affairs*, the party's monthly journal, the war on Vietnam "is illegal; it is immoral; it is militarily untenable; it is diplomatically disastrous; and – perhaps decisive – *it cannot work*…With world opinion horrified, with U.S. opinion at least suspicious, with the vast strength of the Socialist world, with the fierce determination of the people of Vietnam, with the realities of U.S. politics…there is every reason to believe that a cease-fire in Vietnam can be compelled." A peace policy, Aptheker added, "can be forced upon Washington; it must be *forced* since the natural proclivities of monopoly capitalism are towards greater and greater monopolization, exploitation and domination. That is, the

99. Gus Hall, *Communism, Mankind's Bright Horizon* (New Outlook Publishers, 1966), 5 and Christopher Friedrichs, "Hall Says Vietnam Escalation Might Result in Nuclear War," *Daily Columbia Spectator*, December 16, 1965, 1
100. *Niebyl-Proctor* Marxist *Library: Youth and the Communist Party…*, Ibid
101. Herbert Aptheker, *Mission To Hanoi* (International Publishers, 1966)

natural proclivities of monopoly capitalism are towards war [*italic in original*]."[102]

Aptheker, and his delegation, returned to campuses, rallies, protests, teach-ins, and newspapers eager to hear their firsthand accounts.[103] According to *Worker* reporter Tim Wheeler, the right-wing was "enraged." To them, Aptheker was "consorting with the enemy," though he and his travel partners ultimately became "heroes to the anti-war movement."[104] Earlier that year, James E. Jackson was in Moscow at a Consultative Meeting of Communists on the events then unfolding in Vietnam. He said U.S. imperialism would by its actions bring "progressive and peace loving forces, the popular masses," together in condemnation of the "open aggression against the Democratic Republic of Vietnam."[105] Jackson's statement proved prophetic. By March 1973, U.S. imperialism was forced to retreat.

Like their namesake – W.E.B. DuBois, who officially joined the CPUSA in 1961 – the DBC faced unprecedented repression, including the March 1966 bombing of their national headquarters in San Francisco.[106] That same month, Richard Nixon attacked the DBC because of its name. He claimed it apparently misled people due to the similarity in pronunciation to the Boys Clubs of America, a "classic example of Communist deception and duplicity."[107] Students, however, mocked the Republican trickster and his outlandish claim.[108] That July the Fort Hood Three became the first U.S. soldier to refuse to deploy to Vietnam and were later court martialed. That two of the three – PFC James Johnson, who would later become city editor of the party's newspaper, the *Daily World*, and PVT Dennis

---

102. Herbert Aptheker, "Vietnam: Life Or Death," *Political Affairs*, April 1965, 30-32

103. See: Gary Murrell, '*Most Dangerous Communist…*,' Ibid

104. Tim Wheeler, author interview, 10/2/2017

105. NYU, TAM 347, Box 13, Folder 50: *Statement: On the Events in Vietnam by the Communist and Workers' Parties, Participating in the Consultative Meeting*, (James E. Jackson attended in Moscow, March 1-5, 1965), document dated March 3, 1965

106. See: Seth Rosenfeld, *Subversives: The FBI's War on Student Radicals, and Reagan's Rise to Power* (Farrar, Straus and Ciroux, 2012), 318-319

107. Douglas Robinson, "Du Bois 'Duplicity' Decried By Nixon," *The New York Times*, March 9, 1966

108. Jim Sayre, "The Commie-Chasers Get W.E.B. DuBois And Boys," *The Stanford Daily*, March 30, 1966, 6

Mora, a DBC leader – were party members[109] is illustrative of the multifaceted role young Communists would play in the emerging anti-war movement. Communists were also active in Women Strike for Peace. According to CPUSA leader Roberta Wood, "lots of Communists were active and helped organize WSP, like me!"[110] Further, Communists served in the leadership of the Spring Mobilization to End the War in Vietnam (later, New Mobe), which "adhere[ed] to the policy of 'non-exclusion' [of Communists], first and most of all, because it is right in principle, [and] necessary to the political health of the nation." "People of the Left (Communists with or without quotation marks)," it was noted in *Mobilizer*, the organization's bulletin, "should be permitted and expected to function normally in the political life of the country." Secondly, Spring Mobe recognized that "in practice a non-Communist coalition is in danger of becoming an anti-Communist one" and "its program will in the long run tend to be moderate and its resistance to the war restrained in policy." By excluding Communists, "It will tend to seek allies to its right,"[111] the bulletin concluded.

Additionally, during this time Communists, such as Virginia Brodine, were early advocates for environmental sustainability,[112] while others, such as Agnes 'Sis' Cunningham, were leading voices in the folk music revival, publishing the song book *Broadsides* for 25 years.[113]

------

109. Re Johnson and Mora's membership in CPUSA (two of the Fort Hood Three): Elena Mora, long-time Party leader and niece of Dennis Mora, author interview, while in Chicago at a CPUSA National Board meeting, May 29-31, 2015 ; Marc Brodine, author interview, while in Chicago at a CPUSA Marxist Strategy and Tactics conference, February, 18, 2017: Brodine attended Party School with Johnson. Tim Wheeler, a fellow *Daily World* reporter who worked with Johnson in the NY office, author interview, October 2, 2017. See *The Fort Hood Three: The Case Of The Three G.I.'s Who Said "No" To The War In Vietnam* (Fort Hood Three Defense Committee, 1966). For obvious reasons (anti-communism), Mora and Johnson publicly denied membership in the CPUSA. See also: Martin Arnold, "3 Soldiers hold News Conference to Announce They Won't Go to Vietnam," *The New York Times*, July 1, 1966

110. Roberta Wood's comment in Tony Pecinovsky, *Let Them Tremble: Biographical Interventions Marking 100 Years of the Communist Party, USA* (New York: International Publishers, 2019), manuscript; in author's possession

111. NYU, TAM 137, Box 4, Folder 6: *Documents From Cleve.*, Mobilizer (bulletin of the Spring Mobilization Committee to End the War in Vietnam), Vol. 1, No. 1 (December 19), 1966, New York

112. See: Chapter 12 in this collection.

113. See: Agnes 'Sis' Cunningham, Gordon Friesen, and Ronald D. Cohen (ed.), *Red Dust and Broadsides: A Joint Autobiography* (University of

These are just a few examples of how CPUSA members helped build the movements for free speech, civil rights, and peace.

1968-1973: "Hit the nail on the head…"

In 1968, a decade after their 1958 East Coast party conference on youth, Communists would again make history with Charlene Mitchell's campaign for president of the United States. Mitchell, the first African American woman to run for president and Mike Zagarell, Mitchell's vice presidential running mate, continued what had by then become a well-known phenomenon inside and outside of red circles: Communist speaking engagements at college and university campuses across the country.

Mitchell deepened the CPUSA's theoretical outlook on universities. She argued that college and university campuses "should be a self-governing community," just as workers should be empowered to govern themselves. The presidential candidate was expanding upon Karl Marx's well-known analysis, articulating the irreconcilable differences between workers and capitalists inevitably leading to class conflict. She added, students and universities under capitalism have divergent interests. "The interest of the students is to learn how to think: the interest of a capitalist university is to teach them how to behave…The goal of [capitalist] education is the creation of docile people, the essence of general society is the subordination of people to things: commodities and the production of commodities," she concluded.[114]

In early October 1968, Mitchell spoke at the "first political forum" of the San Fernando Valley State College SDS chapter. More than 200 students heard her blast the "dog eat dog" nature of U.S. capitalism. She added, the "racist war in Vietnam should be ended right now. It was started by presidential decree and can be ended by presidential decree." It is time "to turn this country around, and we Communists are ready to do this," she concluded. Mitchell also did numerous TV and newspaper interviews, including a "national CBS-TV show on minority party candidates."[115] A few weeks later, she was at City

Massachusetts Press, 1999)

   114. NYU, TAM 132, Box 123, Folder 13: Charlene Mitchell, *Communist Candidate Speaks On Black Liberation* (CPUSA tri-fold brochure, 1968) and Nicholas Gagarin, "Charlene Mitchell: Silhouette," *The Harvard Crimson*, November 5, 1968

   115. Sam Kushner, "Charlene wowed 'em in LA with her cool," *Daily World*, October 3, 1968, 3

College-New York, telling 100 students there that the "[George] Wallace movement contained the seeds of fascism." She urged the creation of a "Left alternative against the Center and the Right" and "warned against supporting Humphrey" as a "lesser evil" candidate. "We need an effective Left instead," she argued. "The only real alternative is the Left," she added, in alliance with the Communist Party, which "stood for community control of the schools and police,"[116] a call eerily relevant today as the assault on Black lives continues unabated. A few days later, she was in Austin, Texas, where she was greeted by local SNCC leaders and spoke with 120 students at the University of Texas.[117] Days later she spoke at Fisk University.[118]

Just days before the November presidential election, Mitchell spoke at Lowell State College, Harvard, Boston State College, Massachusetts Institute of Technology, and the University of Massachusetts.[119] She told about 150 Harvard students, "the old grey goose of liberalism is dying and after Tuesday, it may be dead." While she exaggerated the impact her candidacy would have on the outcome of the presidential elections, her criticism of liberalism was incisive and withering. "American liberalism has perverted itself," she added. "The liberal coalition brought on the war in Vietnam. Liberals say that violence has brought about the crisis in our country. It is, instead, the failure of liberalism that has driven demonstrators and rebels into the streets." She implored the assembled students to get involved, and asked: "What are you going to do with your lives? Are you going to be on the side of Che Guevara or of [Secretary of State, Robert] McNamara? Are you going to join the movement, or will your life be one of quiet desperation?"[120] In all, Mitchell spoke at 16 colleges in 9 days leading up to the election.[121] Zagarell spoke at Bloomfield College, Northeastern College, Brandeis University, the University of Maine, Colby College, Amherst College, Brown University, and the University of Rhode Island, among others that

---

116. "CUNY students hear Charlene," *Daily World*, October 22, 1968, 9
117. "Texan youths hear Charlene Mitchell," *Daily World*, October 25, 1968, 5
118. Nora North, "Fisk students put searching queries to Mrs. Mitchell," *Daily World*, October 29, 1968, 10
119. "Mrs. Mitchell stumps NE colleges," *Daily World*, November 2, 1968, 10
120. Nicholas Gagarin, "Black Communist Leader Predicts Liberalism's End," *The Harvard Crimson*, November 1, 1968
121. "Charlene Mitchell to top record tour with Daily World fete Nov. 3," *Daily World*, October 29, 1968, 10

October.[122] Their college and university speaking engagements, along with others, reinforced a positive appraisal within the party that the 1950s red scare goal of isolating Communists was far from successful.

Roughly one year later, in fall 1969, 1,500 students called for a general strike throughout the University of California system in support of the recently dismissed Communist professor, Angela Davis.[123] This student activism was reflective of the strategic importance party leaders had placed on youth and students at the 1958 conference and 1959 convention. The Davis frame-up and trial, the worldwide defense, as well as her ultimate acquittal is so well known it doesn't warrant discussion here. However, what came after does, i.e. the birth in May 1973 of the Communist-led National Alliance Against Racist and Political Repression,[124] which helped to lead the fight to free JoAnne Little and Frank Chapman, among other victims of racist and political repression, such as Ben Chavis and the Wilmington 10.

For example, at a July 4, 1974 rally in Raleigh, NC, the NAARPR led 10,000 protesters "past [the] notorious 134-year-old Central Prison" to the State Capital, where they railed against the so called "administration of justice"; 45 people were then on death row, more than in any other state, and 14,000 were housed in that state's prisons, which was "one of the highest prisoner ratios in the nation." The main speaker, Angela Davis, called North Carolina "the No. 1 disaster area in terms of racial justice," which was a partial explanation for the NAARPR's decision to rally there. Davis' goal, to lay "to rest the myth that the oppressed people of this land – Black, Brown, Red, Yellow, and white, and people of varied political and religious beliefs – cannot work together," to lay "to rest the myth that people will no longer take to the streets for freedom and justice." Speaking alongside Davis was the Rev. Ralph D. Abernathy, head of the Southern Christian Leadership Conference. He called North Carolina "the most repressive state in America." Perhaps more damning to the right-wing though, was his willingness to publicly work with Communists, like Davis. "They must be trembling in Washington to see us holding hands today," Davis said as she put her arm around Abernethy. "Because...here is a minister, and here," tapping her

122. Mike Davidow, "CP candidates bring new life to campus," *Daily World*, October 15, 1968, 3

123. A. Brychkov, *American Youth Today* (Progress Publishers, 1973), 208

124. Charlene Mitchell, *For Freedom for Political Prisoners and Victims of Racism and Class Injustice, Party Affairs*, Vol. VII, No. 1, January 1973, 32-40

chest, "is a Communist." The Red-Black alliance Communists had spent decades building still posed a formidable challenge, a challenge that brought the SCLC and the NAARPR together in North Carolina to draw attention to death and prison sentences disproportionately handed out to people of color. "Now we must consolidate our unity, make it firm as a rock," Davis concluded.[125]

Also in 1973, Communists founded the National Anti-Imperialist Movement in Solidarity with African Liberation, which helped to lead the domestic divestment movement against apartheid South Africa. At NAIMSAL's founding convention African American party leader Henry Winston – who was considered "the moving force" behind the organization[126] – called for a "massive anti-imperialist movement to compel the unseating" of South Africa from the United Nations, as well as imposing comprehensive mandatory sanctions against the racist regime. Like the NAARPR, NAIMSAL chapters were established across the country and organized solidarity actions with African National Congress and South African Communist Party leaders, often in defiance of the State Department.

At the founding conference, Winston said, "Black folk in the USA, together with the courageous and valiant fighters of liberation movements in Africa...symbolize to me the road ahead, the road to complete destruction of imperialism in general, and the defeat of U.S. imperialism in particular." Though "we fight on two different fronts," he emphasized, we also fight "against a common enemy...U.S. monopoly, U.S. imperialism," a system then in retreat. For Winston, "The African Liberation movement has given to us...the extended hand – will we accept that hand," he asked? Like Alphaeus Hunton and the Council on African Affairs before him, Winston urged the conference attendees to focus their energies against apartheid South Africa. "These fascist, racist beasts have no place among civilized nations," he added. To him, this was the "test of internationalism...how we Black folk in the United States, together with our allies, white, Black, Yellow, Brown, Red, can unite our voices in such a way as to develop that kind of attack which will compel American imperialism to reverse its policy...We cannot do less," he concluded, "for in doing it we help not only the people of

125. NYU, TAM 132, Box 110, Folder 13: *10,000 March On North Carolina* – "Unity is Our Weapon," National Alliance, 1974 and "Justice Assailed In North Carolina," *The New York Times*, July 5, 1974

126. Gerald Horne, *White Supremacy Confronted: U.S. Imperialism and Anti-Communism vs. the Liberation of Southern Africa, from Rhodes to Mandela* (International Publishers, 2019), 586

Africa, but we are [also] helping to advance the fight of Black folk here at home for full equality."

Communists could justifiably be proud of their history, particularly the struggle against racism. This was a fight Communists had been leading since at least the 1930s with the defense of the Scottsboro Nine. Winston also attacked the remnants of anti-communism, saying, "if you are going to defeat the man, you cannot play the man's game and the man's game is Anti-Communism."[127] Soon Tony Monteiro, considered the "youthful head of the movement that spearheaded the campaign to expel South Africa," was addressing the UN's Special Commission on Apartheid. He told the assembled dignitaries, the "tide of liberation engulfs the entire apartheid regime,"[128] a tide given substantial support by ascendant socialism, particularly from the Soviet Union and Cuba.

Just a few years earlier, in February 1970, the party founded the Young Workers Liberation League. At the YWLL's founding convention, Hall emphasized Popular Front tactics as the party's main organizational direction. He said, "In Marxist-Leninist terms, tactics is a word meaning how to move people into struggle based on their understanding of their own self-interests. How to move the struggles to the next stage. That must be the test of all tactics – how do they move people into struggle." According to Hall, "Social progress is being propelled by a worldwide revolutionary process. It is sweeping capitalism before it – root and branch. The question before mankind is not whether socialism. In a basic sense it is not even how socialism. The only unanswered question is how soon. The founding convention has helped with the answer to this question…it is sooner than you think,"[129] he concluded. YWLL leaders were, according to Hall, part of a world historic movement towards socialism.

According to Jarvis Tyner, a YWLL leader, "The significant thing about it [the YWLL] was that up till then it was assumed that the 'socialist left' was white students…There was this idea of parallel development: Black youth were supposed to go into the Black Panther Party and student radicals into SDS." Though it was never

---

127. NYU, TAM 132, Box 110, Folder 14: Henry Winston, *Remarks of Henry Winston At The Founding Conference of NAIMSAL, Chicago, October 1973*, October 19-21, 1973

128. Victoria Missick, "South Africa condemned at special UN hearings," *Daily World*, June 25, 1976, 3

129. Brian Rubinsky, "Working Class Internationalism: The American Communist Party and Anti-Vietnam War Activism 1961-1971" (Doctoral Dissertation, Rutgers University, October 2014), 58

as large as SDS or as provocative as the Black Panther Party, the YWLL's diversity challenged the "idea of parallel development" and contributed to the various movements and organizations of the day in a multiplicity of ways. James Steele, who served as YWLL national chair from 1974 to 1983, added in retrospect: "The League attracted some of the best radicalized youth of the period" and "broadened their outlook. It helped equip them with tactics based on unity. It made a rather remarkable contribution." According to Judith LeBlanc, "The League hit the nail on the head for me…it exemplified equality and brotherhood." To LeBlanc, the YWLL emphasized "uniting young people from different walks of life and different nationalities."[130]

That LeBlanc, who lived on the Pine Ridge Indian Reservation in 1973 during the historic stand-off at Wounded Knee, found a political home in the CPUSA was not surprising. The American Indian Movement activist recalled, "That experience [Wounded Knee] more than anything else, convinced me to join the Communist Party."[131] Considered part of the "AIM generation,"[132] LeBlanc worked with the Legal Defense/Offense Committee, which helped indicted defendants collect evidence and affidavits. Further, it was at Wounded Knee where she "got to know folks connected to the party who helped me understand the nature of systemic racism."[133] LeBlanc wasn't the only CPUSA leader advocating for Native rights; Lonnie Nelson participated in the 1972 takeover of the Bureau of Indian Affairs building in Washington, D.C. and Wounded Knee.[134] In July 1973, LeBlanc was in the German Democratic Republic as part of an American Indian contingent within the U.S. delegation to the 10th World Festival of Youth and Students. She would go on to spearhead the party's cable access T.V. show *Changing America,* help

---

130. Danny Spector, "The Founding of the Young Workers Liberation League: Combining theory with youthful style," *People's Daily World,* February 7, 1990, 10

131. "New York salutes women in struggle," *People's Weekly World,* March 21, 1998, 4

132. Judith LeBlanc, "Wounded Knee, 1973-1998: In the struggle continues," *People's Weekly World,* April 25, 1998 and "Upsetting Billionaires at Standing Rock [Interview with LeBlanc]," Inequality.org, September 28, 2016, http://inequality.org/standing-standing-rock/

133. "New York salutes women…," Ibid, and Judith LeBlanc, author interview, 10/29/2019

134. "Communism in Washington State: History and Memory Project – Lonnie Nelson," University of Washington, https://depts.washington.edu /labhist/cpproject/nelson_interview.shtml

lead United For Peace & Justice, and the Native Organizers Alliance which has led the campaign to stop the Dakota Access Pipeline.[135]

Communists would also help found and lead Trade Unionists for Action and Democracy and edit the newspaper *Labor Today*,[136] which helped initiate rank and file movements against labor's conservative – perhaps, reactionary – old guard.

Conclusion: A myth of marginality

Though small in number, throughout the 1960s and early 1970s CPUSA members were an integral part of the movements for free speech, civil rights, peace, social, and economic justice. To claim otherwise simply does not square with the historical record.

Unfortunately, some continue to perpetuate a myth of marginality. Today, 58 years after Gus Hall spoke with 12,000 students at the University of Oregon, a simple – yet false – narrative persists. The dominant, "orthodox" narrative of the history of the CPUSA is that it became a "shattered organization" that was "afflicted with a mortal illness" and played a negligible role after 1956 as its "membership plummeted."[137] Of course, after nearly a decade of political repression, the CPUSA was weakened. The Khrushchev revelations, the suppression of the Hungarian Revolution, internal security measures (the elimination of membership lists, for example), sectarianism, and factionalism, coupled with the forced dissolution of most of the party's auxiliary organizations – the Civil Rights Congress, the International Workers Order, the Jefferson School for Social Science, the Council on African Affairs, Sojourners for Truth and Justice, among others – weakened the party considerably. This is not in dispute.

135. See: *Let Them Tremble…*, Ibid

136. Victor Devinatz, "The Antipolitics And Politics Of A New Left Union Caucus: 'The Workers' Voice Committee Of The UAW Local 6, 1970-1975," *Nature, Society & Thought*, Vol. 14, No. 3 (July 2001), 258-321

137. Klehr, Haynes and Firsov, ed *The Secret World Of American Communism*, Ibid, 13, 14. Klehr et al begrudgingly note just a few paragraphs later, that the Party "gained some respectability and some members," but "entered its death throes in 1989." However, contradicting his own statements, Klehr, in 1991, suggested that the Party "is the oldest, largest, wealthiest, best-organized, and most effective Marxist-Leninist group in America." See: Harvey Klehr, *Far Left Of Center: the American radical left today* (Transaction Publishers, 1991), 3; See also: Joseph R. Starobin, *American Communism In Crisis, 1943-1957* (University of California Press, 1972), 224

The study of history is a complicated endeavor. Add into the mix decades upon decades of political vilification and repression, and it is possible to infer why this myth has become so prevalent – even among those sympathetic to the CPUSA and the Left more generally.

One 1969 study of *Black Power And Student Rebellion: Conflict On The American Campus,* simply ignores the CPUSA, arguing, "Until the war in Vietnam emerged, in mid-1965, as the central political issue of the nation, the coalition of faculty, administrators, blacks, and white student activists, while loose and characterized by some mutual suspicion and distrust, was fairly stable; the colleges and universities remained relatively calm." According to this narrative, the tens of thousands of students who fought for free speech, challenged conservative faculty, administration, and community leaders, to hear Communist speakers simply do not exist. On many campuses, it was anything but "calm." In another section it is noted, "If anything, the universities and colleges were benevolent and supportive havens which sanctioned and recognized students' organizations, supplied facilities for meetings, and often served as training and staging areas for the perilous journey south." It was even argued that a "common bond of shared ideology between faculty and students on the race problem…provided additional support for student faith in the university and in what it represented." This is an odd argument, as campus faculty often spearheaded the assault against free speech by attacking Communists, one of the African American community's most consistent allies. Finally, according to this study, it wasn't until the 1964 Berkeley Free Speech Movement, "a student uprising…[that] shocked the world of higher education,"[138] that student discontent was registered as historically relevant.

Even those ostensibly supportive of the CPUSA and socialism got the story wrong. *American Youth Today*, a Progress Publishers book, while sympathetic to the CPUSA and its various youth formations, noted that the Berkeley FSM was the beginning of the youth and student upsurge. To the Soviet author, Bettina Aptheker's leadership in the FSM, as well as her election to student government, "showed that students were beginning to reject anti-communism." As discussed above, this movement actually began in the early 1960s when students defiantly invited Communists to their campuses – most notably Herbert Aptheker, Bettina's father, who, according to his biographer, "traversed the country speaking on college and

138. James McEvoy and Abraham Miller (ed.), *Black Power And Student Rebellion: Conflict On The American Campus* (Wadsworth Publishing, 1969), 3, 9, 77, 419

university campuses." Additionally, much was made of the CIA's financial support of the NSA and that groups anti-communism.[139] Missing, however, are the numerous examples of local NSA chapters bucking official anti-communism by working with Advance and the PYOC.

Perhaps, the best known analysis among sympathetic historians of the period is Maurice Isserman's *If I Had a Hammer...The Death of the Old Left and the Birth of the New Left.* As Isserman argues, Communists "were involved in a doomed enterprise." They were part of "a defeated movement" soon to be surpassed by the New Left. Simply and succinctly, "between 1956 and 1958" the CPUSA "for all intents and purposes collapsed." Isserman correctly notes that "the civil rights movements, the anti-war movements, and the campus radicalism of the 1960s did not just materialize out of thin air." However, like other authors he neglects the early 1960s Communist youth initiatives, the wildly successful university and college speaking engagements, the numerous party-led youth formations, as well as the work of Black Communists during this period. According to him, Communists were now "bereft of the old reliable constituencies and issues," adrift in a world they could not relate to, so the story goes. Though I disagree with Isserman's overall assessment, he does make one astute comment regarding the role of "ex-Communists." He wrote, "It probably would not be going too far to say that the most influential adult radical group in the 1960s was this 'party' of ex-Communists. It was a party that could do *almost everything* that a more formally organized radical group could do in the same situation: everything, that is, except recruit new members [*italics* in original]." Isserman concludes, the CPUSA was "unable to play any direct role in assisting" in the "birth" of the New Left,[140] the content of this essay notwithstanding.

More recently, historian Michael Goldfield, in an article titled "100 Years of American Communism" written for the *Jacobin,* simply omits the second half of the CPUSA's 100 year history. Unfortunately, Goldfield's omission leads to a false claim, a claim that cannot be substantiated. As he wrote, by the 1950s the CPUSA "was easily blown away with nary a trace." Goldfield also quotes James Weinstein, a "bitter detractor," who notes that "the Communist Party was not only the largest and best organized party on the Left, but for

139. A. Brychkov, *American Youth Today* (Progress Publishers, 1973), 64-74, 89 and Murrell, *'The Most Dangerous Communist...,'* Ibid, 153

140. Maurice Isserman, *If I Had a Hammer...The Death of the Old Left and the Birth of the New Left* (Basic Books, Inc., 1987), Preface and Chapter 1

all practical purposes it was the socialist left." Of course, Weinstein qualifies this otherwise correct statement with "until 1956 or so."[141] Goldfield simply dismisses the CPUSA in the 1960s and 1970s with a wave of the hand.

Leaders of SDS and the Maoist Progressive Labor Party, were a bit more supportive than Isserman and Goldfield. Milt Rosen, chairman of the PLP, declared the party-led DBC one of the most important groups in the anti-Vietnam War peace movement, just after SDS and the May 2nd Movement. In retrospect, others were even more generous. The CPUSA's emphasis on diversity was praised; it was "the best-integrated organization, by race, sex and age, that I've ever seen," noted one PLP leader. Robert Greenblatt, national coordinator of the National Mobilization Committee to End the War in Vietnam, noted that the attacks levied against the DBC were a "new witch hunt...designed to destroy the movement and pick off its leadership,"[142] which Communists were very much a part of.

Fortunately, there are a few recent scholarly works highlighting this neglected aspect of the CPUSA's 100 year history. For example, Gary Murrell's biography of Herbert Aptheker,[143] Gerald Horne's biography of William L. Patterson,[144] Keith Gilyard's biography of Louise Thompson Patterson,[145] and Sara Rzeszutek Haviland's biography of James and Esther Cooper Jackson,[146] are excellent additions to the historical record. Unfortunately, though, a general history of the CPUSA during the 1960s and 1970s has not been written, which serves to reinforce this myth of marginality.

In spring 2007, shortly after the CPUSA completed the transfer of its vast archival records to NYU's Tamiment Library historian Gerald Horne noted, "I think historians of the future will be struck by the fact that in attempting to assess the impact of the CPUSA, some scholars spent more time seeking out documents in Moscow, as

141. Tony Pecinovsky, "100 years of CPUSA: A critical reply to 'Jacobin,'" CPUSA, May 8, 2020, https://www.cpusa.org/article/100-years-of-cpusa-a-critical-reply-to-jacobin/. This author emailed Goldfield the "reply."

142. Pecinovsky, *Let Them Tremble...*, Ibid

143. Murrell, *'The Most Dangerous Communist...,'* Ibid

144. Gerald Horne, *Black Revolutionary: William Patterson and the Globalization of the African American Freedom Struggle* (University of Illinois Press, 2013)

145. Keith Gilyard, *Louise Thompson Patterson: A Life of Struggle for Justice* (Duke University Press, 2017)

146. Sara Rzeszutek Haviland, *James and Esther Cooper Jackson: Love And Courage In The Black Freedom Movement* (University of Kentucky Press, 2015)

opposed to this country."[147] Similarly, I believe historians of the future will be struck by the fact that in attempting to assess the impact of the CPUSA they will undoubtedly note – perhaps, in dismay – that some scholars deliberately chose to obfuscate and ignore the CPUSA and its contributions during the 1960s, 1970s, and beyond. For, it is plainly obvious to those willing to look that the CPUSA was far from marginal.

147. Gerald Horne, "Rethinking the History and Future of the Communist Party," *People's World*, April 6, 2007, https://www .peoplesworld.org/article/rethinking-the-history-and-future-of-the-com munist-party/

Virginia Brodine: Deciphering and Communicating the Science of Environmental Sustainability

By Marc Brodine & Tony Pecinovsky

There is a long history of Marxists, starting with Karl Marx and Friedrich Engels themselves, coming to grips with environmental issues and with the scope of the interrelationships between humanity and the rest of nature. The use of Marxist dialectics to understand the mutually impactful, mutually conditioned, mutually interdependent connections helps to illuminate the non-linear aspects of those interactions, often referred to as environmental tipping points.

As Engels wrote in the *Dialectics of Nature*:

[W]e by no means rule over nature like a conqueror over a foreign people, like someone standing outside nature but we, with flesh, blood, and brain, belong to nature, and exist in its midst... and all our mastery of it consists in this fact, that we have the advantage over all other beings of being able to know and correctly apply its laws.[1]

Two books by John Bellamy Foster, editor of *Monthly Review*, explain in detail the history of the Marxist analysis of ecology. In *Marx's Ecology* and *The Return of Nature*,[2] Foster explains not only the work of Marx and Engels, but also of other important Marxists including British scientists J. B. S. Haldane and J. D. Bernal. Foster notes, in his analysis of the growth of the modern movement for environmental

---

1. Fredrick Engels, *Dialectics of Nature*, quoted in Virginia Brodine, *Red Roots, Green Shoots* (New York: International Publishers, 2007), 15

2. John Bellamy Foster, *Marx's Ecology* (New York, Monthly Review Press, 2000), and *The Return of Nature* (New York, Monthly Review Press, 2020)

sustainability, the role of prominent Communist Virginia Warner Brodine, though he does not acknowledge her CPUSA membership.

As the first national expression of socialism, more research needs to be done on the Soviet Union's early approach to ecology. It provided important examples through practical policies adopted by V.I. Lenin and the Bolsheviks, such as the massive national parks system. Other innovations included the integration of green belts in city planning, separating industry from residential areas, and massive investments in public transportation.[3] In the 1930s, much of the early gains of Soviet environmental policy were lost in the forced march to industrialization driven in part by the need to prepare for the struggle against fascism. Many Communists and Marxists were also seduced by the dream of "man's triumph over nature," the idea that humans could control nature for their own benefit. This is part of what led to over-centralization and planning massive public works projects rather than exploring a more decentralized, distributed approach in areas where that would better fit the laws of nature.

Decades later, during the 1970s and 1980s, there was renewed interest among Soviet scientists and the public in environmental issues. For example, there was a protracted struggle against the pulp and paper mills polluting Lake Baikal; this campaign resulted in the cleaning up of the lake, the largest freshwater lake in the world.[4]

Communist Party, USA members were early advocates of what is now called intersectionality. They emphasized the links between peace, equality, economic justice, and environmental sustainability. They were among the most dedicated of the peace activists who circulated the Stockholm Peace Appeal in the early 1950s, a call for all nations to abandon nuclear weapons. Domestically, W.E.B. DuBois led the campaign that ultimately collected 2.5 million signatures despite concerted political repression. Globally, peace activists claimed to have collected 500 million signatures. According to historian Gerald Horne, the petition "though slandered and maligned,

---

3. For a discussion on Soviet environmentalism, see: John Bellamy Foster, "Late Soviet Ecology and the Planetary Crisis," *Monthly Review*, June 1, 2015, https://monthlyreview.org/2015/06/01/late-soviet-ecology-and-the-planetary-crisis/ and Arran Gare, "Soviet Environmentalism," *Historical Materialism*, February 5, 2018, http://www.historicalmaterialism.org/blog/soviet-environmentalism-arran-gare

4. For a more detailed discussion of the positive and negative examples of socialist environmental policies, see: Marc Brodine, *Green Strategy: Path to Fundamental Transformation* (New York: International Publishers, 2018), Chapter 16, Environmental Socialism

may have been signed by more than any other appeal ever devised by human hand and brain."[5] While opposition to nuclear weapons grew out of concerns for peace – and avoiding the devastation of nuclear war – it also came from environmental concerns about the dangers of nuclear waste, nuclear testing, and nuclear fallout.

Modern CPUSA engagement with environmentalism started in the late-1950s. Two radicals, Barry Commoner and Virginia Brodine, along with friends and fellow scientists, founded the Committee for Nuclear Information in St. Louis, Missouri in 1958. The committee organized scientists to speak-out publicly. They provided the general public with an alternative perspective regarding the use a nuclear power, weapons, and radiation. As we will explore below, they were opposed to the efforts of the nuclear power industry and government scientists to promote the use of nuclear power and weapons. Their efforts helped to birth the modern movement for environmental sustainability.

Dr. Commoner had been a member of the Young Communist League while attending college in New York in the 1930s. During 1950s and 1960s, he was a professor in the Biology Department at Washington University in St. Louis.

Virginia Warner joined the CPUSA in the late 1930s in Seattle. After marrying bassist and fellow CPUSA member Russell Brodine in 1941, they moved to Los Angeles, where she became the Hollywood reporter for the *Daily People's World*, the CPUSA's West Coast newspaper. She also took a writing class from the playwright and screenwriter John Howard Lawson[6] – a victim of the Red Scare blacklist in Hollywood[7] – where she began a life-long friendship with Gerda Lerner, a Jewish refugee from fascist Austria who became one of the founders of the modern women's history movement; Brodine worked with Lerner and others in the Communist-led Congress of American Women,[8] under the

---

5. See: Gerald Horne, *Black & Red: W.E.B. DuBois and the Afro-American Response to the Cold War 1944-1963* (State University of New York Press, 1986), 126, 131 and Lawrence S. Wittner, *The Struggle Against The Bomb – One World or None: A History of the World Nuclear Disarmament Movement Through 1953* (Stanford University Press, 1993), 183

6. This history is recounted in Russell Brodine's autobiography *Fiddle and Fight* (New York, International Publishers, 2001)

7. See: Gerald Horne, *The Final Victim of the Blacklist: John Howard Lawson, Dean of the Hollywood Ten* (University of California Press, 2006)

8. For more on Lerner, see: "Gerda Lerner: Historian," http://www.gerdalerner.com/biography/ and Marc Brodine, "Gerda Lerner, pioneering scholar of women's, African-American history," *People's World*, January

leadership of Claudia Jones, a prominent African American later deported to Great Britain.[9] The Brodines moved to St. Louis in 1949 when Russell was hired by the St. Louis Symphony Orchestra. After working as an editor at a medical publishing house, Virginia became Public Relations Director for the Midwest Region of the International Ladies Garment Workers Union,[10] a position she would hold for eight years.

Both now in St. Louis, Commoner and Brodine grew concerned about nuclear fallout from aboveground atmospheric testing of nuclear weapons. Nuclear scientists assured citizens that nuclear power and nuclear fallout were safe, or at least safe enough. They argued that citizens should not worry about such esoteric issues. Conversely, Commoner, Brodine, and a collective of local scientists, physicians, civic leaders, and teachers, knew that families needed information on which to make intelligent decisions regarding nuclear fallout and its effect on children. Their mantra was that these issues were "too important to leave to the experts," especially experts in the pay of the nuclear power and weapons industry. Educating the public about the dangers of nuclear testing and fallout meant deciphering the science, making it intelligible to nonscientists, and then sharing that knowledge widely.

Initially organized as the Greater St. Louis Women's Committee for Ending H-Bomb Tests,[11] the most important project the Committee for Nuclear Information started in the St. Louis area was the Baby Tooth Survey. CNI volunteers collected baby teeth from school children and subjected the teeth to analysis to measure the levels of radioactive strontium 90 ingested from the milk that children drank. Hundreds of thousands of teeth were collected, offering new detailed information for mothers and families about the safety of the milk supply. Children who donated their teeth became official members of Operation Tooth Club, and received a certificate and button that read, "I Gave My Tooth to Science."[12] Volunteers spoke

8, 2013, https://www.peoplesworld.org/article/gerda-lerner-pioneering-scholar-of-women-s-african-american-history/

9. For more on Jones, see: Carole Boyce Davies, *Left of Karl Marx: The Political Life of Black Communist Claudia Jones* (Duke University Press, 2008)

10. Brodine, *Fiddle and Fight*, Ibid

11. Dee Garrison, *Bracing for Armageddon: Why Civil Defense Never Worked* (Oxford University Press, 2006), 66

12. Luke Ritter, "The Baby Tooth Survey in St. Louis," The State Historical Society of Missouri, https://missouriencyclopedia.org/groups-orgs/baby-tooth-survey-st-louis

with dentists and church groups, among others. A TV commercial featuring the tooth fairy urging kids to donate their teeth was aired. The mayor even proclaimed Tooth Survey Week.[13] CNI volunteers were testing to see if radioactive fallout from nuclear bombs were ingested through grass pastures where cows grazed; radiation was then passed on through their milk to children. The baby teeth enabled scientists to gauge the level of radiation ingested and observe radioactive side-effects.

As one historian noted, the results of the original scientific research initiated by CNI "probably contributed to President Dwight Eisenhower's decision to temporarily halt hydrogen bomb tests in 1959," and it was among the factors that pushed President John F. Kennedy to sign the Partial Test Ban Treaty in 1963. By 1969, when the project ended, over 300,000 baby teeth had been collected in St. Louis, and similar studies had been established in New York, Los Angeles, and Montreal, as well as in Japan and Germany. As a "marvel of environmental activism," the survey's findings "led to significant policy changes regarding nuclear weapons testing."[14]

Though red-baited, Brodine and her cohort of activist-scientists approached the contentious issue of peace and nuclear disarmament by circumventing Cold War terminology. They provided powerful evidence of the harmful impacts of the nuclear arms race, especially on children. As the *St. Louis Post-Dispatch* noted in 2013, the Baby Tooth Survey is "recalled as one of the great citizen-scientist collaborations [that] played a part in ending nuclear weapons testing." It was also noted that the CNI's project "represented a public outreach effort that would be nearly impossible to duplicate,"[15] even with modern social media.

---

13. Rosalind Early, "How to Stop a Nuclear Bomb: The St. Louis Baby Tooth Survey, 50 Years Later," *St. Louis Magazine*, September 20, 2013, https://www.stlmag.com/How-to-Stop-a-Nuclear-Bomb-The-St-Louis-Baby-Tooth-Survey-50-Years-Later/

14. Ritter, "The Baby Tooth...," Ibid, Dennis Hevesi, *Dr. Louise Reiss, Who Helped Ban Atomic Testing, Dies at 90," New York Times*, January 10, 2011 and "St. Louis Baby Tooth Survey, 1959-1970," Legacy of Achievement, Washington University School of Dental Medicine, http://beckerexhibits.wustl.edu/dental/articles/babytooth.html

15. "Decades later, Baby Tooth Survey legacy lives on," *St. Louis Post-Dispatch*, August 1, 2013, https://www.stltoday.com/lifestyles/health-med-fit/health/decades-later-baby-tooth-survey-legacy-lives-on/article_c5ad9492-fd75-5aed-897f-850fbdba24ee.html

Fifty years after the Partial Test Ban Treaty, Joseph Mangano, director of the nonprofit Radiation and Public Health Project, noted at a panel celebrating the anniversary of the Baby Tooth Survey that, "It was a factor in speeding the test ban treaty, which to this day was one of the great environmental treaties in history...It sort of started the world on the path from inevitable nuclear war and disaster to disarmament."[16] *St. Louis Magazine* commemorated the Survey with an article titled "How to stop a Nuclear Bomb: The St. Louis Baby Tooth Survey, 50 Year Later." According to journalist Rosalind Early, after the results were published the Survey and its organizers "came under fire from nuclear-program supporters." The names of Washington University faculty members supporting the Survey were revealed; the *St. Louis Globe-Democrat* even called for the professors to be fired.[17] Regardless, as the *Washington Post* noted in 2001, "The original Baby Tooth Survey was a groundbreaking effort. It marked one of the first times the public mobilized en masse to aid scientific research."[18] The *New York Times*, in an obituary of Dr. Louise Reiss, a CNI leader, added that the study "helped persuade the world's leading powers to ban nuclear testing in the atmosphere."[19] Further, according to Ellen Griffith Spears, author of *Rethinking the American Environmental Movement post-1945*, the "study helped reframe the nuclear issue, linking concern about war and peace to public health and environmental impact."[20] Another historian described the Baby Tooth Survey as "a particularly imaginative combination of research and public education" geared towards halting nuclear testing.[21] In short, Commoner, Brodine, and others, helped to shape the course of nuclear history by researching the level of radiation in baby teeth. As Commoner said, "We might be credited with aiding the success of the 1963 test ban treaty...What we did was to educate people on what nuclear war is about. A housewife could write her congressman. She

---

16. "Decades later...," Ibid
17. Early, "How to Stop...," Ibid
18. Stephanie Simon, "Revival of Baby Tooth Study Denounced," *The Washington Post*, December 2, 2001, https://www.washingtonpost.com /archive/politics/2001/12/02/revival-of-baby-teeth-study-denounced /828851ad-e867-4902-9c3f-5a5a55085075/
19. Hevesi, "Dr. Louise Reiss...," Ibid
20. Ellen Griffith Spears, *Rethinking the American Environmental Movement post-1945* (Routledge, 2020)
21. Craig Waddell (ed), *And No Birds Sing: Rhetorical Analyses of Rachel Carson's Silent Spring* (Southern Illinois University, 2000), 25

could spell strontium 90."[22] Decades later, the baby teeth were redis-
covered and provided material for new research.[23]

This strategy, of not taking explicit political positions but rather
providing scientific expertise in lay terms to the general public, was
in part a response to the continuing effects of the anti-communist
McCarthy period. Anti-communism cast a pall over any activity or
organization that included members of the CPUSA. Virginia's husband Russell had been driven away from several jobs due to FBI
intimidation; for example, the Salt Lake City Symphony refused to
renew his contract unless he agreed to cooperate with FBI efforts
to target CPUSA members.[24] Progressive activists were regularly
accused of being sympathizers, fellow travelers, or dupes of the
Communists. Red Squads ran rampant, trampling democratic liberties and civil rights. Actual Communists and many liberals were
labeled subversive and repeatedly called before investigative committees, harassed, jailed, and deported – but the work continued.

During this time, CNI also published one of the first maps issued
to the public of what would happen to a city if a nuclear bomb were
dropped on it. They explained that the initial effects in the immediate area would be followed by radiation poisoning, fires, and
other nuclear contamination in ever-widening circles of impacts far
beyond the drop site. Those impacts were also explained as lasting
over time; the St. Louis metropolitan area was used as an example.[25]

Following the publication in September 1962 of Rachel Carson's
Silent Spring, public awareness of environmental issues and concern for the environment grew rapidly. Carson, a marine biologist,
exposed the long-term negative health impacts of DDT,[26] eventually
leading to this harmful pesticide being banned, over the opposition
of the chemical industry.

In 1963, the CNI newsletter *Nuclear Information* hired Virginia Brodine as editor and first employee – prior to that, the newsletter had

22. Jerome P. Curry, "St. Louis Environment Data Group 10 Years Old,"
St. Louis Post-Dispatch, April 7, 1968, 3G

23. "Decades later…," Ibid and "St. Louis Baby Tooth Survey, 1959-1970,"
Ibid

24. Brodine, *Fiddle and Fight*, Ibid

25. Virginia Brodine, *Red Roots, Green Shoots* (New York: International
Publishers, 2007) Chapter 1 and Brodine, "The Day Before Yesterday: The
Committee for Nuclear and Environmental Information," in Mary Lee
Dunn, *Barry Commoner's Contribution to the Environmental Movement: Science
and Social Action* (Routledge, 2000), 4-11

26. For more on Carson, see: "The Life And Legacy Of Rachel Carson,"
http://www.rachelcarson.org/SilentSpring.aspx

been an all-volunteer effort. According to historian Luke Ritter, Brodine "quickly became a sort of liaison between the scientists who wrote for the journal and readers who did not possess a particular background in science."[27] Deciphering and communicating science became Brodine's calling, a role she would play throughout her life. Though she humbly praised Commoner as the person who carried "the organization along" due to his "unwavering confidence in the importance of information and the ability of the public to understand and use it,"[28] it was Brodine who translated the information and made it digestible to the general reader.

According to Commoner's biographer, *Nuclear Information* "was living up to its long-held intention to diversify the range of information it presented by moving beyond questions of nuclear technology." Brodine hoped to educate the general public on "the use of chemical compounds for pest extermination...[and] the discharge of the wastes from our urban, industrial civilization into the air and water," as well as "the uses of nuclear energy." In August 1964, Brodine told *Nuclear Information* subscribers that the publication had outgrown its "old name when we began to include other subject matters in addition to nuclear information." That summer *Nuclear Information* changed its name to *Scientist and Citizen*, which better reflected the publication's mission as well as Brodine's growing interest in environmental sustainability. As she put it, the new name "bring[s] together the citizen who needs information and the scientist who has a responsibility to inform." The lead article that month was on "Water Pollution in Missouri," illustrating the magazine's broadened coverage.[29]

It was noted in the August 1967 issue of *Science* that *Scientist and Citizen* was "an attractive magazine," with over 6,000 subscribers. Brodine was praised as "full-time staff and an energetic editor." Additionally, *Science* commended the magazine, as "Some of its articles serve as the basis for news stories in the nation's newspapers." Additionally, while most "of the articles are written by CEI scientists; all are subjected to critical appraisal by the members of CEI's Scientific Advisory Board" and although "the material in the magazine is subject to rigorous scientific scrutiny, it is written for the intelligent nonscientist subscriber," a by-product of Brodine's editing skill.

---

27. Ritter, Ibid

28. Michael Egan, *Barry Commoner And The Science Of Survival: The Remaking of American Environmentalism* (Massachusetts Institute of Technology, 2007), 87-88, 195

29. Egan, *Barry Commoner...*, Ibid

The magazine was also considered a "central source for the scientific information movement in the country."[30]

Foreshadowing her later work, in spring 1965 Brodine, along with scientific advisor and Washington University professor Robert Karsh, penned an article titled "Should the Air We Breathe Be Cleaned Up?" It noted that "of all aspects of man's environment it [air] seems the most unchanging, the most inexhaustible; constantly purifying itself, forever free and forever in motion." Unfortunately, "as man has multiplied and increased and changed the earth, he has also changed the composition of the air," for the worse. This change has taken on an "ever more rapid pace," they continued, "[as] we are concentrating ourselves in more and larger cities, with more vehicles and more industry in time of peace, and more destruction in time of war, overwhelming the ability of the atmosphere to disperse the pollutants we create." As Brodine put it, "Because everyone breathes, air is clearly everyone's business." Brodine even went so far as to argue, a "continued increase [of carbon dioxide] might affect the world's climate, even so far, it has been suggested, as to melt the polar ice caps, raising the level of the oceans, and flooding present coastal areas." Articulated 55 years ago, her prediction is now a global reality. The article concludes with a call to action. "Citizens need to balance the risk and cost of continued pollution against the cost of control. They need to decide upon the quality of the air they want to breathe and how much they are willing to pay for it…They must decide what, if anything, we should do to safeguard the world's atmosphere for the future."[31] Her query is still a pertinent question, perhaps even more urgent today.

As its scope expanded, CNI changed its name to the Committee for Environmental Information. CEI collaborated with concerned scientists and citizens around the country and played an important role in founding the Scientists Institute for Public Information along with Margaret Mead, a cultural anthropologist, and others. The renaming of the organization as well as the magazine was an indication of the interconnected scope of the issues beyond just nuclear power. It was also an indication of growing support. CEI and *Scientist and Citizen,* however, did not shift focus too far. For example, there was an effort by the U.S. government to plan non-military nuclear projects, Project Chariot and Project Plowshare, including a plan to use nuclear

30. Bryce Nelson, "Scientist and Citizen: St. Louis Group Broadens Educational Role," *Science*, August 25, 1967, Vol. 157, Issue 3791, 903-907

31. Virginia Brodine and Robert Karsh, "Should the Air We Breathe Be Cleaned Up?," *The Edwardsville Intelligencer*, March 6, 1965, 2

devices to create a harbor in Alaska. A coalition of concerned citizens, Alaska Inuit tribes, and the CEI fought back. They exposed the dangers of such recklessness to the public, ultimately defeating the initiative. The *St. Louis Post-Dispatch* credited CEI for bringing "the situation to the public in its magazine." It was noted that an entire issue of what was then called *Nuclear Information* had been devoted to the "Alaska project."[32]

In 1968, on the 10th anniversary of the founding of CNI, the *St. Louis Post-Dispatch* profiled the organization and some of its work. It noted that the "scope of the committee's work has expanded today to include air pollution, pesticides, herbicides, fertilizers and chemical and biological warfare." It was added that the organization's "most famous work" was the Baby Tooth Survey. Though now called CEI, the "Committee's credo remains the same – that the average citizen has the right and responsibility to decide if scientific advances that may help civilization or hinder its existence should be implemented." To Commoner, scientists have a responsibility "to get the facts before the public and the public must make the decision." Though Brodine said "We use other methods of course…[including] the news media and the Speakers Bureau," *Scientist and Citizen* was still CEI's main way of educating the public. It was added at the end of the article, "The streets of St. Louis often smell. Sewage fills the rivers. The noise level of modern machinery and civilization often reaches schizophrenic proportions. Nitrogen from the uncontrolled use of fertilizers to make the soil richer is upsetting the balance of nature." Then the author quoted a CEI supporter as saying, "The people have to decide. They can't depend on experts…" Deciphering and democratizing science to empower the general public was Brodine's and CEI's mission.[33]

Scientist and Citizen changed its name again in the late 1960s, this time to *Environment*, "one of the nation's major sources of environmental information."[34] Brodine continued as Editor Emeritus, while she worked on two textbooks, *Air Pollution* (1973) and *Radioactive Contamination* (1975),[35] published by Harcourt Brace Jovanovich as part of the Environmental Issues Series by the Scientists Institute for Public Information.

---

32. Curry, "St. Louis Environment Data Group…," Ibid
33. Curry, Ibid
34. Waddell, *And No Birds Sing…*, Ibid
35. Virginia Brodine, *Air Pollution* (Harcourt Brace Jovanovich, 1975), and *Radioactive Contamination* (Harcourt Brace Jovanovich, 1973)

In his early 1974 review of *Air Pollution*, Sheldon Novick, Brodine's replacement as editor of *Environment*, noted, "This is a fine book, with a somewhat misleading title… [as it] deals with more than its brief title normally evokes." In the preface, Brodine explains: "*Air Pollution* differs from other books on the subject in purpose: The book marshals current scientific knowledge that is relevant to the social issue of air pollution, showing how air pollution affects the earth-atmosphere system, how it affects the human body throughout its lifespan, and finally, these matters are related to the need for social and economic change." According to Novick, "A much broader subject matter than the usual review of chemical engineering or epidemiology is presented here." As he noted, "The emphasis here is not on specific laws or regulations but on the strategy, or philosophy, which so far has underlain most pollution control efforts, that treat the air as a simple resource to be apportioned through the marketplace by the use of taxes, fees, and modest regulations." It is "against this prevailing view" that Brodine calls for larger systemic change. To her, pollution taxes, regulations, and controls "exert only a negative control in an area where positive planning and collective social action seem necessary,"[36] a courageous proposal given the context of a Cold War world.

Physicist Walt Patterson, in his review of Brodine's second book *Radioactive Contamination*, noted that it was "a clear, readable and orderly exposition of the scientific details, in the relevant historical, economic, political and social context." Despite Brodine's urgency, it was added that the "language is calm and measured…[though] the source of radioactivity we ought to be most concerned about is the growing arsenal of nuclear weapons," weapons "that can destroy us all," as Brodine points out.[37] Robert Young noted in a 1976 *Physics Today* review that Brodine "has written a readable introduction to the issues involved in the use of nuclear energy." Though Brodine "takes the point of view of the environmentalist…she treats controversial issues such as the determination of the biological effects of chronic low-level radiation exposure accurately and fairly…Stylistically and technically, the book is well done. Brodine has a definite journalistic style, which makes for easy reading."[38] This was high praise. In a

---

36. Sheldon Novick, "Books: *Air Pollution*," *Environment*, Vol. 16, Issue 1, 1974, 41

37. Walt Patterson, "Radioactive contamination," *New Scientist*, November 15, 1975, http://waltpatterson.net/brodine.pdf

38. Robert D. Young, "Radioactive Contamination," *Physics Today*, June 1976, 56, https://physicstoday.scitation.org/doi/abs/10.1063/1.3023525?journalCode=pto

publisher advertisement *Radioactive Contamination*'s goal is clearly articulated: "...the author considers what informed citizens in a nuclear age should know about radioactive contamination and how they can act in their best interests when the decisions about the use of nuclear power are being made."[39] For Brodine, information was always geared toward action. Like Marx, her goal was to change the world. In the Preface to *Radioactive Contamination* she adds, "This book is not primarily for specialists. It is for all who have to live in the nuclear age and who want to understand it."[40] Writing in the *Daily World,* the CPUSA's national newspaper, Hank Starr noted that the subtitle to Brodine's book should have been "The activist's guide to nuclear hazards." To him, the book was "packed with information useful to trade unionists, students, medical people, scientists – all who face the daily struggle of ideas in our turbulent world." He highlights "Brodine's main point...that no previous technology has had the potential for poisoning human life and human environment on such a disastrous scale." According to him, "Brodine shows the actual economic and political processes by which U.S. monopolies came to build the world's most dangerous type of reactor and ped-dle it to much of the 'free world,'" something not likely to be found in other books of this type. "A final chapter on nuclear weapons provides a sane review of the insane situation," Starr concludes, as nuclear war could potentially "destroy us all."[41]

Often the issues addressed in *Environment* were the same issues addressed by Brodine at the grassroots. For example, in the late 1960s, Brodine testified before the St. Louis Board of Aldermen about the necessity of removing lead paint from homes; toddlers in poor neighborhoods were being poisoned by eating paint chips contam-inated with lead, which effected brain development, among other negative consequences. The health problems associated with lead paint disproportionately impacted African American children in St. Louis' predominantly Black northside, where Black Communists, such as Hershel Walker, organized around workers' rights, equal-ity, and peace.[42] Simultaneously, *Environment* devoted its April 1968 issue entirely to lead poisoning. In the Scientists' Institute for Public

---

39. *Environment,* January/February 1975, 41

40. Brodine, *Radioactive Contamination,* Ibid, https://archive.org/stream/in.ernet.dli.2015.138218/2015.138218.Radioactive-Contamination_djvu.txt

41. Hank Starr, "Complex matters made understandable: The activist guide to nuclear hazards," *Daily World,* January 7, 1976, 8

42. See: Clarence Lang, *Grassroots at the Gateway: Class Politics and Black Freedom Struggle in St. Louis, 1936-75* (University of Michigan Press, 2009)

Information statement published in the magazine, it is noted, "Lead poisoning among preschool slum children is an environmental problem resulting from the living conditions of its victims." The statement added, "Since it is a problem of the environment in which the children are living, the only sure cure is a change in that environment." Like Brodine, SIPI urged "scientists to bring information on lead poisoning in understandable terms to their communities, particularly to people living in substandard housing, and to help alert the health community." Article themes in the April issue ranged from "Lead In The Slums: Scientists Inform, Citizens Act," to "The Price of Missing Early Indications of Lead Poisoning," and "Citizens vs. Lead In Three Communities," among others. The "Citizens vs…" article profiled education and awareness efforts in Chicago, New York, and Rochester. Charts and graphs were also used to educate general readers on the "Incidence of Lead Poisoning in Children in New York and Chicago." The cover graphic was a photo of a wall with lead paint crumbling; the caption read: "LEAD – still a child killer in the slums. LEAD – an increasing contaminant in our environment."[43] It wasn't until 1978 that the federal government banned all consumer uses of lead paint, roughly 10 years after *Environment* helped to bring this information into the public spotlight.

In April 1970, the first Earth Day took place; over 20 million people participated in activities ranging from demonstrations and teach-ins to neighborhood cleanup efforts. This was a vindication of what Commoner, Brodine, and others had started roughly 15 years earlier.

Shortly thereafter, Commoner wrote one of the most influential ecology books, *The Closing Circle*.[44] Published in 1971, *The Closing Circle* did not explicitly advocate socialism, but Commoner's analysis was greatly influenced by Brodine and Marxism. It explained that much of the U.S. environmental crises were due to changes in production following World War II.

In 1972 Brodine participated in the Allerton Park Institute Conference, an annual conference that explores areas of emerging or continuing interest to practicing librarians. The 1972 Conference was centered on "information resources in the environmental sciences." Conference papers included topics on "Librarians As Environmental Activists," "Scientific And Educational Society Activity In The Environmental Sciences," "Regional Environmental Libraries," "Federal Resources And Environmental Programs," and "Selecting And Evaluating Environmental Information Resources In Public Libraries,"

---

43. *Environment*, Vol. 10, No. 3, April 1968
44. Barry Commoner, *The Closing Circle* (Alfred A. Knopf, Inc., 1971)

among other topics. Brodine's paper focused on "Environmental Information From Other Organizations." She noted that while some presenters would deal with "the professional and technical societies and their publications as sources of information on the environmental sciences," her subject was "the *other* organizations [*italic* in original]," and their popular journals, like *Environment,* designed to educate a broad audience, not just specialists. Jokingly she queried that "these other organizations" were seen as "somewhat suspect" and asked, how "did we *other* organizations get into this respectable company, alongside government, academic, and professional sources? Is not our scientific purity questionable? Has not our reputation been compromised since we have been seen in nonscientific company – [among] bird watchers, peaceniks, [and] health nuts… people over 50 who could not pass today's high school chemistry courses and people under 20 who find these courses irrelevant?"

For Brodine, the "fact that the planning committee chose to have the *other* organizations discussed at this Institute tells us that the environmental sciences differ in some way from the other physical sciences…[that] the environmental sciences *are* different because they stand at the interface of science and society." Environmental sciences "are immediately relevant to everyone," she continued, "who lives and breathes and wants to continue doing so, to everyone who wants to pass on an environment to the next generation in which living and breathing continues to be possible." She told conference participants that the Scientists' Institute for Public Information, as well as local environmental groups like the St. Louis Committee for Environmental Information, these *other* groups, were "devoted specifically to the dissemination of scientific information on the environment."

Her goal was to democratize scientific information, disseminate it widely, and ensure that it was intelligible to non-specialists as a call to action. Her faith in ordinary, working class people – if properly informed – led her to call for transparency. "Social, economic, and political decisions are constantly being made which have important effects on our environment," she continued. "These decisions range all the way from action to control the waste a particular industry is dumping into a particular stream, to national programs for future sources and uses of electric power. If these decisions are to be sound, they must be based on an understanding of the relevant scientific and technical information. This information must be in the hands of the people who make the decisions. If decision-making is not to be limited to a small group of government officials, advised by a handful of scientists and influenced by another handful of powerful industrialists and financiers, the information must be in the hands of many men and women and all the elements of the decision-making exposed to public scrutiny."

Brodine wasn't naïve, though. She acknowledged in every science "there is, of course, a large gap between what the experts know and what others know – including other scientists, in this age of specialization. No one expects to make experts of us all; we are not trying to fill in the gap by dumping into it mountains of material created by the information explosion. We are trying to bridge it by communicating that part of the information that people need to know in order to participate in social decisions about the environment."

Integral to Brodine's analysis was "social action." Like Marx, she did not want to just interpret the world, she wanted to change it. Such basic change requires empowering others to participate and giving them the information they need to do so effectively. She wanted to "help people who do not know what questions to ask, by asking questions that are or should be in the social arena." To "select and organize" information and "express it in language more understandable to the nonscientist,"[45] was Brodine's life's work.

Coupled with her environmental advocacy as a magazine editor and activist – within and outside of the CPUSA – Brodine also found time to critique U.S. foreign policy and henchmen Richard Nixon and Henry Kissinger. In 1972, she contributed an essay to a book she edited, *Open Secret: The Kissinger-Nixon Doctrine in Asia*. She had been struck, on reading the books written by Kissinger as a professor before entering government, by the ways in which Kissinger's theoretical arguments were now being implemented as U.S. policy in Vietnam. She was convinced that Kissinger's approach was deeply threatening to world peace because it was so focused on the use of U.S. military power as the most important element of foreign policy.

As Mark T. Klare noted in the Bulletin of Concerned Asian Scholars, Brodine and the other authors, "attempt to clear away some of the ambiguities surrounding the Nixon Doctrine in order to expose its neo-colonial foundation. They argue convincingly that the 'Kissinger-Nixon Doctrine' is a plan for continued U.S. domination of Asia, embracing the 'containment' policies of the early Cold Warriors, but clothed in the new rhetoric of regional cooperation and international *détente*." However, Klare added, the United States has

---

45. Virginia Brodine, "Environmental Information From Other Organizations," 1972: Information resources in the environmental sciences, Illinois Digital Environment for Access to Learning and Scholarship, https://www.ideals.illinois.edu/handle/2142/1559

not "abandoned its long-standing goal of restructuring Asian societies so as to most efficiently serve the needs of America's corporate system," i.e., U.S. capitalism. He makes note of Brodine's analysis of Kissinger's "game plan," which was "to inflict losses or to pose risks for the enemy out of proportion to the objectives under dispute," a tactic then being employed in Vietnam.[46] James Chace, in the *New York Times*, reinforces Klare, but with a bit more ambiguity. In his review of *Open Secret*, Chace simply notes, "It would be tempting to dismiss their [Brodine, and the other authors] notion of American aspirations to global hegemony as simply too schematic. But their warnings should be heeded as necessary storm signals." In other words, according to Chace, Brodine et al, are on the right track regarding the Kissinger-Nixon Doctrine, just for the wrong reasons. This is an odd take, as Chase sees an "increasing reliance on nuclear weapons" as a very real possibility if U.S. ambitions aren't curbed.[47] The book included an introduction by well-known scholar Noam Chomsky, and highlighted Brodine's keen understanding of both science and U.S. foreign policy, and of the links between Kissinger's theoretical work and actual U.S. foreign policy.

Concurrently, Virginia Brodine began to advocate within the CPUSA for the adoption of an environmental program. For many years, the party organization had been focused on other issues, with little direct environmental activism. The party's focus on the labor and peace movements, various electoral campaigns, the youth and student upsurge, as well as ongoing legal battles associated with the Smith and McCarran Acts and McCarthyism generally, led many party activists to feel their plate was already too full. This, coupled with a much smaller membership, meant party activists like Brodine often had to struggle on environmental issues with little organizational support – though the party's leadership began to see environmental sustainability as an emerging and important arena of struggle.

Gus Hall, CPUSA national chairman, wrote two short books relevant to environmental issues, *Ecology: Can We Survive Under Capitalism?* (1972) and *The Energy Rip-off* (1974).[48] Both addressed aspects

46. Mark T. Klare, "Restructuring the Empire: The Nixon Doctrine after Vietnam," *Bulletin of Concerned Asian Scholars*, Vol. 5 Issue 2, 1973, https://www.tandfonline.com/doi/pdf/10.1080/14672715.1973.10406337

47. James Chace, "The quasi-Prime Minister of the World," *New York Times*, December 10, 1972

48. Gus Hall, *Ecology: Can We Survive Under Capitalism?* (New York, International Publishers. 1972) and *The Energy Rip-Off* (New York: International Publishers, 1974)

of the interlocked crises capitalism was already experiencing. To him, dependence on fossil fuels coupled with capitalist exploitation of workers and the environment were unsustainable. He saw that capitalism was harmful to both workers and to our shared environment. Hall called for the nationalization of the energy industry, which would have greatly facilitated our current transition to a green, renewable energy system.

Two articles by Brodine in the party's theoretical journal *Political Affairs* in May and June of 1976 explained Marxist dialectics as they relate to environmental issues. These articles were also early arguments for the adoption of a party environmental program.

In the first article, "Rediscovering the Dialectics of Nature," Brodine highlighted the urgency of the movement. She wrote, "we are faced with an environmental crisis on a world scale, intimately related to the world crisis of capitalism. In other words, the material foundation of all human life, all human society, is in danger." She went on, "We must learn to understand nature and nature's laws, the material foundation of society. We must learn to understand the effects upon nature of a given mode of ownership of the means of production and of a given production technology. Then and only then will it be possible to move simultaneously toward socialism and toward the achievement of an equilibrium between the world's people and the natural environment that supports them."[49]

The second article in this two part series, "Toward a Party Program on the Environment," worked to clarify the party's stance on the environment as a class issue. "The ruling class is using the economic crisis consciously to maintain a free hand in the exploitation of the environment," she wrote. "The capitalist line is that environmental measures are a luxury we cannot afford; they would raise prices, cut jobs, and make recovery more difficult. Essentially, this is a confession of failure. It is an admission that this system cannot provide people with both a living and a livable environment."[50]

The article also acknowledged the disparate impacts on people of color, stating that "Both the urban and Western lands aspect of environmental degradation should be included in our program and related to our entire program for Black and Native Americans. Housing struggles of Black people in our cities, occupational struggles in the plants and the Western lands struggle of Native Americans are in the interests of a better environment for the whole nation."[51]

49. Brodine, *Red Roots…*, Ibid, 12, 14
50. Ibid, 27
51. Ibid, 31

In summer 1976 Brodine visited the Soviet Union on behalf of SIPI.[52] That November, she reported on her visit to the members and friends of the New York Association for American-Soviet Friendship and Cultural Relations, an affiliate of the National Council of American-Soviet Friendship. There, with over 700 attendees, Brodine celebrated the 59th anniversary of the October Revolution. She said, "both countries benefit in the exchange of research in the environmental field…[and] both countries have similar problems of an industrial society." However, she noted that the Soviet Union "was able to introduce and effect environmental remedies sooner than in the U.S." Dr. Alexander Bykov, director of ecology at the USSR Academy of Science, also "stressed the need for further cooperation and exchange of information." Other speakers included historian Gerald Horne and Richard Morford, executive director of the National Council.[53]

Brodine's party activism was buoyed by events back home, too. For example, in May 1977 she helped to organize the St. Louis *Daily World*'s annual Paul Robeson awards dinner. Brodine and other Communists, such as Thomas Crenshaw, Hershel Walker, and Earl Clay, recognized Betty Lee, editor of *Proud* magazine, as a "tireless worker for civil rights." Brodine praised Lee, and said, "her devotion to…Black Liberation [has] all been in the great tradition of Paul Robeson." Pearlie Evans, district assistant to Congressman William Clay, also spoke at the dinner.[54] The following March, Brodine was in Chicago, along with "200 faculty, graduate students, cultural workers and workingclass [sic] intellectuals from 17 states" for the Third Midwest Marxist Scholars Conference. Other attendees included historians Philip Foner and Herbert Aptheker; as well as CPUSA leaders Claude Lightfoot and Victor Perlo. According to the *Daily World*, the event "differed from the usual academic conference: theoretical discussions were related to concrete problems,"[55] something Brodine had committed her life to.

In the 1970s, Brodine led the fight to place the party firmly against the rampant development of nuclear power, stressing the nature of the immense potential hazards of nuclear power left in the hands

52. "Rally for peace, détente set for Nov. 21 in N.Y.," *Daily World*, November 13, 1976, 9

53. Mike Giocondo, "NY rally celebrates ties of US-USSR friendship," *Daily World*, November 26, 1976, 8

54. "A leader in the Robeson tradition," *Daily World*, June 18, 1977, M-S

55. "Marxist scholars parley reflects growth of interest," *Daily World*, March 28, 1978, 5

of private industry, loosely regulated by a government committed to further development of nuclear weapons. Some prominent party leaders opposed this view. Victor Perlo, head of the party's Economics Commission, had been convinced by Soviet scientists that under socialism nuclear power was safe and well-regulated; this confidence was later disproven by the 1986 Chernobyl nuclear power plant disaster. Specifically, Brodine challenged Perlo on his article "Over-reacting over reactors," which she called "disappointing." She urged Perlo and the *Daily World* to "use special care to assure accuracy and clarity" with this topic. She also noted, "The hazard is not from the daily operation of nuclear plants if properly operated, continuously monitored and carefully controlled. The hazard is from failures in structure, operation or control in the plants themselves," which proved to be the case at Chernobyl and Three Mile Island. Brodine also repeated a familiar theme, one she had been articulating since at least the late-1950s, while gently criticizing the party's press. She wrote, "Scientists have a duty to provide us with the information we need to decide whether we can accept the risk and responsible newspapers have a duty to publish such information."[56] Brodine stressed not only the dangers of a nuclear disaster but also the dangers of nuclear waste, some of which can remain radioactive for thousands of years. She also stressed the health consequences to uranium miners.

In the late 1970s, after retirement, Brodine and her husband returned to Washington State, continuing her environmental activism and her work to get the party to adopt an environmental program. During the 1980s and 1990s, in addition to local work on water and development issues, she organized the Washington State CPUSA to issue two statements she drafted, one on the clean-up of the Hanford Nuclear Reservation in Eastern Washington in 1985.

The other statement, "Cutting Into The Future: Jobs and Timber in Washington State," was issued in April 1990. It argued that sustainable logging practices were better for workers – ecologically informed logging methods require more workers, provide more jobs, and benefit local communities more. This argument was contrasted to the timber companies, who sought to pit loggers against environmentalists. The later were focused on protecting spotted owls and their habitat from destructive logging practices. The statement made clear that, "A loss of forests can change the climate; a change of climate can make it impossible for the forests to grow back." It went on,

56. Virginia Brodine, "Military and Civilian Nuclear Programs: A Family Likeness," *World Magazine*, September 14, 1974, M-4, M-11

"We already know that all humanity needs forests to help keep our atmosphere, and therefore our climate, in balance. The forests are a natural barrier against the global warming scientists are warning us about. It is not just the tropical forests of Brazil that play this role. Our own Northwest forests, too, cleanse the air and help to stabilize the average global temperature, giving us in the Northwest our temperate climate." The statement continued, "The battle over the spotted owl engenders more heat than light. On one side, the unions are fighting for their jobs; the owl symbolizes for environmentalists, protection of the vanishing old-growth forest from mindless destruction. But workers are not mindless and environmentalists are not heartless. Both need to use the time ahead not to dig trenches for another fight on the same lines, but to understand each other's minds and hearts and find some common ground for both using and protecting the forests that are the heritage for all of us."[57] Brodine's call was profound in its foresight. She also served on the boards of Washington State SANE/Freeze and the Central Washington Peace and Environmental Council (which she helped to found).

In another *Political Affairs* article in January 1989, "The Environment: A Natural Terrain for Communists," Brodine linked environmental destruction to Marx's analysis of surplus value. "Environmental exploitation takes place at three stages of production," she wrote:

It depletes the earth's non-renewable resources (coal, oil, gas, metals of all kinds) and uses some renewable resources (soil, forests) in a manner which destroys the ability of nature to renew them.

In the manufacturing process, it degrades the work environment, putting the health of workers at risk even as it produces waste products which endanger human and other forms of life when released. The products manufactured may also be injurious to people and the environment when they are used (pesticides are just one example).

It discharges waste into air, water, and soil, polluting those life-sustaining components of the biosphere and seriously interfering with their natural cycles.

---

57. Brodine, Red Roots…, Ibid, 33-38

Exploitation has a precise meaning in relation to labor: the expropriation by capital of the surplus value created by labor. What do we mean exactly by the exploitation of the environment? In economic terms, capital uses the environment on one end of the production process as a source of raw material and on the other end as a sewer, without paying the cost of maintaining the capacity of the environment to continue supplying the raw materials and to continue absorbing the waste.

She continued:

Each individual worker and an entire class of people are being robbed for the benefit of a few through the exploitation of labor. All humanity and all nature are being robbed for the benefit of a few through the exploitation of the environment. This is now on such a scale as to threaten earth's survival.[58]

The August 29, 1989 *People's Daily World* included an article by Brodine; it was a condensed version of remarks she had made during a CPUSA workshop on "Global Environmental Problems" at the party's national ideological conference, attended by 500 members. She noted, "The basis of capitalism is private ownership, its engine profit. Capitalism exploits nature, exploits labor, sells at a profit and dumps the waste. This cannot go on forever. It impoverishes the world and threatens it with irreversible damage." This had been a recurring theme for Brodine, who had now been arguing for environmental sustainability for over 30 years.

She went on, "Ecology, the science dealing with the relationship between living organisms and their environment, helps us understand nature's laws. Marxism shows us how this relationship is imbedded in social and economic relations and therefore in class struggle." To Brodine, Marxist dialectics reinforced environmental science, just as socialism reinforced sustainable development. As she put it, "Socialism works for people, not profits, but experience has shown that a socialist country [the Soviet Union] that must defend itself is forced into war production. Desirable production goals can be pursued in environmentally destructive ways. The use of nature's laws as 'a regulating guide to social production,' as Marx proposed, means making environmental exploitation as impermissible as the exploitation of labor." Brodine's distinction here is important as we

---

58. Ibid, 39-48

chart a path towards a sustainable, green future, especially as desirable production goals pursued in environmentally destructive ways ultimately harm people and the planet. Additionally, exploitation of the environment "is broadening and sharpening the class struggle. Those for whom questions of class are muted or obscured in their work relationships come face-to-face with the implications of private ownership when they become involved in environmental struggles that try to affect the production process."

As an author and editor – though perhaps stated more tactfully in *Environment* – Brodine argued that "Environmental issues have revolutionary implications. An economic system that cannot maintain the biosphere that sustains life is not a viable system."[59] Though Brodine often addressed larger ideological issues, she did not ignore local, grassroots struggles. At the conference she told reporter Tim Wheeler, "The timber companies are over-harvesting the trees and it is ecologically and economically damaging." She also noted that unions and environmentalists were "now moving into alliance," before returning to her workshop's theme. "I've felt that our Party has neglected the area [of environmental work] but we had a workshop here with people who are deeply involved in these struggles to bring workers, environmentalists and the peace movement together."[60]

Coupled with Brodine's ongoing analysis was action. For example, in December 1989 she spoke out against a familiar theme: U.S. militarism and environmental destruction. At an Ellensburg, WA City Council meeting she was one of hundreds of protesters who took a stand against the proposed expansion of the U.S. military's Yakima Firing Center; the Firing Center, which already consisted of more than 250,000 acres, was aiming to expand an additional 63,000 acres. Speaking on behalf of Washington State SANE/Freeze, Brodine said, "Only a Rip Van Winkle who has been asleep since 1985 could continue looking at the world through cold war [sic] eyes and advocate further expansion of military facilities like the Firing Center." The City Council had already voted to seek a legal injunction to halt the expansion.[61]

59. Virginia Warner Brodine, "Global environmental problems," *People's Daily World*, August 29, 1989, 9

60. Tim Wheeler, "Taking the 'high road,'" *People's Daily World*, July 20, 1989, 14-15

61. "Ellensburg, Wash. – Residents protest firing range expansion," *People's Daily World*, December 22, 1989, **5**

In the early 1990s, Brodine became the chair of the CPUSA's first Environmental Commission; it began to draft a party environmental program. Her advocacy was one factor in overcoming the reluctance felt by some party members. She saw this arena of struggle as important to the working class, important to electoral politics, and important for the survival of humanity.

Brodine visited Cuba in spring 1992. She noted, despite being "mired in its deepest economic crisis since Castro took power," that something "is going on in Cuba that neither environmentalists nor socialists have given the attention it deserves." She called Cuba's process for "developing a healthy, sustainable relationship between people and nature," revolutionary. Despite the collapse of socialism in the Soviet Union and Eastern Europe, which had a devastating impact on Cuba, she asked: "Why is it that Cuba is, in the main, fighting for survival with, not against, its natural environment?" Her answer. "The secret lies in another revolutionary process: a revolution in the relation of people to people. Without this," she added, "a healthier relationship of people to nature would be impossible." To her, Cuba's socialist path was central to its ability to balance human welfare with the laws of nature. "Humanity cannot deal with nature one individual at a time. A society that describes its highest goal as the opportunity for the individual to get ahead – as in 'the American dream' – is turning its back on the kind of collective goals and collective action that are essential for a sustainable human/nature relationship. The Cuban dream is a collective dream. Cuba's program is a collective program, first for all the people, now for the people's environment."

She noted recent UN reports on the health of Cuban citizens and added that "Cuba's fight for survival has been taken on by a healthy, well-fed, well-educated people, with a national purpose, a collective purpose, a purpose of coming through the current crisis with an environment that can continue to sustain them into the future." Specifically, Brodine noted Cuban efforts at reforestation, the use of biomass fuels, which accounted for "30 percent of Cuba's energy supply," and organic farming, among other renewable energy sources, like solar.[62] If recent reports are accurate, Cuba continues to lead the world in the health of its citizens, as well as in the health of its environment.

---

62. Virginia Brodine, "Cuba & the environment: A revolutionary process," *People's Weekly World*, June 6, 1992, 17 and Brodine, "Green Cuba," Multinational Monitor, November 1992, https://www.multinational monitor.org/hyper/mm1192.html

In the spring of 1993, Brodine critiqued the Timber Summit held in Portland, OR for the *People's Weekly World*. President Bill Clinton spoke at the Summit and noted that he cannot "legislate against the laws of change." Brodine took this comment to task and added, "The capitalist law, 'profit is sacred,' will continue to be followed, and the natural laws that govern the growth and renewal of forests will be ignored." With a keen eye for the long-term issues raised by "old-growth cutting," Brodine added, "If Clinton permits all or some of the old-growth cutting the [logging] companies want, there will be a few more jobs now but the long slide down the clear-cut hillside that has been destroying both trees and jobs will go on." Challenging the contention that environmentalists cost timber workers jobs, she placed the blame squarely with timber companies. "The timber companies like to make environmentalists the scapegoats but the corporate engine of change began reducing jobs long ago, when the great forests of the northwest, from northern California into Canada, were cut as if they had no end."[63]

As the 1990s grew closer to the 2000s, Brodine's voice became more and more emphatic. In an April 1994 opinion piece, titled "Capitalism is dangerous to earth's health," she provided an analysis of post-World War II industrial capacity and its impact on the environment. She noted, "Our crisis-prone system has been building toward an environmental crisis since World War II," though the "seeds of this crisis were planted long ago in the private ownership of natural resources," in the very foundation of capitalism. The private ownership of natural resources was as old as capitalism itself. However, since "World War II and accelerating throughout the post-war years, new scientific and technological developments [have] made it possible to degrade the environment in ways that were both wider in scope and less reversible. All too often technology was put into practice without understanding its effects on nature." Brodine concluded with a call to action and noted the potential for CPUSA growth. "The worsening environmental crisis has brought about a new wave of environmental concern today [that is] much wider and much better informed than ever before. Youth especially are environmentally conscious and looking for the kind of leadership that the Communist Party and Young Communist League can give."

As a life-long CPUSA member *and* founder of the modern movement for environmental sustainability, Brodine's insights were unique. The collapse of socialism in the Soviet Union and Eastern

---

63. Virginia Warner Brodine, "Timber: Saving the environment and jobs, too," *People's Weekly World*, April 17, 1993, 11

Europe did not dampen her spirits, though. She had been a Communist for almost 60 years by this point. She approvingly quoted another party member, noting, "As one Party member put it, 'Nothing needs the Communist *plus* more than the environmental movement [*italic* in original].'"[64]

In 1994, the first CPUSA Environmental Program was published, *People and Nature Before Profits: our jobs, our environment, our future.* The program stated:

Fundamental change, the scientists tell us, will be needed to meet the global environmental threats. As important and valuable as grassroots local movements and coalitions are, as necessary and significant as changes in state and federal administration, state legislatures and Congress can be, as hopeful as international cooperation on environmental issues may appear, no change is truly fundamental unless it grapples with the economic causes of the problems of the present and the threats to our future. Fundamental change means *economic* change, and a new politics built on the new economic base [*italic* in original].

It went on:

To sum up: The need for a sustainable environment is overpowering, but within this system, impossible. The pressure of the capitalist system on nature is so ingrained, so pervasive, and so severe, that it is not too much to say that it is an *unnatural* as well as an *inhumane* system [*italic* in original].

In a March 1995 article in *Political Affairs*, Brodine provided a little history. She wrote that, "In spite of Gus Hall's *Ecology: Can We Survive Under Capitalism*...and some statements and activities around particular environmental problems, the Communist Party as a whole did not in the '70s and '80s play the visible and important role it could have. Concern within the Party grew however, and a workshop at the 1989 Ideological Conference stimulated a party-wide discussion during which the present Communist environmental program developed."[65]

---

64. Virginia Brodine, "Capitalism is dangerous to earth's health," *People's Weekly World*, April 23, 1994, 17

65. Brodine, *Red Roots...*, Ibid, 82

At a public event in Seattle earlier that year, Brodine outlined how she saw the CPUSA environmental program contributing to the various movements emerging around sustainability. She said, "We Communists do not fight just for what is possible, but for what is necessary…The assault on the environment by the profits-first system in our own country and around the globe means that a fightback program, a strategy for today and for the future, is necessary to the continued existence of the human race. Our contribution to such a program and strategy is in 'People and Nature Before Profits.' We believe it can help get us started on the way to making the necessary possible." Among the trade unionists, youth and student activists, and environmentalists in attendance was also Hazel Wolf of the Audubon Society, who noted that she "is proud to have endorsed the pamphlet."[66]

In a January 1998 *People's Weekly World* article, Brodine critiqued the recently concluded United Nations Global Warming Conference held in Kyoto, Japan in December 1997. This particular conference adopted the Kyoto Protocol, which outlined greenhouse gas emissions reduction obligations of between 6 to 8 percent below 1990 levels between the years 2008 and 2012. While then President Clinton signed the treaty, Congress did not ratify it and the George W. Bush administration rejected it.

Perhaps too optimistically, Brodine said the Conference "signaled the end of the debate over whether the activities of human societies are increasing global warming, and moved the discussion into the arena of doing something about it. The concern of the people of the world is now whether there will be action commensurate with the danger." She squarely placed the burden of action "in the hands of governments, including our own, and of the corporations." Though she was also quick to point out the role of grassroots organizing, protesting, lobbying and other actions in support of environmental sustainability, and added, "Without people's movements to affect when, what, and how much action, it is likely to be too little, too late." Her projections have proved remarkably prophetic.

She called out the hypocrisy and ignorance on display in the U.S. Senate over ratification of the treaty. Opponents, she wrote, were "trying to frame the debate in term of patriotism." Disingenuously, they claimed ratification of the Kyoto Protocol means "to give up our national sovereignty and submit to international pressure." With a keen eye for the larger economic issue at stake, Brodine didn't mince

---

66. Thorun Robel, "'Close encounters of the environmental kind,'" *People's Weekly World*, March 25, 1995, 11

words. She added, opponents "are speaking for the industrial and financial giants who are making very nice profits now, thank you, and want to go right on doing things their own way."

Foreshadowing protests soon to erupt against the World Trade Organization, Brodine also noted that, "We won't win the prize [a green, sustainable economy] without working for it. People and people's organizations, especially trade unions and environmental organizations, need a program which will work seriously for the kind change that puts people and nature before profits."[67]

Virginia Brodine's last paper, given to a Socialist Scholars Conference and printed in *Political Affairs* in October 1999, was titled "Working Class Globalism." The final paragraphs are as follows:

Understanding the environmental need for socialism is one thing. Getting there is something else. Each struggle to solve an issue in the present is part of the path toward socialism and a determinant of the kind of socialism we will have. We fight for democracy because we need it today, and because that fight will help create Bill of Rights socialism tomorrow.

We need to raise the level of awareness of environment as a local, national, and especially a global issue, and learn how to link it with peace, equality, democracy, jobs, and socialism.

That will help to save the threatened global environment and help build socialism. When that great victory is achieved, we will be ready to begin making those fundamental changes in production that are basic to a livable and sustainable environment.[68]

Her work over four decades resulted in linking the call for a sustainable environment with the fight for a sustainable and just economy, and for working class solutions. She opposed the trend in parts of the environmental movement to blame workers rather than corporations for environmentally destructive practices. She was a Communist who sought to promote environmental sustainability as a working class issue.

---

67. Virginia Brodine, "Corporations won't save the earth," *People's Weekly World*, January 17, 1998, 9
68. Brodine, *Red Roots…*, Ibid, 106-110

400 FAITH IN THE MASSES

Brodine lived to participate in the Battle in Seattle against the World Trade Organization, which linked the international and inter-sectional issues of environmental crisis, economic and racial justice, working class organization, and an end to imperialism. While press attention focused on the divisive tactics of a handful of anarchists (who burned dumpsters and broke storefront windows in downtown Seattle), the demonstration sponsored by unions and environmental groups among others included over 45,000 people – including CPUSA members such as Judith LeBlanc.[69] At the time, weak from breast cancer, Brodine was not able to march, but participated in the main rally. With the chant of "Teamsters and Turtles United," the unity between movements gave her great hope for the future and validated her life's work.

When Brodine passed away at the age of 85 on May 12, 2000, Alan H. McGowan, a co-editor at *Environment,* traced her pioneering contributions from the early 1960s. He credited her with "wrestling with scientists's [sic] words to turn them into English, a distinction that has been the hallmark of the magazine ever since." As McGowan put it, Brodine had been an "activist and writer her entire life, she saw information as a tool for empowerment and [she] worked to get the science right and the words eloquent." Brodine deciphered scientific and technical jargon at a time when "most scientists were not convinced that writing for the public was important." According to McGowan, "In Virginia's hands words were weapons. The beauty of her work as with every great editor, is that she turned the words of others into weapons as well. Under her leadership, the magazine became an important and effective instrument, able to illuminate and explain the science imbedded in many important policy issues." He concluded by saying, "We miss her, but the magazine that we have today is in no small part her legacy. We thank her for *Environment.*"[70] Years later *Monthly Review* noted that Brodine was part of the "prefigurative moment" of ecosocialism, a group of "writers [who] saw the relation between Marxism and ecology as relatively unproblematic."[71] The *People's Weekly World* lauded Brodine as "a

69. See: Tony Pecinovsky, *Let Them Tremble: Biographical Interventions Marking 100 Years of the Communist Party, USA* (New York: International Publishers, 2019)

70. Alan H. McGowan, "A Tribute to Virginia Brodine, *Environment Maga-zine,* Vol. 42, Issue 6 (July/August) 2000, https://search.proquest.com/openview/12aeef0568c3e161faf7305a9d64f4b9/1?pq-origsite=gscholar&cbl=34866

71. "Notes From The Editors," *Monthly Review*, July-August 2018 (Vol. 70, No. 3), https://monthlyreview.org/2018/07/01/mr-070-03-2018-07_0/

lifelong activist in the causes of political, social and environmental justice."[72] *Political Affairs*, in 2014, noted that it was Brodine's "experiences in environmental struggles stretching back to the 1950s through the 1990s that led her to insist that nature be added to our central slogan." It was as a participant in "class and racial aspects of environmental struggles...combined with Brodine's deep theoretical probing that she reached the conclusion that nature and the environment had to be included in our day-to-day work. The slogan People and Nature Before Profits was born."[73] Now Brodine's pioneering research, deciphering and communicating for environmental sustainability, is referenced by state and city governments across the country. For example, the New Jersey Department of Environmental Protection, the United States Department of Agriculture, as well as the environmental resource guide for the City of Santa Barbra refence Brodine's work.[74]

The CPUSA was committed to continuing Brodine's pioneering work. In 2004, a second edition of *People and Nature Before Profits: Towards a Sustainable Society* was issued, updating the science, addressing climate change in a more central fashion, and acknowledging that environmental issues had played an ever larger role in electoral politics.[75]

In the September/October 2007 issue of *Political Affairs*, Virginia's son Marc (co-author of this essay) published an article entitled "Nature, Society and Human Survival." In it, he noted:

All value to humanity comes either directly from nature, or from nature altered by human labor. If we compromise nature's

---

72. "Remembering two who made a difference," *People's Weekly World*, May 20, 2000, 2

73. Len Yanelli, "Nature before profits: some history, some theory," *Political Affairs*, March 7, 2014, http://www.politicalaffairs.net/nature-before -profits-some-history-some-theory/

74. "Coastal Zone Information Center – Air Resources and the Coast: A Staff Working Paper," New Jersey Department of Environmental Protection, Division of Marine Services Office of Coastal Zone Management, November 1976, https://www.govinfo.gov/content/pkg/CZIC-hc79-a4-n42-1976 /html/CZIC-hc79-a4-n42-1976.htm , "Electronic Outlook Report from the Economic Research Service: Cuba's Tropical Fruit Industry," United States Department of Agriculture, April 2004, https://naldc.nal.usda.gov /download/34811/PDF and "2011 Environmental Resources Element," City of Santa Barbra, https://www.santabarbaraca.gov/civicax/filebank /blobdload.aspx?BlobID=16904

75. Brodine, *Red Roots...*, Ibid, 111-165

ability to regenerate the materials we need for our survival, we compromise our own ability to survive. We face a series of linked environmental problems – from climate changes, to water use, to soil depletion – which have the potential to negatively affect sea levels, weather systems, our ability to grow food and drink water, and other essential aspects of human life. We can't endlessly alter the balance of natural systems like the atmosphere or the oceans without suffering the consequences of that alteration.

He continued, "The real question is: will we continue to force these natural systems to work together against humanity? Or will we restructure our social, economic, agricultural, and industrial systems to work more in harmony with them?" This article was an excerpt from a longer essay "The Dialectics of Climate Change," which used Marxist dialectics to explain climate change and other environmental crises, and environmental examples to explain Marxist dialectics.[76]

In 2008, Marc gave a report to the CPUSA National Committee on climate change, the first such discussion there. He said:

Global warming is more than an inconvenient truth. Understanding the root causes of global warming and most other major environmental problems can lead to revolutionary truth. Or the results from ignoring those root causes will be much more than inconvenient...Capitalism is using the natural world as an experimental hot house, playing with the future of all humanity for short-term profit. We can't risk finding out the absolute limits of various environmental support systems by passing those limits and creating a world profoundly more inhospitable to human life.

The conclusion called on party activists to find ways to merge their current work with the movements for environmental sustainability.

Too often we have looked at environmental issues as one more in a long list of things we ought to be doing something about but can't. We've approached environmental issues as if that meant dropping what we are currently doing to switch to a

---

76. Marc Brodine, "Nature, Society and Human Survival," *Political Affairs*, August 28, 2007, http://www.politicalaffairs.net/nature-society-and-human-survival/

different movement, a different organization. But the reality is that whatever struggles we are already involved in have an environmental side, and these aspects are only going to increase in importance.

We have to integrate environmental issues into our current work, and recognize the interconnections between environmental struggles and other issues. It is part of the job of Communists to take care of the future in the struggles of today.

At the 2014 CPUSA National Convention, an environmental panel was one of three plenary panels presented to the whole convention. Marc Brodine chaired the panel. In his opening remarks, he said:

Communists oppose the rapacious, irresponsible exploitation of nature by capitalists just as we oppose capitalist economic exploitation and oppression of workers.

Environmental struggles are fundamental to the future of humankind. If we live in a world increasingly inhospitable to human life and to the agriculture which feeds us, basic survival needs will trump everything else, including the potential for socialism.

We can't sideline environmental problems – they speak to the most basic needs of all humanity. To feed the hungry, we need to be able to grow food. To shelter the homeless, we need to be able to build sustainable housing. To create peace, we need to protect peoples and nations from environmental devastation. To produce for human needs, we must have natural resources to draw on. In order for humanity to survive, we need a healthy natural world that we work with, not against.

As an understanding of environmental crises became more widespread in the Party, more and more Party activists made the connections between workers struggles on the job, the struggles of working class communities against the depredations of fossil fuel corporations, chemical corporations, and other environmentally destructive capitalist practices.[77]

---

77. The proceeding reports are in Brodine's possession

In the preparations for the CPUSA's 100th Anniversary Convention in 2019, the CP Labor Commission proposed a resolution, adopted by the Convention, on "The U.S. Working Class, Climate Change, and the Green New Deal." It highlighted House Resolution 109, the Green New Deal, sponsored by Representative Alexandria Ocasio Cortez and over 90 other members of Congress. "This resolution is a sweeping set of proposals that aims to dramatically reduce greenhouse gas emissions in the US; create millions of good high-paying jobs; make massive investments in the infrastructure; secure universal access to clean air, water, food, and a sustainable environment; and promote justice and equality for 'frontline and vulnerable communities.'" It also constitutes "a far-reaching and radical plan for economic reconstruction of the U.S., expansion of democracy, and major steps toward achieving a 'just transition' to an environmentally sustainable economy," something Virginia Brodine had been calling for since at least the mid-to late-1950s.[78]

Marc Brodine went on to write the book *Green Strategy: Path to Fundamental Transformation*. It not only discussed the dangers threatening humanity from environmental degradation and pollution and climate change. It also covered aspects of Marxist philosophy that help explain environmental issues, lessons for the movement from mass struggles like the Civil Rights Movement and the labor movement, and projected some programmatic demands for the immediate future. The book argued that socialism is necessary to solve the imbalance between humanity and the environment on which we depend. In the Preface, he wrote:

What is destructive to the natural world is also destructive to all of us, and it is up to all of us to take action. We can't count on our current political system nor on our current economic system to solve climate change for us, we must all join to create fundamental transformation in the many human systems which surround us, in order to protect the natural systems which are essential for humans to survive and thrive.

Green Strategy argues for unity between the environmental movement and the labor movement, alongside all other progressive movements for change. It is an attempt to bridge the gap left by most environmental writing. Whereas many books on the environment

---

78. "Final Resolutions for the 31st National Convention," CPUSA, June 10, 2019, https://www.cpusa.org/article/final-resolutions-for-the-31st-national-convention/

work to explain the science, and advocate changes that individuals can make, these approaches leave out an essential step: building a movement powerful enough to create the change we need. Such an approach requires an understanding of organizations, of the history of struggles in the U.S., and a willingness to work to bridge divides and conflicts between sections of those movements.

The book ends by arguing that:

> Socialism is crucial to the environmental, industrial, agricultural, and distribution changes we need to make, but by itself that won't be enough. We need to integrate socialist economics with environmental science. When Marx and Engels were developing their theories, they paid great attention to the latest in scientific discoveries and research, but science has developed extensively since then, and the human impact on the environment has worsened significantly. Our new environmental realities must be integrated with our understanding of social and economic processes.

> In order to achieve the changes that we need in the world, we need a comprehensive, long-range strategy for building a movement capable of creating those changes. I invite you to join me on this path, the path of developing the strategy we need, and then together organizing the broad, working-class based movement for social, political, and environmental transformation.

> A better world is not only possible, a better world is necessary.[79]

In 2020, facing a global pandemic, a burgeoning fascist attack on democracy, a worldwide economic downturn, and rising people's movements against racist injustice, for democracy, and for serious action to combat climate change, the CPUSA is reorganizing its Environmental Commission. It will continue to tackle the crucial issues of human survival, environmental and economic sustainability, and building socialism – something Communists, like Virginia Brodine, have been fighting for since the late-1950s.

---

79. Marc Brodine, *Green Strategy: Path to Fundamental Transformation* (New York: International Publishers, 2018)

About the Authors

Norman Markowitz teaches 20th century U.S. political history at Rutgers University. He writes and teaches from a Marxist perspective, and has written many articles for the History News Service, the History News Network, the journal *Political Affairs* and various Encyclopedias, including the *Encyclopedia of American National Biography*, and the *Encyclopedia of Social Movements* on a variety of topics, including biographical entries on Jimmy Hoffa, Julius and Ethel Rosenberg, the Civil Rights movement, 1930-1953, and Poor Peoples Movements in American history.

C.J. Atkins holds a Ph.D. in political science from York University, with a research and teaching background in political economy and the politics and ideas of the American left. His dissertation focused on factional struggle within the U.S. Democratic Party from 1985 to 2016; his prior research dealt with the topics of economic reform in China and Marxist theory. He previously taught at the School of Public Policy and Administration at York University and currently serves on the editorial board of *People's World*.

Joshua J. Morris studied Cold War history at UCSB, has a Master's in Communist Party history from CSU Pomona, and a PhD in American History from Wayne State. He has published in journals of labor and critical studies and is currently working on a history of American Communism for Lexington Books (Rowman & Littlefield). He examines American Communist history through a Gramscian maxim and emphasizes the need for a historical materialist assessment of working class movements.

Al Neal is a journalist, historian, photographer, former mid-west coordinator for the Fight for $15 and A Union; he also served as a union representative for the Service Employees International Union. He splits his time between St. Louis, Missouri and London, England. Neal focuses on the study of American radicalism, its history, and far-reaching impact and influence on art, culture, labor, and sports. He writes regularly for *People's World*.

Timothy V Johnson is the editor of the academic journal *American Communist History* and serves on the editorial board of *Science & Society*. His scholarship focuses on the relation of the African American community and the Communist Party, USA. His authored articles include "Death for Negro Lynching!" The Communist Party, USA's Position on the African American Question" and "'We Are Illegal Here': The Communist Party, Self-Determination and the Alabama Sharecroppers Union."

Robert M. Zecker is professor of history at Saint Francis Xavier University in Nova Scotia, Canada. He teaches U.S. history with specializations in immigration, race, and ethnicity. He is the author of numerous articles and four books, most recently *A Road to Peace and Freedom: The International Workers Order and the Struggle for Economic Justice and Civil Rights, 1930-1954.*

Denise Lynn is Associate Professor of History and Director of Gender Studies at the University of Southern Indiana in Evansville, Indiana. She serves as the Vice-President of the Historians of American Communism. She writes a regular blog for *Black Perspectives*, a publication of the African American Intellectual History Society. Her research focuses on gender and race in the American Communist Party.

Joel Wendland-Liu is the author of *The Collectivity of Life: Spaces of Social Mobility and the Individualism Myth*. He teaches courses on diversity, intercultural competence, immigration, and civil rights. He is a former editor of *Political Affairs* and occasionally writes for media outlets such as CGTN.com, *People's World*, and *Common Dreams*. He is currently working on a book on racial formation in west Michigan.

Rachel Rubin is Professor of American Studies at the University of Massachusetts Boston. She is author of *Creative Activism: Conversations on Music, Film, Literature, and Other Radical Arts, Merle Haggard's "Okie from Muskogee," Well Met: Renaissance Faires and the American Counterculture, Immigration and American Popular Culture* (with Jeffrey Melnick), and *Jewish Gangsters of Modern Literature*, and co-editor of *Radicalism in the South Since Reconstruction, American Popular Music: New Approaches to the Twentieth Century*, and *American Identities: An Introductory Textbook*. She is currently working on *People's Friendship in the Cold War: The Patrice Lumumba Peoples' Friendship University in Moscow.*

James Smethurst is Professor of Afro-American Studies at the University of Massachusetts Amherst. He is the author of *The New Red Negro: The Literary Left and African American Poetry, 1930-1946, The Black Arts Movement: Literary Nationalism in the 1960s and 1970s, The African American Roots of Modernism: From Reconstruction to the Harlem Renaissance*, and *Brick City Vanguard: Amiri Baraka, Black Music, Black Modernity*. He also co-edited *Left of the Color Line: Race, Radicalism and Twentieth-Century Literature of the United States, Radicalism in the South Since Reconstruction*, and *SOS—Calling All Black People: A Black Arts Movement Reader*. He is currently working on *Behold the Land: A History of the Black Arts Movement in the South.*

Elisabeth Armstrong is a Professor in the Program for the Study of Women and Gender at Smith College. She has published two books, *Gender and Neoliberalism: The All India Democratic Women's Association and Globalization Politics* and *The Retreat from Organization: US Feminism Reconceptualized*. She is currently working on a book about women's internationalism in the mid-20th century called *To Bury the Corpse of Colonialism: The 1949 Asian Women's Conference and the Praxis of Anti-Imperialist Solidarity.*

Tony Pecinovsky is the author of *Let Them Tremble: Biographical Interventions Marking 100 Years of the Communists Party, USA.* He has written for numerous publications, including the *St. Louis Labor Tribune, People's World, Shelter Force, Political Affairs, Z-Magazine, Alternet* and *American Communist History,* among other publications. He is the president of the St. Louis Workers Education Society, a 501c3 non-profit dedicated to ongoing adult education centered on labor history, workers' rights, and political education.

Marc Brodine is Chair of the Washington State CPUSA. A former member and local officer of the American Federation of State, County, and Municipal Employee, he is currently an artist and guitar player. Marc writes on environmental issues for the *People's World* and answers environmental questions on the CPUSA web site. Brodine is the author of *Green Strategy: Path to Fundamental Transformation.*

Bibliography

Abt, John J. and Myerson, Michael, *Advocate and Activist: Memoirs of an American Communist Lawyer* (University of Illinois Press, 1993)

Aptheker, Bettina, *Intimate Politics: How I Grew Up Red, Fought for Free Speech, and Became A Feminist Rebel* (Seal Press, 2011)

Barrett, James R., *William Z. Foster and the Tragedy of American Radicalism* (University of Illinois Press, 2001)

Bart, Phillip (ed), *Highlights of a Fighting History: 60 Years of the Communist Party, USA* (International Publishers, 1979)

Bontemps, Arna, and Rampersad, Arnold, *Black Thunder* (Beacon Press, 1992)

Brodine, Marc, *Green Strategy: Path to Fundamental Transformation* (New York: International Publishers, 2018)

Brodine, Russell, *Fiddle and Fight* (New York, International Publishers, 2001)

Brodine, Virginia, *Red Roots, Green Shoots* (New York: International Publishers, 2007)

Brown, Lloyd L. and Wald, Alan, *Iron City* (Northeastern University Press, 1994 [1951])

Brown, Michael E. (ed.), *New Studies In The Politics And Culture Of U.S. Communism* (Monthly Review Press, 1993)

Boyce Davies, Carole, *Left of Karl Marx: The Political Life of Black Communist Claudia Jones* (Duke University Press, 2008)

Bosteels, Bruno, *The Actuality of Communism* (Verso Books, 2011)

Buelna, Enrique M., *Chicano Communists And The Struggle For Social Justice* (University of Arizona Press, 2019)

Cannon, James, *A History of American Trotskyism* (Pathfinder Press, 2002)

Chakravartty, Renu, *Communists in Indian Women's Movement* (New Delhi: People's Publishing House, 1980)

Chapman, Jr., Frank Edgar, *The Damned Don't Dry* (Lulu Press, 2019)

Cohen, Robert, *When the Old Left Was Young: Student Radicals and America's First Mass Student Movement, 1929-1941* (Oxford University Press, 1993)

Cole, Lester, *Hollywood Red: The Autobiography of Lester Cole* (Ramparts Press, 1981)

Cunningham, Agnes, Friesen, Gordon, and Cohen, Ronald D. (ed.), *Red Dust and Broadsides: A Joint Autobiography* (University of Massachusetts Press, 1999)

Dean, Jodi, *The Communist Horizon* (Verso, 2012)

Denning, Michael, *The Cultural Front: The Laboring of American Culture in the Twentieth Century* (Verso, 1998)

Dennis, Michael, *Blood On Steel: Chicago Steelworkers And The Strike Of 1937* (Johns Hopkins University Press, 2014)

Dennis, Peggy, *The Autobiography of an American Communist* (Berkley: Creative Arts Book Co., 1977)

Dolinar, Brian, *The Black Cultural Front: Black Writers and Artists of the Depression Generation* (University Press of Mississippi, 2014)

Draper, Theodore, *The Roots of American Communism* (New York: Transaction Publishers, 2003)

DuBois, W.E.B. *Black Reconstruction in America, 1860-1880* (New York: Touchstone Books, 1992 [1935])

Duffy, Peter, *The Agitator: William Bailey and the First American Uprising against Nazism* (Public Affairs, 2019)

Dutt, R. Palme, *Fascism and Social Revolution* (Proletarian Publisher, 1934)

Feurer, Rosemary, *Radical Unionism In The Midwest, 1900-1950* (University of Illinois Press, 2006)

Finkelstein, Sidney, *Existentialism and Alienation in American Literature* (New York: New World Publishers, 1967)

Foner, Philip S. (ed.), *The Bolshevik Revolution: Its Impact on American Radicals, Liberals, and Labor* (International Publishers, 2017)

Foster, William Z., *Pages from a Worker's Life* (New York: International Publishers, 1970)

———. *History of the Communist Party of the United States* (New York: International Publishers, 1952)

Freeman, Joshua, *In Transit: The Transport Workers Union in New York, 1933-1966* (Temple University Press, 2001)

Fowler, Josephine, *Japanese and Chinese Immigrant Activists: Organizing in America and International Communist Movements, 1919-1933* (Rutgers University Press, 2007)

Gellman, Erik S., *Death Blow to Jim Crow: The National Negro Congress and the Rise of Militant Civil Rights* (University of North Carolina Press, 2014)

Ghodsee, Kristen, *Second World, Second Sex: Socialist Women's Activism and Global Solidarity during the Cold War* (Duke University Press, 2018)

Gilmore, Glenda, *Defying Dixie: The Radical Roots of Civil Rights, 1919-1950* (W. W. Norton & Company, August 10, 2009)

Gilyard, Keith, *Louise Thompson Patterson: A Life of Struggle for Justice* (Duke University Press, 2017)

Grant, Nicholas, *Winning Our Freedoms Together: African Americans and Apartheid, 1945–1960* (University of North Carolina Press, 2017)

Green, Gil, *Cold War Fugitive: A Personal Story of the McCarthy Years* (New York: International Publishers, 1984)

Gore, Dayo, *Radicalism at the Crossroads: African American Women Activists in the Cold War* (New York University Press, 2011)

Hall, Gus, *Ecology: Can We Survive Under Capitalism?* (New York, International Publishers. 1972)

———. *The Energy Rip-Off* (New York: International Publishers, 1974)

Haviland, Sara Rzeszutek, *James and Esther Cooper Jackson: Love And Courage In The Black Freedom Movement* (University Press of Kentucky, 2015)

Heideman, Paul (ed.), *Class Struggle and the Color Line* (Chicago: Haymarket Books, 2018)

Higashida, Cheryl, *Black Internationalist Feminism: Women Writers of the Black Left, 1945-1995* (University of Illinois Press, 2011)

Holsaert, Noonan, Richardson, Robinson, Young and Zellner, ed., *Hands On The Freedom Plow: Personal Accounts By Women In SNCC* (University of Illinois Press, 2012)

Honey, Michael K., *Southern Labor and Black Civil Rights: Organizing Memphis Workers* (University of Illinois, 1993)

Horne, Gerald, *Black and Red: W. E. B. DuBois and the Afro-American Response to the Cold War, 1944-1963* (University of New York Press, 1986)

———. *W.E.B DuBois: A Biography* (Greenwood, 2009)

———. *White Supremacy Confronted: U.S. Imperialism and Anti-Communism vs. the Liberation of Southern Africa, from Rhodes to Mandela* (New York: International Publishers, 2019)

———. *Black Liberation/Red Scare: Ben Davis and the Communist Party* (University of Delaware Press, 1994)

———. *Black Revolutionary: William Patterson and the Globalization of the African American Freedom Struggle* (University of Illinois Press, 2013)

———. *Communist Front?: The Civil Rights Congress, 1946-1956* (Associated University Presses, 1988)

———. *Fighting In Paradise: Labor Unions, Racism, And Communists In The Making Of Modern Hawai'i* (University of Hawaii Press, 2011)

———. *Paul Robeson: The Artist as Revolutionary* (Pluto Press, 2016)

———. *Class Struggle In Hollywood, 1930-1950: Moguls, Mobsters, Stars, Reds, & Trade Unionists* (University of Texas Press, 2001)

———. *Red Seas: Ferdinand Smith and Radical Black Sailors in the United States and* Jamaica (New York University Press, 2009)

———. *Race Woman: The Lives Of Shirley Graham DuBois* (New York University Press, 2000)

———. *The Final Victim of the Blacklist: John Howard Lawson, Dean of the Hollywood Ten* (University of California Press, 2006)

———. *The End of Empires: African Americans and India* (Temple University Press, 2009)

Inge, M. Thomas, (ed.), *Dark Laughter: The Satiric Art of Oliver W. Harrington* (University Press of Mississippi, 1993)

Isserman, Maurice, *Which Side Were You On?: The American Communist Party During the Second World War* (Wesleyan University Press, 1982)

Johanningsmeier, Edward P., *Forging American Communism: The Life of William Z. Foster* (Princeton University Press, 1994)

Johnson, Howard Eugene; Johnson, Wendy; Naison, Mark D., ed., *A Dancer in the Revolution: Stretch Johnson, Harlem Communist at the Cotton Club* (Fordham University Press, 2014)

Johnson, Oakley, *The Day is Coming: Life and Work of Charles E. Ruthenberg* (New York: International Publishers, 1957

Kaplan, Judy and Shapiro, Linn, ed., *Red Diapers: Growing Up In The Communist Left* (University of Illinois Press, 1998)

Keeran, Roger, *The Communist Party and the Auto-Workers' Union* (New York: International Publishers, 1986)

Kelley, Robin D. G., *Hammer And Hoe: Alabama Communists During The Great Depression* (University of North Carolina Press, 1990)

———. *Freedom Dreams: The Black Radical Imagination* (Beacon Press, 2002)

———. *Race Rebels: Culture, Politics, and the Black Working Class* (The Free Press, 1994)

Korstad, Robert, *Civil Rights Unionism: Tobacco Workers and the Struggle for Democracy in the Mid-Twentieth-Century South* (University of North Carolina Press, 2003)

Lang, Clarence, *Grassroots at the Gateway: Class Politics and Black Freedom Struggle in St. Louis, 1936-75* (University of Michigan Press, 2009)

Larson, Eric (ed.), *Jobs With Justice: 25 Years, 25 Voices* (PM Press, 2013)

Leonard, Aaron J. and A. Gallagher, Conor, *A Threat of the First Magnitude: Counterintellegence & Infiltration from the Communist Party to the Revolutionary Union – 1962-1974* (Repeater Press, 2018)

Levering Lewis, David; Nash, Michael H.; Leab, Daniel J., ed., *Red Activists and Black Freedom: James and Esther Jackson and the Long Civil Rights Revolution* (Routledge, 2010)

———. *When Harlem was in Vogue* (Penguin Book, 1997)

Liberman, Robbie and Lang, Clarence (ed.), *Anticommunism and the African American Freedom Movement: "Another Side of the Story"* (Palgrave Macmillan, 2009)

Lightfoot, Claude and Johnson, Tim, (ed.), *Autobiography of Claude M. Lightfoot: Chicago Slums to World Politics* (New Outlook Publishers, 1985)

Lipsitz, George, *Rainbow at Midnight: Labor and Culture in the 1940s* (University of Illinois Press, 1994)

———. *The Possessive Investment in Whiteness* (Temple University Press, 1998)

Locke, Alain. "Values and Imperatives." In Leonard Harris, ed., *The Philosophy of Alain Locke: Harlem Renaissance and Beyond* (Temple University Press, 1991 [1935])

Lorence, James L., *The Unemployed People's Movement: Leftists, Liberals, And Labor In Georgia, 1929-1941* (University of Georgia Press, 2011)

Lumpkin, Beatrice, *Always Bring A Crowd: The Story of Frank Lumpkin Steelworker* (International Publishers, 1999)

———. *Joy in the Struggle* (New York: International Publishers, 2013)

Martelle, Scott, *The Fear Within: Spies, Commies, and American Democracy on Trial* (Rutgers University Press, 2001)

Maund, Alfred, *The International* (McGraw-Hill, 1961)

———. and Wald, Alan, *The Big Boxcar* (University of Illinois Press, 1998)

May, Vivian, *Pursuing Intersectionality, Unsettling Dominant Imaginaries* (Routledge, 2015)

McKay, Claude, *Banjo: A Novel Without a Plot* (New York: Mariner Books, 1970 [1929])

McDuffie, Erik S., *Sojourning For freedom: Black Women, American Communism, and the Making of Black Left Feminism* (Duke University Press, 2011)

Mickenberg, Julia L., *American Girls In Red Russia: Chasing the Soviet Dream* (University of Chicago Press, 2017)

Mildo Hall, Gwendolyn, ed., *A Black Communist In The Freedom Struggle: The Life Of Harry Haywood* (University of Minnesota Press, 2012)

Mishler, Paul, *Raising Reds: The Young Pioneers, Radical Summer Camps, and Communist Political Culture in the United* States (Columbia University Press, 1999)

Mortimer, Wyndham, *Organize: My Life as a Union Man* (Beacon Paperback, 1972)

Murrell, Gary, *"The Most Dangerous Communist in the United States": A Biography of Herbert Aptheker* (University of Massachusetts Press, 2015)

Naison, Mark, *Communists in Harlem during the Depression* (University of Illinois Press, 2005)

Nelson, Bruce, *Workers on the Waterfront: Seaman, Longshoremen, and Unionism in the 1930s* (University of Illinois Press, 1990)

Nesbitt, Francis Njubi, *Race for Sanctions: African Americans against Apartheid, 1946-1994* (Indiana University Press, 2004)

Ottanelli, Fraser M., *The Communist Party Of The United States: From the Depression to World War II* (Rutgers University Press, 1992)

Painter, Nell Irvin, *The Narrative of Hosea Hudson: The Life and Times of a Black Radical* (W.W. Norton & Co., 1993)

Patterson, William L., *The Man who Cried Genocide: An Autobiography of William L. Patterson.* (New York: International Publishers, 1971)

Pecinovsky, Tony, *Let Them Tremble: Biographical Interventions Marking 100 Years of the Communist Party, USA* (New York: International Publishers, 2019)

Pintzuk, Edward, *Reds, Racial Justice, and Civil Liberties* (MEP Publications, 1997)

Prashad, Vijay, *Everybody was Kung Fu Fighting: Afro-Asian Connections and the Myth of Cultural Purity* (Beacon Press, 2002)

———. *The Karma of Brown Folk* (University of Minnesota Press, 2001)

Reed, John, *Ten Days That Shook the World* (New York: International Publishers, 2001)

Reed, T.V., *Robert Cantwell and the Literary Left: A Northwest Writer Reworks American Fiction* (University of Washington Press, 2014)

Renu, Chakravartty, *Communists in Indian Women's Movement.* (New Delhi: People's Publishing House, 1980)

Richmond, Al, *A Long View from the Left: Memoirs of an American Revolutionary* (Houghton Mifflin, 1973)

Robeson, Taj Fraizier, *The East Is Black: Cold War China in the Black Radical Imagination* (Duke University Press, 2015)

Roman, Meredith L., *Opposing Jim Crow: African Americans And The Soviet Indictment Of U.S. Racism, 1928-1937* (University of Nebraska Press, 2012)

Rukeyser, Muriel, *Savage Coast* (New York: The Feminist Press, 2013)

Ryan, James G., *Earl Browder: The Failure of American Communism* (University of Alabama Press, 2005)

Sabin, Author J., *Red Scare in Court: New York Versus the International Workers Order* (University of Pennsylvania Press, 1993)

Saxton, Alexander, *Bright Web in the Darkness* (University of California Press, 1997 [1958])

Schwarz, A.B. Christa, *Gay Voices of the Harlem Renaissance* (Indiana university Press, 2003)

Sear, John Bennett, *Generation of Resistance: The Electrical Workers Unions and the Cold War* (Infinity Publishing Co., 2008)

Shields, Art, *On the Battle Lines, 1919-1939* (New York: International Publishers, 1986)

Silber, Irwin, *Press Box Red, The story of Lester Rodney, the Communist who helped break the color line in American Sports* (Temple University Press. 2003)

Smedley, Agnes, *Daughter of Earth* (New York: The Feminist Press, 1993 [1928])

Spears, Ellen Griffith, *Rethinking the American Environmental Movement post-1945* (Routledge, 2020)

Solomon, Mark, *The Cry Was Unity: Communists and African Americans, 1917-1936* (University Press of Mississippi, 1998)

Somerville, John, *The Communist Trials and the American Tradition: Expert Testimony on Force, and Violence and Democracy* (International Publishers, 2000)

Spencer, Robyn, *Angela Davis: Radical Icon* (Westview Press, 2020)

Stepan-Norris, Judith and Zeitlan, Maurice, *Left Out: Reds and America's Industrial Unions* (Cambridge University Press, 2002)

Stranton, Mary, *Red, Black, White: The Alabama Communist Party, 1930-1950* (University of Georgia Press, 2019)

Storch, Randi, *Red Chicago: American Communism at its Grassroots, 1928-1935* (University of Chicago Press, 2007)

Swerdlow, Amy, *Women Strike For Peace: Traditional Motherhood and Radical Politics in the 1960s* (University of Chicago Press, 1993)

Takaki, Ronald, *Strangers from a Different Shore: A History of Asian Americans* (New York: Little, Brown and Company, 1998)

Taruc, Luis, *Born of the People* (New York: International Publishers, 1953)

Taylor, Clarence, *Reds At The Blackboard: Communism, Civil Rights, and the New York City Teachers Union* (Columbia University Press, 2011)

Tsiang, H.T., *And China Has Hands* (New York: Ironweed Press, 2003 [1937])

Vapnek, Lara, *Elizabeth Gurley Flynn: Modern American Revolutionary* (Westview Press, 2015)

Von Eschen, Penny M., *Race Against Empire: Black Americans and Anticolonialism, 1937-1957* (Cornell University Press, 1997)

Washington, Mary Helen, *The Other Blacklist: The African American Literary and Cultural Left of the 1950s* (Columbia University Press, 2014)

Wendland, Joel, *The Collectivity of Life: Spaces of Social Mobility and the Individualism Myth* (Lexington Books, 2016)

Williamson, John, *Dangerous Scot: The Life and Work of an American "Undesirable"* (New York: International Publishers, 1969)

Yates, James, *Mississippi to Madrid: Memoir of a Black American in the Abraham Lincoln Brigade* (Open Hand Publishing, LLC, 1989)

Zecker, Robert M., *"A Road to Peace and Freedom": The International Workers Order and the Struggle for Economic Justice and Civil Rights, 1930-1954* (Temple University Press, 2018)

Zipser, Arthur and Pearl, *Fire and Grace: The Life of Rose Pastor* Stokes (University of Georgia Press, 1989)

Zumoff, Jacob, *The Communist International and US Communism, 1919-1929* (Brill Academic Publishers, 2014)

www.ingramcontent.com/pod-product-compliance
Lightning Source LLC
Chambersburg PA
CBHW020601270326
41927CB00005B/119